The first edition of this book was written by Edward de la Billière and Keith Carter, with additional information by Charlie Loram. The second edition was updated and partly rewritten by Chris Scott with additional research by Lucy Ridout. This third edition was updated by Jim Manthorpe.

**JIM MANTHORPE** has trekked in many of the world's mountainous regions from Patagonia to the Himalaya and Scandinavia to the Canadian Rockies. The author of three other Trailblazer guidebooks, *Pembrokeshire Coast Path*, *South Downs Way* and *Scottish Highlands – The Hillwalking Guide*, he has also researched and updated six other g

H
speake                                                                                          asional public
where                                                                                          s of Scotland

D1325242

**Pennine Way**
First edition: 2004; this third edition: 2011

**Publisher**
Trailblazer Publications
The Old Manse, Tower Rd, Hindhead, Surrey, GU26 6SU, UK
Fax (+44) 01428-607571, info@trailblazer-guides.com
www.trailblazer-guides.com

**British Library Cataloguing in Publication Data**
A catalogue record for this book is available from the British Library

**ISBN 978-1-905864-34-8**

© **Trailblazer 2004, 2008, 2011**
Text and maps

**Editor**: Anna Jacomb-Hood
**Layout**: Nick Hill
**Proofreading**: Jane Thomas
**Photographs (B&W)**: © Jim Manthorpe: p10, p265;
© Chris Scott p9, p11, p18, p51ᵗ, p54, p83
**Photographs (flora)**: © Bryn Thomas except: C1 top right © Jim Manthorpe
**All other photographs**: © Jim Manthorpe (unless otherwise indicated)
**Illustrations**: © Nick Hill (pp69-70)
**Cartography**: Nick Hill
**Index**: Jane Thomas & Anna Jacomb-Hood

**Warning: hillwalking can be dangerous**
Please read the notes on when to go (pp23-6) and outdoor safety (pp56-8).
Every effort has been made by the author and publisher to ensure that the information
contained herein is as accurate and up to date as possible. However, they are unable
to accept responsibility for any inconvenience, loss or injury sustained by anyone
as a result of the advice and information given in this guide.

Printed on chlorine-free paper by
D'Print (☎ +65-6581 3832), Singapore

# Pennine Way

**EDALE TO KIRK YETHOLM**
planning, places to stay, places to eat,
includes 138 large-scale walking maps
and 235 GPS waypoints

**EDWARD DE LA BILLIÈRE**
**KEITH CARTER & CHRIS SCOTT**
THIRD EDITION RESEARCHED AND UPDATED BY
**JIM MANTHORPE**

# TRAILBLAZER PUBLICATIONS

## Dedications

**From Edward**: To Pips, who carried the real load
while I was out walking and having fun in the name of work.

**From Keith**: For Annie

## Acknowledgements

**From Jim:** One of the joys of long-distance walking is meeting folk along the way and I'd like to thank everyone I met for their company. Particular thanks to Helen and Norman. I'm very grateful to the many readers who have helped with advice and recommendations, most notably Chris Sainty and Nigel Jarvis, and thanks also to: Robert W Harvey, Giles Cooper, Bill Houlder, Mike Mayor, Em Weirdigan, Susan Lever, Bryan Hirst, Lynda Bares, Paul Drinkwater, Andrew Markland, Lucy Ridout, Dave Goodfellow, Tom Read, Peter Stott, the Bayes family at the Pen-y-ghent Café in Horton-in-Ribblesdale, David Livesey, Julie Francis, David Harrison, Ian Hinks, Ian Molloy, Ian Potts, Justin Turner, Rosalyn Vahter and Peter White.

At Trailblazer I'd like to thank everyone involved, especially Bryn, Nick, Anna and Jane for all their help and hard work; also Roderick Leslie for reading the bird text.

Thanks, too, to the original authors of this book: Edward de la Billière, Keith Carter and Chris Scott who, with Charlie Loram, put together such a comprehensive guide; it made my job a lot easier.

## A request

The author and publisher have tried to ensure that this guide is as accurate and up to date as possible. Nevertheless things change. If you notice any changes or omissions that should be included in the next edition of this book, please write to Trailblazer (address on p2) or email us at info@trailblazer-guides.com. A free copy of the next edition will be sent to persons making a significant contribution.

Updated information will be available on the internet at:
**www.trailblazer-guides.com**

**Front cover**: Above Laddow Rocks (see p89) near Crowden. © Jim Manthorpe

# CONTENTS

# INTRODUCTION

Of all the long-distance trails in the British Isles the Pennine Way, 256 miles/412km (268 miles/429km including optional side routes) along the backbone of northern England, is pre-eminent. The first to be opened as a National Trail, to some it's the best; it's certainly the best known and it's arguably the hardest.

Anyone who completes the Pennine Way will refute the suggestion that it was easy. It isn't. It requires fitness, determination, good humour and adaptability because your walk won't go smoothly all the time. There will be days when you wish you'd never crawled out of bed, but there will be others when you feel invincible, when you can walk all day and arrive at your next stop, raring to go.

The Way takes you through most of the inland habitats of flora and fauna in this country and you'll see a wonderful variety of plant and animal life. You'll start with a testing trudge over the peat moors of the Peak District and continue into the South Pennines past such milestones as Stoodley Pike and Calder Vale. You then move into Brontë country and will pass Top Withins, said to be the Wuthering Heights of Emily's novel.

Your path continues past reservoirs and windswept moorland until Lothersdale, the last former mill town, now a village with an incongruous factory chimney. The bedrock now turns to limestone and you enter the lowlands of the Airedale Gap where a delightful riverside walk leads to Malham. The climbing resumes, up onto Fountains Fell and Pen-y-ghent and then down into Horton-in-Ribblesdale in Three Peaks country, a land of wide skies and magnificent views. Through Swaledale the Way continues, where Hawes and Keld lead to lonely and deserted Baldersdale: the halfway point.

Passing Teesdale's churning waterfalls, the Way then breaches the North Pennines to behold the stunning glaciated chasm of High Cup and thereafter the homely village of Dufton. Here begins the much-dreaded traverse of Cross Fell, at 2930ft/893m the walk's highest point. Gradually descending from the wilds of the North Pennines you reach Hadrian's Wall, archaeologically and historically one of the most evocative places in Britain. Along with High Cup, the walk along the Wall is one of the most outstanding days on the trail.

North of the Wall you enter the vast forests of Wark and Redesdale, eventually reaching the village of Bellingham. One more day to the lonely forest outpost of Byrness is followed by the suitably climactic 27-mile (43km) slog over the Cheviots to the end at Kirk Yetholm.

An unexpected bonus of the walk, particularly for city-based walkers, is the pleasing time-warp effect evoked in some villages; Garrigill being a good example. Here you'll enjoy a kind of Blytonesque rural British apogee: the tranquil village green with the village shop overlooking it and a church.

For some the walk changes their lives. Certainly completing the Way proves there's nothing you can't do once you set your mind to it and, however you do it, the Pennine Way stands supreme.

## About this book

This guidebook contains all the information you need; the hard work has been done for you so you can plan your trip from home without the usual pile of books, maps, guides and tourist brochures. It includes:

- Guidelines on where to stay; from wild camping to B&Bs and hotels
- Walking companies if you want an organised tour
- A number of suggested itineraries for all types of walkers
- Answers to all your questions: when to go, degree of difficulty, what to pack and the approximate cost of the whole walking holiday

When you're all packed and ready to go, there's detailed information to get you to and from the Pennine Way as well as 138 detailed maps (1:20,000) to help you find your way along it. The route guide section includes:

- Walking times in both directions & GPS waypoints as a back-up to navigation
- Reviews of accommodation; campsites, hostels, B&Bs and hotels
- Cafés, pubs, tea-shops, restaurants, and shops for buying supplies
- Rail, bus and taxi information for the towns and villages on or near the Way
- Street maps of the main towns
- Historical, cultural and geographical background information

## Minimum impact for maximum insight

*Nature's peace will flow into you as the sunshine flows into trees. The winds will blow their freshness into you and storms their energy, while cares will drop off like autumn leaves.*
**John Muir** (one of the world's first and most influential environmentalists, born in 1838)

Why is walking in wild and solitary places so satisfying? Partly it is the sheer physical pleasure: sometimes pitting one's strength against the elements and the lie of the land. The beauty and wonder of the natural world and the fresh air restore our sense of proportion and the stresses and distractions of everyday life slip away. Whatever the character of the countryside, walking in it benefits us mentally and physically inducing a sense of well-being, an enrichment of life and an enhanced awareness of what lies around us.

All this the countryside gives us and the least we can do is to safeguard it by supporting rural economies, local businesses, low-impact methods of farming and land-management and by using environmentally sensitive forms of transport – walking, of course, being the best.

In this book there is a detailed and illustrated chapter on the wildlife and conservation of the region and a chapter on minimum impact walking with ideas on how to tread lightly in this fragile environment; by following its principles we can help to preserve our natural heritage for future generations.

# PLANNING YOUR WALK

## About the Pennine Way

### HISTORY

In 1935 the journalist Tom Stephenson used the title 'Wanted: A long green trail' for an article. He was the first to suggest a public trail along the backbone of England, the Pennines, ending just over the Scottish border.

His quest was taken up by many and over the years new rights of way were created until eventually one long chain of 256* miles (412km) was established from Edale in Derbyshire to Kirk Yetholm in Scotland. It officially opened as the Pennine Way in 1965, making it the first official long-distance footpath in Britain. In its early days the Pennine Way was hard-going because a substantial part of the route crossed water-logged bogs which made sodden feet a guarantee at some stage. Today walkers never get wet as often as 20 years ago because of the Herculean efforts that have been made to lay a trail of reclaimed stone slabs. Most welcome these, others scorn them. They are but an example of how the face of the British countryside has changed, and will continue to change, over the relatively short time that this route has been open.

Who'd begrudge this slab causeway across sodden Black Hill?

### HOW DIFFICULT IS THE PENNINE WAY?

If attempted in a single continuous slog, the Pennine Way is tough. Although only a few days might be really challenging, walking daily for at least a fortnight come rain or shine will take it out of

> **If attempted in a single continuous slog, the Pennine Way is tough.**

you. The weather can whip in unchallenged from the west coast and leave you drenched or even frozen. Without GPS, navigation is sometimes tricky, especially for those unfamiliar with map reading.

* now 268 miles (429km) including optional side routes

Half the Pennine Way is on open moorland and one quarter on rough grazing; only a tenth passes through forest, woodland or along riverbanks.

This level of difficulty is what gives the Pennine Way its kudos. You'll end most days feeling the strain but ideally will recover overnight, and once the aches subside you'll be able to bask in the glory of your achievement.

Do not be put off. Although the walk is not as popular as it used to be and fewer than 4000 people attempt the trek annually, overall the **gradients** are pretty tame; it's the duration that does you in. There are 178 miles (286km) on gentle slopes of less than five degrees, 20 miles (32km) on slopes of ten to fifteen degrees, and only 3½ miles (6km) on steep slopes of more than fifteen degrees. All in all this totals 40,000ft/12,000m of ascent but if you can both read a map and comfortably walk at least 12 miles (19km) in a day you should manage it; just don't expect every day to be a walk in the park.

## ROUTE FINDING

Winding your way through villages and farmyards and out over open moorland, navigation along the Pennine Way can – depending not insignificantly on your route-finding experience – be notoriously tricky.

There are plenty of helpful photogenic wooden signposts along the route but there are also plenty of places where you'll be left guessing. Fortunately, on some open moorlands, the presence of slabbed causeways not only make

for easy going across the mire but also act as an easy-to-follow trail, even in zero visibility. Nevertheless, there are enough places on the Pennine Way, both in the valleys and on unslabbed moors, where poor visibility could leave you helpless. In such conditions, if you've lost track of your position, the traditional map and compass are of little use. With the absence of visible landmarks to correlate with a map, at best you can guess your position and head off cross-country on a bearing hopefully leading to a recognisable track or road. In some conditions such actions can be a recipe for a hill-walking disaster.

## GPS

*I never carried a compass, preferring to rely on a good sense of direction... I never bothered to understand how a compass works or what it is supposed to do... To me a compass is a gadget, and I don't get on well with gadgets of any sort.* **A Wainwright**

While modern Wainwrights will scoff, more open-minded walkers will accept GPS technology as an inexpensive, well-established if non-essential, navigational aid. To cut a long story short, within a minute of being turned on and with a clear view of the sky, GPS receivers will establish your position and altitude in a variety of formats including the British OS grid system (see p40), anywhere on earth to an accuracy of within a few metres.

One thing must be understood however: **treating GPS as a replacement for maps, a compass and common sense is a big mistake**. Although current units are robust, it only takes the batteries to go flat or some electronic malfunction to leave you in the dark. GPS is merely a **navigational aid or backup** to conventional route finding and, in almost all cases, is best used in conjunction with a paper map. All a GPS does is stop you exacerbating navigational errors or save you time in correcting them.

Using GPS with this book is *an option*. Without it you could find yourself staggering around mist-clad moors all night, or ambling confidently down the wrong path. With it you can reliably establish your position, or quickly find out how far and in what direction it is to a known point on the trail.

## Using GPS with this book

It's anticipated you won't tramp along day after day, ticking off the book's waypoints as you pass them because the route description and maps are more than adequate most of the time. Only when you're **unsure of your position** or which way to go might you feel the need to turn on the unit for a quick affirmation.

Most of the book's maps feature numbered waypoints from Edale to Kirk Yetholm. These correlate to the list on pp259-65 which gives the longitude/ latitude position in a decimal minute format as well as a description. You'll find more waypoints on bleak moorland sections such as Cross Fell, where a walk can degenerate into a prolonged stumble through thick mist. Typically the end or start of a slabbed section is also marked, as well as cairns and other significant landmarks or turnings. In towns and villages waypoints are less common but in places can still be useful to pin down an unsigned turn down an alleyway, for example.

You can either manually key the nearest presumed waypoint from the list in this book into your unit as and when the need arises. Or, much less laboriously and with less margin for keystroke error, download the complete list for free as a GPS-readable file (but not the descriptions) from the Trailblazer website. You'll need the right cable and adequate memory in your unit (typically the ability to store 500 waypoints or more). This file, as well as instructions on how to interpret an OS grid reference, can be found at: ⌨ **http://trailblazer-guides .com/gps-waypoints**.

You'll soon discover that it's possible to buy state-of-the-art **digital mapping** to import into a GPS unit with sufficient storage capacity. Advanced GPS users may like this option but it has to be said it's about as useful as internet on a mobile phone. Reliability and battery/charging issues aside, the pocket-sized receiver you'll typically

Some days are clearly better than others.

use will have a screen far too small to give you the 'big picture' and currently the cost of this digital mapping will exceed a set of easy-to-use OS paper maps which, while bulky, are always preferable.

It's worth repeating that 98.2% of the people who've ever walked the Pennine Way did so without GPS so there's no need to rush out and buy one. Your spending priorities ought to be on good waterproofs and a sturdy pair of boots. However, all those thousands will have had their frustrating moments of navigational uncertainty and reliable technology now exists to reduce mistakes. Correctly using this book's GPS waypoints will get you back on track and dozing in front of the pub fireplace or tucked up in bed all the sooner.

## HOW LONG DO YOU NEED?

It's no surprise: the slower you go the more you'll take in and get out of the Pennine Way, if for no other reason than you're not continually preoccupied by aching limbs and attaining your next destination. Nevertheless some stages along

**... most mortals average 17 days over the walk**

are simply not able to be shortened without resorting to the flexibility of wild camping (see p14) and for many, time is money; not all of us can afford to dally. The Pennine Way record stands at an absurd if impressive 2 days, 17 hours, 20 minutes and 15 seconds (Mike Hartley, 1989); most mortals average 17 days over the walk, and even then not without some gnashing of teeth. On this schedule there'll be some long days of well over 20 miles (32km), but at least one rest day. Anything less, even a couple of days, can be really pushing your luck and is best left to fit walkers or second attempts when you know the lie of the land and how to pace yourself.

Before you plan anything read the comments from Pennine Way walkers in the boxes on p27, p30, p31 and p33 and look at the suggested itineraries (see pp32-4).

---

### ❏ Doing the walk in several stages

While most walkers set out to do the Pennine Way in as short a time as possible, they include those who fail early or wage an increasingly miserable battle of mind over matter. Doing it in a single stage you get the weather and conditions you're given. There is no time to nurse injuries, exhaustion or low moods as, especially if you've booked accommodation, you must always press on.

My recollection of doing the Pennine Way in the 1970s was much like this: a gruelling march from hostel to booked hostel. Thirty years after my first walk, my update for the second edition was undertaken in four four-day stages (partly because of the amount of research required). At this pace I found the combined 16-day walk never came close to being a chore. Within reason I was also able to pick good spells of weather while avoiding crowded weekends with their need to book accommodation. Each four-day morsel was anticipated with pleasure rather than dreaded, as some days had been in my teens.

Although I had no choice this time round and a part of me still itches to bang it out in one go, I feel sure I got more out of doing the walk in stages and met as many doing it like this as those taking it on in one fell swoop.

**Chris Scott**

# Practical information for the walker

## ACCOMMODATION

Places to stay are numerous and well spaced along most of the Pennine Way, allowing for a modest flexibility in your schedule. Apart from in the high season (mid-summer), it's not necessary to **book** bunkhouses, hostels and B&Bs weeks ahead but doing so a few days in advance adds to peace of mind (see box below).

Unless you take the hardcore camping option, accommodation adds up to the **biggest expense** of your walk.

### Camping

Campsites along the Way range from a sloping field shared with livestock and a basic toilet, to offer-it-all caravan parks with widescreen DVDs to rent. Short of wild camping, this is by far the cheapest option at generally around £5 per person per night although, in these crowded British Isles, for a walker campsites might not be considered the best of all worlds. You lack the freedom and exhilaration

---

❏ **Should you book your accommodation in advance?**

When walking the Pennine Way it's advisable to have your night's accommodation booked at least by the time you set off in the morning. Although it may compromise your spontaneity, most daily stages are pretty clear cut and booking enables you to enjoy the walk (or suffer its torments) knowing you have a secure bed come nightfall.

That said, there's a certain amount of hysteria regarding the booking of accommodation, some insisting you start booking at least six months in advance. Whilst it's true that the earlier you book the more chance you'll have of getting precisely the accommodation you want, booking so far in advance does leave you vulnerable to changing circumstances.

The situation is often not as bad as some suggest, at least not outside the high season (the school holidays from the middle of July to the first week of September). Outside this period, and particularly in April/May or September, as long as you're flexible and willing to take what's offered you should get away with booking just a few nights in advance, or indeed often just the night before. The exceptions to this rule are **weekends** and places where accommodation is limited.

If you're planning on staying in **hostels** the same applies though do be careful when travelling out of high season as some YHA hostels have limited opening days/hours in winter. Once again, it's well worth booking at least one night before, and well before that if it's a weekend or the summer holidays, to make sure the hostel isn't fully booked or shut. Note that **bunkhouses** are often booked by groups, particularly in holiday periods so it is best to book in advance.

Some **tourist information centres** are able to book accommodation; they generally charge 10% of the first night's accommodation or of the whole stay; this is then deducted from your actual bill. See pp21-2 for details of accommodation-booking services.

If you have to **cancel** do try and telephone your hosts; it saves a lot of worry and allows them to provide a bed for someone else.

of sleeping out in the wilds (see below) and the negligible sound proofing of close-packed tents means a rowdy group can ruin your evening.

Furthermore, many 'campsites' these days are just caravan parks with a small patch of grass allocated to the dwindling numbers of backpackers. You end up in the corner of what feels like a grassy car park surrounded by static, sat-dished caravans occupied by weekenders. You'll spend little money of course, but the only real advantage over wild camping is a perceived sense of security, the ablutions block and a pub meal down the road. Compared with B&B-ing, your rucksack will be heavier and the rub is that the price you pay for good-quality lightweight gear (4-6kgs for a tent, mat and bag) would pay for a week of B&Bs.

However, as long as you can avoid packed campsites, autonomy in sleeping arrangements lightens the load in other ways; there's no need to book accommodation, you can change your plans as you go and so treat yourself to something more comfy whenever it's available.

As you'll typically be in or near a village or town, carrying **cooking gear and food** is not really necessary; the Pennine Way may be tough but it's not remote. Consider making life easier for yourself by combining inexpensive camping with the convenience of eating in local cafés and pubs.

### Wild camping

[See also box p32]  The Scots have a more enlightened attitude but the official line in England and Wales is that sleeping wherever you like is not allowed **unless you have the permission of the landowner**. Attempting to acquire this permission is in most cases totally impractical and may be fruitless but, up to a point, in the hills wild camping is generally **tolerated on the uncultivated open fells** beyond the last farm wall or fence and well away from any livestock.

And so it should be; if walking along England's backbone is a great adventure, in good weather how much better can it be to watch the sun set and rise in some of these wild places? Indeed, if you're attempting the walk in less than a fortnight, some nights in the wild will be your only option. Whether you have to or you want to, the chance to spend the night out in the Pennine wilderness cannot fail to make your experience all the more memorable.

The key to this activity is **discretion and respect**:
● Camp late or out of sight (use green tents or bivi bags) and leave early
● Camp in very small groups; two tents maximum
● Never make open fires
● Bury or pack out your toilet waste (see pp53-4)
● Leave no trace of your passing

If you get spotted by the landowner, as long as you clearly look like a walker in transit he probably won't shoot you, but if he asks you to move on, you must comply. Bedding down late and leaving early should avoid the chances of such a confrontation.

As for **eating**, as suggested on p17, eliminate the paraphernalia and chores involved with cooking. Eat locally then walk on to your pitch with a back-up of ready-to-eat foods. Try and plan your camp spot so that you can get to a café within an hour or two of setting off next day.

In the Pennines one wild camping black spot is the **Kinder Scout**; the first day out of Edale. Because of the high peat-fire risk during very dry and always busy summers it's not unknown for rangers to set out of an evening to harry wild campers. Spare the hassle and save your wild nights until you're over the Snake Pass, if not the A62. Ever busy **Hadrian's Wall** is also a place you'd want to camp discreetly or just keep going; head for the Wark Forest instead.

## Camping barns, bunkhouses and hostels [see box p33]

It's possible to stay in this type of accommodation on almost every night of your walk, so keeping your expenses to a minimum. However, some nights will be in basic stone barns and others in hostels that are frequently crowded.

Apart from the good value, the other appeal of this type of accommodation is the ease of **meeting fellow walkers** and having the time to get to know them, rather than a transient 'ow do' on the trail. This bonhomie can get tested when the kitchen resembles Dresden circa 1945 or a snorer gets into their stride (earplugs are a must), but you get what you pay for.

The simplest and cheapest of all are **camping barns** (£6-8 per person) which, at a minimum, provide a roof over your head, a sleeping platform on which to lay your bag and mat, a cooking area for your stove and a toilet. You'll need to bring full camping gear apart from a tent but some barns also provide hot water, showers, cooking facilities and a wood-burning stove. There's also a **bothy** on Cross Fell (see p201).

**Bunkhouses** (£8-14) are independent hostels in all but name; they are sometimes part of the YHA but not always. They are equipped with bunk beds, full cooking facilities, showers and a drying room. Most assume you will have your own sleeping bag with you, although it's often possible to hire bedding for the night. A few even provide breakfast and an evening meal.

Accommodation is usually in bunk-bedded same-sex rooms; there's always a self-catering kitchen. In addition, a good-value three-course evening meal costing about £10 and a packed lunch (about £5) are available at some places.

To stay at a **YHA/SYHA hostel** it is cheaper to be a member (YHA ☎ 0800-019 1700 or ☎ 01629-592700, 🖳 www.yha.org.uk, SYHA ☎ 0845-293 7373, 🖳 www.syha.org.uk,or join at any hostel), especially if you expect to stay in hostels more than a few nights; non-members pay an additional £3 per night. Annual membership costs £9.95 for under-26s or £15.95 for over-26s (which includes under-18s travelling with you); 10% discount if you pay by direct debit. You can either book accommodation online through the YHA/SYHA website or by phone. If booking less than a week in advance phone the hostel direct.

The YHA/SYHA hostels along or close to the Pennine Way vary in size and facilities from simple cottages, as at Mankinholes, to purpose-built buildings like Hawes or Malham, or former country houses turned into activity centres where uncorked kids drugged by the country air bounce off the walls; Edale YH springs to mind. Prices start from £13 per night. All hostels have a self-catering kitchen and the majority also provide meals for an additional charge (see p23).

## Bed and breakfast (B&B)

B&Bs are a British institution, although not always for the right reasons. For anyone unfamiliar with the concept, you get a bedroom in someone's home along with in most cases the legendary cooked Full English Breakfast the following morning. The main advantage on the Pennine Way is you can travel light, sleep well and start the day with a good feed. At the more rural places, or those with friendly owners, you also gain an insight into how the locals live.

**What to expect**  British B&Bs in popular or seaside locations can be notorious for both jamming in beds and crumby facilities; it has to be said B&Bs along the Pennine Way are of a much higher standard. Tacky or fussy joints with 'polite' notices on all surfaces are far outnumbered by well-kept town establishments, unpretentious old farmhouses or characterful country homes with enthusiastic owners.

Any B&B depending on Pennine Way custom can be considered 'walker friendly' and arriving looking like a drowned rat is expected. Some places have drying facilities and understand that you may well want to do nothing more than collapse.

---

❑ **B&B-style accommodation**

● **Rooms**  **Single** rooms are usually poky 'box' rooms and are rarely available. **Twin** rooms have two single beds while a **double** is supposed to have one double bed though sometimes has two single beds that are pushed together to make a double when required. **Family** rooms sleep three or more; often they have a double bed with a single or bunk beds, or three/four single beds. They can therefore also be used as a double or twin.

● **Facilities**  An **en suite** room attracts a premium although often this can be just for a cramped shower cubicle squeezed in next to a loo. So don't automatically turn your nose up at a **bathroom** across the corridor which is often more spacious with a deep, inviting bath just waiting for you to turn the taps on and ease away the aches with a long hot soak. In some places the bathroom is shared with other rooms (**shared facilities**) but it may be for the sole use of the guests in a particular room (**private facilities**).

● **Rates**  These are usually quoted on a **per person** per night basis and range from a very rare £20 for a bed in a room with a shared bathroom up to £50 or more per person for a very comfortable room with private bathroom and all mod cons. Most places listed in this guide are around £30-40, though a night in some of the hotels en route could be up to £60 per person. Also hotel rates do not always include breakfast so check in advance.

Be warned that if you're staying on your own most places will charge you a **single occupancy supplement** of between £5 and £10 if only a twin or double are available – some even charge you the full rate and, unless you pay for two people, many won't accept bookings from solo travellers at **weekends** as they can usually be sure to fill them with two people.

If the rate quoted is for a **room** there may be a discount for single occupancy.

Owners change their tariffs at a moment's notice in response to the number of visitors, so use the prices in this book as a rough guide. In the low season (Sep-Mar) prices may come down to some extent.

Some B&Bs offer an **evening meal**, particularly if there is no pub or restaurant nearby. Check what the procedure is when you book. Many will do a **packed lunch**, too; ask the night before.

## Guesthouses, hotels, pubs and inns

**Guesthouses** are hotel-like B&Bs. They're generally slightly more expensive but can offer more space, an evening meal and a comfortable lounge for guests.

**Pubs** and **inns** often turn their hand to mid-range B&B accommodation in country areas and although these businesses are less personal; you may find the anonymity preferable. They can be good fun if you plan to get hammered at the bar, but not such fun if you're worn out and trying to sleep within sound of the same rowdy bar. In this case it's best to ask to see the room first or specifically ask for a quiet room.

Some **hotels** are fantastic places with great character and worth the treat – but more likely they are places you're forced to go to when all the cheaper alternatives are full.

## FOOD AND DRINK

There's nothing that rounds off a hard day's walk quite as well as a good meal and a drink. There are some wonderful old pubs and restaurants in the towns and villages along the Way and while it's true that many pub menus are a celebration of mediocrity there are still places which cook good home-made traditional grub. And for fans of real ale you can be spoilt for choice in the better pubs, especially in Yorkshire which has a strong tradition of brewing. So, rather than plump for burger and chips and a pint of gassy bitter, with what looks like a head of shaving foam on top, try something from the lists in the boxes on p18 and p19.

### Breakfast

Served in B&Bs, hotels, pubs and cafés across the country a cooked breakfast is a great way for a Pennine Way walker to start the day. Depending on where you are the items on the plate will vary but often include sausages, bacon, fried egg, hash browns, tomatoes, black pudding and mushrooms. This will be served with toast and marmalade, orange juice and tea/coffee. However, many places now offer a lighter option – a continental breakfast. If you want to get an early start some places may be happy to provide a packed lunch instead of breakfast.

### Lunch, cream tea and evening meals

For lunch you may like to take a **packed lunch** from wherever you stayed the night before or buy something in the many bakeries, cafés, and local shops en route. If you need sustenance in the afternoon look out for places serving **cream teas** (a scone served with jam and cream, possibly with a cake or two, and a pot of tea).

Pennine pubs are a great place to unwind in the evening and, apart from the few towns with restaurants, are often your only choice for a meal. With Britain's long overdue food revolution continuing apace, pubs have also been forced to become more than drinking dens. Places where your meal flips from freezer

❏ **Traditional food**

● **Cumberland sausage** Common on pub menus, this is a long, coiled or curved sausage where the meat (pork) inside is chopped rather than minced. Served with chips or mashed potato.

● **Yorkshire pudding** You may find this on the menu throughout the week served on its own (with/without gravy) but many pubs go to a special effort with this dish on a Sunday when it is served with roast beef.

● **Lamb Henry** With all those sheep out on the hills it comes as no surprise that lamb is popular. Lamb Henry is lamb shanks/shoulder cooked on the bone, often with mint or rosemary. It's

Lamb Henry and chips

a cheap but filling meal though is mostly served in the winter months.

● **Parkin** A Yorkshire ginger cake, said to be the ideal accompaniment to a cup of strong Yorkshire tea.

● **Wensleydale cheese** It's been around a long time and has had a surge of popularity recently thanks to its endorsement by global superstars Wallace and Gromit. You can visit the factory and shop in Hawes (see p151).

● **Bilberry pie** A pastry pie filled with bilberries which are found growing wild across the northern moors in late summer.

● **Curd tarts** Pastry tarts of curd cheese often with currants, best served as an afternoon snack with a cup of tea.

to microwave to plate are thankfully in decline. Despite the name, **bar meals** can be eaten at a regular table and at best have a home-cooked appeal which won't find you staring bleakly at an artfully carved radish entwined around a lone prawn. All menus include some token vegetarian options and, if there is a traditional Pennine Way dish it must be **lamb Henry** (see box above), found on menus from Edale to Dufton and beyond. How better to recharge your stomach than with a quivering shank of Pennine lamb slathered in gravy, two veg and of course a pint of Black Sheep. It makes the walk worth walking.

## Buying camping supplies

With a bit of planning ahead there are enough shops to allow self-sufficient campers to buy supplies along the way. All the known shops are listed in Part 4. The longest you should need to carry food for is **two days**. Hours can be irregular in village shops although camp stoves, gas canisters or meths are usually available in general stores. Coleman Fuel is not so widely found.

## Drinking water

Even in our day-to-day lives most of us are usually under hydrated. On the trail it's now widely accepted that an adequate intake of water is essential to your well being. What is adequate will depend on the individual but a person of average height and build needs between two and four litres a day.

These days many walkers use a plastic water bag (eg a Camelbak) which

**... a person of average height and build needs between two and four litres of water a day**

often slots into a purpose-built sleeve in their pack. The drinking tube enables you to effortlessly sip on demand without breaking your stride. This system is by far the best way to ensure you drink regularly and frequently, but because the unseen bladder can run out (or may not be big enough on a hot day) carry a **500ml bottle as a back up**.

On longer days over wild country you'll need **extra water** so look out for opportunities for refills: farmsteads will often oblige. There are days, however, when taps are in short supply and you have to resort to natural sources. Many people are squeamish about using such water – the 'dead sheep upstream' is a commonly invoked scenario. The fact is, on the **high fells** away from livestock, agricultural run-off and former mine workings, water is as pure as it gets in the UK. Using these sources can **reduce your water payload** or give you a good drink (or even a cooling wash) without cutting into your own supplies.

What is safe is really just a matter of using your common sense and intuition. The higher the source or the faster the river the better; avoid slow-moving or stagnant sources although sipping from transient rockpools filled by recent rains is fine. If you still have visions of a rotting ewe's eye staring at you just upstream, use one of the many compact, pump-action **water filters** (tablets are too slow). Near running water wild campers in particular should employ the toilet guidelines given on pp53-4.

Note that whatever the adverts imply, beer is not a thirst-quenching substitute for water, while tea and coffee are diuretics which shoot through the body. Along with food to help absorb it, **fresh water** is best, its loss minimised by a **hat** and backed up by a handful of rehydration sachets, such as Dioralyte (see p39).

---

❑ **Real ales**
● **Black Sheep Brewery** (🖳 www.blacksheepbrewery.com) have been brewing since 1992. They produce a number of cask ales but their most popular is simply called Black Sheep. You'll see it in pubs up and down the Pennine Way.
● **Peak Ales** (🖳 www.peakales.co.uk) produce three different brews: Swift Nick, a fruity, hoppy beer; DPA, their take on the traditional IPA; and Bakewell Best, a proper pint of bitter. You might find some of these in the pubs at the southern end of the Way.
● **Timothy Taylor** (🖳 www.timothy-taylor.co.uk) is a famous brewery that has been in the business for over 150 years. Their Landlord is a strong pale ale while the Timothy Taylor's Best is a classic bitter popular throughout the country.

---

## MONEY AND OTHER SERVICES

**Cash** and a couple of credit/debit cards are the best means of paying your way on the walk. Don't expect an **ATM** (cash machine) in every village but remember that many shops now have ATMs or offer 'cashback' when you buy something. It's also worth knowing that most accommodation places including

PLANNING YOUR WALK

B&Bs will take **cheques** from a British bank though many shops no longer do so. **Travellers' cheques** are of limited use on the Pennine Way.

While there may not be **banks** or ATMs in every village, several **post offices** now allow cash withdrawals with a debit card and PIN number, or a chequebook and debit card. However, as the era of the country post office is in decline, check with the Post Office Helpline (☎ 08457-223344) that the post offices en route are still open. Alternatively visit 🖳 www.postoffice.co.uk and click on 'Counter services', then 'Counter money services', then 'Pay in and withdraw money' under 'Use your bank account' for a full list of banks offering withdrawal facilities through post offices and for a list of branches with an ATM.

Post offices also provide a useful **poste restante** service (see box p33 and 🖳 www.royalmail.com). Where they exist, special mention is made in Part 4 of **other services** such as **outdoor gear shops, laundrettes, pharmacies, medical centres** and **tourist information centres**.

---

❑ **Information for foreign visitors**

● **Currency** The British pound (£) comes in notes of £100, £50, £20, £10 and £5, and coins of £2 and £1. The pound is divided into 100 pence (usually referred to as 'p', pronounced 'pee') which comes in silver coins of 50p, 20p, 10p, and 5p and copper coins of 2p and 1p.

● **Rates of exchange** Up-to-date rates of exchange can be found on 🖳 www.xe.com/ucc; alternatively ask at banks, post office or travel agencies.

● **Business hours** Most **shops** and main **post offices** are open at least from Monday to Friday 9am-5pm and Saturday 9am-12.30pm but many shops choose longer hours and some open on Sunday as well. Occasionally, especially in rural areas, you'll come across a local shop that closes at midday during the week, usually a Wednesday or Thursday. Many **supermarkets** are open 12 hours a day. **Banks** typically open at 9.30am Monday to Friday and close at 3.30pm or 4pm though in some places they may open only two or three days a week and/or in the morning only; ATM machines though are open all the time. **Pub** hours are less predictable; although many open Mon-Sat 11am-11pm and Sun to 10.30pm, often in rural areas opening hours are Mon-Sat 11am-3pm & 6-11pm, Sun 11am/noon-3pm & 7-11pm.

● **National (bank) holidays** Most businesses are shut on 1 January, Good Friday (March/April), Easter Monday (March/April), first and last Monday in May, last Monday in August, 25 December and 26 December.

● **School holidays** State-school holidays in England are generally as follows: a one-week break late October, two weeks over Christmas and the New Year, a week mid-February, two weeks around Easter, one week at the end of May/early June (to coincide with the bank holiday at the end of May) and five to six weeks from late July to early September. State-school holidays in Scotland are basically the same apart from the summer when term ends late June/early July and starts again in mid-August. Private-school holidays fall at the same time, but tend to be slightly longer.

● **EHICs and travel insurance** Although Britain's National Health Service (NHS) is free at the point of use, that is only the case for residents. All visitors to Britain should be properly insured, including comprehensive health coverage. The European Health Insurance Card (EHIC) entitles EU nationals (on production of the EHIC card so ensure you bring it with you) to necessary medical treatment under the NHS while on a temporary visit here. For details, contact your national social security institution. However, this is not a substitute for proper medical cover on your travel insurance for

## WALKING COMPANIES

If you prefer the planning and baggage carrying done for you, or like the company of other walkers, the companies below will be of interest to you.

### Baggage-forwarding/accommodation-booking services

**Baggage forwarding** means collecting your gear and delivering it to your next accommodation by late afternoon; all you need on the hill is a daypack with essentials. The cost is around £8 a day and you can book collection for your whole walk or any stage you need it. Most of the companies offering walking holidays provide baggage forwarding. Alternatively you can use local taxi companies; some B&Bs also provide a luggage-transfer service.

Don't overlook the ethical and ecological issues of such services: a fleet of half-empty vans trundling around the Dales doesn't do much for your hitherto pristine carbon footprint.

unforeseen bills and for getting you home should that be necessary. Also consider cover for loss and theft of personal belongings, especially if you are camping or staying in hostels, as there may be times when you'll have to leave your luggage unattended.
● **Weights and measures** The European Commission is no longer attempting to ban the pint or the mile: so, in Britain, milk can be sold in pints (1 pint = 568ml), as can beer in pubs, though most other liquid including petrol (gasoline) and diesel is sold in litres. Distances on road and path signs will continue to be given in miles (1 mile = 1.6km) rather than kilometres, and yards (1yd = 0.9m) rather than metres. The population remains divided between those who still use inches (1 inch = 2.5cm), feet (1ft = 0.3m) and yards and those who are happy with millimetres, centimetres and metres; you'll often be told that 'it's only a hundred yards or so' to somewhere, rather than a hundred metres or so. Most food is sold in metric weights (g and kg) but the imperial weights of pounds (lb: 1lb = 453g) and ounces (oz: 1oz = 28g) are frequently displayed too. The weather – a frequent topic of conversation – is also an issue: while most forecasts predict temperatures in Celsius (C), many people continue to think in terms of Fahrenheit (F; see the temperature chart on p24 for conversions).
● **Smoking** The ban on smoking in public places relates not only to pubs and restaurants, but also to B&Bs, hostels and hotels. These latter have the right to designate one or more bedrooms where the occupants can smoke, but the ban is in force in all enclosed areas open to the public – even if they are in a private home such as a B&B. Should you be foolhardy enough to light up in a no-smoking area, which includes pretty well any indoor public place, you could be fined £50, but it's the owners of the premises who carry the can if they fail to stop you, with a potential fine of £2500.
● **Time** During the winter, the whole of Britain is on Greenwich Meantime (GMT). The clocks move one hour forward on the last Sunday in March, remaining on British Summer Time (BST) until the last Sunday in October.
● **Telephone** From outside Britain the international country access code for Britain is ☎ 44 followed by the area code minus the first 0, and then the number you require. Within Britain, to call a landline number from a landline phone in the same telephone code area, the code can be omitted: dial the number only.
  If you're using a **mobile (cell) phone** that is registered overseas, consider buying a local SIM card to keep costs down.
● **Emergency services** For police, ambulance, fire and mountain rescue dial ☎ 999.

If you don't want to have to book all your accommodation it is worth using an **accommodation-booking service**. Tourist information centres (see box p13) are able to book accommodation but mostly only in their area.

● **Sherpa Van Project** (accommodation ☎ 01609-883731; baggage ☎ 01748-826917, 🖳 www.thepennineway.co.uk) Sherpa does not offer the walk as such but operates an accommodation-booking service as well as baggage collection (late Mar/early Apr to mid Oct; minimum of two bags and maximum of 20kg per bag) from Malham northwards; they also have an online forum.

## Self-guided walking holidays

Packages usually include accommodation with breakfast, transport arrangements, minibus back-up and baggage transfer. However, each company is different so check the details carefully.

● **Brigantes Walking Holidays** (☎ 01729-830463, 🖳 www.brigantesenglish walks.com; Skipton) Self-guided holidays, accommodation booking and baggage collection along the entire route as well as free car parking at their base in Kirkby Malham and free transport to the start of the walk in Edale for anyone who has booked a full package.

● **Discovery Travel** (☎ 01904-632226, 🖳 www.discoverytravel.co.uk; York) They have a 21-day self-guided holiday covering the whole route but can also tailor-make holidays.

● **Macs Adventure** (☎ 0845-527 7871 or ☎ +44-141 530 8886, 🖳 www.macs adventure.com) They offer the whole walk over 20 days, or just from Horton-in-Ribblesdale in 13 days, or just the central section in 8 or 9 days. They also offer a highlights trip and can tailor-make itineraries to suit.

● **UK Exploratory** (part of Alpine Exploratory ☎ 01729-823197, 🖳 www.alpineexploratory.com; Settle) The whole walk over three weeks (19 days plus two rest days), or individual weeks over the southern, central or northern parts of the route. In addition they can tailor-make holidays.

# Budgeting

Compared to its neighbours England is no longer a cheap place to go travelling. Your trip budget depends on the level of comfort you're prepared to lavish upon yourself – and, up to a point, how fast you can walk!

Obviously the least expensive scenario would be walking flat out on the fast pace schedule in the itinerary boxes on pp32-4, wild camping every night and living off wild roots, berries and roadkill. At the other extreme you could stay in comfortable hotels and B&Bs and make use of a baggage transfer service.

Even if you may think that opportunities for spending are rather limited along the Pennine Way, there is still a tendency among many walkers to budget over optimistically.

## ACCOMMODATION STYLES

### Camping
You can get by on less than £6 per person per day if you wild camp and cook all your own food; if visiting a campsite add another £6. Most walkers would find it tough to live this frugally and know that part of the fun is the odd shower, pint and a Full English every now and then, in which case £12-15 per day would be more realistic.

### Bunkhouses, camping barns and hostels
You can't always cook your own food in bunkhouses/camping barns (though all YHA hostels have a kitchen) so costs can rise: £20-25 per day will allow you to have the occasional meal out and enjoy a few local brews.

If staying in a YHA hostel expect to pay around £17 per night; breakfast costs £4.95, a packed lunch is £5.50 and an evening meal £6.95-9.25.

### B&B-style accommodation
B&B rates per person can range from £20 to £50 or more a night but of course you get a good feed to set you up for the day. On top of that add £12-17 to cover a packed lunch and a pub meal in the evening. You'll soon find doing the walk at a relaxed three-week pace could put your budget into four figures.

## OTHER EXPENSES

Think carefully about how you're going to **get to Edale** – fairly straightforward – **and back from Kirk Yetholm** – more convoluted. If using trains, buy a flexible ticket well in advance to gain a reasonable fare. Incidental expenses can add up: pub lunches, soft drinks or beer, taxis to take you to a distant pub or back onto the trail in the morning. This does not include finding out that some vital item of your equipment has been left at home or is not performing well. Add another £5 a day to cover such eventualities.

# When to go

## SEASONS

The **main walking season** in England is from Easter (March/April) through to October; in terms of weather and the lack of crowds the best months in which to do the walk are **May, June** and **September**.

## Spring
The month of **April** is one of the most unpredictable for walkers. The weather can be warm and sunny, though blustery days with showers are more typical; there might be snow still lying on the hills. On the plus side, the land is just waking up to spring, there won't be many other walkers about but there will be plenty of wild flowers and the birdsong will be at its best.

**PLANNING YOUR WALK**

**May** and **June** are a great time for walking the Pennine Way; the school holidays and associated mayhem are weeks away and all you'll meet are fellow walkers. Temperatures are not too warm, the weather is as dry and clear as can be expected, wild flowers are out in their full glory and the daylight will outlast your stamina. Make the most of it.

## Summer

**July** and **August** herald the arrival of the tourist hordes. Places such as Haworth, Malham and the Dales become leisure battle zones at weekends, tiny villages are congested with traffic and accommodation gets booked out. But, as always in England, there's still a good chance of at least some rain during this time.

## Autumn

A slower pace of life returns as schooling resumes. Late **September** and early **October** see stunning colours in the woods and on the hills. You're less likely to meet other walkers, but more likely to encounter rain and strong winds. Temperatures remain mild.

## Winter

Late **October** and **early November** reliably bring up a crop of glorious crisp clear days, but winter is on its way. The days shorten, the temperature drops noticeably and with it many B&Bs, campsites and even shops close.

You need to be pretty hardy to walk between late **November** and mid-**March**. True, some days might be bright and sunny, and snow can add a magical element to the hills, but you are far more likely to be walking through driving rain and sleet, accommodation is what you can get and the short days are a problem on longer stages.

## TEMPERATURE, RAINFALL AND DAYLIGHT HOURS

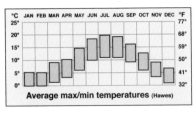

**Average max/min temperatures** (Hawes)

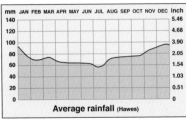

**Average rainfall** (Hawes)

These days the Pennines are certainly less wet than their reputation suggests and if you pick your time of year you can minimise your chances of spending days encased in a rustling cagoule.

Just don't expect your plan to be totally foolproof. If there's one thing you can plan on with the English weather it is unpredictability. The charts here and opposite can only provide a guide.

If walking in autumn, winter and early spring, you must take account of how far you can walk in the **available daylight**. It's not possible to cover the same distance you can in mid-summer.

The chart on the right gives the sunrise and sunset times for the middle of each month at Hawes, a town about halfway along the Pennine Way which gives a reasonably accurate picture for daylight for the whole trail.

Depending on the weather you can get a further 30-45 minutes of

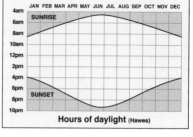

Hours of daylight (Hawes)

usable twilight after sunset. By this time you should be nearly done anyway, following a clear path to a village bathed in warm lamplight.

PLANNING YOUR WALK

## ANNUAL EVENTS ALONG THE PENNINE WAY

The events below are listed according to when they are held in the year (April to September); however, in some places events are held throughout the year so check the websites listed.

● **Three Peaks Challenge** (🖥 www.threepeaksrace.org.uk, see box p145) Held on the last Saturday in April in the area around Horton-in-Ribblesdale.

● **Fellsman Hike** (🖥 www.fellsman.org.uk) A 60-mile high-level traverse from Ingleton to Threshfield via Dodd Fell (see Map 53, p150) held over two days in mid-May. The event challenges the competitors' navigational skills and fitness.

● **Swaledale Arts Festival** (🖥 www.swaledale-festival.org.uk) Brass bands, jazz and various art events; held over two weeks from the end of May to mid June.

● **Yetholm Festival Week** (🖥 www.yetholmonline.org.uk) Second week in June climaxing with Trolley Dolly Jean's duck race.

● **Edale Country Day** (🖥 www.edalecountryday.org.uk) Jazz, wacky races, wood turning, sheep shearing, bands and maypole dancing; held mid-June.

● **Twice Brewed Roman Wall Show** (🖥 www.northumberlandnationalpark. org.uk/romanwallshow) Sheep and shepherds show on a Saturday in mid-June.

● **Malham** (🖥 www.malhamdale.com/events.htm) Several summer events from the kiddy-oriented Safari in late June to late August's agricultural show. See p136 for details about peregrine-falcon viewing from April to August.

● **Hawes Gala** (🖥 www.wensleydale.org/events this seems more relevant) A Saturday in late June as well as Craft Fairs most summer weekends and several Yorkshire Dales National Park events.

● **Hebden Bridge Arts Festival** (🖥 www.hebdenbridge.co.uk/festival) Music, comedy, drama, talks and exhibitions held at the end of June and start of July.

● **Thornton-in-Craven Village Fête** (🖥 www.thorntonincraven.co.uk) Mid-July.

● **Middleton-in-Teesdale Carnival** (🖥 www.middleton-carnival.org.uk) Carnival Queens, Scarecrow Trails and much more; held last Saturday in July. According to their website the 2010 carnival may have been the last one so check for the latest before getting too excited about it.

- **Gargrave Show** (⌨ www.gargraveshow.org.uk)  Over a century old, an agricultural show featuring prize cattle and sheep dog trials; mid-August.
- **Dufton Show** (⌨ www.theduftonshow.co.uk) Agricultural show and sheepdog trials; last Saturday in August.
- **Bellingham Show** (⌨ www.bellinghamshow.com)  Last Saturday in August.
- **Bowes Show** (⌨ www.bowesshow.org.uk) Farming show in early September.
- **Three Peaks Cyclocross** (⌨ www.3peakscyclocross.org.uk)  Held on the last Sunday in September in the area around Horton-in-Ribblesdale.
- **Hardraw Brass-band Contest** (⌨ www.yhbba.org.uk/Hardraw1)  Running since 1884 in the grounds of the Green Dragon Inn; second Sunday in September.

## WALKING WITH DOGS

Dogs are a pleasure to walk with providing they are well behaved and fit. They must be under control at all times and kept on the lead when near livestock (see box below). You may know that your dog doesn't chase sheep but farmers don't. You'll be walking through many conservation areas so you must also carefully control your dog when there are nesting birds or fledglings around; they make tasty meals for a dog, and even if chased and not caught they can sometimes die later.

Be sure your dog is up to the task; it's not unknown for dog walkers to have to end their Pennine walk early because their pet has injured or exhausted itself. Accommodation too can be a chore; however, places that accept dogs are specified in the route guide.

---

### ❑ Walking through fields of cattle

It is very rare that cows will attack walkers but it does happen; in 2009 a woman was trampled to death on the Pennine Way near Hawes. Cows get particularly nervous when dogs are about so if you are walking with a dog be aware of this. Cows with calves can be even more twitchy.

But don't get alarmed; a walk along the length of the Pennine Way will involve walking through dozens and dozens of fields with cattle in them. Most of the time they will just watch you pass. Cattle are usually docile animals. If you walk calmly past they will invariably ignore you. If you feel nervous or unsure about a herd, you are entitled to walk round the edge of the field to avoid them and rejoin the path later.

Very rarely they will wander over out of curiosity but if they do you should be on your guard. Ramblers (see box p42) offer the following guidelines for safely crossing fields of cattle:

- Try not to get between cows and their calves
- Be prepared for cattle to react to your presence, especially if you have a dog with you
- Move quickly and quietly, and if possible walk around them
- Keep your dog close and under proper control
- Don't hang onto your dog. If you are threatened by animals – let it go as the cow will chase after that
- Don't put yourself at risk. Find another way round the cows and rejoin the footpath as soon as possible.
- Don't panic! Most cows will stop before they reach you. If they follow just walk on quietly. Don't forget to report any problems to the highway authority.

# Itineraries

All walkers are individuals. Some like to cover large distances as quickly as possible, others like to stroll along and stop frequently. (Indeed this natural variation in pace is what causes most friction in groups.) You may want to walk the Pennine Way all in one go, tackle it over a series of weekends, or use the trail for linear day walks; the choice is yours. To accommodate these differences this book has not been divided up into rigid daily stages, though many will use it that way. Instead, it's been designed to make it easy for you to plan your own optimal itinerary.

The **planning map** (see inside back cover) and **table of village/ town facilities** (see pp28-31) summarise the essential information. Alternatively, have a look at the **suggested itineraries** (pp32-4) and choose your preferred type of accommodation and pace. There are also suggestions (see pp34-6) for those who want to experience the best of the trail over a day or a weekend. The **public transport maps** and service table (pp45-50) will also be useful.

Having made a rough plan, turn to **Part 4**, where you will find summaries of the route; full descriptions of the accommodation, suggestions for where to eat and information about other services in each village and town; as well as the detailed trail maps.

> **Most people walk the Pennine Way south to north... the prevailing south-westerly wind and rain are behind you, as is the sun.**

Most people walk the Pennine Way **south to north**. There are practical reasons for this; the prevailing south-westerly wind and rain are behind you, as is the sun. Head north–south if you want a better face tan! The maps in Part 4 give timings for both directions and, as route-finding instructions are on the maps rather than in blocks of text, it ought to be straightforward using this guide back to front.

---

❑ **The next time I do the Pennine Way...**
... will be in 2013, marking 50 years since my first south–north odyssey.

Next time I shall take my time, and that will be a first! I'll book all my accommodation in advance, ensuring a framework of low daily mileages. I'll gratefully stop and stare – and even divert from the trail – wherever the fancy takes me. If the weather hits me hard, I'll be able to pass my spare hours in the occasional pub and tea-room. I'll carry only what I need for the day: baggage transport rules OK, so I'll have a wardrobe of clean clothes to wear in the evenings, books to read, and enough money to eat and sup well.

Next time won't be remotely like the first time, and it will be the last time, book-ending a fascinating and fulfilling series of treks along this inspiring trail.

**Peter Stott**

PLANNING YOUR WALK

| Place name<br>(Places in brackets<br>are a short walk<br>off the Pennine<br>Way) | Distance from<br>previous<br>place<br>(approx<br>miles/km) | Cash<br>Machine/<br>ATM<br>(in bank, shop<br>or post office) | Post<br>office | VILLAGE AND<br>Tourist<br>Information<br>Centre (TIC)/<br>Point (TIP)<br>National Park<br>Centre (NPC) |
|---|---|---|---|---|
| Edale/Nether Booth | | ✔ | ✔ | NPC |
| Upper Booth | 2 (3) | | | |
| Torside, (Padfield & Hadfield) | | | | |
| Crowden | 14 (23) | | | |
| Standedge | 11 (18) | | | |
| (Diggle) | | | | |
| Blackstone Edge | 7 (11.5) | | | |
| Mankinholes | 4 (6.5) | | | |
| Hebden Bridge* | 3 (5) | ✔ | ✔ | TIC |
| Blackshaw Head | 1 (1.5) | | | |
| Colden | 1 (1.5) | | | |
| Widdop | 2.5 (4) | | | |
| (Haworth) | | ✔ | ✔ | TIC |
| Ponden & Stanbury | 7.5 (12) | | | |
| Ickornshaw & Cowling | 4 (6.5) | | | |
| Lothersdale | 2 (3) | | | |
| Thornton-in-Craven | 4 (6.5) | | | |
| (Earby) | | | ✔ | |
| East Marton | 1.5 (2) | | | |
| Gargrave | 2.5 (4) | ✔ | ✔ | |
| Airton | 3.5 (6) | | | |
| Kirkby Malham | 1.5 (2.5) | | | |
| Malham | 1 (2) | | | NPC |
| Horton-in-Ribblesdale | 15 (24) | | ✔ | TIP |
| Hawes | 14 (23) | ✔ | ✔ | NPC/TIC |
| Hardraw | 1.5 (2) | | | |
| Thwaite | 8 (13) | | | |
| (Muker) | | | | |
| Keld | 3 (5) | | | |
| Tan Hill | 4 (6) | | | |
| (Bowes) | | | | |
| Baldersdale | 10 (16) | | | |
| Lunedale | 3 (5) | | | |
| Middleton-in-Teesdale | 3.5 (6) | ✔ | ✔ | TIC |
| Holwick | 2.5 (4) | | | |
| High Force | 2.5 (4) | | | |
| Forest-in-T'dale/Langdon Beck | 3.5 (6) | | ✔ | |
| Dufton | 12 (19) | | | |
| Garrigill | 16 (26) | | ✔ | |

*(continued on p30)*

* distance is to the Rochdale Canal towpath. HB is a further 1mile (2km off route)

**PLANNING YOUR WALK**

**TOWN FACILITIES**

| Restaurant/ Café/pub $\checkmark$ = one; $\checkmark\!\checkmark$ = two; $\checkmark\!\checkmark\!\checkmark$ = 3 + | Food Store | Camp-site | Hostels YHA/H (IndHostel)/ CB (Camping Barn)/B (Bunkhouse) | B&B-style accommodation $\checkmark$ = one; $\checkmark\!\checkmark$ = two; $\checkmark\!\checkmark\!\checkmark$ = 3+ | Place name (Places in brackets are a short walk off the Pennine Way) |
|---|---|---|---|---|---|
| $\checkmark\!\checkmark\!\checkmark$ | $\checkmark$ | $\checkmark$ | YHA, CB | $\checkmark\!\checkmark\!\checkmark$ | **Edale/Nether Booth** |
| | | $\checkmark$ | CB | | **Upper Booth** |
| $\checkmark$ | | $\checkmark$ | B | $\checkmark\!\checkmark\!\checkmark$ **Torside, (Padfield & Hadfield)** |
| | | $\checkmark$ | YHA | | **Crowden** |
| $\checkmark\!\checkmark\!\checkmark$ | | $\checkmark$ | | $\checkmark\!\checkmark\!\checkmark$ | **Standedge** |
| $\checkmark$ | | | | $\checkmark\!\checkmark\!\checkmark$ | **(Diggle)** |
| $\checkmark$ | | | | | **Blackstone Edge** |
| $\checkmark$ | | $\checkmark$ | YHA | $\checkmark$ | **Mankinholes** |
| $\checkmark\!\checkmark\!\checkmark$ | $\checkmark$ | | H | $\checkmark\!\checkmark\!\checkmark$ | **Hebden Bridge** |
| | | $\checkmark$ | | $\checkmark$ | **Blackshaw Head** |
| $\checkmark$ | $\checkmark$ | $\checkmark$ | | | **Colden** |
| $\checkmark$ | | | | $\checkmark$ | **Widdop** |
| $\checkmark\!\checkmark\!\checkmark$ | $\checkmark$ | | YHA | $\checkmark\!\checkmark\!\checkmark$ | **(Haworth)** |
| $\checkmark$ | | $\checkmark$ | | $\checkmark\!\checkmark\!\checkmark$ | **Ponden & Stanbury** |
| $\checkmark$ | $\checkmark$ | $\checkmark$ | | $\checkmark\!\checkmark$ | **Ickornshaw & Cowling** |
| $\checkmark$ | | | | | **Lothersdale** |
| | | | | $\checkmark$ | **Thornton-in-Craven** |
| $\checkmark\!\checkmark$ | $\checkmark$ | | YHA | | **(Earby)** |
| $\checkmark\!\checkmark$ | | $\checkmark$ | | | **East Marton** |
| $\checkmark\!\checkmark\!\checkmark$ | $\checkmark$ | $\checkmark$ | | $\checkmark\!\checkmark$ | **Gargrave** |
| | | | H | $\checkmark$ | **Airton** |
| $\checkmark$ | | | | | **Kirkby Malham** |
| $\checkmark\!\checkmark\!\checkmark$ | | $\checkmark$ | YHA, B | $\checkmark\!\checkmark\!\checkmark$ | **Malham** |
| $\checkmark\!\checkmark$ | $\checkmark$ | $\checkmark$ | B | $\checkmark\!\checkmark\!\checkmark$ | **Horton-in-Ribblesdale** |
| $\checkmark\!\checkmark$ | $\checkmark$ | $\checkmark$ | YHA | $\checkmark\!\checkmark\!\checkmark$ | **Hawes** |
| $\checkmark$ | | $\checkmark$ | B | $\checkmark\!\checkmark$ | **Hardraw** |
| $\checkmark$ | | $\checkmark$ | | $\checkmark$ | **Thwaite** |
| $\checkmark\!\checkmark$ | $\checkmark$ | | | $\checkmark\!\checkmark\!\checkmark$ | **(Muker)** |
| | | $\checkmark$ | B | $\checkmark\!\checkmark$ | **Keld** |
| $\checkmark$ | | $\checkmark$ | B | $\checkmark$ | **Tan Hill** |
| $\checkmark$ | | $\checkmark$ | | $\checkmark$ | **(Bowes)** |
| | | $\checkmark$ | CB | $\checkmark$ | **Baldersdale** |
| | | $\checkmark$ | | | **Lunedale** |
| $\checkmark\!\checkmark$ | $\checkmark$ | $\checkmark$ | | $\checkmark\!\checkmark\!\checkmark$ | **Middleton-in-Teesdale** |
| $\checkmark$ | | $\checkmark$ | CB | $\checkmark$ | **Holwick** |
| $\checkmark$ | | | | $\checkmark$ | **High Force** |
| $\checkmark$ | | | YHA | $\checkmark\!\checkmark\!\checkmark$ **Forest-in-T'dale/Langdon Beck** |
| $\checkmark$ | | $\checkmark$ | YHA | $\checkmark\!\checkmark\!\checkmark$ | **Dufton** |
| | $\checkmark$ | $\checkmark$ | | $\checkmark\!\checkmark\!\checkmark$ | **Garrigill** |

*(continued on p31)*

PLANNING YOUR WALK

VILLAGE AND

*(continued from p28)*

| Place name (Places in brackets are a short walk off the Pennine Way) | Distance from previous place (approx miles/km) | Cash Machine/ ATM (in bank, shop or post office) | Post office | Tourist Information Centre (TIC)/ Point (TIP) National Park Centre (NPC) |
|---|---|---|---|---|
| Alston | 4 (6) | ✔ | ✔ | TIC |
| Slaggyford & Knarsdale | 6 (10) | | | |
| Greenhead | 11 (18) | | | |
| Burnhead | 4 (6) | | | |
| Once Brewed | 2.5 (4) | | | NPC/TIC |
| (Stonehaugh) | | | | |
| Hetherington | 9.5 (15) | | | |
| Bellingham | 3 (5) | ✔ | ✔ | TIC |
| Byrness | 15 (24) | | | |
| (Upper Coquetdale) | | | | |
| Kirk Yetholm/Town Yetholm | 27 (43) | | ✔ | |

**Total distance** 256 miles (412km) – or 268 miles (429km) including optional side routes

---

❑ **The next time I do the Pennine Way...**
... I'll pick the long but uncrowded days of early summer again. Knowing some good spots now, if the weather's good I'll pace myself to wild camp most nights, but to save the hassle of cooking I'll eat meals in the towns and pubs. Thanks to the 16-hour days I'll be able to walk slowly from early morning into the dusk, and still have regular rests or even a siesta while keeping on target. I'd also make more use of the natural springs and other potable water sources to reduce the amount of water carried.

The hill camping will greatly enhance the wilderness experience, with towns only passed through by day rather than slept in overnight. Although I will probably regret it, instead of an expensive lightweight tent I'll just use a flysheet, either as a groundsheet on fine nights or pegged out and kept up with walking poles. (I may also make an effort to get into using walking poles by day.)

I wouldn't expect to wild camp all the time and every third or fourth day (or if the weather's crap) I'd check into a B&B, bunkhouse or whatever for a wash and a proper night's sleep and a full English breakfast (FEB). **Chris Scott**

---

❑ **The next time I do the Pennine Way...**
... I'll do it just the same way as the first time; with a bivi bag for sleeping on the high, windswept moors when the weather behaves itself and splashing out on a snug B&B when it doesn't. I'll not bother with a camping stove and all the clutter that comes with it, instead getting a good feed in a pub before heading off to the wild moors to sleep with the curlews. The next morning I'll get breakfast in a bakery or café. And I will take my time (on the Way and in the café). **Jim Manthorpe**

## TOWN FACILITIES

*(continued from p29)*

| Restaurant/ Café/pub ✔ = one; **WW** = two; **WWW** = 3 + | Food Store | Camp-site | Hostels YHA/H (IndHostel)/ CB (Camping Barn)/B Bunkhouse | B&B-style accommodation ✔ = one; **WW** = two; **WWW** = 3+ | Place name (Places in brackets are a short walk off the Pennine Way) |
|---|---|---|---|---|---|
| **WWW** | ✔ | ✔ | YHA, B | **WWW** | Alston |
| ✔ | | ✔ | | **WW** | Slaggyford & Knarsdale |
| **WW** | | ✔ | YHA/H, CB | **WWW** | Greenhead |
| ✔ | | | | ✔ | Burnhead |
| ✔ | | ✔ | YHA, B | **WWW** | Once Brewed |
| | | ✔ | | | (Stonehaugh) |
| | | | | ✔ | Hetherington |
| **WW** | ✔ | ✔ | B | **WWW** | Bellingham |
| | | ✔ | H | ✔ | Byrness |
| | | ✔ | CB | ✔ | (Upper Coquetdale) |
| | | | YHA | **WWW** | Kirk Yetholm/Town Yetholm |

---

### ❑ The next time I do the Pennine Way...

... I'd change little from the first. I'd walk south to north, facing the more demanding terrain towards the northern end. I'd take 20 days again, giving time to relax between shower and dinner each evening.

Having a couple of days under ten miles in the final week provided encouragement, while staying at Uswayford* made the Cheviots a fine two-day traverse. I'd again use YHA hostels, B&Bs and baggage forwarding, and dine at some fine hostelries along the way.

I'd again use Bridgedale socks and liners, and two walking poles, train in advance and use whey protein daily to aid muscle recovery. But I'd make an earlier start on the first day and this time get a quality rucksack. I'd navigate more carefully off Bleaklow summit.

I might slip a bottle of real ale into my luggage for that first night at Crowden YH, which is nowhere near a boozer although I would take more parental responsibility in moderating the consumption of Brenda's superb homemade sherry trifle at Ponden House.

I'd never again try to squeeze my wet clothes into a packed-out YH drying room but hang them out in the dormitory. And I would never again drink keg bitter after consecutive days of real ale. **Tom Read**

*\*Note from editor*: B&B is no longer available in Uswayford.

PLANNING YOUR WALK

## WILD CAMPING* AND CAMPSITES (▲)

| | Relaxed pace | | Medium pace | | Fast pace | |
|---|---|---|---|---|---|---|
| **Night** | **Place** | **Approx distance** miles (km) | **Place** | **Approx distance** miles (km) | **Place** | **Approx distance** miles (km) |
| 0 | Edale | | Edale | | Edale | |
| 1 | Crowden ▲ | 16 (26) | Crowden ▲ | 16 (26) | Black Hill | 20 (32) |
| 2 | Standedge ▲ | 11 (18) | Blackstone Edge | 15 (24) | Blackshaw* | 20 (32) |
| 3 | Withens Moor | 10 (16) | Walshaw Reservoir | 17 (27) | Pinhaw | 20 (32) |
| 4 | Withins Height | 14 (22.5) | Pinhaw Beacon | 13 (21) | Fountains Fell | 20 (32) |
| 5 | East Marton ▲ | 13.5 (22) | Fountains Fell | 20 (32) | Hawes ▲ | 21 (34) |
| 6 | Fountains Fell | 15 (24) | Dodd Fell | 17 (27) | Sleightholme | 20 (32) |
| 7 | Old Ing Moor | 12 (19.5) | Keld ▲ | 16 (26) | Middleton | 20.5 (33) |
| 8 | Gt Shunner Fell | 14 (22.5) | (Rest day) | 0 | Rail wagon | 19 (30.5) |
| 9 | Tan Hill Inn ▲ | 11.5 (18.5) | Deepdale Beck | 12 (19.5) | Greg's Hut | 23.5 (38) |
| 10 | Deepdale Beck | 7.5 (12) | Rail wagon | 15 (24) | Glendue Burn | 24.5 (39.5) |
| 11 | Middleton ▲ | 9 (14.5) | High Cup Nick | 10 (16) | Wark Forest | 18 (29) |
| 12 | Rest day | 0 | Greg's Hut | 13.5 (22) | Byrness Hill | 23 (37) |
| 12 | High Cup | 16 (26) | Alston ▲ | 11.5 (18.5) | Kirk Yetholm | 25 (40) |
| 13 | Greg's Hut | 13.5 (22) | Glendue Burn | 14 (22.5) | | |
| 14 | Alston ▲ | 11.5 (18.5) | Wark Forest | 15 (24) | | |
| 15 | Glendue Burn | 14 (22.5) | Deer Play | 15 (24) | | |
| 16 | Wark Forest | 15 (24) | Coquet Head | 15 (24) | | |
| 17 | Deer Play | 15 (24) | Kirk Yetholm | 19 (30.5) | | |
| 18 | Byrness Hill | 11.5 (18.5) | | | | |
| 19 | Windy Gyle | 12 (19.5) | | | | |
| 20 | Kirk Yetholm | 12 (19.5) | | | | |

|  |  |  |
|---|---|---|
| **20 nights** | **17 nights** | **12 nights** |
| **Average 12.8 miles/day** | **Average 15 miles/day** | **Average 21.3 miles/day** |

\* Wild camping obviously allows overnighting where you please. Where possible the approximate locations of wild camps have been proposed on the fells, ie where discreet and unobtrusive stays are most easily made. Most places have also been chosen for their scenic appeal, the vicinity of Glendue Burn being a notable but unavoidable exception. On other days the ideal distance – be it 'relaxed' or 'fast' – puts you so near a town it's simpler to stay on a campsite or even at a B&B. In Kirk Yetholm B&Bs are the only option unless you camp out around White Law on the alternative route, a couple of miles from the end.

The flexibility of wild camping enables greater daily distances to be covered which is why the three proposed itineraries above are a little faster than the accommodated options given on pp33-4.

## STAYING IN HOSTELS, BUNKHOUSES AND CAMPING BARNS

| | Relaxed pace | | Medium pace | | Fast pace | |
|---|---|---|---|---|---|---|
| **Night** | **Place** | **Approx distance** miles (km) | **Place** | **Approx distance** miles (km) | **Place** | **Approx distance** miles (km) |
| 0 | Edale | | Edale | | Edale | |
| 1 | Crowden | 16 (26) | Crowden | 16 (26) | Crowden | 16 (26) |
| 2 | Standedge* | 11 (18) | Standedge* | 11 (18) | Mankinholes | 21 (34) |
| 3 | Mankinholes | 10 (16) | Mankinholes | 10 (16) | Ick & Cowling* | 20 (32) |
| 4 | Haworth§ | 15 (24) | Ick & Cowling* | 20 (32) | Malham | 16 (26) |
| 5 | Earby• | 9 (14.5) | Malham | 16 (26) | Horton-in-Rib | 15 (24) |
| 6 | Malham | 12 (19.5) | Horton-in-Rib | 15 (24) | Keld | 26.5 (42.5) |
| 7 | Horton-in-Rib | 15 (24) | Hawes | 14 (22.5) | Middleton-in-T* | 20.5 (33) |
| 8 | Hawes | 14 (22.5) | (Rest day) | | Dufton | 20.5 (33) |
| 9 | (Rest day) | | Keld | 12.5 (20) | Alston | 20 (32) |
| 10 | Keld | 12.5 (20) | Baldersdale* | 14 (22.5) | Greenhead | 17 (27) |
| 11 | Bowes* | 12.5 (20) | Langdon Beck | 15 (24) | Bellingham | 21.5 (34.5) |
| 12 | Middleton-in-T* | 15 (24) | Dufton | 12 (19.5) | Byrness | 15 (24) |
| 13 | Langdon Beck | 9 (14.5) | Alston | 20 (32) | Kirk Yetholm | 27 (43.5) |
| 14 | Dufton | 12 (19.5) | Greenhead | 17 (27) | | |
| 15 | Garrigill* | 16 (26) | Once Brewed | 7 (11.5) | | |
| 16 | Knarsdale* | 10 (16) | Bellingham | 14.5 (23) | | |
| 17 | Greenhead | 11 (18) | Byrness | 15 (24) | | |
| 18 | Once Brewed | 7 (11) | Kirk Yetholm | 27 (43.5) | | |
| 19 | Bellingham | 14.5 (23) | | | | |
| 20 | Byrness | 15 (24) | | | | |
| 21 | Upper Coquetdale | 12 (19.5) | | | | |
| 22 | Kirk Yetholm | 15 (24) | | | | |

**22 nights Av 12 miles/day**　　**18 nights Av 14.2 m/d**　　**13 nights Av 19.6 m/d**

*\* No hostel/bunkhouse/barn; stay in B&B　§ 3½ miles (6km) off-route therefore +3½ miles each way　• 1½ miles (2km) off-route therefore +1½ miles each way*

---

### ❏ The next time I do the Pennine Way...

... I will endeavour to allow more time in the day to lounge around and watch the world go by. Previously I'd sometimes reached my destination by 2pm, regardless of the time in hand. I should have spent longer at viewpoints, village centres and points of interest and simply arrived later. I'll definitely take more photos by carrying my camera around my neck or in a pocket; it was amazing how few photos I took with the camera in my rucksack. I'll also make more journal entries during and at the end of each day. Over time the brain muddles the facts and a more permanent record of my trip would be perfect. I'll definitely research the villages along the way for fêtes, village days or festivals. I just missed two on my route and both sounded spectacular. I'll also make use of the Post Office's 'Poste Restante' service to allow maps, clean clothes, guidebooks etc to be picked up along the way.

　　And I will definitely not leave a pair of shorts drying on the line at the Tan Hill Inn after a few too many the night before.　　　　　　　　　　　　**Dave Goodfellow**

## STAYING IN B&Bs

| Relaxed pace | | Medium pace | | Fast pace | |
|---|---|---|---|---|---|
| **Place** | **Approx distance** | **Place** | **Approx distance** | **Place** | **Approx distance** |
| **Night** | miles (km) | | miles (km) | | miles (km) |
| 0 Edale | | Edale | | Edale | |
| 1 Torside | 15 (24) | Torside | 15 (24 | Torside | 15 (24) |
| 2 Standedge | 12 (19.5) | Standedge | 12 (19.5) | Mankinholes | 22 (35.5) |
| 3 Hebden Bridge | 14 (22.5) | Hebden Bridge | 14 (22.5) | Ponden | 17 (27) |
| 4 Ponden | 12 (19.5) | Ickornshaw | 16 (26) | Malham | 22.5 (36) |
| 5 Thornton-in-C | 14 (22.5) | Malham | 16 (26) | Horton-in-Rib | 15 (24) |
| 6 Malham | 10 (16) | Horton-in-Rib | 15 (24) | Keld | 26.5 (42.5) |
| 7 Horton-in-Rib | 15 (24) | Hawes | 14 (22.5) | Middleton-in-T | 20.5 (33) |
| 8 Hawes | 14 (22.5) | (Rest day) | | Dufton | 20.5 (33) |
| 9 (Rest day) | | Keld | 12.5 (20) | Alston | 20 (32) |
| 10 Keld | 12.5 (20) | Baldersdale | 14 (22.5) | Greenhead | 17 (27) |
| 11 Baldersdale | 14 (22.5) | Langdon Beck | 15 (24) | Bellingham | 21.5 (34.5) |
| 12 Langdon Beck | 15 (24) | Dufton | 12 (19.5) | Byrness | 15 (24) |
| 13 Dufton | 12 (19.5) | Alston | 20 (32) | Kirk Yetholm | 27 (43.5) |
| 14 Garrigill | 16 (26) | Greenhead | 17 (27) | | |
| 15 Knarsdale | 10 (16) | Once Brewed | 7 (11.5) | | |
| 16 Greenhead | 11 (18) | Bellingham | 14.5 (23) | | |
| 17 Once Brewed | 7 (11.5) | Byrness | 15 (24) | | |
| 18 Bellingham | 14.5 (23) | Kirk Yetholm | 27 (43.5) | | |
| 19 Byrness | 15 (24) | | | | |
| 20 Upper Coquetdale | 12 (19.5) | | | | |
| 21 Kirk Yetholm | 15 (24) | | | | |
| **21 nights Av 12 miles/day** | | **18 nights Av 14.2 m/d** | | **13 nights Av 19.6 m/d** | |

## ❏ THE BEST DAY AND WEEKEND (TWO-DAY) WALKS

One great way of experiencing the Pennine Way without burning yourself out is to do it in a series of days or weekends that take in a section at a time, not necessarily consecutively. Over a period of time it would be quite possible to complete the entire route this way. Another advantage is to walk only the best sections, leaving the intermediate dross to the end-to-enders.

The following are some suggestions for linear walks intended to get the most out of the time available. Getting back to the start is not always straightforward but by using bus and train timetables, taxi firms and some ingenuity it's possible.

### Day walks

● **Edale to Kinder Downfall via Upper Booth, Jacob's Ladder and Kinder Low** (see pp77-81) There and back is a popular walk of 10 miles (16km) which gives a true taste of the Dark Peak and the groughs and edges of the Kinder Plateau. The area gives a fine feeling of wilderness yet is not very far at any time from civilisation.

(continued opposite)

**Day walks** *(continued from opposite)*

● **Thornton-in-Craven to Malham via East Marton and the Leeds–Liverpool Canal** (see pp122-36)  10 miles (16km) of easy, low-level walking initially through meadows and fields, then on the canal towpath before visiting Gargrave. Beyond Gargrave you follow a lovely riverside path along the River Aire via Airton and Kirkby Malham to arrive at Malham where, if time allows, a visit to the Cove is a must.

● **Malham to Horton-in-Ribblesdale via Fountains Fell and Pen-y-ghent** (see pp136-45)  A 15-mile (24km) walk which is one of the best day walks as you surmount the Cove and follow the dry gorge behind it to the Tarn and beyond. You soon rise out of farmland to gradually surmount Fountains Fell where you drop down again in time to take the stiffer trek up Pen-y-ghent followed by the long, long descent to the lovely village of Horton.

● **Middleton-in-Teesdale to Langdon Beck** (see pp182-9)  This low-level walk of 9 miles (15km) follows the banks of the River Tees, an area rich in wild flowers and birds offering constant variety and many diversions. The falls of Low Force and High Force are passed, the latter in spate is an awesome sight. By crossing the footbridge at Holwick Head, a visit to High Force Hotel can be made for lunch or a pint and a night in the remote hamlet of Langdon Beck is a treat.

● **Dufton to Garrigill over Cross Fell** (see pp197-205)  This one needs an early start so perhaps stay in Dufton the night before. It is 16 miles (26km) to Garrigill and the weather over Cross Fell is likely to be unpredictable so go well prepared. There's a mountain refuge hut just below the summit (Greg's Hut) where shelter can be sought if necessary. Then there's a long foot-numbing walk down the miners' track to the quaint village of Garrigill.

● **Greenhead to Once Brewed** (see pp220-5)  This walk is a great introduction to Hadrian's Wall following the ramparts themselves as they swoop and soar along Whin Sill. It's 7 miles (11km) and will only take a morning. Thirlwall Castle can also be visited, a later fortification than the Romans yet built using stone from the Wall itself.

● **Kirk Yetholm to The Schil and back** (see pp257-253 and vice versa)  This 10-mile (16km) walk follows the high-level alternative route southwards, returning by the low-level route via Old Halterburnhead (ruin) and the road along the Halter Burn. It visits White Law and Steer Rig before topping out on The Schil (1985ft/605m). In good weather you should have fine views and if you've done the Kinder Downfall to Edale walk described above, all that remains is the 240-odd miles in between.

**Weekend (two-day) walks**

● **Edale to Standedge** (see pp77-95)  This 27-mile (43km) walk takes in the Kinder Scout, Bleaklow and Black Hill massifs and offers a chance to experience the true meaning of the name 'Dark Peak' or 'peat' for short. A night at Crowden hostel, or a Torside B&B, comes as a welcome break in the route, much of it mercifully slabbed to ensure you keep your boots dry and your spirits high.

● **Thornton-in-Craven to Horton-in-Ribblesdale** (see pp122-45)  A 25-mile (40km) route following a pleasant and then outstanding section of the Way, taking in the best of the limestone country. After the lovely riverside walk along the meandering River Aire you arrive in Malham. On day two you have some climbing to do over Fountains Fell, then up to the windy heights of Pen-y-ghent to end an exhilarating weekend at Horton and a train home.

● **Hawes to Tan Hill** (see pp156-67)  This 16½-mile (27km) walk could be done in a day but what's the rush? Plan an overnight stop in the tiny hamlet of Thwaite, perhaps taking advantage of a mini-break at the charming Kearton Country Hotel. *(cont'd overleaf)*

**Weekend (two-day) walks**

*(continued from p35)* Tan Hill could be reached for a late lunch on the second day, allowing the rest of the day to call a taxi to take you down into Kirkby Stephen where there's a train station. The walking is superb and includes Great Shunner Fell and a lovely stretch high above the Swale.

● **Middleton-in-Teesdale to Alston** (see pp182-210)  Fancy a stiff training walk incorporating the crème-de-la-crème of the North Pennines? Then this 40-mile (64km) stretch will give you something to get your teeth into. Up to High Force is tame, but beyond the wild moors move in, ending at the glorious amphitheatre of High Cup. After a night in quiet Dufton it's a tougher trek up over Cross Fell followed by the truly interminable tramp along the Corpse Road down to Garrigill (consider overnighting here, it's much nicer than Alston, five tiresome miles away). Once completed the lure of the Pennine Way will be all but irresistible!

● **Byrness to Kirk Yetholm** (see pp243-57)  This easy weekender explores the heart of The Cheviots – and overnighting at one of the refuges is great fun if the weather is on your side; or there's always the B&Bs in Upper Coquetdale (see p250). The full 27-mile (43km) crossing follows the Border fence, switching from England into Scotland and back again. Luckily most of the boggy upland sections are slabbed for your walking and route-finding pleasure. As you arrive at Kirk Yetholm you can only imagine what it must feel like to have come all the way up from Edale.

# What to take

Not ending up schlepping over the fells like an overloaded mule with a migraine takes experience and some measure of discipline. **Taking too much** is a mistake made by first-time travellers of all types, an understandable response to not knowing what to expect and not wanting to be caught short.

By UK standards the Pennine Way is a long walk but it's not an expedition into the unknown. Experienced independent hill walkers trim their gear down to the essentials because they've learned that an unnecessarily heavy pack can exacerbate injuries and put excess strain on their already hard-pressed feet. For those not camping or intent on carrying the complete works of Dostoyevsky in hardback, it's hard to see how you'd need more than 10kg of gear.

Note that if you need to buy all the gear listed, keep an eye for the ever-frequent online **sales** and at outdoor gear shops; time it right and you could get it all half price.

## TRAVELLING LIGHT

Organised tours apart, baggage-forwarding services (see p21-2) are tempting for walkers but partially miss the point of long-distance walking: the satisfaction of striking out from Edale knowing that you're carrying with you everything you need to get to Kirk Yetholm. However, if you've chosen to carry it all you must be ruthless in your packing choices.

## HOW TO CARRY IT

Today's **rucksacks** are hi-tech affairs that make load-carrying as tolerable as can be expected. Don't get hung up on anti-sweat features; unless you use a wheelbarrow your back will always sweat. It's better to ensure there is thick padding and a **good range of adjustment**. In addition to hip belts, use an unelasticated **cross-chest strap** to keep the pack snug; it makes a real difference.

If camping you'll need a pack of at least 60-litres' capacity. Staying in hostels 40 litres should be ample, and for those eating out and staying in B&Bs a 20- to 30-litre pack should suffice; you could even get away with a daypack.

Although many rucksacks claim to be waterproof, use a strong plastic **bin liner**. It's also handy to **compartmentalise** the contents into bags so you know what is where. Take **plastic bags** for wet things, rubbish etc; they're always useful. Finally, pack the most frequently used things so they are readily accessible.

## FOOTWEAR

### Boots

Not surprisingly on a walk of around half a million steps, choosing a good pair of boots is vital. Scrimp on other gear if you must, but not on boots. Expect to spend at least £100 on quality three-season items which are light, breathable and waterproof and have ankle support and the key feature – flexible but thick **soles** to insulate your own pulverised soles as you limp down the stony Corpse Road off Cross Fell. With modern fabric boots **breaking-in** is a thing of the past but arriving in Edale with new unworn boots is unwise – try them out beforehand with a full pack over a weekend.

An old and trusted pair of boots can be transformed with shock-absorbing after-market **insoles**. Some are thermally moulded to your foot in the shop but the less expensive examples are also well worth the investment even if the need for replacement by the end of the walk is likely. If you get bad blisters refer to p39 for blister-avoidance strategies. Although not essential, it's a treat to have **alternative footwear** when not on the trail to give your feet a break or let boots dry. Sport sandals or flip-flops are all suitable as long as they're light.

### Socks

As with all outdoor gear, the humble sock has not escaped the technological revolution (with prices to match). But to paraphrase L'Oréal, 'your feet are worth it' so invest in two pairs designed for walking. Although cushioning is desirable, avoid anything too thick which will reduce stability. A correctly sized boot with an anatomically shaped insole gives a sure-footed feel. As well as the obvious olfactory benefits, frequent washing will maintain the socks' springiness.

## CLOTHES

### Tops

The proven system of **layering** is still a good principle to follow. A quick-drying synthetic or a less-odiferous merino-wool **base layer** transports sweat away from your skin; the mid-layer(s), typically a **fleece** or woollen jumper, keep(s) you warm; and when needed, an outer 'shell' or **jacket** protects you from the wind and rain.

Maintaining a comfortable temperature in all conditions is essential; this means not **overheating** just as much as the more obvious effects of **wind chill**. Both can prematurely tire you. Trudging out of the Calder Valley on a warm day will have you down to your base layer, but any exposed and prolonged descent or rest on an unsheltered summit with the blowing wind will soon chill you. Although tedious, the smart walker is forever fiddling with zips and managing their layers and headwear to maintain an optimal level of comfort.

Avoid cotton; as well as being slow to dry, when soaked it saps away body heat but not the moisture – and you'll be wet from sweat if not rain. Take a change of **base layers** (including underwear), a **fleece** suited to the season, and the best **waterproof** you can afford. **Soft shells** are an alternative to walking in rustling nylon waterproofs when it's windy but not raining.

It's useful to have a **spare set of dry clothing** so you're able to get changed should you arrive chilled at your destination, but choosing **quick-drying clothes** and washing them reduces your load. Once indoors your body heat can quickly dry out a synthetic fleece and nylon leggings. However, always make sure you have a **dry base layer** in case you or someone you're with goes down with hypothermia (see p57). This is why a quality waterproof is important.

## Leg wear
Your legs are doing all the work and don't generally get cold so your trousers can be light which will also mean quick-drying. Although they lack useful pockets, many walkers find leg-hugging cycling polyester **leggings** very comfortable (eg Ron Hill Tracksters). Poly-cotton or microfibre trousers are excellent. Denim jeans are cotton; a disaster when wet.

If the weather's good, **shorts** are very agreeable to walk in, leaving a light pair of trousers clean for the evenings. On the other hand **waterproof trousers** would only suit people who really feel the cold; most others will find them unnecessary and awkward to put on and wear – quick drying legwear is better. As the worst of the peat bogs are tamed by slabs, **gaiters** are not essential but are still useful when walking through wet vegetation.

## Headwear and other clothing
Your head is both exposed to the sun and loses most of your body heat so have two **hats**: a woolly beany for warmth and a peaked cap for UV protection; a bandana makes a good back up. Between them they'll conserve body heat or reduce the chances of dehydration. **Gloves** are a good idea in wintry conditions (carry a spare pair in winter).

## TOILETRIES

Besides **toothpaste** and a brush, **liquid soap** can also be used for shaving and washing clothes, although a ziplock bag of **detergent** is better if you're laundering regularly. Carry **toilet paper** and a lightweight **trowel** to bury the results out on the fells (see p54).

Less obvious items include **ear plugs**, **sun screen, moisturiser** and, particularly if camping, **insect repellent** and a **water purification system**.

## FIRST-AID KIT

Apart from aching limbs your most likely ailments will be blisters so a first-aid kit can be tiny. **Paracetamol** helps numb pain, **Ibuprofen** is more effective against pain with inflammation although rest, of course, is the cure. '**Moleskin**', '**Compeed**', or '**Second Skin**' all treat blisters. An **elastic knee support** is a good precaution for a weak knee. A few sachets of **Dioralyte** or **Rehydrat** powders will quickly remedy mineral loss through sweating. Also consider taking a small selection of different-sized **sterile dressings** for wounds.

## GENERAL ITEMS

### Essential

Carry a **compass** and know how to use it with a map; also take a **whistle** (see p56) and a **mobile phone** for emergencies; a **water pouch** (at least two litres); a **headtorch** with spare batteries; **emergency snacks** which your body can quickly convert into energy; a **penknife, watch, plastic bags, safety pins** and **scissors.**

### Useful

If you're not carrying a proper bivi bag or tent a compact foil **space blanket** is a good idea in the cooler seasons. Many would list a **camera** as essential but it's liberating to travel without one once in a while – instead take a **notebook** in which to record your memories; a reading **book** will help you enjoy midsummer wild camps and a **vacuum flask** is great for carrying hot drinks in cooler seasons. Studies have shown that nothing improves a hilltop view on a chilly day like a cup of hot tea or soup. Also consider taking **sunglasses**, **binoculars** and **walking poles**.

PLANNING YOUR WALK

---

❏ **Walking poles – must have or don't need?**
I decided to find out and, turning back just in time from splashing out £90 on some Leki Super Makalus, I bought a similarly sprung pair for £15 off eBay.

The first thing serious walkers must know is that one pole is as useful as one boot. You'll often see 'leisure walkers' along tow paths and the like using single poles as walking sticks but on the hill **you need two** if you want them to work for you.

The most effective application was found to be on long steady ascents such as Great Shunner or Fountains Fell. Here, as long as you could maintain your rhythm, they had a positive aerobic value, adapting your arms into 'forelegs' to bear some weight and propel you forward faster than normal, though of course using more energy. After a good day of uphill poling you'll notice some soreness in your chest muscles.

Only on the very steepest, slipperiest downhills, like that off Kinder Scout, might poles be an aid to steadying yourself. At any other time or on the flat they're a hindrance. Do you collapse them and tuck them away or carry them? I never got fully into them because my pack was fairly light and I was content to slog unpoled up most hills. With a heavy pack or on a fast end-to-end schedule, making the effort to get acclimatised to walking poles would be worthwhile. **Chris Scott**

PLANNING YOUR WALK

## SLEEPING BAG

If you're camping or planning to stay in camping barns you'll need a sleeping bag. Some bunkhouses offer bedding but you'll keep your costs down if you don't have to hire it. All YHA hostels provide bedding and insist you use it.

A **two-season bag** will do for indoor use, but if you can afford it or anticipate outdoor use, go warmer. The choice over a **synthetic or down** filling is a debate without end. Year by year less expensive synthetic-filled bags (typically under £100) approach down's enviable qualities of good compressability while expanding or 'lofting' fully once unpacked to create maximum warmth. But get a down bag wet (always a risk in the UK) and it clogs up and loses all its thermal qualities; and washing down bags takes half a day at the laundrette.

## CAMPING GEAR

If committed to the exposure of wild camping you'll need a **tent** you can rely on; light but able to withstand the rain and wind. At campsites you may just get away with a £7 tent from Argos. Otherwise, a good one-man item suited to the wilds can cost less than £100 and weigh just 1.5kg, with a sub-2kg two-man example costing around £220.

An inflatable **sleeping mat** is worth many times its weight. As for **cooking**, is it really worth the bother on the Pennine Way; the extra weight and hassle is only viable when shared by a group of three or more.

> ❏ **Talking the talk**
>
> Although we all speak English after a fashion, the finely honed ear will perceive at least **five** distinct accents along the Pennine Way, each with its own dialects, with greetings being most evident to the walker. These will be most noticeable in deeply rural areas, particularly among agricultural workers who may sound unintelligible to an unacclimatised foreigner.
>
> From the High Peak of northern Derbyshire ('*ahyallrait*?') you'll flit between the cultural frontier of erstwhile county rivals, Yorkshire and Lancashire, who both share a curt '*ow do*?'. Then, as you leave the Dales another invisible boundary is crossed and the accent takes on the distinctive 'Geordie' tones of County Durham and Northumberland ('*allreet*?') before your final linguistic watershed over the Cheviots into Scotland where a barely discernible nod means you've a new friend for life.

## MAPS

The hand-drawn maps in this book cover the trail at a scale of 1:20,000 but are in a strip the scale equivalent to two miles wide. In some places, particularly on high moors where navigation points are scant, a proper **topographical map and a compass** could be of great use. But, as mentioned on p11, when the mist comes down and all landmarks disappear, a **GPS** used with a map comes into its own.

In Britain the **Ordnance Survey** (🖳 www.ordnancesurvey.co.uk; 🖳 http://leisure.ordnancesurvey.co.uk) series is peerless. Their orange 1:25,000-scale 'Explorer' features pin-sharp cartography and detail that makes navigation a doddle. From south to north nine sheets cover the Pennine Way: **OL1** *The Peak District – Dark Peak area;* **OL21** *South Pennines;* **OL2** *Yorkshire Dales – Southern & Western areas;* **OL30** *Yorkshire Dales Northern & Central Areas;* **OL31** *North Pennines – Teesdale & Weardale;* **OL19** *Howgill Fells & Upper Eden Valley;* **OL43** *Hadrian's Wall;* **OL42** *Kielder Water and Forest;* **OL16** *The Cheviot Hills.*

Packing such a stack of maps, especially the bulky laminated weatherproof versions, is a chore. Walkers either post them ahead or mark the Way and trim off the flab with a pair of scissors. Alternatively, members of the **Ramblers** (see box p42) can borrow these maps for up to six weeks at 50p per map from their library and members of the **Backpackers Club** (see box p42) can buy OS maps at a significant discount through their map service.

OS Explorers are the ultimate Pennine maps but there are two handy map series which give the big picture during planning and work fine on the trail as a back up to this book's maps. Both use 50-years-old out-of-copyright OS maps as bases and then add or update contemporary information (although you may still spot the odd long out-of-date detail).

**Footprint Maps** (🖳 www.footprintmaps.co.uk) produces a compact set of two double-sided sheets: *Pennine Way Part 1 – South: Edale–Teesdale* and *Part 2; Teesdale–Kirk Yetholm* (both 2005) printed on waterproof paper. Each 60cm x 40cm sheet has 16 panels at around 1:50,000 scale. With a commentary of recommended daily stages, incremental mileages from 1 to 255 and an uncluttered design, their only drawback is the lack of a grid to work with GPS.

**Harvey Maps** (🖳 www.harveymaps.co.uk) produce a similar set of maps: three waterproof sheets covering *Edale to Horton*, *Horton to Greenhead* and *Greenhead to Kirk Yetholm* (all 2005) in a series of north-oriented strip panels at a scale of 1:40,000 and with similar information. The panels cover a broader area each side of the path but being one-sided like an OS can be a bit cumbersome in windy conditions although crucially they include the OS grid to work with GPS.

---

❏ **Online satellite imagery**

More for inspiration and planning than navigation on the trail, free online satellite mapping like Google Maps (🖳 maps.google.co.uk) helps bring your surroundings alive. And it's made all the more impressive with basic free software packages such as Google Earth (🖳 earth.google.com) or NASA World Wind (🖳 worldwind.arc.nasa. gov; PC only).

This 'Earth browsing' software allows you to effortlessly zoom in and steer from 25,000km out in space to within a few metres above the tip of Stoodley Pike monument. Once there you can then tilt the projection and glide off along the Pennine Way at your preferred altitude, tracing the exact course of the trail which is usually clearly visible.

In fact you could do a lot worse than export this book's GPS waypoints (see p11) as a .KML file, open it up in Google Earth and press 'play'. You can then sit back and let the software 'fly' you from waypoint to waypoint from Edale all the way to Kirk Yetholm. It's no exaggeration to say the experience will blow your mind!

## ❏ SOURCES OF FURTHER INFORMATION
### Trail information
**Pennine Way National Trail** (💻 www.nationaltrail.co.uk/PennineWay) The website provides an up-to-date accommodation guide as well as FAQs and even GPS waypoints. **Pennine Way Association** (💻 www.penninewayassociation.co.uk) A charity that campaigns to protect the national trail. Their website has lots of useful info including updates and news on the path.

The two main **online** sources of chat covering the Pennine Way are: 💻 **www .coast2coast.co.uk/ubb/cgi-bin/Ultimate.cgi** which has its own Pennine Way forum and 💻 **www.ramblers.co.uk/forum** which covers walking in Britain. A thorough scan over the previous months' postings on the former forum is bound to come up with some useful nuggets of information.

### National parks and tourist information centres along the Pennine Way
The Pennine Way goes through the Peak District, Yorkshire Dales and Northumberland **national parks**; see box p62 for contact details.

Most **tourist information centres** (TICs) are open daily from Easter to September/ October, and thereafter more limited days/hours, often weekends only. Unless you're stuck for accommodation or have a specific query, they're of little use to an organised walker once underway. Some TICs are also national park centres. **Edale** (see p75); **Hebden Bridge** (see p106); **Haworth** (see p115); **Malham** (see p133); **Horton-in-Ribblesdale** (see p144); **Hawes** (see p153); **Middleton-in-Teesdale** (see p180); **Alston** (see p208), **Once Brewed** (see p225); **Bellingham** (see p233).

### Organisations for walkers
● **Backpackers Club** (💻 www.backpackersclub.co.uk) For people interested in lightweight camping. Members receive a quarterly magazine, access to a comprehensive information service (including a library), discounts on maps (see p41) and a farm-pitch directory. Membership is £12 per year, family £15, under 18s and over 65s £7.

● **The Long Distance Walkers' Association** (💻 www.ldwa.org.uk) An association of people with the common interest of long-distance walking. Membership includes a journal, *Strider*, three times per year giving details of challenge events and local group walks as well as articles on the subject. Information on over 730 paths is presented in their *UK Trailwalkers' Handbook*. Individual membership is £13 a year whilst family membership for two adults and all children under 18 is £19.50 a year.

● **Ramblers** (formerly Ramblers Association; ☎ 020-7339 8500, 💻 www.ramblers .org.uk) Looks after the interests of walkers throughout Britain. They publish a large amount of useful information including their quarterly *Walk* magazine (£3.40 to non-members), and *Walk Britain: Great Views* (£14.99), a guide to Britain's top 50 viewpoints via 50 walks. The website also has a discussion forum (see above). Membership costs £31/41/19.50 individual/joint/concessionary.

### Some books
*Laughs Along the Pennine Way,* Pete Bog (Cicerone, 1987; OP) A collection of hit-and-miss cartoons, some of which will have you chuckling with recollection; *The Pennine Way,* Tony Hopkins (Zymurgy, 2005) Medium-format picture book with good background text but spoiled by the occasional less-than-crisp shot;
● **Flora and fauna** *Collins Complete Guide – British Wildlife,* Paul Sterry (Collins, 2008) Birds, wild flowers, trees, insects, wild animals, butterflies and moths but not entirely comprehensive; *RSPB Pocket Guide to British Birds,* Simon Harrap (RSPB, 2007); *Collins Bird Guide,* Lars Svensson (Collins, 2010); *Collins Complete Guide – British Wild Flowers,* Paul Sterry (Collins, 2008) User friendly tome.

# Getting to and from the Pennine Way

Travelling to the start of the Pennine Way by public transport makes sense. There's no need to trouble anyone for a lift or worry about your vehicle while walking, there are no logistical headaches about how to return to your car when you've finished the walk and it's obviously a big step towards minimising your ecological footprint. Quite apart from that, you'll simply feel your holiday has begun the moment you step out of your front door, rather than when you've slammed the car door behind you.

## NATIONAL TRANSPORT

**Manchester** and **Sheffield** can both be used as gateways to the start of the Pennine Way being only 30-45 minutes from Edale by train, the most convenient way to get there. At the northern end of the walk **Berwick-upon-Tweed** is the main transport hub, reached from Kirk Yetholm in about four hours by changing buses at Kelso.

---

❏ **Getting to Britain**
● **By air**  There are plenty of cheap flights from around the world to London's airports: Heathrow, Gatwick, Luton, London City and Stansted. However, Manchester (🖳 www. manchesterairport.co.uk) and Edinburgh (🖳 www.edinburghairport.com) airports are the closest to the start and finish points of the Pennine Way and both have a number of international flights. There are also airports at Newcastle (🖳 www.newcastleairport. com) and Leeds (🖳 www.leedsbradfordairport.co.uk).
● **From Europe by train**  Eurostar (🖳 www.eurostar.com) operates a high-speed passenger service via the Channel Tunnel between a number of cities in Europe (particularly Paris and Brussels) and London (St Pancras International). St Pancras is located between King's Cross and Euston stations from where trains operate to the north; these stations also have connections to the London Underground. For more information about rail services from Europe contact your national rail company or Railteam (🖳 www.railteam.eu).
● **From Europe by coach**  Eurolines (🖳 www.eurolines.co.uk) have a huge network of long-distance coach services connecting over 500 cities in 25 European countries to London. Check carefully, however: often, once such expenses as food for the journey are taken into consideration, it does not work out that much cheaper than taking a flight, particularly when compared to the fares on some of the budget airlines.
● **From Europe by car**  P&O Ferries (🖳 www.poferries.com) and Norfolk Line (🖳 www.norfolkline-ferries.co.uk) are just two of the many ferry operators from Europe. The main routes are between all the major North Sea and Channel ports of mainland Europe and the ports on Britain's eastern and southern coasts. Direct Ferries (🖳 www. directferries.com) lists all the main operators/routes and sells discounted tickets.
   Eurotunnel (🖳 www.eurotunnel.com) operates the shuttle train service for vehicles via the Channel Tunnel between Calais and Folkestone taking one hour between the motorway in France and the motorway in Britain.

## By rail

Manchester and Sheffield are served by frequent trains from the rest of Britain, and Berwick-upon-Tweed is on the east-coast main line between London, Newcastle and Edinburgh. There are stations on the Pennine Way at Edale, Hebden Bridge, Gargrave and Horton-in-Ribblesdale. Other useful stations with good bus services linking them to various parts of the Way include Huddersfield, Skipton, Penrith, Darlington, Haltwhistle and Hexham. The main rail operators are Northern (see box p50), East Coast (🖥 www.eastcoast.co.uk), Virgin (🖥 www.virgintrains.co.uk) and Trans-Pennine Express (see box p50). Megatrain (🖥 www.megatrain.com/uk) also serves Manchester, Leeds and Berwick-upon-Tweed.

**National Rail Enquiries** (☎ 0845-748 4950, 24hrs, 🖥 www.nationalrail.co.uk) will be able to give you the timetable and fare information for rail travel in the whole of Britain. Tickets can be bought by phone or online through the relevant rail operator (see box p50) or online at 🖥 www.thetrainline.com or 🖥 www.qjump.co.uk. It's worth planning ahead, at least two weeks, as it's the only way to save a considerable amount of money. It helps to be as flexible as possible and don't forget that most discounted tickets carry some restrictions; check what they are before you buy your ticket. Travel on a Friday may be more expensive than on other days of the week.

For a comprehensive list of taxi companies operating from railway stations contact Train Taxi (🖥 www.traintaxi.co.uk).

## By coach

**National Express** (☎ 0871-781 8181, lines open 8am-8pm daily; 🖥 www.nationalexpress.com) is the principal coach (long-distance bus) operator in Britain. There are services from most towns in England and Wales to a number of towns and cities on or near the route including: Manchester, Sheffield, Crowden, Keighley, Skipton, Otterburn, Byrness and Berwick-upon-Tweed (see box p49). **Megabus** (🖥 www.megabus.com/uk) also serves Manchester and Berwick-upon-Tweed; fares start from £1 plus a 50p booking fee.

Travel by coach is usually cheaper than by train but takes longer. Advance bookings carry discounts so be sure to book at least a week ahead. If you don't mind an uncomfortable night there are overnight services on some routes.

## By car

Both Edale and Kirk Yetholm are easily reached using the motorway and A-road network from the rest of Britain. Unless you're just out for a day walk however, you'd be better leaving the car at home as there is nowhere safe to leave a vehicle unattended for a long period.

## LOCAL TRANSPORT

Getting to and from most parts of the Pennine Way is relatively simple due to the public transport network including trains, coaches and local bus services. This opens up the potential for linear walks from an hour to several days without the nuisance of parking and getting back to your car.

The **public transport map** on pp46-7 gives an overview of routes which are of particular use to walkers and the table below and on pp48-50 lists the operators (and their contact details), the route details and the approximate frequency of services in both directions. Note that services may be less frequent in the winter months or stop completely. It is also essential to **check services before travelling** as details may change.

If the operator details prove unsatisfactory contact **traveline** (☎ 0871-200 2233, daily 7am-9pm, 🖳 www.traveline.org.uk) or **Transport Direct** (🖳 www. transportdirect.info), or **Public Transport Information** (🖳 www.pti.org.uk), which have timetable information for the whole of the UK. Local timetables can also be picked up from tourist information centres along the Way.

Note: many services in rural areas operate on a **hail and ride** basis ie the driver will stop to set passengers down or pick them up as long as it's safe to do so.

---

## PUBLIC TRANSPORT SERVICES

### Bus services
**Alston Road Garage** (☎ 01833-640213)
73    Langdon Beck to Middleton-in-Teesdale, Mon-Sat 3/day plus 1/day if pre-booked or requested to driver + Wed 2/day to/from Barnard Castle. If pre-booked the service will also go to Forest-in-Teesdale, Holwick, Lunedale & Baldersdale; contact the company for details.

**Arriva** (🖳 www.arrivabus.co.uk)
X26/27/X27/28  Catterick to Darlington via Richmond, Mon-Sat 4/hr, Sun 2/hr
75    Darlington to Barnard Castle via Staindrop, daily 1/hr
76    Darlington to Barnard Castle via Winston, Mon-Sat 1/hr
95/96 Barnard Castle to Middleton-in-Teesdale, Mon-Sat 1/hr, Sun 4/day
685   Newcastle to Carlisle via Hexham, Haltwhistle & Greenhead, Mon-Sat 12/day, Newcastle to Hexham Sun 1/hr, Hexham to Carlisle via Haltwhistle & Greenhead Sun 4/day (route also operated by Stagecoach North West)
X85   Newcastle to Hexham, Mon-Fri 3/day (two in morning and one in evening)
X59   Darlington to Hawes via Richmond & Leyburn, Mon-Fri 1/day

**Central Coaches**
72    Barnard Castle to Bowes, Mon-Sat 4/day (+1/day term-time Mon-Fri)

**Dales and District** (☎ 01677-425203, 🖳 www.dalesanddistrict.co.uk)
156/157 Northallerton to Hawes, Mon-Sat 9/day, Sun 4/day

**First** (🖳 www.firstgroup.com/ukbus)
184   Huddersfield to Manchester via Marsden, Standedge & Diggle, Mon-Sat 1/hr, Sun 5/day
272   Sheffield to Castleton, Mon-Sat 9/day (see also Hulleys of Baslow)
590   Halifax to Rochdale via Hebden Bridge & Todmorden, daily 1/hr
591   Halifax to Heptonstall via Hebden Bridge, Mon-Sat 1/hr
592   Halifax to Burnley via Hebden Bridge & Todmorden, daily 1/hr
593   Halifax to Old Town via Hebden Bridge, Mon-Sat 1/hr
594   Halifax to Todmorden via Hebden Bridge, Mon-Sat 2/hr, Halifax to Hebden Bridge, Easter to Sep Sun 4/day
E     Hebden Bridge circular route via Mytholm and Blackshaw Head, daily 1/hr

*(continued on p48)*

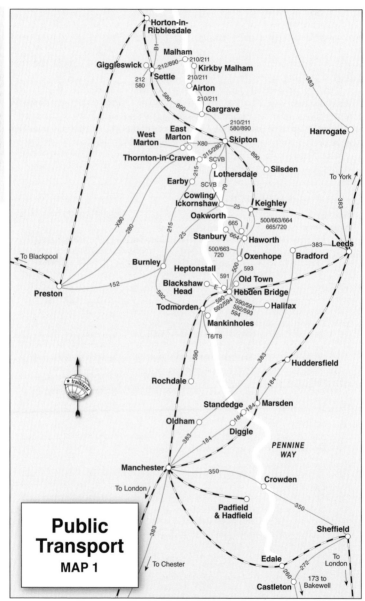

**Public Transport MAP 1**

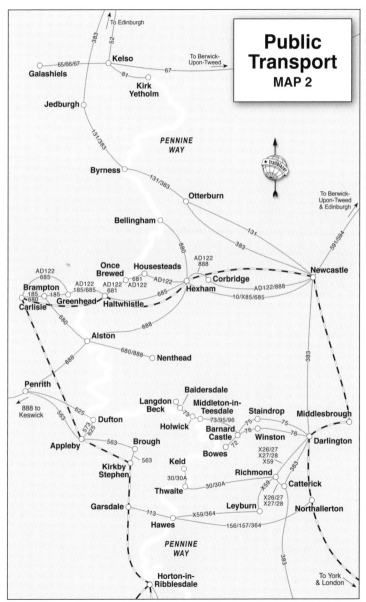

PLANNING YOUR WALK

PLANNING YOUR WALK

## PUBLIC TRANSPORT SERVICES

**Bus services** *(continued from p45)*
**First Borders** (🖳 www.firstborders.co.uk)
65/66  Kelso to Galashiels, Mon-Fri 2/day
81  Kelso to Kirk Yetholm circular route, Mon-Sat 7/day

**Go North East** (🖳 www.simplygo.com)
10  Newcastle to Hexham, Mon-Sat 3/hr, Sun 1/hr

**Grand Prix Coaches** (☎ 01768-341328, 🖳 www.grandprixservices.co.uk)
563  Penrith to Kirkby Stephen via Appleby & Brough, Mon-Sat 6/day

**Hadrian's Wall Bus Service** (🖳 www.hadrians-wall.org)
AD122  Carlisle to Hexham via Greenhead, Haltwhistle & Once Brewed, Apr-Oct
daily 5/day + Walltown to Hexham via Once Brewed and Housesteads, Apr-
Oct daily 3/day, 1/day continues to Newcastle

**Hulleys of Baslow** (☎ 01246-582246, 🖳 www.hulleys-of-baslow.co.uk)
173  Bakewell to Castleton, daily 3/day
260  Castleton to Edale, Sun & Bank Hol Mon only 6/day
272  Sheffield to Castleton, Mon-Sat 3/day (see also First)

**Jacksons of Silsden** (☎ 01535-652376, 🖳 www.jacksonsofsilsden.com or 🖳 www
.dalesbus.org)
890  Settle to Malham circular route (Malham Tarn Shuttle), Sat, Sun & bank hols
5/day, mid July to end Aug. Note: the bus starts in the morning in Silsden
goes to Skipton, then Gargrave and on to Settle and Malham, it then shuttles
between these two during the day and goes back to Gargrave, Skipton and
Silsden in the evening.

**Keighley & District** (☎ 01535-603284, 🖳 www.keighleybus.co.uk)
79  Skipton to Cowling, Mon-Fri 1-2/day
500  Keighley to Hebden Bridge via Haworth & Oxenhope, daily 1/hr
663/5  Keighley to Oxenhope (663)/Oakworth (665) via Haworth, daily 1/hr
664  Keighley to Stanbury via Haworth, Mon-Sat 1/hr
720  Keighley to Oxenhope via Haworth, Mon-Sat 1/hr

**Little Red Bus** (🖳 www.littleredbus.co.uk; call ☎ 01423-526655 for more details of
the 30/30A, 113 and B1; ☎ 01756-795666 for the 211 and to book a seat on the SCVB;
and ☎ 01524-262753 to book a journey on the 212)
30/30A  Keld to Richmond via Thwaite, Muker (Farmer's Arms), Gunnerside Bridge
and Reeth, Mon-Sat 2/day; Gunnerside Bridge to Richmond Mon-Sat 2/day;
and Reeth to Richmond Mon-Sat 2/day. (Note: book to be sure of a place as
the bus has 16 seats only)
113  Garsdale to Hawes, Mon-Sat 4/day
B1  Settle to Horton-in-Ribblesdale, Mon-Sat 3/day
211  Skipton to Malham via Gargrave, Airton and Kirkby Malham, Mon, Wed &
Fri 2/day (see also Pennine Motor Services No 210)
SCVB  Skipton to Lothersdale & Cowling (Mon-Fri 9am-2.45pm)
212  Giggleswick/Settle to Malham via Malham Cove (Mon-Fri)
Note: the SCVB and 212 are dial-a-ride services so call to book a seat.

**Munro's of Jedburgh** (☎ 01835-862253, 🖳 www.munrosofjedburgh.co.uk)
52  Edinburgh to Kelso, Mon-Sat 11/day, Sun 5/day
131  Newcastle to Jedburgh via Otterburn & Byrness, Mon-Sat 1-2/day

**National Express** (☎ 08717-818181, 🖳 www.national express.com)
350  Manchester to Sheffield via Crowden, daily 4/day
383  Chester to Edinburgh via Manchester, Bradford, Leeds, Harrogate, Catterick, Darlington, Newcastle, Otterburn, Byrness & Jedburgh, 1/day
591  London to Edinburgh via Newcastle & Berwick-upon-Tweed, 1/day
594  London to Edinburgh via Newcastle & Berwick-upon-Tweed, 1/day (night service)

**Pennine Motor Services** (☎ 01756-795515, 🖳 www.pennine-bus.co.uk or 🖳 www .dalesbus.org)
210  Skipton to Malham via Gargrave, Airton & Kirkby Malham Mon-Fri 2/day (see also Little Red Bus); Skipton to Malham via Airton Sat 2/day (operated by Hutchinsons)
215  Burnley to Skipton via Earby & Thornton-in-Craven, Mon-Sat 1-2/hr, Sun 8/day
580  Skipton to Giggleswick via Gargrave & Settle, Mon-Sat 11/day

**Perryman's Buses** (🖳 www.perrymansbuses.co.uk)
67  Galashiels to Berwick via Kelso, Mon-Sat 7-8/day, Sun 4/day

**Robinson's** (☎ 01768-351424)
573  Appleby circular route including Dufton, Fri 2/day
625  Appleby to Penrith via Dufton, Tue & Sat 1/day

**Royal Mail Postbus** (🖳 www.postbus.royalmail.com)
364  Leyburn to Northallerton via Hawes, Mon-Sat 1/day plus Northallerton to Hawes circular route Mon-Fri 2/day

**Stagecoach** (🖳 www.stagecoachbus.co.uk)
680  Carlisle to Nenthead via Brampton & Alston, Mon-Sat 2/day plus Sat 1/day (see also Telford's Coaches and Wright Brothers' Coaches)
685  Newcastle to Carlisle (see Arriva for details)

**Telford's Coaches** (☎ 013873 75677; 🖳 www.telfordscoaches.com)
185  Carlisle to Haltwhistle via Crosby-on-Eden, Brampton, Gilsland, Longbyre, Greenhead & Walltown, Mon-Sat 1/day, 2/day to Brampton only (not all stops shown on map)
680  Carlisle to Nenthead (see Wright Brothers' Coaches and Stagecoach)

**Transdev Lancashire (Mainline)**(☎ 0845-604 0110, 🖳 www.lancashirebus.co.uk
25  Burnley to Keighley via Cowling, Mon-Sat 1/hr, Sun 6/day

**Transdev Lancashire United** (☎ 0845-272 7272, 🖳 www.lancashirebus.co.uk)
152  Preston to Burnley, Mon-Sat 2/hr, Sun 1/hr
X80  Skipton to Preston via West Marton, Mon-Sat 4/day, Sun 2/day
280  Skipton to Preston via Thornton-in-Craven, Mon-Sat 5/day

**Tyne Valley Coaches** (☎ 01434-602217, 🖳 www.tynevalleycoaches.co.uk)
880  Hexham to Bellingham, Apr-Oct Mon-Sat 3/day                *(continued overleaf)*

## PUBLIC TRANSPORT SERVICES

**Bus services** *(continued from p49)*

**Tyrer Tours** (☎ 0845-130 1716)
T6    Mankinholes to Todmorden circular, Mon-Sat 12/day
T8    Mankinholes to Todmorden circular, Sun 12/day

**Wright Brothers' Coaches** (☎ 01434-381200, 🖵 www.wrightscoaches.co.uk)
680    Carlisle to Nenthead via Brampton & Alston, Mon-Fri termtime 2/day plus
          2/day Brampton to Nenthead (operated with Telford's and Stagecoach)
681    Haltwhistle to Housesteads via Once Brewed, Mon-Sat 3/day
888    Newcastle to Keswick via Corbridge, Hexham, Alston & Penrith, July-Sep
          daily 1/day

## Rail services

**DalesRail** (🖵 www.dalesrail.com)
● Blackpool to Carlisle via Preston, Horton-in-Ribblesdale, Garsdale, Kirkby Stephen
& Appleby, Apr/May to Sep/Oct Sun 1/day

**Keighley & Worth Valley Railway** (☎ 01535-645214, 🖵 www.kwvr.co.uk)
● Keighley to Oxenhope via Haworth, July & Aug daily 5-11/day, Sep-June weekends
& bank holidays only 5-11/day

**Northern Rail** (🖵 www.northernrail.org)
● Manchester Piccadilly to Sheffield via Edale, daily 10-12/day
● Manchester Victoria to Leeds via Marsden and Huddersfield, Mon-Sat 1/hr, Sun 7/day
● Manchester Piccadilly to Hadfield, daily 2/hr
● Leeds to Manchester Victoria via Hebden Bridge & Todmorden, Mon-Sat 2/hr,
Sun 1/hr
● Leeds to Carlisle via Keighley, Skipton, Settle, Horton-in-Ribblesdale, Garsdale,
Kirkby Stephen & Appleby, Mon-Sat 5-6/day, Sun 3-4/day
● Newcastle to Carlisle via Hexham & Haltwhistle, daily1/hr

**Trans Pennine Express** (🖵 www.tpexpress.co.uk)
● Manchester to Newcastle via Leeds, York, Northallerton, Darlington &
Middlesborough, Mon-Sat 1/hr, Sun 8/day

# MINIMUM IMPACT & OUTDOOR SAFETY

## Minimum impact walking

Britain has little wilderness, at least not by the dictionary definition of land that is 'uncultivated and uninhabited'. But parts of the Pennine Way include the closest we have and it's a fragile environment. Trapped between massive conurbations, the Peak District and South Pennines in particular are among the most crowded recreational areas in England and inevitably this has brought its problems. As more and more people enjoy the freedom of the hills so the land comes under increasing pressure and the potential for conflict with other land-users is heightened. Everyone has a right to this natural heritage but with it comes a responsibility to care for it too.

You can do this while walking the Pennine Way by practising many of the suggestions in this section. Rather than being seen as a restriction, learning how to minimise your impact brings you closer to the land and to those who work it.

### ECONOMIC IMPACT

Rural businesses and communities in Britain have been hit hard in recent years by a seemingly endless series of crises but there is a lot that the walker can do to help.

Playing your part today involves much more than simply closing the gate and not dropping litter; the new ethos which is fast becoming fashionable is 'local' and with it come huge social and environmental benefits.

The family-run **Pen-y-ghent Café** (see p144) provides not only sustenance and information for passing walkers but also keeps a Pennine Way book for wayfarers to sign.

#### Support local businesses
In light of the economic pressures that many businesses are under there is something else you can do: buy local. Look and ask for local produce (see box p18) to buy and eat. Not only does this

cut down on the amount of pollution and congestion that the transportation of food creates (the so-called 'food miles'), but also ensures that you are supporting local farmers and producers; the very people who have moulded the countryside you have come to see and who are in the best position to protect it. If you can find local food which is also organic so much the better.

It's a fact of life that money spent at local level – perhaps in a market, or at the greengrocer, or in an independent pub – has a far greater impact for good on that community than the equivalent spent in a branch of a national chain store or restaurant. While no-one would advocate that walkers should boycott the larger supermarkets, which after all do provide local employment, it's worth remembering that businesses in rural communities rely heavily on visitors for their very existence. If we want to keep these shops and post offices, we need to use them.

### Encourage local cultural traditions and skills

No part of the countryside looks the same. Buildings, food, skills and language (see box p40) evolve out of the landscape and are moulded over hundreds of years to suit the locality. Encountering these cultural differences is a great part of the pleasure of walking in new places. Visitors' enthusiasm for local traditions and skills brings awareness and pride, nurturing a sense of place; an increasingly important role in a world where economic globalisation continues to undermine the very things that provide security and a feeling of belonging.

## ENVIRONMENTAL IMPACT

By choosing a walking holiday you've already taken a positive step towards minimising your impact on the wider environment. By following these suggestions you can also tread lightly along the Pennine Way. Some of the latter practices become particularly relevant if you are wild camping.

### Use public transport

Traffic congestion is becoming the norm in Britain although where there is a demand for it, public transport is improving and gets better with use. There are days in the Peak District, particularly after Bank Holidays, when a brown band of pollution smothers the horizon. Once the cars have gone, the band disperses.

The Pennines, especially the southern end, are not as remote as we like to think and these days noise pollution is also a growing problem. The wilderness of Kinder Scout is often now marred by the noise of planes heading for Manchester Airport. Elsewhere there's nothing more disappointing than sitting on top of a hill in front of a beautiful view only to have the background hum of traffic intrude on the peace. Nearly all of us contribute to this pollution in some way and the best way to stop it is to stay out of our cars and use public transport instead, becoming part of the solution rather than part of the problem.

### Do you really need to use a baggage-forwarding service?

Think twice about effectively negating all the good you do in arriving by public transport and walking by then having your baggage vanned from one end of the Pennine Way to the other. For those who are able-bodied and not camping, it's hard to imagine what needs cannot be easily fitted into a 30-litre backpack. This self-sufficiency is part of the satisfaction of long-distance walking.

## Never leave litter
A piece of orange peel left on the ground takes six months to decompose; silver foil 18 months; a plastic bag 10 years; clothes 15 years; and a can 85 years.

Although you'll encounter it in popular areas, become fanatical about taking out all your litter and even that left by others; if you enjoyed the countryside, show it some respect by keeping it clean. As well as being unsightly litter kills wildlife, pollutes the environment and can be dangerous to farm animals. One good idea is to repackage any pre-packaged food into reusable containers as this reduces the amount of rubbish you have to get rid of.

### Is it OK if it's biodegradable?
Not really. Apple cores and especially banana skins and orange peel are unsightly, encourage flies, ants and wasps and so ruin a picnic spot for others. In high-use areas such as the Pennine Way bury them or better still take them with you.

## Erosion
**Stay on the main trail** The effect of your footsteps may seem minuscule but when they are multiplied by thousands of walkers each year they become rather more significant. Although it can be a bit much to ask when the actual pathway is waterlogged, avoid taking shortcuts, widening the trail or creating more than one path; your footprints will be followed by many others.

**Consider walking out of season** The maximum disturbance caused by walkers coincides with the time of year when nature wants to do most of its growth and recovery. In high-use areas, like that along much of the Pennine Way, the trail often never recovers. Walking at less busy times eases this pressure while also generating year-round income for the local economy. Not only that, but it may make the walk more enjoyable as there are fewer people on the path and (where it's open) there's less competition for accommodation.

## Respect wildlife
Care for all wildlife you come across and tempting as it may be to pick wild flowers leave them so the next people who pass can enjoy them too. Don't break branches off or damage trees in any way. If you come across wildlife keep your distance and don't watch for too long. Your presence can cause considerable stress particularly if the adults are with their young or in winter when the weather is harsh and food scarce. Young animals are rarely abandoned. If you come across deer calves or young birds keep away so that their mother can return.

## Outdoor toiletry
As more and more people discover the joys of the outdoors, answering the call of nature is becoming an important issue. In some national parks in North America visitors are required to pack out their excrement. This could soon be necessary here. Human excrement is not only offensive to our senses but, more importantly, can infect water sources.

MINIMUM IMPACT WALKING & OUTDOOR SAFETY

**Where to go**  Wherever possible **use a toilet**. Public toilets are marked in this guide and you'll also find facilities in pubs and cafés and on campsites.

If you do have to go outdoors choose a site at least **30 metres away from running water**. Carry a small trowel and **dig a hole** about 15cm (6") deep to bury your excrement. It will decompose quicker when in contact with the top soil or leaf mould. Do not squash it under rocks as this slows down the composting process. However, do not attempt to dig any holes on land that is of historical or archaeological interest, such as around Hadrian's Wall.

**Toilet paper and tampons**  Toilet paper decomposes slowly and is easily dug up by animals. It can then blow into water sources or onto the trail. The best method for dealing with it is to **pack it out**, along with **tampons** and **sanitary towels**.

## ACCESS AND THE RIGHT TO ROAM

Britain is a crowded island with few places where you can wander as you please. But in November 2005 the Countryside & Rights of Way Act 2000 (CRoW), or 'Right to Roam' as dubbed by walkers, came into effect after a long campaign to allow greater public access to areas of countryside in England and Wales deemed to be uncultivated open country; this essentially means moorland, heathland, downland and upland areas. Some land is covered by restrictions (ie high-impact activities such as driving, cycling, horse-riding) and some land is excluded (gardens, parks and cultivated land). Full details are given on the Countryside visitors page on 🖥 www.naturalengland.org.uk.

This confusing sign does not mean 'no access for walkers' but advises that you're leaving a Right to Roam area and thereafter must stick to footpaths.

With more freedom in the countryside comes a need for more responsibility from the walker. Remember that wild open country is still the workplace of farmers and home to all sorts of wildlife. Have respect for both and avoid disturbing domestic and wild animals.

### The Countryside Code

The Countryside Code seems like common sense but some people still appear to have no understanding of how to treat the countryside they walk in. Every visitor has a responsibility to minimise their impact so that others can enjoy the same peaceful landscapes; it doesn't take much effort.

The Countryside Code was revised and relaunched in 2004, in part because of the changes brought about by the CRoW Act (see above). Below is an expanded version of the new Code, launched under the logo '**Respect, Protect and Enjoy**':

● **Be safe**  You're responsible for your own safety: follow the guidelines on pp56-8.

● **Leave all gates as you find them**  Normally a farmer leaves gates closed to keep livestock in but may sometimes leave them open to allow livestock access to food or water.

● **Leave livestock, crops and machinery alone**  Help farmers by not interfering with their means of livelihood.

● **Take your litter home**  'Pack it in, pack it out'. Litter is not only ugly but can be harmful to wildlife. Small mammals often become trapped in discarded cans and bottles. Many walkers think that orange peel and banana skins do not count as litter. Even biodegradable foodstuffs attract common scavenging species such as crows and gulls to the detriment of less-dominant species.

> ❑ **The Countryside Code**
> ● Be safe, plan ahead and follow any signs
> ● Leave gates and property as you find them
> ● Protect plants and animals and take your litter home
> ● Keep dogs under close control
> ● Consider other people

● **Keep your dog under control**  Across farmland dogs should be kept on a lead. During lambing time they should not be taken with you at all (see box p26).

● **Enjoy the countryside and respect its life and work**  Access to the countryside depends on being sensitive to the needs and wishes of those who live and work there. Being courteous and friendly to those you meet will ensure a healthy future for all based on partnership and co-operation.

● **Keep to paths across farmland**  Stick to the official path across arable or pasture land. Minimise erosion by not cutting corners or widening the path.

● **Use gates and stiles to cross fences, hedges and walls**  The Pennine Way is well supplied with stiles where it crosses field boundaries. If you have to climb over a gate because you can't open it always do so at the hinged end.

● **Guard against all risk of fire**  Accidental fire is a great fear of farmers and foresters. Never make a camp fire and take matches and cigarette butts out with you to dispose of safely.

● **Help keep all water clean**  Leaving litter and going to the toilet near a water source can pollute people's water supplies. See pp53-4 for advice.

● **Take special care on country roads**  Drivers often go dangerously fast on narrow winding lanes. To be safe, walk facing the oncoming traffic and carry a torch or wear highly visible clothing when it's getting dark.

● **Protect wildlife, plants and trees**  Care for and respect all wildlife you come across along the Way. Don't pick plants, break trees or scare wild animals. If you come across young birds that appear to have been abandoned leave them alone.

● **Make no unnecessary noise**  Enjoy the peace and solitude of the outdoors by staying in small groups and acting unobtrusively.

**MINIMUM IMPACT WALKING & OUTDOOR SAFETY**

> ❑ **Lambing and grouse shooting**
> **Lambing** takes place from mid-March to mid-May when dogs should not be taken along the path. Even a dog secured on a lead can disturb a pregnant ewe. If you see a lamb or ewe that appears to be in distress contact the nearest farmer.
> **Grouse shooting** is an important part of the rural economy and management of the countryside. Britain is home to 20% of the world's moorland, and is under a duty to look after it. The season runs from 12 August to 10 December but shooting is unlikely to affect your walk.

# Outdoor safety

## AVOIDANCE OF HAZARDS

Along with thoughtful judgments, good planning and preparation ensure most hazards can be dealt with. This information is just as important for those out on a day walk as for those walking the entire trail. Always make sure you have suitable **clothes** (see pp37-8) to keep you warm and dry, whatever the conditions and a spare change of inner clothes. Carry adequate food and water too.

A compass, whistle and torch are also advisable, as are a GPS, additional mapping, a first-aid kit and a mobile phone. The **emergency signal** is six blasts on the whistle or six flashes with a torch. For **Mountain Rescue** dial ☎ 999 although this should be treated as the last resort.

### Safety on the Pennine Way

It's vital you take every precaution to ensure your own safety:

● Avoid walking on your own if possible.
● Make sure that somebody knows your plans for every day that you are on the trail. This could be a friend or relative whom you have promised to call every night, or the establishment you plan to stay in at the end of each day's walk. That way, if you fail to turn up or call that evening, they can raise the alarm.
● If visibility is suddenly reduced and you become uncertain of the correct trail, wait. You'll find that mist often clears, at least for long enough to allow you to get your bearings. If you are still uncertain, and the weather does not look like improving, return the way you came to the nearest point of civilisation, and try again another time when conditions have improved.
● Fill your water container at every opportunity; carry some high-energy snacks.
● Always carry a torch, compass, map, whistle and wet-weather gear with you.
● Wear proper walking boots, not trainers.
● Be extra vigilant if walking with children or the unfit.

### Dealing with an accident

● Use basic first aid to treat the injury to the best of your ability.
● Try to work out exactly where you are. If possible leave someone with the casualty while others go to get help. If there are only two people, you have a dilemma. If you decide to get help leave all spare clothing and food with the casualty.
● In an emergency dial ☎ 999; ask for Police and mountain rescue – they will need to know your exact location, the nature of the injuries, the number of casualties, and your phone number.

## WEATHER FORECASTS

The Pennines suffer from enormously unpredictable weather, so for the more remote northern sections it's advisable to find out the forecast before you set off for the day. Many hostels and TICs have a summary of the weather forecast pinned up somewhere. Alternatively you can call the premium-rate weather line (see below), or check the websites also listed below. Pay close attention to it and base your plans for the day on what you hear. That said, even if the forecast is for a fine sunny day, always assume the worst and pack some wet-weather gear.

### Telephone and online forecasts

**Telephone forecasts** are frequently updated and generally reliable. However, calls are charged at the expensive premium rate (60p per minute from a landline; network operators may impose a surcharge for calls from a mobile). **Weather Call:** ☎ 09068-500419 (Cumbria); ☎ 09068-500418 (Northumberland); ☎ 09068-500417 (Yorkshire). However, to minimise the call time Weathercall has introduced a four-digit code to make it easier to use the forecasting services. Relevant codes include: Bakewell 1202, Huddersfield 1712, Bradford 1716; Skipton 1707; Darlington 1801; Kelso 2203. They also have a website 🖳 www.weathercall.co.uk. For detailed **online** weather outlooks, including local five-day forecasts, log on to 🖳 www.bbc.co.uk/weather or 🖳 www.metoffice.gov.uk.

The **Mountain Weather Information Service** (MWIS; 🖳 www.mwis.org.uk) gives out detailed daily forecasts for the upland regions of Britain including the Peak District and Cumbria.

### BLISTERS

It is important to try new boots before embarking on a long trek. Make sure the boots are comfortable and try to avoid getting them wet on the inside. Airing and massaging your feet at rest stops does wonders. If you feel any hot spots stop immediately and apply a few strips of zinc oxide tape and leave it on until it is pain free or the tape starts to come off.

If you have left it too late and a blister has developed you should surround it with 'moleskin' or any other blister kit to protect it from abrasion. Popping it can lead to infection. If the skin is broken keep the area clean with antiseptic and cover with a non-adhesive dressing material held in place with tape.

### HYPOTHERMIA

Also known as exposure, hypothermia occurs when the body can't generate enough heat to maintain its normal temperature, usually as a result of being wet, cold, unprotected from the wind, tired and hungry. It's usually more of a problem in upland areas on the moors or of course outside summer. Hypothermia is easily avoided by wearing suitable clothing, carrying and eating enough food and drink, being aware of the weather conditions and keeping an eye on the condition of your companions. Besides feeling cold and tired, early signs to watch for include shivering. Find shelter as soon as possible and give them another warm layer of clothing and allow them to rest until feeling better. If possible warm the victim up with a hot drink and some chocolate or other high-energy food. If allowed to worsen, erratic behaviour, slurring of speech and poor co-ordination will become apparent and the victim can quickly progress into unconsciousness, followed by coma and death. Quickly get the victim out of any wind and rain, improvising a shelter if necessary. Rapid restoration of bodily warmth is essential and best achieved by bare-skin contact: someone should get into the same sleeping bag as the patient, both having stripped to the bare essentials, placing any spare clothing under or over them to build up heat. Send urgently for help.

## HYPERTHERMIA

**Heat exhaustion**   As the planet warms unprepared or careless walkers suffering heat exhaustion will become more common, even in the north of England. Trudging up hill on a hot day in a singlet and no headwear is asking for it and simply drinking water is not enough. Attention must also be paid to **minerals** lost in sweat. The correct combination and concentration of salts is vital to the body's electrolytic balance. This governs the transmission of nervous signals to the brain and explains why your senses become impaired as you become seriously dehydrated. A slight salt deficiency manifests itself in headaches, lethargy and muscle cramps, though it can take a day or two for salt levels to run down enough for these symptoms to become noticeable.

If you feel groggy, taking some **salt in solution** may make you feel better. In fact, after any exertion on a hot day a cup of slightly salty water or, better still, a swig of an isotonic drink instantly replenishes the minerals and water you lost during that activity. If you don't want to contaminate your water bottle with salty water and don't have a cup handy, lick the back of your hand, sprinkle on some salt, lick it off and swig it down with some water. **Too much salt** in one go (easily done with salt tablets so avoid them) will make you nauseous and may induce vomiting, which means that you lose fluid and so return to Square One. Remember, salt must be ingested with a substantial volume of water.

A sachet of **rehydration powder** such as Dioralyte or Rehydrat replenishes lost minerals in the correct proportions and is a worthwhile part of a first-aid kit. Both are expensive for what they are, so you want to save them for when you're feeling really rough. So-called **isotonic sports drinks** like Gatorade or Game are a more economical way of doing the same thing but they do lack the precise medicinal range and balance of minerals found in pharmaceutical rehydration powders. Alternatively a lunchtime mug of instant soup will do wonders.

**Heatstroke**   Heatstroke is another matter altogether; much more serious. A high body temperature and an absence of sweating are early indications, followed by symptoms similar to hypothermia (see p57) such as a lack of co-ordination, convulsions and coma. Death will follow if treatment is not given instantly. Rehydration sachets are not enough: shade the victim and sponge them down, wrap them in wet towels, fan them, and get help immediately.

## SUNBURN

It can happen, even in northern England and even on overcast days. The only surefire way to avoid it is to cover exposed skin, especially your head or smother yourself in factor 15+ sunscreen throughout the day.

# THE ENVIRONMENT & NATURE

## 3

For such a small place Great Britain has an extraordinarily wide range of habitats. They include orchid-strewn grasslands, woodland, heathland, moorland and mountains as well as coastal and freshwater areas.

What follows is a brief description of some of the many animals and plants you may encounter so you can understand what their business is as they scuttle, fly or run past you, or if a plant simply bows its head in the breeze as you walk by. Just as it's good to have some background knowledge before visiting a new country, so it is with the glories of the countryside.

The countryside is a community; the birds, animals and insects have evolved to be able to exploit different food sources so they are not in competition with each other. Please try and fit into this community by taking note of the points made in the following chapter on minimum impact walking.

Conservation issues are also explored in this chapter on the premise that to really learn about a place you need to know more than just the names of all the plants and animals in it. It is just as important to understand the interactions going on between them and man's relationship with this ecological balance.

## Conserving the Pennines

Some of us are painfully aware of the destruction of the countryside that followed the end of the Second World War. In that time Britain lost some of its most precious habitats: over 150,000 miles of hedgerow, 95% of lowland hay meadows and 80% of chalk and limestone grassland to name but three. The otter which was once common is only now beginning to make a comeback, the large blue butterfly has become extinct, as have ten species of plant; several types of bat are endangered and even the common frog has become uncommon. The figures go on and on and are a sad reflection of our once-abundant countryside.

We now live in a time when 'conservation' and 'the environment' are well-used terms and it's tempting to be complacent in the belief that the countryside is in safe hands. While there have been a few significant improvements in recent years, many areas have continued to decline. Populations of wild birds, for instance, are good indicators of biodiversity as they are near the top of the food chain. The State of the Countryside 2001 report showed the serious decline in populations of 41 common farmland and woodland birds because of habitat destruction and pollution. In the Pennines the number of skylarks has dropped by 39% since 1990.

As a nation we have lost touch not only with country matters, but with nature itself. Today most people's only contact with nature is through anthropomorphising books or wildlife documentaries on television. This is hardly surprising. In the first census, in 1801, 70% of British people lived in the countryside. In the year 2000 that figure had fallen to a staggering 10%. Even though they may live in the countryside many in that 10% category have no real contact with the land or interest in rural affairs.

As walkers we are in a privileged position to re-establish our relationship with nature and become interested and active in how it is looked after. It is after all, to some extent, all of our land; we depend on it for physical and spiritual sustenance. It's therefore useful to have some understanding of how it is being managed on our behalf.

## GOVERNMENT AGENCIES AND SCHEMES

Government responsibility for the countryside is handled in England by **Natural England**. Natural England is responsible for 'enhancing biodiversity and landscape and wildlife in rural, urban, coastal and marine areas; promoting access, recreation and public well-being, and contributing to the way natural resources are managed, so they can be enjoyed now and by future generations'. Amongst other things it designates the level of protection for areas of land, as outlined below, and manages England's national trails (see box opposite).

### National Parks

National Park status is the highest level of landscape protection available in Britain and recognises the importance of the area in terms of landscape, biodiversity and as a recreational resource.

The Pennine Way passes through three National Parks: the Peak District, the Yorkshire Dales and Northumberland. Although they wield a considerable amount of power and can easily quash planning applications from the local council, their management is always a balance between conservation, the needs of visitors, and protecting the livelihoods of those who live within the park.

Following the Foot and Mouth outbreak in 2001 when footpaths countrywide were closed for months, the National Park Authorities suggested that Parks be used as a test bed for rural revival by setting up task forces to explain funding available to small rural businesses, generating ideas for projects, acting as the public element where necessary (eg in setting up farmers' markets) and advising on how to build on successes. It is hoped that these measures will help the

THE ENVIRONMENT & NATURE

❏ **National Trails**
The Pennine Way is one of 15 National Trails in England and Wales. These are Britain's flagship long-distance paths which grew out of the post-war desire to protect the country's special places, a movement which also gave birth to National Parks and AONBs.

National Trails in England are designated and largely funded by Natural England and are managed on the ground by a National Trail Officer. They co-ordinate the maintenance work undertaken by the local highway authority and landowners to ensure that the trail is kept to nationally agreed standards.

government's stated objective, 'to move environmental and social goals closer to the heart of agricultural policy alongside its economic objectives'.

The existence of the National Parks does, however, raise the question of what is being done to conserve and protect the countryside outside their boundaries? The policy of giving special protection to certain areas suggests that those areas not protected tend to be ignored when funding comes to be allocated. Since only 7% of the British Isles has National Park status, the conclusion to be drawn is that vast areas remain neglected and under threat.

## Areas of Outstanding Natural Beauty (AONBs)
Land which falls outside the remit of a National Park but which is nonetheless deemed special enough for protection may be designated an AONB, the second level of protection after National Park status. The North Pennines is one such AONB. Designated in 1988, it is valued for its upland habitats and wildlife, containing a third of England's upland heathland and a third of its blanket bog. These fragile habitats make the North Pennines one of England's most important regions for upland wildlife – it is home to the majority of England's black grouse along with 22,000 breeding pairs of waders. Of course, it wouldn't get AONB status unless it was a beautiful area; the moors, hills and wooded valleys certainly make it so. And it is the underlying geology that gives the region its character which led to the area being designated a UNESCO European Geopark (🖳 www.europeangeoparks.org) in 2003, the first in Britain. A year later it became a founding member of the Global Geoparks Network (🖳 www.globalgeopark.org).

## National Nature Reserves (NNRs) and Local Nature Reserves (LNRs)
**NNRs** are places where wildlife comes first. They were established to protect the most important areas of wildlife habitat and geological formations in Britain, and as places for scientific research. This does not mean they are 'no-go areas' for people. It means that we must be careful not to damage the wildlife of these fragile places. Kinder Scout (see p80) is now a NNR.

**LNRs** are for both people and wildlife. They are living green spaces in towns, cities, villages and countryside which are important to people, and support a rich and vibrant variety of wildlife. They are places which have wildlife or geology of special local interest.

THE ENVIRONMENT & NATURE

❑ **Statutory bodies – contact details**
● **Department for Environment, Food and Rural Affairs** (🖳 ww2.defra.gov.uk)
Government ministry responsible for sustainable development in the countryside.
● **Natural England** (🖳 www.naturalengland.org.uk) See p60.
● **English Heritage** (🖳 www.english-heritage.org.uk) Organisation whose central aim
is to make sure that the historic environment of England is properly maintained. It is
officially known as the Historic Buildings and Monuments Commission for England.
Housesteads Fort (see p223) on Hadrian's Wall is managed by English Heritage as is
Bowes Castle (see p169).
● **Forestry Commission** (🖳 www.forestry.gov.uk). Government department for
establishing and managing forests for a variety of uses (see box p67).
● National parks: **Peak District National Park** (🖳 www.peakdistrict.gov.uk);
**Northumberland National Park** (🖳 www.northumberlandnationalpark.org.uk); and
**Yorkshire Dales National Park** (🖳 www.yorkshiredales.org.uk).
● **National Association for Areas of Outstanding Natural Beauty** (🖳 www.aonb
.org.uk) and **North Pennines AONB** (🖳 www.northpennines.org.uk).

## Sites of Special Scientific Interest (SSSIs)

SSSIs purport to afford extra protection to unique areas against anything that
threatens the habitat or environment. They range in size from a small site where
orchids grow, or birds nest, to vast swathes of upland, moorland and wetland.

The country through which the Pennine Way passes has its share of SSSIs
but they are not given a high profile for the very reason that this would draw
unwanted attention. They are managed in partnership with the owners and
occupiers of the land but it seems this management is not always effective.

## Special Areas of Conservation (SACs)

SACs are areas which have been given special protection under the European
Union's Habitats Directive. They provide increased protection to a variety of
wild animals, plants and habitats and are a vital part of global efforts to conserve
the world's biodiversity.

❑ **Campaigning and conservation organisations – contact details**
● **Royal Society for the Protection of Birds** (RSPB; 🖳 www.rspb.org.uk, see opposite).
● **National Trust** (NT; 🖳 www.nationaltrust.org.uk) A charity with 3.4 million
members which aims to protect, through ownership, threatened coastline, countryside,
historic houses, castles and gardens, and archaeological remains for everybody
to enjoy. NT land/properties on the Pennine Way includes Kinder Scout (see p80),
Housesteads Fort (see p223; though it is managed by English Heritage), Malham Tarn
and Moor (see pp137-8) in Yorkshire Dales NP, Marsden Moor and Hardcastle Crags
near Hebden Bridge.
● **The Wildlife Trusts** (🖳 www.wildlifetrusts.org) The umbrella organisation for
the 47 wildlife trusts in the UK; the trust is concerned with all aspects of nature
conservation and owns over 50 nature reserves. Wildlife trusts along the Pennine Way
include Derbyshire, Durham, Northumberland and Yorkshire.
● **Woodland Trust** (🖳 www.woodlandtrust.org.uk) The trust aims to conserve,
restore and re-establish native woodlands throughout the UK.

THE ENVIRONMENT & NATURE

## CAMPAIGNING AND CONSERVATION ORGANISATIONS

The idea of conservation started back in the mid-1800s with the founding of the **Royal Society for the Protection of Birds** (RSPB; see box opposite). The rise of its membership figures accurately reflect public awareness and interest in environmental issues as a whole: it took until the 1960s to reach 10,000, but then rocketed to 200,000 in the 1970s and mushroomed to over one million by the year 2000. A major spur to the movement's metamorphosis came in 1962 when Rachel Carson published a book called *Silent Spring* documenting the effects of agricultural and industrial chemicals on the environment. It was the long overdue wake-up call needed to bring environmental issues into the public eye. The RSPB now has 200 nature reserves in the UK; the closest to the Pennine Way are Geltsdale, off the A689 west of Knarsdale (off Map 99, p215) and Dove Stone, west of Wessenden Head (off Map 12, p91).

There are now a large number of campaigning and conservation groups (see box opposite). Independent of government but reliant on public support, they can concentrate their resources either on acquiring land which can then be managed purely for conservation purposes, or on influencing political decision-makers by lobbying and campaigning.

The huge increase in public interest and support during the last 20 years indicates that people are more conscious of environmental issues and believe that it cannot be left to our political representatives to take care of them for us without our voice. We are becoming the most powerful lobbying group of all; an informed electorate.

# Flora and fauna

## WILD FLOWERS, GRASSES AND OTHER PLANTS

Many grasses, wild flowers, heather, mosses and liverworts (lichen-type plant with liver-shaped leaves) owe their continued existence to man's land management; global warming notwithstanding, if left to its own devices much of the land would return to the natural state of temperate regions: the woodland of 10,000 years ago.

Rare breeds of livestock are often excellent grazers for rough grassland because they are hardier so do not have to be fed extra food that will then over fertilise the ground. They also seem to be more selective in what they eat, and taste better too.

Spring and early summer is the best time to see wild flowers. You may be amazed by how many are edible. Some examples are given below, but seek expert identification before trying any as some plants are poisonous.

Intensive agriculture took its toll on the wild flower population in the same way that it did on the birds and mammals. The flowers are making a comeback but it is illegal to pick many types of flowers now and the picking of most

THE ENVIRONMENT & NATURE

❑ **Why are flowers the colour they are?**
The vast majority of British wild flowers range in colour from yellow to magenta and do not have red in them. The poppy is the most notable exception. This is because most flowers are insect pollinated as opposed to being pollinated by birds. Birds see reds best, insects see yellow to magenta best.

others is discouraged; it is always illegal without the landowners' permission, no matter what the type. Cut flowers only die, after all. It is much better to leave them to reseed and spread and hopefully magnify your or someone else's enjoyment another year.

## Bogs and wet areas
Look out for **cotton grass** (see opposite; not actually a grass but a type of sedge), **deer-grass**, **cloudberry** (a dwarf blackberry with a light orange berry when ripe that can be used as a substitute for any fruit used in puddings and jams) and the insect-eating **sundew**. Drier areas of peat may be home to **crowberry** (a source of vitamin C) and **bilberry** (see below).

Peat itself is the ages-old remains of vegetation, including **sphagnum mosses**. This type of moss is now rare, but may be found in 'flushes' where water seeps out between gritstone and shale. Also look out for **bog asphodel**, **marsh thistle** and **marsh pennywort**.

## Woodlands
Not much grows in coniferous plantations because the dense canopy prevents light getting in. But in oak woodlands the floor is often covered with interesting plants such as **bilberries**, whose small, round black fruit is ripe for picking from July to September and is much tastier than the more widely commercially sold American variety. It's recommended in jams, jellies, stews and cheesecake. Bilberry pie is known in Yorkshire as 'mucky-mouth pie', for reasons you can work out, and is eaten at funerals. Moorland **cowberry** (also used in jams),

❑ **Orchids**
These highly prized plants, the occasional object of professional thefts, are often thought to grow only in tropical places. They come from one of the largest families in the world and their range is in fact widespread, right up to the Arctic Circle in some places. In Britain over 40 types grow wild and you'd be unlucky not to see any on the Pennine Way, especially in quarries and on hillsides. The **lady's-slipper**, first discovered in Ingleborough in 1640; the **narrow-lipped helleborine**, which grows in Northumberland and the **frog orchid** are just some you may come across. The **early-purple orchid** (see photo opposite) is made into a drink called Saloop, which was popular before coffee became the staple.

Although they have a tendency to grow on other plants, orchids are not parasites, as many believe; they simply use them for support. They are distinctive as having one petal longer than the other two and many growers say they're no more difficult to grow at home than many other houseplants. With their flowers being generally spectacular and the wonderful strong scent they're well worth the effort.

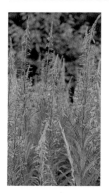

Rosebay Willowherb
*Epilobium angustifolium*

Spear Thistle
*Cirsium vulgare*

Cotton Grass
*Eriophorum*

Rowan (tree)
*Sorbus aucuparia*

Herb-Robert
*Geranium robertianum*

Red Campion
*Silene dioica*

Early Purple Orchid
*Orchis mascula*

Common Knapweed
*Centaurea nigra*

Foxglove
*Digitalis purpurea*

Hemp-nettle
*Galeopsis speciosa*

Hogweed
*Heracleum sphondylium*

Yarrow
*Achillea millefolium*

Dog Rose
*Rosa canina*

Common Hawthorn
*Crataegus monogyna*

Honeysuckle
*Lonicera periclymemum*

Ramsons (Wild Garlic)
*Allium ursinum*

Silverweed
*Potentilla anserina*

Bluebell
*Endymion non-scriptus*

Gorse
*Ulex europaeus*

Meadow Buttercup
*Ranunculis acris*

Marsh Marigold (Kingcup)
*Caltha palustris*

Tormentil
*Potentilla erecta*

Birdsfoot-trefoil
*Lotus corniculatus*

Ox-eye Daisy
*Leucanthemum vulgare*

Common Ragwort
*Senecio jacobaea*

Primrose
*Primula vulgaris*

Cowslip
*Primula veris*

Common Dog Violet
*Viola riviniana*

Heartsease (Wild Pansy)
*Viola tricolor*

Meadow Cranesbill
*Geranium pratense*

Self-heal
*Prunella vulgaris*

Germander Speedwell
*Veronica chamaedrys*

Common Fumitory
*Fumaria officinalis*

Lousewort
*Pedicularis sylvatica*

Water Avens
*Geum rivale*

Scarlet Pimpernel
*Anagallis arvensis*

Bell Heather
*Erica cinerea*

Heather (Ling)
*Calluna vulgaris*

Common Vetch
*Vicia sativa*

**wavy hair grass** and **woodrush** are other species you may see. Other shrubs to look out for include **guelder rose** and **bird cherry**.

### Higher areas

Much of the high land is peaty and many types of grass turn brown in winter. Those present include **matgrass**, **heath rush**, **bent**, **fescues** and **wavy hair grass**. Flowers include **tormentil** and **harebell**.

**Heather** is the main plant of higher areas and is carefully farmed for grouse. It is burnt in strips over the winter to ensure new growth as a food supply for the birds. It has many uses, including as a tea and flavouring beer, and makes a very comfortable mattress on a warm, sunny afternoon. When it flowers around August time, the moors can turn purple. **Bracken**, **gorse** and **tufted hair grass** are all signs that the land is not being intensively managed.

### Lower areas

These places are where you'll see the most flowers, whose fresh and bright colours give the area an inspiring glow, particularly if you have just descended from the browns and greens of the higher, peaty areas.

On valley sides used for grazing you may see **self heal**, **cowslips** (used to make wine and vinegar), **bloody cranesbill** and **mountain pansy**. **Hawthorn** seeds dropped by birds sprout up energetically and determinedly but are cropped back by sheep and fires. This is a good thing; these shrubs can grow to 8 metres (26ft) and would try to take over the hillsides to the detriment of the rich grasslands. They do, however, have a variety of uses: the young leaves are known as 'bread and cheese' because they used to be such a staple part of a diet; the flowers make a delicious drink and when combined with the fruit make a cure for insomnia. **Rushes** indicate poor drainage. Also look out for **bird's eye primrose**, **white clover** and the grasses such as **crested dog's tail** and **bent**.

## TREES, WOODS AND FORESTS

Woods are part of our natural heritage as reflected in our folklore, Little Red Riding Hood and Robin Hood for example, and also in our history with the hunting grounds of Henry VIII and his subsequent felling of the New Forest to construct the fleets that led to Britannia 'ruling the waves'. To the west of Edale, at the start of the walk, is the small town of Chapel-en-le-Frith. Translated, its name means 'chapel in the forest' because it used to be a small clearing in an enormous forest that stretched to Edale and beyond.

Ten thousand years ago as Europe emerged from the Ice Age but before man started to exert his influence on the landscape, 90% of the country was wooded. In 1086 when William the Conqueror ordered a survey it had declined to 15% and it then shrank to 4% by the 1870s. Today, however, about 12% of the UK (2.8 million hectares) is wooded; 5000 hectares of new woodland were created in the UK in 2009-10, much of this in private ownership. What these figures disguise is that a huge proportion of the tree cover today, as opposed to 900 years ago or even 100 years ago, is made up of plantations of conifers (see box p67).

THE ENVIRONMENT & NATURE

It is hoped that by 2020 woodland will cover 20% of England and that a large proportion will be made up of indigenous species, such as oak. Despite this progress England will still be one of the least-wooded countries in Europe where the average wood cover is 36%.

## Oak and broadleaf woodlands

The number of **oak** trees has increased by 20% in 20 years. They are now the commonest species in England. There are two native species: the **common** and the **sessile**. Sessile woodlands are generally remnants of the woodland of William the Conqueror's time and before. Broadleaf woods, that is deciduous (annual leaf-shedders) hardwood, including **beech**, **sycamore**, **birch**, **poplar** and **sweet chestnut**, have grown by 36% since 1980. However, they still only account for 1% of the Yorkshire Dales National Park.

In areas of poorer soil you will also see 'pioneer' species such as **rowan**, **silver birch**, **downy birch** and the much rarer **aspen**. In a natural environment these improve the soil for longer-lasting species such as oak.

## Coniferous woodland

The full extent of the demise of our native woodlands was not fully comprehended until the Second World War when politicians realised we had an inadequate strategic reserve of timber. The immediate response was to plant fast-growing low-management trees such as the North American **Sitka spruce** across the agriculturally unviable land of the British uplands. The mass-planting continued apace into the 1970s and '80s with big grants and tax breaks available to landowners and wealthy investors.

You can see the result of this 'blanket planting' in the northern Pennines; acres of same-age trees with such a dense canopy that nothing grows beneath. As with all monocultures pests easily build up and have to be controlled with chemicals. The deep ploughing damages soil structure and also leads to a higher incidence of flash floods as drainage patterns are altered. It's also been found that acid rain gets trapped in the trees and is released into the streams during a downpour killing young fish and invertebrates.

What's more, the end product from this environmentally damaging land use is a low-grade timber used mainly for paper, a waste of a valuable raw material. Perversely and misleadingly this is often advertised as 'paper from sustainable forestry'. There are now efforts under way to replant felled coniferous timber

---

❏ **Fungi, micro-organisms and invertebrates**

In the soil below your feet and under the yellow leaves of autumn are millions, possibly billions, of organisms beavering away at recycling anything that has had its day and fallen to decay. One gram of woodland soil contains an estimated 4-5000 species of bacteria. Almost all of them are unknown to science and the vitally important role they play in maintaining the natural balance of our ecosystems is only just beginning to be appreciated. Many scientists now believe these organisms actually run the earth. Research into them is at an early stage but as one American academic put it, 'As we walk across leaf litter we are like Godzilla walking over New York City.'

❏ **The Forestry Commission**
The Forestry Commission (see box p62) is the governmental body in charge of Britain's forests. It states its mission to be 'To protect and expand Britain's forests and woodlands and increase their value to society and the environment'. It manages 800,000 hectares of woodland throughout Britain, and although it was largely responsible for encouraging the vast numbers of acres of coniferous woodland, it is now a driving force behind diversification of tree species in woodlands.

with a wider range of species and the number of conifer plantations has fallen by 7% in the past 20 years. These new woodlands are not only planted for timber, but also promote recreation, tourism and are good for wildlife.

## BIRDS

One thing you will see a lot of on your walk is birds and the best way of identifying birds is through their song. Each species sings a different tune, and not just for your pleasure. It is their way of letting others know that their territory is still occupied and not up for grabs, as well as a mating signal. The dawn chorus is such a cacophony because most avian fatalities take place at night, so when they wake and are still alive they have to let opportunist home-hunters know it. They also have a call, or alarm, which is different again from the song.

Birds evolved from reptiles. Their feathers are made from keratin, as are reptile scales. Feathers give birds their shape, warmth, distinctive colour, waterproofing and the ability to fly. All birds moult at least once a year.

A bird's beak is an extension of its upper jaw. It is used for nest building, eating, preening and as a weapon and has evolved to suit individual needs. A wading bird, for instance, will have a probing beak of a length to suit its feeding ground, whether it be mud, sand or shallow water. Different types of waders can therefore feed in the same area without competing. Because its brain is suspended by quasi-ligaments a woodpecker can bang its bill against wood in a way that would leave other birds and most humans brain-damaged.

Birds' feet have evolved to particular tasks too. Perching birds use a tendon along the back of their legs that tightens the toes as the leg is bent. This keeps it on the perch as it sleeps. Feet have different coverings too, being either feathers or bristles, scales or leathery skin. Owls can turn their outer toe backwards to help them grasp branches and their prey. Claws help with this too, and they have also evolved to perform different tasks. Birds of prey tend to have stronger, curved talons; short, strong blunt claws are good for scratching the ground; the heron has adapted a comb-like claw for preening.

Some birds, such as the swallow, perform incredible annual migrations, navigating thousands of miles to exactly the same nest they occupied the previous summer. Recent research suggests that some birds ingest their own organs to keep themselves fuelled for the flight. Swifts are believed to fly non-stop for up to two years, only coming down at the end of that period to lay eggs. They can also survive cold periods by entering a state of torpor.

## Streams, rivers and lakes

Both the **great-crested grebe** and the **little grebe** live on natural lakes and reservoirs. In spring you can see the great-crested grebe's 'penguin dance', where they raise themselves from the water breast to breast by furiously paddling their feet, and then swing their heads from side to side. They also have their full plumage, including an elaborate collar that could well have served as inspiration for the Elizabethans. They nearly became extinct in Britain in the nineteenth century, but have now recovered despite plenty of enemies including pike, rooks, mink and even the wake from boats, which can flood their nests. The **little grebe** is small and dumpy but very well designed for hunting sticklebacks under water.

**Yellow wagtails** are summer visitors that are as likely to be seen on lakesides as in water meadows, pasture and even moors. How do you recognise them? They have a yellow underneath, unlike the **grey wagtail** which has a black chin and then a yellow belly. If the bird is by a fast-flowing stream it will almost certainly be a grey wagtail.

Reservoir water tends to be relatively acidic so supports little wildlife except wildfowl including **goosanders**, especially in winter, and the similar-looking **red-breasted mergansers**. They are both members of the sawbill family which use serrated bill edges to seize and hold small fish. The trout in the reservoirs will have been introduced for anglers.

In streams and rivers you may see **common sandpipers**. Most of them head for Africa in the winter, but about 50 are thought to brave it out in ever-milder Britain. You might see them stalking insects, their head held slowly and horizontally before a sudden snap marks the hunt to an end. **Dippers** are the only songbirds that can 'fly' underwater or walk along streambeds. You may see them 'curtseying' on rocks in the middle of swift-flowing streams before they dive under the surface. They fly extremely quickly, because their small wings were designed for maximum efficiency in the water and are far too small to keep the huge bodies airborne without enormous amounts of flapping and momentum.

## Woodland

Although rare in the Pennines, broad-leaved woodland harbours a variety of bird-life. You may see, or more likely hear, a **green woodpecker**, the largest woodpecker in Britain. They are very shy and often hide behind branches. They trap insects by probing holes and cavities with their tongue, which has a sticky tip like a flycatcher.

The further north you go the more likely you are to see **pied flycatchers**, summer visitors from Africa. The male can have multiple mates and is known to keep territories well over a mile apart, perhaps to keep a quiet life.

**Nuthatches** are sparrow sized with blue backs, orange breasts and a black eye-stripe, and have the almost unique ability to clamber up and down trunks and branches. Here all year, in summer they eat insects and in the autumn crack open acorns and hazel nuts with hard whacks of their bill.

**Treecreepers** cling to trees in the same way as nuthatches and woodpeckers. They have a thin, downward-curved bill that is ideal for picking insects out of holes and crevices. They are brown above and silvery-white underneath, which should help you distinguish them from the similar sized and behaviourally similar **lesser-spotted woodpecker**, which is black and white and not seen on the more northern sections of the Pennine Way. The male woodpecker also has a red crown.

Coniferous woodland is not home to much wildlife at all, because the tree canopy is too dense. You may, however, see nesting **sparrowhawks**, Britain's second commonest bird of prey. It suffered a big decline in the 1950s due to the use of pesticides in farming. In all the British raptor (bird of prey) species the female is larger than the male, but the male sparrowhawk is one of the smallest raptors in Britain. It feeds entirely on fellow birds and has long legs and a long central toe for catching and holding them. It has a square-ended tail and reasonably short wings for chasing birds into trees.

You may also see **short-eared owls** in young plantations because of the preponderance of their principal prey, the short-tailed vole. It also hunts over open moors, heaths and rough grasslands. This owl is probably the one that is most often seen in daylight. It has two ear-tufts on the top of its head which are, you've guessed it, shorter than the long-eared owl's.

**BLACK GROUSE**
**L: 580MM/23"**

You may also see a **black grouse** (see box p161), also known as **black game**. Conifer plantations are providing temporary havens for them while they try to regain some of their numbers. The males, black cocks, perform in mock-fights known as a lek in front of the females, **grey hens**. This happens throughout the year and if you see one fluffing up the white of its tail and cooing like a dove don't necessarily expect to see a female present, because they are quite happy to perform for anyone.

Coniferous woods are also home to the greeny-yellow **goldcrest**, Britain's smallest bird. It weighs less than 10 grams but along with the **coal tit** is possibly the dominant species in coniferous woods. Because it is one of the few species that can exploit conifers it is growing in number.

## Moor, bog and grazing

Many birds have developed to live in the wettest, windiest, most barren places in England; the places along which the best of the Pennine Way passes. On heather moors you will almost certainly see **red grouse**, for whom the heather is intensively managed to ensure a good supply of young shoots for food. They are reddy brown, slightly smaller than a pheasant and likely to get up at your feet and fly off making a lot of noise.

Moorland is also home to Britain's smallest falcon, the **merlin**. The male is slate-grey, the female a reddish brown. They eat small birds, catching them with low dashing flights. Their main threat comes from the expense of maintaining moorland for grouse shooting; as costs grow fewer and fewer farmers are doing this and with the disappearance of the moor we will see the disappearance of the merlin. Another moorland raptor is the **short-eared owl** (see above).

THE ENVIRONMENT & NATURE

**CURLEW**
**L: 600MM/24"**

Bogs are breeding grounds for many species of waders, including the **curlew**, the emblem of Northumberland National Park, if not the Pennine Way. Long-legged, brown and buff coloured, they probe for worms and fish with their long, downward-curving bill. The curlew's forlorn bleat will follow you across many a moor.

**Snipe** live in wet areas. They are smaller than a grouse, but they share very similar plumages. They have particularly long bills for feeding in water and rely on being camouflaged rather than escaping predators by flight, and hence often get up right at your feet. Once airborne their trajectory is fast and zigzags.

In summer **golden plover** live in upland peaty terrain, are seen in pairs and will be visible to walkers (as well as audible because of their plaintive call); in winter they are seen in flocks and in lowland grassland. They are a little larger than a snipe, have golden spotted upper parts and can be recognised by their feeding action of running, pausing to look and listen for food (seeds and insects) and bobbing down to eat it. **Dunlins** also live in peaty terrain and are half the size of a golden plover but not dissimilar in colouring to the inexperienced eye. They are a very common wader.

**SKYLARK**
**L: 185MM/7.25"**

You may also see but are more likely to hear the continuous and rapid song of the **skylark**. They tend to move from moorland to lower agricultural land in the winter. Just bigger than a house sparrow, they have brown upper parts and chin with dark flakes and a white belly.

Patches of gorse and juniper scrub are often chosen as a nesting site for **linnets**, which flock together during the winter but operate in small colonies at other times. They are small birds that will also be seen on open farmland, as will the slightly larger **yellowhammer**, recognisable by its yellow head and chest. It too nests in gorse and juniper bushes.

The **lapwing** is relatively common, quite large and can be recognised by its wispy black plume on the back of its head and, in summer, the aerial acrobatics of the male. They fly high to dive steeply down, twisting and turning as if out of control before pulling out at the last minute.

The **meadow pipit** is a small, and a classic LBJ (little brown job), they make plenty of noise

**LAPWING/PEEWIT**
**L: 320MM/12.5"**

and on a still day will climb to about 15 metres (50ft) and then open their wings to parachute gently down. They can sometimes be recognised by their white outer tail feathers as they fly away from you.

The **peregrine falcon** had a hard time in the 20th century, being shot during the Second World War to protect carrier pigeons and then finding it hard to rear their young after eating insects that had fed on pesticide-soaked plants. Their recent comeback is therefore a sign that things are picking up again in the British countryside.

### Buildings and cliffs

**Swallows**, **house martins** and **swifts** all nest in barns and other buildings. They are hard to tell apart, but as a simple guide: swallows are the largest, are blue-black above and have a white belly and a long-forked tail; swifts are the next down in size, are essentially all black with a shallow forked tail that is usually closed and probably fly the fastest; house martins are the smallest, have a relatively short tail and a completely white underneath and, most usefully for identification purposes, a white rump (on top, near the tail). As a walker, you may be able to relate to why a non-breeding swift will fly 100 miles to avoid rain. If insects are bugging you, thank nature for swifts. A single one will eat 10,000 of the pesky buzzers a day, so think how many more bites you would suffer if it were not for them.

**Peregrine falcons**, **kestrels** and **jackdaws** (similar to a crow but with a whitish back of the head) nest on cliffs. At Malham Cove the RSPB have set up a peregrine viewing site (see p136) allowing visitors to see the resident pair on the limestone cliffs. The kestrel, Britain's commonest and most familiar bird of prey, also nests in man-made structures and is sometimes seen in city centres. It can be distinguished from the sparrowhawk, the second most common raptor, by its pointed wings and hovering when hunting. The male has a blue-grey head and a rich chestnut above, while the female is a duller chestnut both above and on her head. Jackdaws are very common in villages and towns; if you see a crow-like bird sitting on a chimney top, reckon on it being a jackdaw.

**Owls** may also nest in cliffs and barns. You are most likely to see a **little owl**, which is a non-native resident that will often occupy the same perch day after day. Local knowledge can be useful for finding one of these. **Barn owls** have been affected by intensive agriculture and are on the decline but are also one of the most widely distributed birds in the world.

## MAMMALS

**Roe deer** are the smallest of Britain's native deer, and are hard to see. They normally inhabit woodland areas but you may see one in grassland or, if you're very lucky, swimming in a lake. The males (bucks) claim a territory in spring and will chase a female (doe) round and round a tree before she gives in to his pursuit. This leaves circles of rings round the base of the tree, which are known as 'roe rings'.

**Badgers** like to live in deciduous woodland. Their black-and-white striped head makes them highly recognisable, but you're most likely to see them at

THE ENVIRONMENT & NATURE

night. They are true omnivores eating almost anything including berries, slugs and dead rabbits. The female (sow) gathers dry grasses and bracken in February for her nest. She then tucks them between her chin and forequarters and shuffles backwards, dragging them into her home (sett). The young are born blind in February and March and stay underground until spring.

Badgers were thought to spread TB to cows and for this unproven allegation 25,000 were culled in the 1980s and 1990s. The jury is still out, but there's no doubt they do contract and carry the disease. Some conservationists argue that it is more likely that they catch it from cows rather than the other way round. Much hope for a solution is placed in a possible vaccine.

**Foxes** are common wherever there are animals or birds to be preyed on, or dustbins to scavenge from, which is just about everywhere. Britain is estimated to have forty times the fox population of northern France. They are believed to have been here since before the last Ice Age when the sabre-toothed tiger would have prevented them from enjoying their current supremacy in the food chain.

Although now banned, fox hunting is an emotive countryside issue. A lot of conservationists believe that the fox itself is the best control of its numbers. If an environment is unsuitable they tend not to try and inhabit it and, like some marsupials, a pregnant vixen will reabsorb her embryos if conditions are unfavourable for raising cubs.

Foxes do a useful job eating carrion, which sometimes includes dead lambs, and rabbits and if they could learn to lay off the capercaillie and other protected birds they'd even get the RSPB on their side.

The **otter** is a sensitive indicator of the state of our rivers. They nearly died out in the last century due to a number of attacks on them, their habitat and their environment, but law has protected them since 1981. Due to the work of conservationists they're now making a comeback, but even small amounts of pollution can set back the efforts to give them a strong foothold in the wild. They are reclusive so you'll be incredibly lucky if you see one. They not only eat fish, but water voles and small aquatic birds. Their most successful hunting tactic is to launch a surprise attack from below as an otter's eyes are set on the top of its head and they have unique muscles that compensate for the visual distortion caused by water.

**Mink** were introduced from North America and only exist in the wild because they escaped or were set free from mink farms. They are one of the most serious pests in the countryside; being an alien species nature has yet to work out how to balance their presence. They spend a lot of time in rivers feeding on aquatic birds and fish and can be distinguished from otters by their considerably smaller size and white chin patch.

The **stoat** is a small but fierce predator. They are native and fairly widespread and can be recognised by their elongated and elegant form, reddy-brown coats and white bellies. They are very adaptable, moving in wherever they can find a den, including old rabbit burrows, and may live for up to ten years. Minks, stoats, polecats, otters, badgers, weasels (the world's smallest carnivores) and pine martens are all from the same family.

The **red squirrel** is native, unlike the grey squirrel, but it is now rare to see one. They are smaller than their reviled grey cousins and feature a vibrant red coat and fabulously bushy tail (although their coat turns a little browner in winter). Note, too, the tufts that grow at the tips of their ears.

The alien **grey squirrel** has played a big part in the demise of the red squirrel, partly because it is able to eat the red squirrel's food before it ripens. Efforts to reintroduce the red squirrel have not had a great deal of success, partly because they're reluctant to move from tree to tree along the ground and therefore need a dense tree canopy, but also because they lack traffic sense, which forshortens their lives in urban areas.

The **common shrew** is a tiny animal that lives in woodland and hedgerows. It needs to eat every four hours, and in a 24-hour period will eat insects weighing twice its body weight, using its long sensitive nose to sniff them out. It spends a lot of time underground eating earthworms. The mother and babies are sometimes seen traversing open ground in a train-like procession, with each shrew holding the tail of the one in front. It is the second most common British mammal.

The **mole** is armed with powerful forearms that it uses to burrow a network of underground tunnels that act as traps for unsuspecting earthworms. They patrol these every four hours, either eating all the visitors on the spot or gathering them up to save for later after immobilising them through decapitation.

In woodland or anywhere near buildings you may see the smallest of Britain's 15 resident species of **bat**, the **pipistrelle**. Bats have been here consistently since the Ice Age and are now a protected species. Even though the pipistrelle weighs a tiny 3-8 grams (about the same as a single clove of garlic, or two sheets of kitchen roll), in one night it may eat as many as 3500 insects. Bats and **dormice** are the only British mammals to truly hibernate throughout the whole winter from October to April. They will wake, however, if the temperature increases to unseasonal levels.

## REPTILES

The **adder**, or viper, is Britain's only poisonous snake but is harmless if left alone. It can be recognised by a black ziz-zag down its back and found in woodland and moorland. They hibernate in winter and when possible laze around in the morning and evening sun in spring and summer, eating everything from slugs to small birds. The males fight for females by rearing up and twisting themselves round each other as if trying to climb a tree; victory is often down to length. While this strenuous activity is going on the females are still asleep. They wake to find the victorious male rubbing his body against her and sticking his tongue out. It may sound all too familiar to many.

Although the **slow worm** looks like a snake it is, in fact, a lizard, sharing their notched tongue (rather than a snake's forked tongue), moveable eyelids (snakes have no eyelids) and fixed jaw (snakes have a free jaw for swallowing large prey). They eat slugs and insects and inhabit thick vegetation and rotting wood. The **common lizard** inhabits grass, in woods, moorland or grassland. They feed on insects and spiders.

THE ENVIRONMENT & NATURE

# ROUTE GUIDE & MAPS

## Using this guide

The trail guide and maps have been divided into 15 stages (walking from south to north, the direction taken by 80% of walkers on the Pennine Way), though these are not to be taken as rigid daily itineraries since people walk at different speeds and have different interests.

The **route overviews** introduce the trail for each of these stages. They're followed by information about **route-finding troublespots** highlighting places where even experienced walkers may want to pay close attention to navigation. To enable you to plan your itinerary, **practical information** is presented on the trail maps. This includes walking times for both directions, all places to stay and eat, as well as useful shops and other services. Further **details** are given in the text under the entry for each place. For an overview of all this information see the **town and village facilities table**, pp28-31.

### TRAIL MAPS

#### Scale and walking times

The trail maps are to a scale of **1:20,000** (1cm = 200m; $3^{1}/_{8}$ inches = one mile). **Walking times** are given along the side of each map; the arrow shows the direction to which the time refers. The black triangles indicate the points between which the times have been taken. **See box below about walking times**.

These time-bars are a rough guide and are not there to judge your walking ability. There are so many variables that affect walking speed from the weather conditions to how many beers you drank the previous evening. After the first hour or two of walking you'll be able to see how your speed relates to the timings on the maps.

#### Up or down?

The trail is shown as a dashed line. An arrow across the trail indicates the slope; two arrows show that it is steep. Note that the arrow points

---

❏ **Important note – walking times**
Unless otherwise specified, all times in this book refer only to the time spent walking. You will need to add 20-30% to allow for rests, photography, checking the map, drinking water etc. When planning the day's hike count on 5-7 hours' actual walking.

towards the higher part of the trail. If, for example, you are walking from A (at 80m) to B (at 200m) and the trail between the two is short and steep, it would be shown thus: A- – – >>- – -B. Reversed arrow heads indicate a downward gradient.

## Accommodation
Apart from in large towns where some selection has been necessary, all accommodation on or close to the trail is marked (or indicated off the maps) with details in the accompanying text.

Unless otherwise specified, **B&B rates** are either per person (pp) or per room for the summer (high) season assuming two people sharing a room; see also pp16-17. The number and type of rooms are given after each entry: S = single room, T = twin room, D = double room, F = family room (sleeps at least three people; may also be let as a twin or double). Where possible places where facilities include a bath are specified (bath available) and also those that accept dogs.

## Other map features
The numbered GPS waypoints refer to the list on pp259-65. Features are marked on the map when they are pertinent to navigation. In order to avoid cluttering the maps and making them unusable not all features have been marked each time they occur.

# The route guide

## EDALE
For many whose dream it has been to walk the Pennine Way, Edale will have assumed mystical significance. The very name conjures up a vision of gritstone cottages on the edge of wild moorland, and should you drive over Mam Tor and see the valley unrolling far below the impression is indeed auspicious.

A stone church set against green pastoral hills, a single-lane road winding through the middle to a dead end and some beautiful old houses.

Having arrived by train or car would-be Pennine wayfarers make their way up the lane to the Old Nag's Head (see p77) for their farewell pint. Most will be eager to set off early the next morning on the longest long-distance footpath of them all, the fabled Pennine Way.

See p25 for details about Edale Country Day in June.

## Transport
[See also pp45-50] Unless you get dropped off, the **train** is by far the easiest way to get to and from Edale. It's just half an hour from Sheffield and 45 minutes from Manchester. **Bus** services are limited: the only one is Hulley's No 260 between Castleton and Edale and that operates on Sundays/Bank Holiday Mondays only.

Parking in the car park shown on the map costs £4 a day or £5 overnight. For a **taxi** try Simon Cork (☎ 01433-650740 or ☎ 07879-881515), Chris Hudson (☎ 07828-122 390), or Andy Owens (☎ 0786-7988690).

## Services
Pop into the **Moorland Centre** (☎ 01433-670207, ⌨ www.visitpeakdistrict. com; Easter to end Oct Mon-Fri 9.30am-5pm, Sat & Sun 9.30am-5.30pm; Nov to Easter Mon-Fri 10am-3.30pm, Sat & Sun 9.30am-4.30pm). In addition to **tourist information** and details of accommodation

ROUTE GUIDE AND MAPS

in the area (but not booking) there are maps, guidebooks, snacks and souvenirs as well as a collection box for the Edale Mountain Rescue Team (🖥 www.edalemrt.co.uk).

At the top end of the village there's a **post office** (☎ 01433-670220; Mon, Tue & Thur 9am-1pm) with an **ATM** (available in shop hours) and a basic village **shop** (Easter to Sep daily 8am-5pm, rest of year Mon & Tue, Thur-Sat 9am-1pm & 2-4.30pm, Wed & Sun to 1pm only). **This is the last ATM and last shop you will see until Hebden Bridge, unless you take a bus off route.** There is no mobile phone coverage in the village but you may get a weak signal near the train station and there are three **public phones**.

### Where to stay

If you're coming from any distance it makes sense to spend a night in Edale before

starting your walk giving you a whole day to complete the fairly arduous section to Torside. Most walkers choose to stay in the centre of the village but make sure you've booked ahead at peak times or at weekends. The local community website 🖥 **www.edale-valley.co.uk** lists many local establishments and activities in the area. Note that some B&Bs may not be keen to take solo travellers at weekends unless they pay the full room rate.

**In Edale** There are two **campsites** in the centre of the village both of which are open all year. *Fieldhead* (☎ 01433-670386, 🖥 www.fieldhead-campsite.co.uk; space for 45-50 tents) by the Moorland Centre, costs £5-6.50 per adult per night; showers cost 20p; there are also toilet and drying facilities. Booking is recommended at weekends in the summer months. *Cooper's Camp*

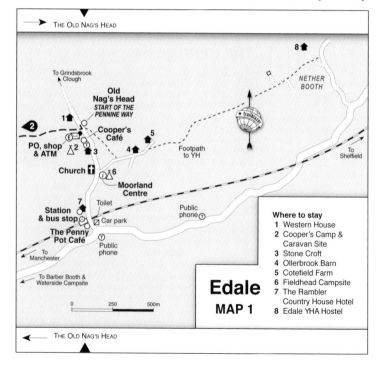

THE OLD NAG'S HEAD

To Grindsbrook Clough

Old Nag's Head
**START OF THE PENNINE WAY**

1

2

PO, shop & ATM

Cooper's Café

5

3    4

Footpath to YH

Church

6

Moorland Centre

Toilet

Station & bus stop

The Penny Pot Café

Car park

Public phone

NETHER BOOTH

🌐 trailblazer

To Sheffield

Public phone

To Manchester

To Barber Booth & Waterside Campsite

0    250    500m

8

**Where to stay**
1  Western House
2  Cooper's Camp & Caravan Site
3  Stone Croft
4  Ollerbrook Barn
5  Cotefield Farm
6  Fieldhead Campsite
7  The Rambler Country House Hotel
8  Edale YHA Hostel

# Edale

## MAP 1

THE OLD NAG'S HEAD

*and Caravan Site* (☎/🖥 01433-670372, 🖥 www.edale-valley.co.uk/camping.php; space for 120 tents), up the hill by the post office, charges £5 per person. Shower (20p) and toilet facilities are available. Booking is essential for Bank Holiday weekends and is subject to a minimum of three nights; at other times it is first come first served.

There's a simple **camping barn** (sleeping eight) with outside toilet, water tap and cooking area ten minutes' walk to the east of the village at *Cotefield Farm* (☎ 0800-019 1700 or ☎ 01629-592700, 🖥 www.yha.org.uk). It costs £7pp (bring your own sleeping bag).

Walkers requiring B&B have a limited choice. *Ollerbrook Barn* (☎ 01433-670200, 🖥 www.ollerbrook-barn-cottage .co.uk; 1D/3T, D or F, two rooms en suite, two share facilities, bath available) is a beautiful ivy-clad converted barn in a quiet spot away from the village. B&B here is from £35pp, packed lunches (£5) are available and dogs are welcome. If arranged in advance they are happy to pick people up from Edale station. Between the church and the pub is *Stone Croft* (☎ 01433-670262, 🖥 www.stonecroftguesthouse.co .uk; 2D, both with private facilities) which costs £75-85 per room.

Another cosy spot is *Western House* (☎ 01433-670014, 🖥 www.westernhouse edale.co.uk; 1D with private facilities/1D, T or F en suite with bath), just above the Nag's Head pub, which charges £65-80 (£50-60 single occupancy) but requires a minimum stay of two nights at the weekend. Dogs are accepted.

*The Rambler Country House Hotel* (☎ 01433-670268, 🖥 www.theramblerinn .com; 3D/2T/4F, all en suite, bath available) charges £60-76 for two sharing, £45 for single occupancy and £75-90 in the family rooms.

**In Nether Booth** Most nights you may find *Edale YHA Hostel* (bookings ☎ 0845-371 9514, 🖥 edale@yha.org.uk; open all day and all year) more of a 157-bed 'hyperactivity centre' over-run with school kids than the old ramblers' hostel it once was so beware before making the 1½-mile walk east of Edale village, especially in the summer holidays as the hostel is usually fully booked with groups but at any time of the year it is best to book in advance. Dorm beds cost from £17 for adults, £13 for under 18s. There are 30 rooms; six twins and six triples, the rest have 4-10 beds. You can get there via a network of footpaths from the village or along the road. Evening meals are available and there is a bar.

**In Barber Booth** This small hamlet is about half a mile south-west of Edale (off Map 1) or just under one mile south-east of Upper Booth (off Map 2) and if you're really stuck for accommodation *Waterside Campsite* (☎ 01433-670215; Easter to Sep; 40 pitches) offers camping for £3pp plus the same per tent and per vehicle. Showers, toilets and hot/cold water are available. Booking is essential for bank holiday weekends.

**Where to eat and drink**
Being the traditional start of the Pennine Way, a meal at the *Old Nag's Head* (☎ 01433-670291; bar open Mon-Sat noon-11pm, Sun to 10.30pm, food served Mon-Sat daily noon-9.30pm, Sun to 8pm) at the top of the village is a must. Try the 'Nag's Special', a giant Yorkshire pudding full of lamb stew and chips for £11.45.

The alternative is the less iconic *Rambler Country House Hotel* (daily noon-9.30pm) down the road or in the daytime try *Penny Pot Café* near the station or *Cooper's Café* next to the post office.

## EDALE TO CROWDEN                    MAPS 1-9

### Route overview
Traversing the peaty wastes of both the Kinder plateau and the tellingly named Bleaklow, distance-wise this **16-mile (26km, 5¾-7¼hrs)** stage is a jump in the deep end, not least because, at over **900m**, it includes the **second biggest total**

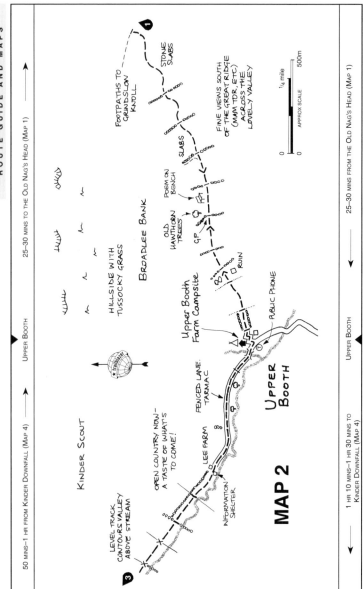

50 MINS–1 HR FROM KINDER DOWNFALL (MAP 4) —→   UPPER BOOTH   25-30 MINS TO THE OLD NAG'S HEAD (MAP 1) —→

1 HR 10 MINS–1 HR 30 MINS TO
KINDER DOWNFALL (MAP 4)   UPPER BOOTH   25-30 MINS FROM THE OLD NAG'S HEAD (MAP 1)

FOOTPATHS TO
GRINDSLOW
KNOLL

STONE
SLABS

HILLSIDE WITH
TUSSOCKY GRASS

BROADLEE BANK

SLABS

POEM ON
BENCH

OLD
HAWTHORN
TREES

GP

FINE VIEWS SOUTH
OF THE GREAT RIDGE
(MAM TOR, ETC.)
ACROSS THE
LOVELY VALLEY

RUIN

KINDER SCOUT

OPEN COUNTRY NOW –
A TASTE OF WHAT'S
TO COME!

FENCED LANE.
TARMAC

LEE FARM

Upper Booth
Farm Campsite

PUBLIC PHONE

UPPER
BOOTH

LEVEL TRACK
CONTOURS VALLEY
ABOVE STREAM

INFORMATION
SHELTER

MAP 2

0   APPROX SCALE   500m

0   ¼ mile

**ascent** of the Pennine Way (the Cross Fell stage being nearly 1100m). A solid day's walk, it's a classic nevertheless, but these days for the right reasons.

The route was once so boggy and confusing that reputedly half of all who set out gave up. Today the worst of the mire has been subdued with stone slabs salvaged from demolished cotton mills and laid end to end to ensure the twin blessings of dry feet and a clearly navigable path.

The inaugural stage passes through the hamlet of **Upper Booth** (Map 2), a pleasant amble through the upper pastures of the valley. Thereafter follows the stiff ascent of **Jacob's Ladder** (Map 3) before open moorland is reached near **Edale Cross**. You'll meet the first of a handful of 'trig points' on top of **Kinder Low** where the route descends to take an impressive arc along the **Kinder Edges**, the plateau's western rim that at weekends can become thronged with day walkers.

### Kinder Scout route                                                      Map 3, p81
The Pennine Way used to go up Grindsbrook Clough to strike across the summit wastes of Kinder Scout, a challenging route that usually resulted in walkers becoming enmired and confused in the labyrinthine maze of peat channels. As generations of wandering boots eroded the peat the decision was taken to re-route the Way via the current, much more easily navigable, westerly path. But purists and the ignorant still march straight past the Old Nag's Head and up Grinds Brook. This is not a good idea.

For those who like to ignore this advice, the best way to cross the wilderness to Kinder Downfall is to follow a bearing of 310° from the top of Grindsbrook Clough where it emerges onto the plateau (SK105872 or N53° 22.9' W01° 50.6'). This should allow you to hit the easier edge path south of the Downfall (see Map 4 for the waypoint). With only a compass it's important not to stray north, even by a few degrees.

Up there, there are no landmarks or useful signs; misleading piles of stones or stakes indicating nothing. Even the wildlife lays low. The occasional golden plover pipes its warning call, a hare may spring up and run off at speed. Otherwise – nothing. Heed the plea of the golden plover and give it a wide berth, and don't think for a moment that you'll find any good wild camping spots (see p15).

Beyond the impressive but rarely flowing **Kinder Downfall** (Map 4) you leave the plateau rim for the steep stepped descent to William Clough (a Clough is a stream) and the Snake Path junction near **Mill Hill**. Here a slab causeway unrolls invitingly across the bare moorland to **Snake Pass** (Map 6) on the A57. If you've had enough, hobble down to **Snake Pass Inn** (see p84) and drown your sorrows. Otherwise it's a good three hours to Torside, so buckle down and point your feet towards the sunken track known as **Devil's Dyke**, with Bleaklow your next objective.

In poor visibility (a caveat that can be invoked for any of the hill sections along the entire Pennine Way) the route to **Bleaklow Head** (Map 7) can be confusing and will need careful navigation. There are very few signs or waymarks to see you safely there, but if all is going well the meandering ascent along peat-lined gullies and past clear-water streams is an intimate, sheltered counterpoint to the preceding expanses of Kinder. Bleaklow itself is not so much

❑ **Kinder Scout – a bit of history**

Kinder Scout, a hugely popular recreational area, with Manchester and Sheffield just a curlew's whistle away, became synonymous with the so-called 'right to roam' when in 1932 it was the scene of a mass 'trespass' in which thousands of people demonstrated their belief that wild land should be accessible to all by marching across the plateau (💻 www. kindertrespass.com). It took a while but the event eventually led to the National Parks and Access to the Countryside Act of 1949. Today rights of access to the countryside have improved further with the Countryside & Rights of Way Act 2000 (see p54).

In October 2009 the Kinder Scout plateau became a National Nature Reserve (see p61). In all, 800 hectares of blanket bog and sub-alpine dwarf shrub heath were afforded the protection that national nature reserve status should bring. The National Trust, who own the land, have plans to restore much of the damaged habitat; repairing eroded patches and aiding the recovery of sphagnum moss, so allowing future generations to enjoy this wild area. One way they plan to do this is to fence off up to 1370 hectares of Kinder Scout to keep sheep off. This should help the vegetation recover and ease erosion. Although the fence could be in place for up to 15 years as of spring 2011, the public will still be able to access the land via stiles and gates.

a mountain as a peat soufflé that failed to rise and with good intuition or plain luck you'll reach the summit pile of stones skewered with a stake or two.

From this point it's all downhill to the Longendale Valley along the rim of **Clough Edge** (Map 8), a deep heather-clad gully, from where an underwhelming panorama of reservoirs and plantations reveal themselves far below.

Once the **B6105** (Map 9) is reached take heart as there's a good B&B close by (see p84). On the north side of the reservoir, **Crowden** is no more than a campsite and hostel-cum-activity centre, bringing you wearily but satisfyingly to the end of your first day. Only 240 miles to go.

### Route-finding trouble spots (Edale to Crowden)

Even in thick mist the pathway to the summit to Kinder Low should present no difficulties, but watch out: the short hop from the trig point to the Kinder Edges path (Map 3) is not blatantly obvious, even in clear conditions.

It's the same story leaving Bleaklow Head (Map 7) where no single path leads to the mile post by the fence (GPS waypoint 006, see p259) at which point the route is clear. If in doubt or experiencing poor visibility follow a compass bearing or use GPS.

### UPPER BOOTH                [Map 2, p78]

Located 1¼ miles (2km) into the Pennine Way, Upper Booth can make a nice warm up the night before you start your walk proper. There's a **public phone** here but the main reason you would come here is to stay at *Upper Booth Farm Campsite* (☎ 01433-670250, 💻 www.upperboothcamping.co .uk; Feb-Nov). **Camping** costs £4pp and a space in the **camping barn** for up to 12 people is from £6pp. Booking is essential for weekends in the summer and Bank Holiday weekends. There are toilet and shower facilities and packed lunches and 'take to your tent' basic meals are available if arranged in advance.

Fresh free-range eggs and milk can be bought at this award-winning farm where conservation and business can be seen working hand in hand; an excellent example of how hill farming can be a sustainable and integral part of the local economy and community.

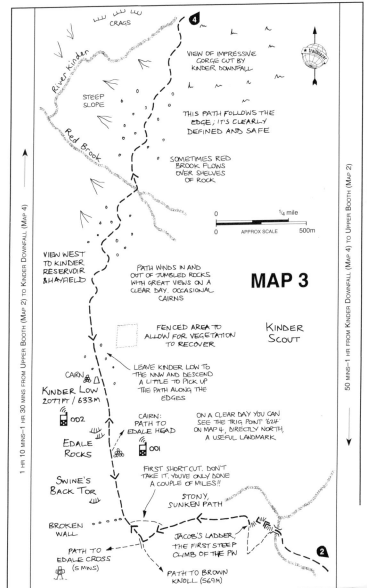

CRAGS

River Kinder

VIEW OF IMPRESSIVE GORGE CUT BY KINDER DOWNFALL

STEEP SLOPE

THIS PATH FOLLOWS THE EDGE; IT'S CLEARLY DEFINED AND SAFE

Red Brook

SOMETIMES RED BROOK FLOWS OVER SHELVES OF ROCK

0          ¼ mile
0                    500m
APPROX SCALE

VIEW WEST TO KINDER RESERVOIR & HAYFIELD

PATH WINDS IN AND OUT OF JUMBLED ROCKS WITH GREAT VIEWS ON A CLEAR DAY. OCCASIONAL CAIRNS

**MAP 3**

FENCED AREA TO ALLOW FOR VEGETATION TO RECOVER

KINDER SCOUT

LEAVE KINDER LOW TO THE NNW AND DESCEND A LITTLE TO PICK UP THE PATH ALONG THE EDGES

CAIRN
KINDER LOW
2077FT / 633M

002

CAIRN: PATH TO EDALE HEAD

001

ON A CLEAR DAY YOU CAN SEE THE TRIG POINT '624' ON MAP 4, DIRECTLY NORTH, A USEFUL LANDMARK

EDALE ROCKS

SWINE'S BACK TOR

FIRST SHORT CUT. DON'T TAKE IT, YOU'VE ONLY DONE A COUPLE OF MILES!!

STONY, SUNKEN PATH

BROKEN WALL

JACOB'S LADDER, THE FIRST STEEP CLIMB OF THE PW

PATH TO EDALE CROSS (5 MINS)

PATH TO BROWN KNOLL (569M)

1 HR 10 MINS–1 HR 30 MINS FROM UPPER BOOTH (MAP 2) TO KINDER DOWNFALL (MAP 4)

50 MINS–1 HR FROM KINDER DOWNFALL (MAP 4) TO UPPER BOOTH (MAP 2)

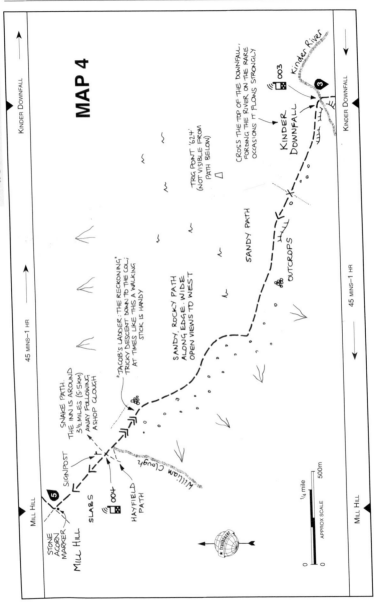

MAP 4

KINDER DOWNFALL

KINDER DOWNFALL

45 MINS–1 HR

MILL HILL

MILL HILL

Kinder River

003

3

CROSS THE TOP OF THE DOWNFALL, FORDING THE RIVER ON THE RARE OCCASIONS IT FLOWS STRONGLY

KINDER DOWNFALL

TRIG POINT '624' (NOT VISIBLE FROM PATH BELOW)

SANDY PATH

OUTCROPS

SANDY, ROCKY PATH ALONG EDGE: WIDE OPEN VIEWS TO WEST

"JACOB'S LADDER: THE RECKONING". TRICKY DESCENT DOWN TO THE COL; AT TIMES LIKE THIS A WALKING STICK IS HANDY

SNAKE PATH. THE INN IS AROUND 3½ MILES (5.5km) AWAY FOLLOWING ASHOP CLOUGH

SIGNPOST

William Clough

5

STONE ACORN MARKER

MILL HILL

MILL HILL

SLABS

004

HAYFIELD PATH

45 MINS–1 HR

¼ mile

500m

APPROX SCALE

trail blazer

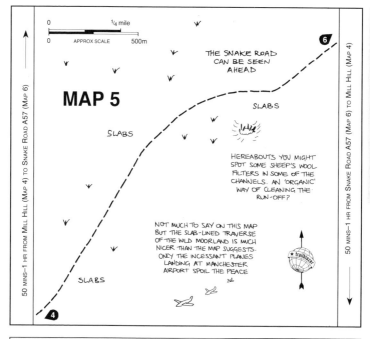

0          ¼ mile
APPROX SCALE
0                    500m

**MAP 5**

THE SNAKE ROAD
CAN BE SEEN
AHEAD

**6**

SLABS

SLABS

HEREABOUTS YOU MIGHT
SPOT SOME SHEEP'S WOOL
FILTERS IN SOME OF THE
CHANNELS. AN 'ORGANIC'
WAY OF CLEANING THE
RUN-OFF?

NOT MUCH TO SAY ON THIS MAP
BUT THE SLAB-LINED TRAVERSE
OF THE WILD MOORLAND IS MUCH
NICER THAN THE MAP SUGGESTS.
ONLY THE INCESSANT PLANES
LANDING AT MANCHESTER
AIRPORT SPOIL THE PEACE

★ trailblazer

SLABS

**4**

50 MINS–1 HR FROM MILL HILL (MAP 4) TO SNAKE ROAD A57 (MAP 6)

50 MINS–1 HR FROM SNAKE ROAD A57 (MAP 6) TO MILL HILL (MAP 4)

## ❑ Peat

The Way has not become synonymous with miles of spirit-sapping bogs for nothing. Paving slabs have alleviated much of the misery, but why is it so darn soggy?

Peat and the underlying geology are to blame. The British Isles (and indeed much of the landmass of planet earth) was once covered in trees. Everywhere

except the highest mountains and sandy beaches was wooded. Sabre-toothed tigers prowled in the forests alongside elephants and rhinos. Today these ancient woodlands and rampaging carnivores are no longer around. The reason for the disappearance of this habitat is not a natural phenomenon but the activities of early man.

When early Britons felled primeval forests for building and farming, groundwater was no longer absorbed and evaporated by the trees. Add the

Wet feet? Blame the cavemen!

impermeability of the underlying gritstone and the saturated vegetation rotted where it lay, forming the peat, which you squelch through today. So, next time your boots fill with black peaty soup, don't curse nature, curse your axe-wielding forebears instead.

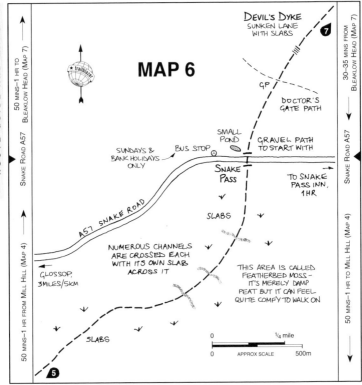

DEVIL'S DYKE
SUNKEN LANE
WITH SLABS
**7**

30-35 MINS FROM BLEAKLOW HEAD (MAP 7)

50 MINS-1 HR TO BLEAKLOW HEAD (MAP 7)

SNAKE ROAD A57

**MAP 6**

★ trailblazer

GP

DOCTOR'S GATE PATH

SMALL POND

GRAVEL PATH TO START WITH

SNAKE ROAD A57

SUNDAYS & BANK HOLIDAYS ONLY

BUS STOP

SNAKE PASS

TO SNAKE PASS INN, 1 HR

A57 SNAKE ROAD

SLABS

50 MINS-1 HR FROM MILL HILL (MAP 4)

NUMEROUS CHANNELS ARE CROSSED EACH WITH ITS OWN SLAB ACROSS IT

GLOSSOP, 3 MILES/5KM

THIS AREA IS CALLED FEATHERBED MOSS – IT'S MERELY DAMP PEAT BUT IT CAN FEEL QUITE COMFY TO WALK ON

50 MINS-1 HR TO MILL HILL (MAP 4)

SLABS

0        ¼ mile
0        500m
APPROX SCALE

**5**

## SNAKE PASS [off Map 6]

From Snake Pass, *Snake Pass Inn* (☎ 01433-651480; 🖳 www.snakepassinn.co.uk; 4S or D/4D or T/4 apartments sleeping up to 5; all en suite, bath available) charges £40 for single occupancy and £60 for two sharing, from £75 per room in an apartment. Dogs are welcome in the apartments. The inn, 2½ miles east down the A57, is full of history and character with a good choice of beer and meals in the bar.

The pub is open all day (food served Wed-Sat noon-9pm, Sun noon-6pm; in summer food may also be served on Mon and Tue). Of course a detour here means you probably wouldn't make the Torside Valley that night.

## TORSIDE [Map 9, p87]

As you descend the Pennine Way from Clough Edge you reach Torside and the B6105 road. *The Old House B&B* (☎ 01457-857527, 🖳 www.oldhouse.torside.co.uk; 1D/1T/1F, all en suite, bath available), only 500m west up the road, is friendly and a walkers' favourite. Facilities include a nice TV lounge and a drying cupboard. Evening meals, such as steak pie and lamb shank, are available. *(cont'd on p88)*

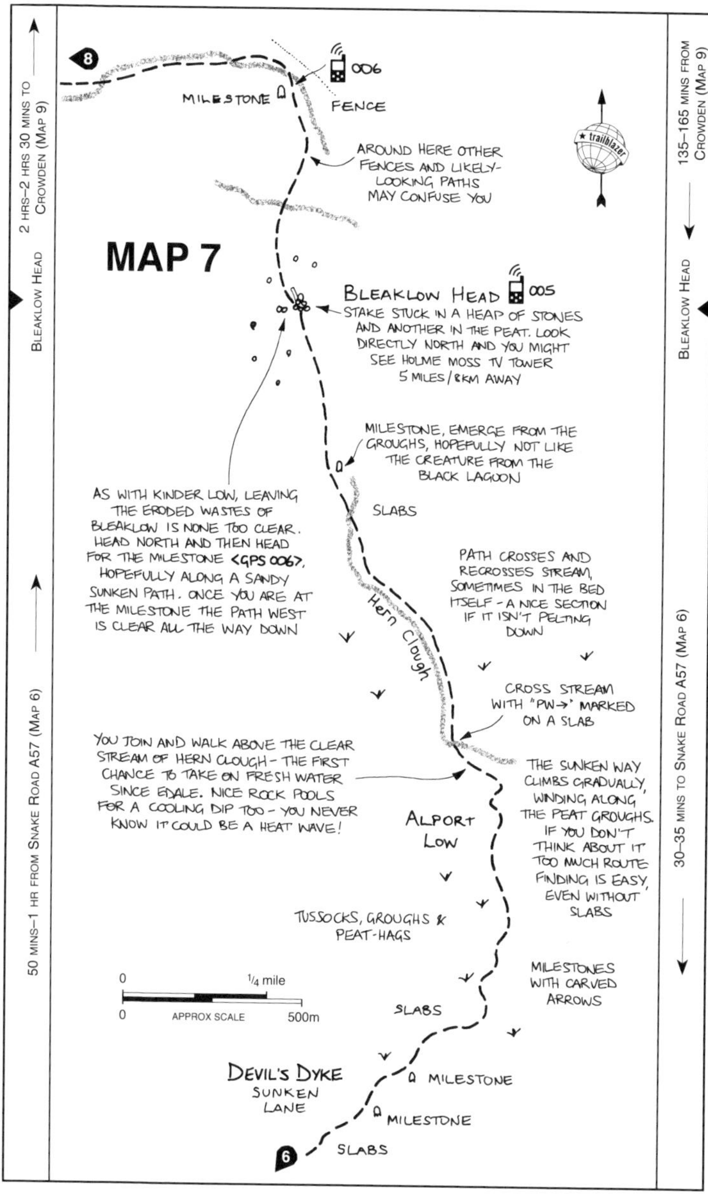

**8**

MILESTONE

006

FENCE

AROUND HERE OTHER
FENCES AND LIKELY-
LOOKING PATHS
MAY CONFUSE YOU

trailblazer

**MAP 7**

BLEAKLOW HEAD 005

STAKE STUCK IN A HEAP OF STONES
AND ANOTHER IN THE PEAT. LOOK
DIRECTLY NORTH AND YOU MIGHT
SEE HOLME MOSS TV TOWER
5 MILES/8KM AWAY

MILESTONE, EMERGE FROM THE
GROUGHS, HOPEFULLY NOT LIKE
THE CREATURE FROM THE
BLACK LAGOON

SLABS

AS WITH KINDER LOW, LEAVING
THE ERODED WASTES OF
BLEAKLOW IS NONE TOO CLEAR.
HEAD NORTH AND THEN HEAD
FOR THE MILESTONE <GPS 006>,
HOPEFULLY ALONG A SANDY
SUNKEN PATH. ONCE YOU ARE AT
THE MILESTONE THE PATH WEST
IS CLEAR ALL THE WAY DOWN

PATH CROSSES AND
RECROSSES STREAM,
SOMETIMES IN THE BED
ITSELF – A NICE SECTION
IF IT ISN'T PELTING
DOWN

Hern Clough

CROSS STREAM
WITH "PW→" MARKED
ON A SLAB

YOU JOIN AND WALK ABOVE THE CLEAR
STREAM OF HERN CLOUGH – THE FIRST
CHANCE TO TAKE ON FRESH WATER
SINCE EDALE. NICE ROCK POOLS
FOR A COOLING DIP TOO – YOU NEVER
KNOW IT COULD BE A HEAT WAVE!

THE SUNKEN WAY
CLIMBS GRADUALLY,
WINDING ALONG
THE PEAT GROUGHS.
IF YOU DON'T
THINK ABOUT IT
TOO MUCH ROUTE
FINDING IS EASY,
EVEN WITHOUT
SLABS

ALPORT
LOW

TUSSOCKS, GROUGHS &
PEAT-HAGS

MILESTONES
WITH CARVED
ARROWS

0        1/4 mile
0    APPROX SCALE    500m

SLABS

**DEVIL'S DYKE**
SUNKEN
LANE

MILESTONE

MILESTONE

**6**    SLABS

2 HRS-2 HRS 30 MINS TO
CROWDEN (MAP 9)

BLEAKLOW HEAD

50 MINS-1 HR FROM SNAKE ROAD A57 (MAP 6)

135-165 MINS FROM
CROWDEN (MAP 9)

BLEAKLOW HEAD

30-35 MINS TO SNAKE ROAD A57 (MAP 6)

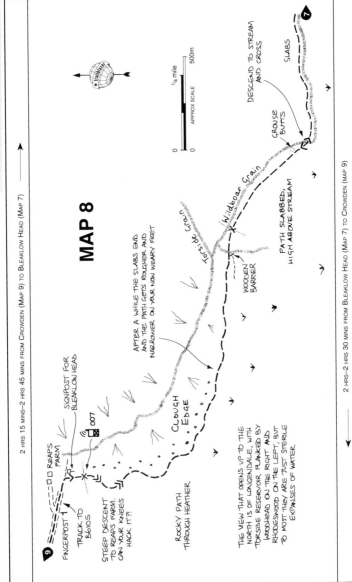

## MAP 8

REAPS FARM

FINGERPOST

TRACK TO B6105

STEEP DESCENT TO REAPS FARM. CAN YOUR KNEES HACK IT?!

SIGNPOST FOR BLEAKLOW HEAD

007

AFTER A WHILE THE SLABS END AND THE PATH GETS ROUGHER AND NARROWER ON YOUR NOW WEARY FEET

CLOUGH EDGE

ROCKY PATH THROUGH HEATHER

THE VIEW THAT OPENS UP TO THE NORTH IS OF LONGDENDALE, WITH TORSIDE RESERVOIR FLANKED BY WOODHEAD ON THE RIGHT AND RHODESWOOD ON THE LEFT, BUT TO MOST THEY ARE JUST STERILE EXPANSES OF WATER

Torside Grain

Wildboar Grain

WOODEN BARRIER

PATH SLABBED, HIGH ABOVE STREAM

GROUSE BUTTS

DESCEND TO STREAM AND CROSS

SLABS

¼ mile

500m

APPROX SCALE

trailblazer

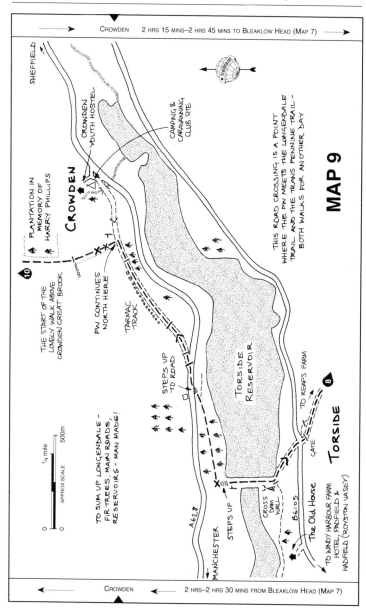

CROWDEN    2 HRS 15 MINS–2 HRS 45 MINS TO BLEAKLOW HEAD (MAP 7)

SHEFFIELD

CROWDEN YOUTH HOSTEL

CAMPING & CARAVANNING CLUB SITE

CROWDEN

PLANTATION IN MEMORY OF HARRY PHILLIPS

MAP 9

THIS ROAD CROSSING IS A POINT WHERE THE PW MEETS THE LONGDENDALE TRAIL AND THE TRANS PENNINE TRAIL – BOTH WALKS FOR ANOTHER DAY

THE START OF THE LOVELY WALK ABOVE CROWDEN GREAT BROOK

PW CONTINUES NORTH HERE

TARMAC TRACK

STEPS UP TO ROAD

TORSIDE RESERVOIR

TO REAPS FARM

TORSIDE

TO SUM UP LONGDENDALE – FIR TREES, MAIN ROADS, RESERVOIRS – MAN MADE!

STEPS UP

A628

MANCHESTER

CROSS DAM WALL

STEPS UP

B6105

GATE

The Old House

TO WINDY HARBOUR FARM HOTEL, PADFIELD & HADFIELD (ROYSTON VASEY)

APPROX SCALE

0    ¼ mile

0    500m

CROWDEN    2 HRS–2 HRS 30 MINS FROM BLEAKLOW HEAD (MAP 7)

*(continued from p84)* Alternatively they offer a lift to The Peels Arms (see below; a taxi back costs about £8). Ask in advance if you would like a packed lunch. They also have an **annex** which can be let on a B&B basis (2F, double bed and bunk beds and one room with bunk beds; shared facilities) or for a group as a **bunkhouse** (the rate includes bedding; towels are available for hire). The annex has a basic kitchen so walkers staying on a bunkhouse basis can make their own breakfast. They also offer a two-night Pennine Way package with, for example, transport to Edale on the first morning and will then take your luggage to Standedge, Marsden or Diggle after the second night, though variations are possible. Contact them for all prices.

*Windy Harbour Farm Hotel* (☎ 01457-853107, 🖳 www.peakdistrict-hotel.co.uk; 5D/1T, all en suite) is two miles along the B6105 en route to Padfield, but if you call or book ahead they'll come and pick you up. For B&B they charge £60 (£40 for single occupancy). Packed lunches are available (£5) and evening meals are offered Mon-Fri (or take a 10-min walk to The Peels Arms); they also offer basic **camping** (£4pp) as long as the field is not too wet. Dogs (£5) are welcome but booking is essential.

## PADFIELD AND HADFIELD
**[off Map 9, p87]**

Padfield is about 2½ miles to the west, adjacent to Hadfield, better known to many as the fictional 'Royston Vasey' from the *League of Gentlemen* TV series; not a distinction most 'local people' would cherish in reality. Hadfield also has a **railway station** with a frequent service to Manchester Piccadilly (see the public transport table and map pp45-50).

*The Peels Arms* (☎ 01457-852719, 🖳 www.peelsarms.co.uk, Temple St; 1T/1D share facilities, 1D en suite) is the best place for a meal (food served Mon-Fri noon-2.30pm & 5-9pm, Sat noon-9pm, Sun noon-8pm, all day on Bank Holiday Mondays) and a drink (bar open Mon-Fri noon-3pm & 5-11pm, all day at weekends). B&B costs £50-70 for two sharing; from £25 for single occupancy but the full rate must be paid at weekends in the summer.

Just over the road is *White House Farm* (☎ 01457-854695, 🖳 www.thepen nineway.co.uk/whitehousefarm; 2T shared bathroom/1D private bathroom) with B&B from £50 (£30 for single occupancy); they welcome dogs if booked in advance and provide packed lunches (£4.50).

## CROWDEN  [Map 9, p87]

Crowden has long been synonymous with *Crowden YHA Hostel* (bookings ☎ 0845-371 9113, 🖳 crowden@yha.org.uk; Easter-Oct). Part of the YHA franchise scheme, there are 38 beds; two single rooms, two twins and eight 4-bed rooms (adults from £17, under-18s from £13) and a kitchen; evening meals are available. Like many YHA hostels it is often block-booked with groups in the school holidays.

The only other accommodation is the *Camping and Caravanning Club Site* (☎ 01457-866057 or 0845-130 7633; non-members £4.60-6.40pp; Apr to end Oct; 45 pitches) nearby, with good facilities including a shop and a drying room. Booking is advised; however, non-members can't book till January.

The only bus service is the National Express **coach** (No 350) between Manchester and Sheffield (see the public transport map and table, pp45-50). If you need to call a **taxi**, try Goldline Taxis (☎ 01457-857777 or ☎ 01457-853333).

## CROWDEN TO STANDEDGE                MAPS 9-15

### Route overview

This section is a modest **11 miles (18km, 5-6¼hrs)**, one of the shortest days on the trail, and a fairly undemanding tonic after yesterday's baptismal exertions

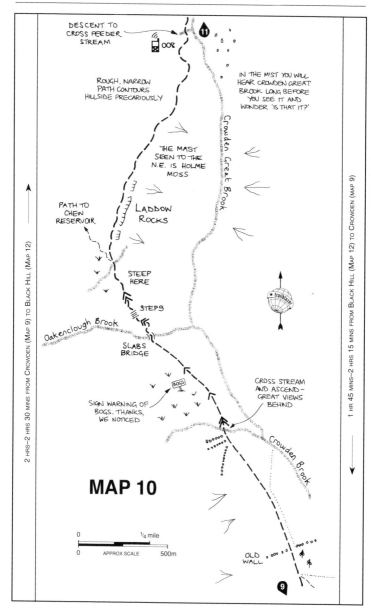

DESCENT TO CROSS FEEDER STREAM

008

ROUGH, NARROW PATH CONTOURS HILLSIDE PRECARIOUSLY

IN THE MIST YOU WILL HEAR CROWDEN GREAT BROOK LONG BEFORE YOU SEE IT AND WONDER 'IS THAT IT?'

Crowden Great Brook

THE MAST SEEN TO THE N.E. IS HOLME MOSS

PATH TO CHEW RESERVOIR

Laddow Rocks

STEEP HERE

STEPS

Oakenclough Brook

SLABS BRIDGE

BOGS

SIGN WARNING OF BOGS. THANKS, WE NOTICED

CROSS STREAM AND ASCEND – GREAT VIEWS BEHIND

Crowden Brook

MAP 10

0          ¼ mile
0   APPROX SCALE   500m

OLD WALL

9

11

trailblazer

2 HRS–2 HRS 30 MINS FROM CROWDEN (MAP 9) TO BLACK HILL (MAP 12)

1 HR 45 MINS–2 HRS 15 MINS FROM BLACK HILL (MAP 12) TO CROWDEN (MAP 9)

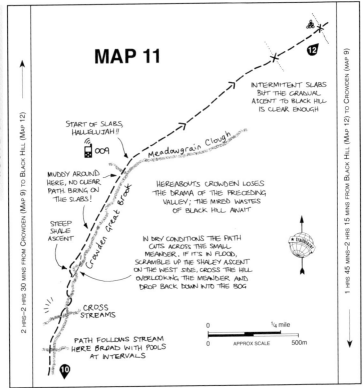

**MAP 11**

START OF SLABS, HALLELUJAH!!

009

Meadowgrain Clough

INTERMITTENT SLABS BUT THE GRADUAL ASCENT TO BLACK HILL IS CLEAR ENOUGH

12

MUDDY AROUND HERE, NO CLEAR PATH. BRING ON THE SLABS!

HEREABOUTS CROWDEN LOSES THE DRAMA OF THE PRECEDING VALLEY; THE MIRED WASTES OF BLACK HILL AWAIT

STEEP SHALE ASCENT

Crowden Great Brook

IN DRY CONDITIONS THE PATH CUTS ACROSS THE SMALL MEANDER. IF IT'S IN FLOOD, SCRAMBLE UP THE SHALEY ASCENT ON THE WEST SIDE, CROSS THE HILL OVERLOOKING THE MEANDER AND DROP BACK DOWN INTO THE BOG

CROSS STREAMS

★ trailblazer

PATH FOLLOWS STREAM HERE BROAD WITH POOLS AT INTERVALS

10

0 ............ 1/4 mile
0 ...... APPROX SCALE ...... 500m

*Left margin (rotated):* 2 HRS–2 HRS 30 MINS FROM CROWDEN (MAP 9) TO BLACK HILL (MAP 12)

*Right margin (rotated):* 1 HRS 45 MINS–2 HRS 15 MINS FROM BLACK HILL (MAP 12) TO CROWDEN (MAP 9)

(although realistically, unless you plan to curl up in a ditch you must add another mile or two at the end to get to a place to stay).

The gradual ascent out of Torside to the gritstone outcrops of **Laddow Rocks** (Map 10) lining the Crowden Great Brook characterise an area of classic south Pennine countryside. In late spring bright bilberry bushes adorn the hillsides while below them dried and now soggy bracken takes on rich coppery hues. The march along the tops of Laddow has its moments of exposure – a sudden westerly gust while on the precipitous path could be most inopportune. But as you descend again to the brook, just at the right moment wet feet are all but averted by a mill slab causeway that leads to the peat-soaked morass that answers aptly to the name of **Black Hill** (Map 12).

Many of these southerly days on the Pennine Way are bisected rather too frequently by east–west roads which intrude on the wilderness. At **Wessenden Head** the A635 carves its way across the moors, on a good day accompanied by the tantalising aroma of frying bacon from the roadside snack van.

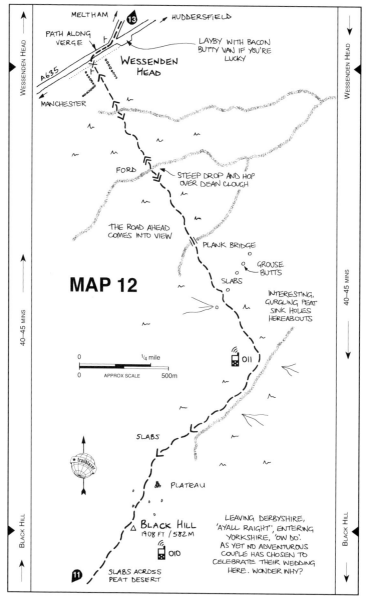

MELTHAM

**13**

HUDDERSFIELD

PATH ALONG VERGE

LAYBY WITH BACON BUTTY VAN IF YOU'RE LUCKY

WESSENDEN HEAD

A635

MANCHESTER

FORD

STEEP DROP AND HOP OVER DEAN CLOUGH

THE ROAD AHEAD COMES INTO VIEW

PLANK BRIDGE

GROUSE BUTTS

SLABS

**MAP 12**

INTERESTING, GURGLING PEAT SINK HOLES HEREABOUTS

0    1/4 mile

0    APPROX SCALE    500m

011

SLABS

*trailblazer*

PLATEAU

△ BLACK HILL
1908 FT / 582 M

010

LEAVING DERBYSHIRE, 'AYALL RAIGHT', ENTERING YORKSHIRE, 'OW DO'. AS YET NO ADVENTUROUS COUPLE HAS CHOSEN TO CELEBRATE THEIR WEDDING HERE. WONDER WHY?

**11**

SLABS ACROSS PEAT DESERT

WESSENDEN HEAD

40–45 MINS

BLACK HILL

WESSENDEN HEAD

40–45 MINS

BLACK HILL

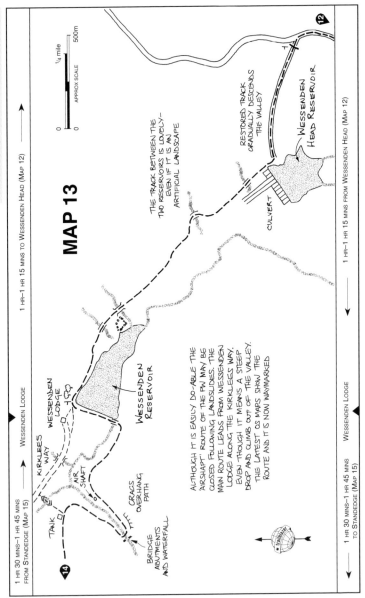

# MAP 13

1 HR 30 MINS–1 HR 45 MINS FROM STANDEDGE (MAP 15) ⟶ WESSENDEN LODGE ⟶ 1 HR–1 HR 15 MINS TO WESSENDEN HEAD (MAP 12) ⟶

THE TRACK BETWEEN THE TWO RESERVOIRS IS LOVELY– EVEN IF IT IS AN ARTIFICIAL LANDSCAPE

RESTORED TRACK GRADUALLY DESCENDS THE VALLEY

WESSENDEN HEAD RESERVOIR

¼ mile
APPROX SCALE
500m

CULVERT

WESSENDEN RESERVOIR

WESSENDEN LODGE

KIRKLEES WAY

AIR SHAFT

CRAGS OVERHANG PATH

TANK

BRIDGE ABUTMENTS AND WATERFALL

ALTHOUGH IT IS EASILY DO-ABLE THE "AIRSHAFT" ROUTE OF THE PW MAY BE CLOSED FOLLOWING LANDSLIDES. THE MAIN ROUTE LEADS FROM WESSENDEN LODGE ALONG THE KIRKLEES WAY. EVEN THOUGH IT MEANS A STEEP DROP AND CLIMB OUT OF THE VALLEY, THE LATEST OS MAPS SHOW THE ROUTE AND IT IS NOW WAYMARKED

1 HR 30 MINS–1 HR 45 MINS TO STANDEDGE (MAP 15) ⟶ WESSENDEN LODGE ⟶ 1 HR–1 HR 15 MINS FROM WESSENDEN HEAD (MAP 12) ⟶

12

14

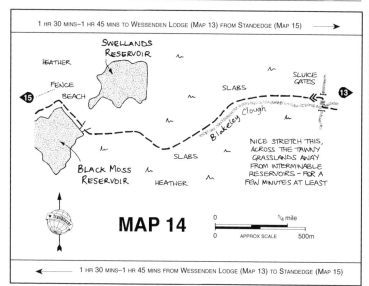

1 HR 30 MINS–1 HR 45 MINS TO WESSENDEN LODGE (MAP 13) FROM STANDEDGE (MAP 15) ⟶

SWELLANDS RESERVOIR

HEATHER

FENCE

BEACH

⑮

SLABS

SLUICE GATES

⑬

*Blakeley Clough*

NICE STRETCH THIS, ACROSS THE TAWNY GRASSLANDS AWAY FROM INTERMINABLE RESERVOIRS – FOR A FEW MINUTES AT LEAST

SLABS

BLACK MOSS RESERVOIR

HEATHER

MAP 14

★ trailblazer

0          ¼ mile
0    APPROX SCALE    500m

1 HR 30 MINS–1 HR 45 MINS FROM WESSENDEN LODGE (MAP 13) TO STANDEDGE (MAP 15)

ROUTE GUIDE AND MAPS

The successive hours string together a necklace of **reservoirs**: Wessenden Head and Wessenden (Map 13), Swellands and Black Moss (Map 14), Redbrook and Brun Clough (Map 15), a series of holding tanks serving the former industrial towns. The eye will be drawn to these successive stretches of water, scanning the surface for birdlife and rewarded, probably, by some Canada geese, a species of fowl which many birdwatchers dismiss as having no charm (an opinion which a goose might consider the kettle calling the pot black!). They were introduced in the 17th century as human migrants flowed in the opposite direction and have adapted readily to life in public parks in towns as well as in the countryside.

The approach to **Standedge Cutting** (Map 15) aims directly for the Great Western Inn (see below) but turns sharp left along an old packhorse route before reaching the west end of the cutting at the Brun Clough Reservoir car park.

### Route-finding trouble spots

The only place you could briefly go astray is on Map 11 where in heavy rain you might need to navigate round the flooded meander of Crowden Great Brook and squelch uncertainly north to thankfully meet the slabs (GPS Waypoint 009, see p259) leading up to Black Hill.

### STANDEDGE       [Map 15, p95]

First's No 184 **bus** service passes through Standedge en route between Huddersfield and Manchester; see the public transport map and table, pp45-50.

### East of the Cutting

Arriving on the busy A62 at Standedge, the prospect of a bed for the night does not look too promising. There's **The Great Western Inn** (☎ 01484-844315; bar Apr-Oct Tue-

Sun noon-11pm, rest of year noon-3pm & 5-11pm; food served Tue-Fri noon-2.30pm & 5-9pm, Sat noon-9pm, Sun noon-7pm; closed Mon all year), which you'll have spotted from the Way. They also offer basic **camping** (late Mar to late Oct); facilities (toilet/sink) are only available when the pub is open; there's no charge for camping but donations (to the Air Ambulance appeal) are welcomed. Breakfast is served if requested the night before.

*The Carriage House* (☎ 01484-844419, 🖥 www.carriage-house.co.uk), on the road towards Marsden, has less basic **camping** for £5 with shower/toilet facilities; if booked in advance they can provide breakfast for campers and will do basic food shopping as well. They also do **B&B** for £30pp (£40 for single occupancy). The pub specialises in Turkish food but they also have a full pub menu (food served Mon & Wed 6-8.30pm, Thur 5.30-9pm, Fri 5.30-9.30pm, Sat noon-10pm, Sun noon-8.30pm). The pub is closed on Tuesdays but is open from noon on Fridays.

Otherwise, short of waiting for the hourly bus (see p93), the quickest way into **Marsden** (two miles) is to take the Standedge Trail eastwards from the Marker Stone on the PW at the south end of Redbrook Reservoir (Map 15; GPS waypoint 013, see p259).

There's surprisingly little choice in Marsden but the *Olive Branch Restaurant* (☎ 01484-844487, 🖥 www.olivebranch.uk.com; 3D, all en suite; food served Mon-Sat 6.30-9.30pm, Sun 1-8.30pm), on the main Manchester Rd, has a mouthwatering menu of seafood, game and poultry. A fixed price menu (two/three courses £15.95/18.95) is available (Mon-Thur 6.30-8pm and all day Sun). A double costs £80 (single occupancy £60) for room only (breakfast costs £12.50pp); from Monday to Thursday they do a £135 dinner, bed and breakfast deal for two sharing (£160 at the weekend).

There is a Co-op **supermarket** in Marsden and an **ATM**. Marsden has a **train station** and is a stop on the Manchester to Huddersfield/Leeds line. First's **bus** service No 184 stops here en route between Huddersfield and Manchester.

### West of the Cutting
B&B options west of the Cutting are not much more convenient. The closest to the Pennine Way on the **Diggle** side is *Rock Farm* (☎ 0790-955 6024 or ☎ 01457-870325; 1D shared bathroom/1T en suite; £25pp) at the top of Manor Lane, Dean Head. Dogs are welcome if prebooked. To get there it's actually easier to continue over the A62 along the Pennine Bridleway track (west of the Pennine Way) which leads right to the farm. In the evening they will drop you at the pub for a meal. You can get a taxi or walk back. They have drying facilities and also offer packed lunches (£5).

A bit further south but about as close (15 mins from the Way) is *Wellcroft House* (☎ 01457-875017; 🖥 www.wellcrofthouse .co.uk; 1D/2D or T, all with private facilities, bath available) on Bleak Hey Nook Lane. A listed 18th-century weavers' cottage, the rooms are very well equipped and there's a guest lounge. B&B costs £55-65 (£35-45 for single occupancy). Evening meals are available; if booked in advance you will get a full meal but they are happy to make something if you haven't booked and decide not to go to the pub. Although most walkers seem to manage it, they'll pick you up if you can't walk another mile and they can do a packed lunch too. Dogs (£5) are welcome if prebooked.

### DIGGLE                          [off Map 15]
On the outskirts of Diggle about 1½ miles south-west of the PW (all steeply downhill) is *New Barn* (☎ 01457-873937 or ☎ 0797-959 8232; 1S/1T/1D en suite/1F shared bathroom), Harrop Green Farm, which charges £28pp. They have drying facilities and offer packed lunches (£5). You can take

First's No 184 **bus** (see the public transport map and table, pp45-50) from the stop opposite back up to the Way next morning.

A minute or two east of the Diggle Hotel, *Sunfield Accommodation* (☎ 01457-8740 30, 🖥 www.sunfieldaccom.co.uk; 4D/1T/ 1F, all en suite) charges £60 (£35 for single

ROUTE GUIDE AND MAPS

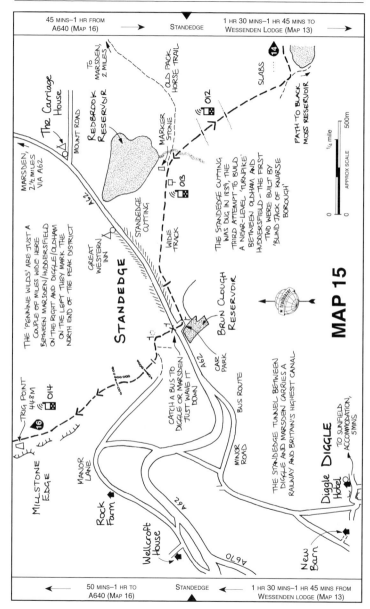

45 MINS–1 HR FROM A640 (MAP 16) → ▼ STANDEDGE 1 HR 30 MINS–1 HR 45 MINS TO WESSENDEN LODGE (MAP 13) →

STANDEDGE

MAP 15

TO MARSDEN, 2 MILES

OLD PACK HORSE TRAIL

The Carriage House

MOUNT ROAD

REDBROOK RESERVOIR

MARSDEN, 2½ MILES VIA A62

A62

STANDEDGE CUTTING

GREAT WESTERN INN

MARKER STONE

☐12

☐13

SLABS

☒14

PATH TO BLACK MOSS RESERVOIR

¼ mile

500m

0

0    APPROX SCALE

THE STANDEDGE CUTTING WAS DUG IN 1839, THE THIRD ATTEMPT TO BUILD A NEAR-LEVEL 'TURNPIKE' BETWEEN OLDHAM AND HUDDERSFIELD – THE FIRST TWO WERE BUILT BY 'BLIND JACK OF KNARSE BOROUGH'

WIDE TRACK

THE 'PENNINE WILDS' ARE JUST A COUPLE OF MILES WIDE HERE BETWEEN MARSDEN/HUDDERSFIELD ON THE RIGHT AND DIGGLE/OLDHAM ON THE LEFT. THEY MARK THE NORTH END OF THE PEAK DISTRICT

BRUN CLOUGH RESERVOIR

CAR PARK

BUS ROUTE

A62

TRIG POINT 448M

☒15

☐14

MILLSTONE EDGE

CATCH A BUS TO DIGGLE OR MARSDEN JUST WAVE IT DOWN

MANOR LANE

ROCK FARM

MINOR ROAD

THE STANDEDGE TUNNEL BETWEEN DIGGLE AND MARSDEN CARRIES A RAILWAY AND BRITAIN'S HIGHEST CANAL

WELLCROFT HOUSE

A670

DIGGLE

Diggle Hotel

TO SUNFIELD ACCOMMODATION, 5 MINS

NEW BARN

← 50 MINS–1 HR TO A640 (MAP 16) ▲ STANDEDGE ← 1 HR 30 MINS–1 HR 45 MINS FROM WESSENDEN LODGE (MAP 13)

occupancy). Packed lunches are available if requested at the time of booking. Dogs also welcome if booked in advance.

Down in Diggle why not treat yourself at *Diggle Hotel* (☎ 01457-872741; 2T/1D/1D, T or F, en suite; bar Mon-Fri noon-3pm & 5pm-midnight, Sat & Sun all day; food served Mon-Fri noon-2.30pm & 5.30-9pm, Sat noon-9pm, Sun noon-8pm), a family-run free house with several real ales. Look out on the extensive menu for their home-made pies (£6.95) or on weekdays for their two-course lunch (£11); in winter the succulent *Lamb Henry* (see p18; the official dish of the Pennine Way) may be on the specials board. Accommodation is also available here at £55 if you're sharing (£35 for single occupancy).

## STANDEDGE TO CALDER VALLEY                              MAPS 15-22

### Route overview

It has to be said that while much flatter than the previous two days and not without its agreeable moments, the **14 miles (23km, 5¾-7½hrs**; plus an extra 30 minutes each way walking to and from Hebden Bridge) to the Calder Valley is not the greatest day's walking on the Pennine Way. It starts enthusiastically enough with a traverse along **Millstone Edge** (Map 15), the first of several gritstone edges, but several road crossings (not least of which is the vertigo-inducing crossing high above the M62), along with the frequent hum of distant traffic and a string of man-made reservoirs does not distinguish this stage. The presence of rogue dirt bikers who gain easy access onto the moors between the A640 and the A58 can also spoil the day. Quite simply, the Lancashire and Yorkshire conurbations press in too close to the Pennine Way and almost smother it.

As the numerous reservoirs testify, the soggy moorland is well adapted to water catchment for these towns, but luckily the worst of the bogs are slabbed for your walking pleasure. Just beyond the M62, the wastes of **Redmires** (Map 18) certainly used to exact their annual tribute of walkers' boots and souls; now they quiver, subdued beneath the mighty flagstones.

Overlooking Littleborough, **Blackstone Edge** is an airy rampart. Soon you encounter the ancient **Aiggin Stone** and descend a short section of time- and cartwheel-worn 'Roman' pavement. Thereafter a less salubrious drain accompanies you nearly all the way to the White House pub (see p98) in preparation for the afternoon's level track circumventing several **reservoirs** (Map 19) before another moorland drain leads to a view of the distant monument of Stoodley Pike. You reach Stoodley by way of **Coldwell Hill** (Map 20), along slabs which wend their way through stunted heather and grass, the Way designated intermittently with piles of stones, and come to another ancient crossroads known as **Withen's Gate**. If you're heading for **Mankinholes** (see p103), turn left here down the Calderdale Way for a mile and a bit.

If your objectives lie in the Calder Valley or beyond, **Stoodley Pike** (Map 21; see box p103) demands a short rest to either admire the view or cower wretchedly from the rain. Underway again, it's downhill into farmland and through light woodland to the Rochdale Canal where a decision has to be made whether to follow the towpath a mile or two into **Hebden Bridge** (see p105) or trek the same distance up some gruelling gradients to the nearest accommodation

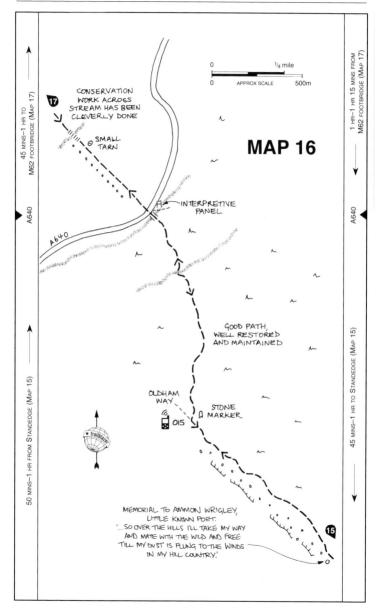

45 MINS–1 HR TO M62 FOOTBRIDGE (MAP 17)

A640

50 MINS–1 HR FROM STANDEDGE (MAP 15)

1 HR–1 HR 15 MINS FROM M62 FOOTBRIDGE (MAP 17)

A640

45 MINS–1 HR TO STANDEDGE (MAP 15)

17

CONSERVATION
WORK ACROSS
STREAM HAS BEEN
CLEVERLY DONE

SMALL
TARN

INTERPRETIVE
PANEL

MAP 16

A640

0        ¼ mile

0        APPROX SCALE        500m

GOOD PATH,
WELL RESTORED
AND MAINTAINED

OLDHAM
WAY

015

STONE
MARKER

trailblazer

MEMORIAL TO AMMON WRIGLEY,
LITTLE KNOWN POET.
'... SO OVER THE HILLS I'LL TAKE MY WAY
AND MATE WITH THE WILD AND FREE
TILL MY DUST IS FLUNG TO THE WINDS
IN MY HILL COUNTRY.'

15

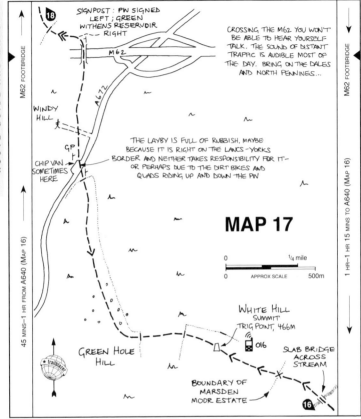

**MAP 17**

at Blackshaw Head (see p108). Alternatively you can take First's E bus (see public transport map and table, pp45-50).

### Route-finding trouble spots

Good news, even in day-long 100-metre visibility, the only place the route is difficult to follow is along the braided paths alongside Blackstone Edge. Luckily, poles or cairns loom out of the murk just in time.

### BLACKSTONE EDGE/A58
**[Map 19, p100]**

It's rare that a pub pops up so opportunely so enjoy the **White House** (☎ 01706-378456, 🖥 www.thewhitehousepub.co.uk; bar Mon-Sat noon-2.45pm & 6.30-11pm, food served Mon-Sat noon-2pm & 6.30-9.30pm, Sun noon-9pm), a former packhorse inn on the A58 near Blackstone Edge Reservoir, a perfectly serviceable place for a pint or a meal.

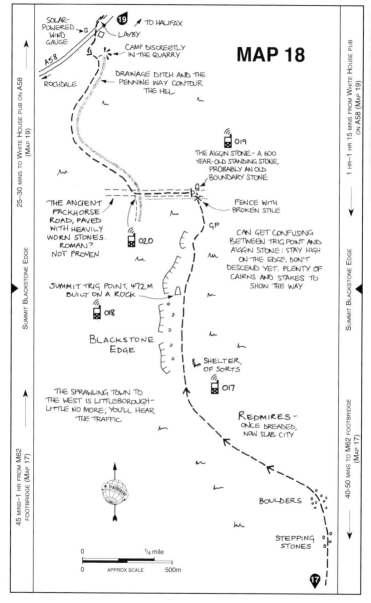

**MAP 18**

SOLAR-POWERED WIND GAUGE

LAYBY

TO HALIFAX

CAMP DISCREETLY IN THE QUARRY

A58

ROCHDALE

DRAINAGE DITCH AND THE PENNINE WAY CONTOUR THE HILL

019

THE AIGGIN STONE – A 600 YEAR-OLD STANDING STONE, PROBABLY AN OLD BOUNDARY STONE

FENCE WITH BROKEN STILE

THE ANCIENT PACKHORSE ROAD, PAVED WITH HEAVILY WORN STONES. ROMAN? NOT PROVEN

020

GP

CAN GET CONFUSING BETWEEN TRIG POINT AND AIGGIN STONE: STAY HIGH ON THE EDGE, DON'T DESCEND YET. PLENTY OF CAIRNS AND STAKES TO SHOW THE WAY

SUMMIT TRIG POINT, 472M BUILT ON A ROCK

018

BLACKSTONE EDGE

SHELTER, OF SORTS

017

THE SPRAWLING TOWN TO THE WEST IS LITTLEBOROUGH– LITTLE NO MORE; YOU'LL HEAR THE TRAFFIC

REDMIRES – ONCE DREADED, NOW SLAB CITY

trailblazer

0      ¼ mile

0                              500m
APPROX SCALE

BOULDERS

STEPPING STONES

17

25–30 MINS TO WHITE HOUSE PUB ON A58 (MAP 19)

SUMMIT BLACKSTONE EDGE

45 MINS–1 HR FROM M62 FOOTBRIDGE (MAP 17)

1 HR–1 HR 15 MINS FROM WHITE HOUSE PUB ON A58 (MAP 19)

SUMMIT BLACKSTONE EDGE

40-50 MINS TO M62 FOOTBRIDGE (MAP 17)

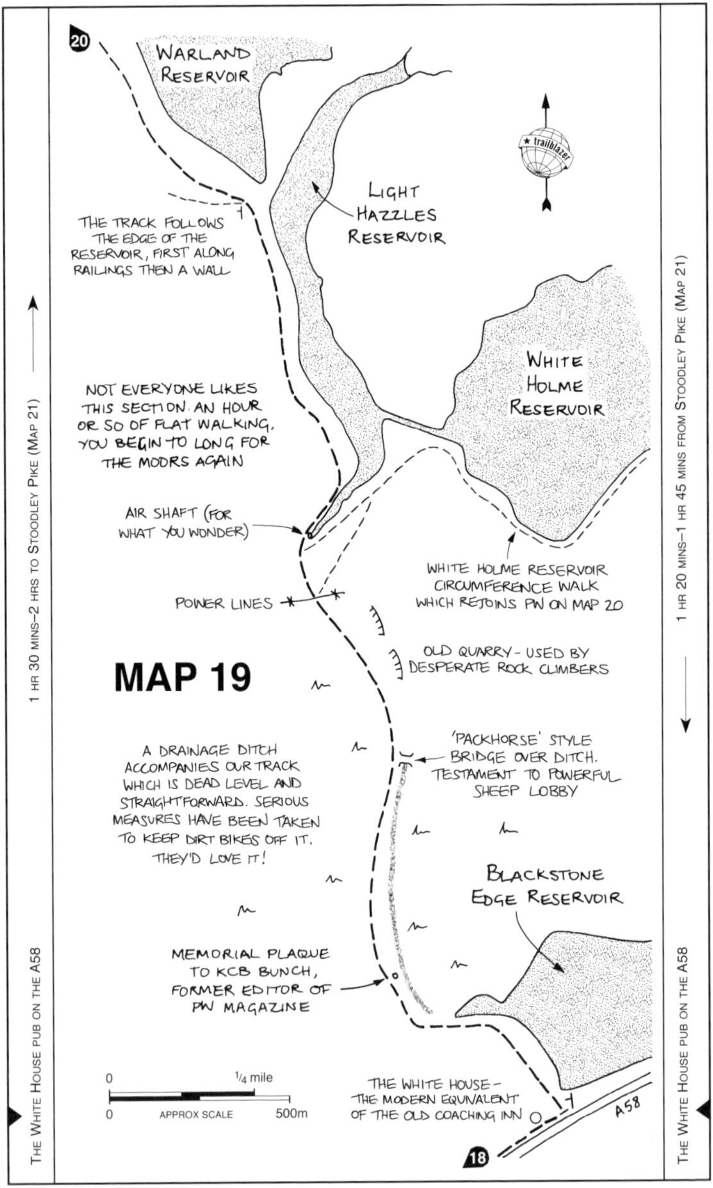

ROUTE GUIDE AND MAPS

**20**

WARLAND
RESERVOIR

LIGHT
HAZZLES
RESERVOIR

★ trailblazer

WHITE
HOLME
RESERVOIR

THE TRACK FOLLOWS
THE EDGE OF THE
RESERVOIR, FIRST ALONG
RAILINGS THEN A WALL

NOT EVERYONE LIKES
THIS SECTION. AN HOUR
OR SO OF FLAT WALKING.
YOU BEGIN TO LONG FOR
THE MOORS AGAIN

AIR SHAFT (FOR
WHAT YOU WONDER)

WHITE HOLME RESERVOIR
CIRCUMFERENCE WALK
WHICH REJOINS PW ON MAP 20

POWER LINES

OLD QUARRY – USED BY
DESPERATE ROCK CLIMBERS

# MAP 19

A DRAINAGE DITCH
ACCOMPANIES OUR TRACK
WHICH IS DEAD LEVEL AND
STRAIGHTFORWARD. SERIOUS
MEASURES HAVE BEEN TAKEN
TO KEEP DIRT BIKES OFF IT.
THEY'D LOVE IT!

'PACKHORSE' STYLE
BRIDGE OVER DITCH.
TESTAMENT TO POWERFUL
SHEEP LOBBY

BLACKSTONE
EDGE RESERVOIR

MEMORIAL PLAQUE
TO KCB BUNCH,
FORMER EDITOR OF
PW MAGAZINE

| 0 | | 1/4 mile |
|---|---|---|
| 0 | APPROX SCALE | 500m |

THE WHITE HOUSE –
THE MODERN EQUIVALENT
OF THE OLD COACHING INN

A58

**18**

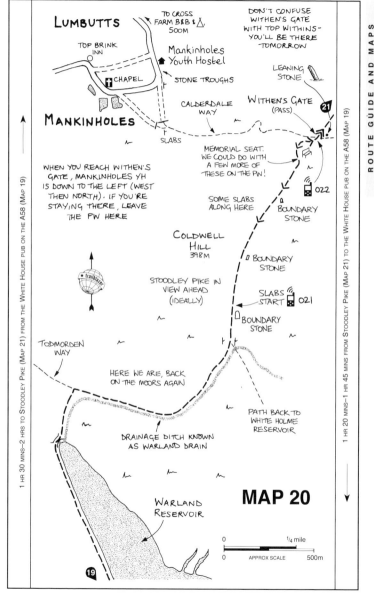

LUMBUTTS

TOP BRINK INN

✝ CHAPEL

MANKINHOLES

TO CROSS FARM B&B & ⛺, 500M

Mankinholes Youth Hostel

STONE TROUGHS

CALDERDALE WAY

SLABS

DON'T CONFUSE WITHEN'S GATE WITH TOP WITHINS— YOU'LL BE THERE TOMORROW

LEANING STONE

WITHEN'S GATE (PASS)

**21**

MEMORIAL SEAT. WE COULD DO WITH A FEW MORE OF THESE ON THE PW !

WHEN YOU REACH WITHEN'S GATE, MANKINHOLES YH IS DOWN TO THE LEFT (WEST THEN NORTH). IF YOU'RE STAYING THERE, LEAVE THE PW HERE

SOME SLABS ALONG HERE

022

BOUNDARY STONE

★ trailblazer

COLDWELL HILL 398M

STOODLEY PIKE IN VIEW AHEAD (IDEALLY)

BOUNDARY STONE

SLABS START 021

BOUNDARY STONE

TODMORDEN WAY

HERE WE ARE, BACK ON THE MOORS AGAIN

PATH BACK TO WHITE HOLME RESERVOIR

DRAINAGE DITCH KNOWN AS WARLAND DRAIN

**MAP 20**

WARLAND RESERVOIR

**19**

0          ¼ mile

0          500m
APPROX SCALE

1 HR 30 MINS–2 HRS TO STOODLEY PIKE (MAP 21) FROM THE WHITE HOUSE PUB ON THE A58 (MAP 19)

1 HR 20 MINS–1 HR 45 MINS FROM STOODLEY PIKE (MAP 21) TO THE WHITE HOUSE PUB ON THE A58 (MAP 19)

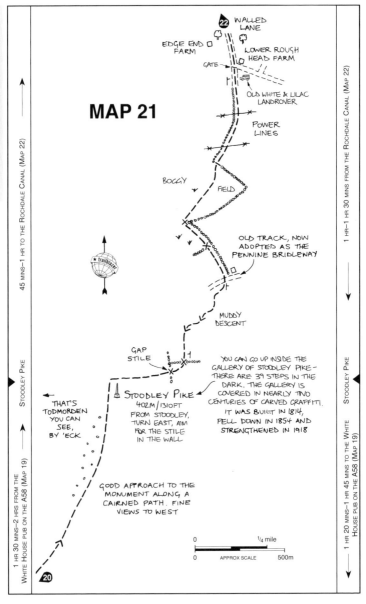

**MAP 21**

45 MINS–1 HR TO THE ROCHDALE CANAL (MAP 22)

1 HR–1 HR 30 MINS FROM THE ROCHDALE CANAL (MAP 22)

22  WALLED LANE

EDGE END FARM

LOWER ROUGH HEAD FARM

GATE

OLD WHITE & LILAC LANDROVER

POWER LINES

BOGGY

FIELD

OLD TRACK, NOW ADOPTED AS THE PENNINE BRIDLEWAY

★ trailblazer

MUDDY DESCENT

GAP STILE

YOU CAN GO UP INSIDE THE GALLERY OF STOODLEY PIKE – THERE ARE 39 STEPS IN THE DARK. THE GALLERY IS COVERED IN NEARLY TWO CENTURIES OF CARVED GRAFFITI. IT WAS BUILT IN 1814, FELL DOWN IN 1854 AND STRENGTHENED IN 1918

STOODLEY PIKE

STOODLEY PIKE
402M/1310FT
FROM STOODLEY, TURN EAST, AIM FOR THE STILE IN THE WALL

THAT'S TODMORDEN YOU CAN SEE, BY 'ECK

GOOD APPROACH TO THE MONUMENT ALONG A CAIRNED PATH. FINE VIEWS TO WEST

1 HR 30 MINS–2 HRS FROM THE WHITE HOUSE PUB ON THE A58 (MAP 19)

1 HR 20 MINS–1 HR 45 MINS TO THE WHITE HOUSE PUB ON THE A58 (MAP 19)

STOODLEY PIKE

0        ¼ mile
0                          500m
APPROX SCALE

20

## MANKINHOLES        [Map 20, p101]

Unless you're content to curl up in a curlew's nest, the only accommodation between Standedge and the Calder Valley is in Mankinholes. It means a diversion off the route and unless you retrace your steps to Withen's Gate to rejoin the trail proper, you'll have missed out part of the Pennine Way and the resultant guilt could torment you for eternity.

Most walkers continue down to the Calder Valley but unless you haul on up the other side, the bright lights of Hebden Bridge also require a diversion of a mile or two. The traditional *Mankinholes YHA Hostel* (☎ 0845-371 9751, 💻 mankin holes@yha.org.uk; Feb-Dec) is an old manor house charging from £13 (under 18s from £10) for one of its 32 beds (eight rooms with 2-6 beds). It is licensed but does not provide meals so you'll have to cook your own or go to the *Top Brink Inn* (☎ 01706-812696, 💻 http://topbrink.com; bar

Mon-Fri noon-3pm & 5.30-11pm, all day Sat & Sun; food served Mon-Fri noon-2.30pm & 5.30-9.30pm, Sat noon-10pm, Sun and Bank Holidays noon-9.30pm). The menu includes Cumberland sausage with chips and a fried egg (£5.85), sirloin steak (£12.65) and a range of vegetarian dishes. There is also a specials board and home-made desserts.

B&B is available at *Cross Farm* (☎ 01706-813481; 2D/2T, all with private facilities, bath available) from £30pp; basic **camping**, with shower (50p) and toilet facilities in a barn, costs £4pp.

If you are short of cash or need some retail therapy, catch the bus into **Todmorden** (or simply 'Tod' to locals; 💻 www.todmor den.org) for **shops**, **supermarkets**, **pubs**, **restaurants** and **ATMs**. Tyrer Tours' T6/T8 **bus** runs regularly from Mankinholes (see public transport map and table, pp45-50).

**ROUTE GUIDE AND MAPS**

---

### ❑ Stoodley Pike                                          [see Map 21]

This needle-shaped monument above the Calder Valley (Calderdale) was erected on a site where there had been an ancient burial cairn, assumed to be that of a chieftain. It seems plausible, the height being a commanding one and the ideal spot to erect a memorial.

It was also an ideal site for a beacon since the chain that warned of the approach of the Spanish Armada included Halifax's Beacon Hill and Pendle Hill above Clitheroe, Stoodley being the link between the two.

Be that as it may, in 1814 it was decided to celebrate the defeat of Napoleon by erecting a monument by public subscription and local bigwigs were quick to put their name down. Then as now a chance to appear influential was not to be missed. Unfortunately Napoleon escaped from Elba, raised his armies and overthrew the restored monarchy, cutting short the erection of the monument. After Wellington finally put paid to Napoleon at Waterloo, the work began again and it was completed before the end of 1815.

Disaster struck in 1854 when the tower collapsed as the country was going to war again, this time in the Crimea, an evil omen indeed. Rebuilt, it has survived to this day although they do say it wobbled a bit on the eve of the Falklands War.

For walkers along the Pennine Way the 37-metre (120ft) high spire is a landmark that beckons from afar. Inside the graffiti-decked gallery you can climb the 39 steps in the dark.

Roughly at the 40-mile (60km) mark from Edale, Stoodley Pike marks a change in the countryside. The peat moors are largely behind you and ahead lie more pastoral scenes as the gritstone gives way to limestone.

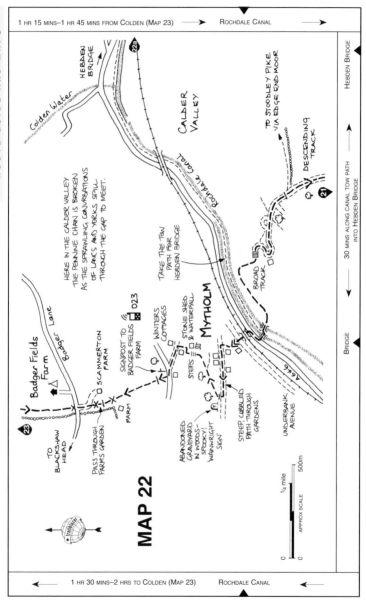

1 HR 15 MINS–1 HR 45 MINS FROM COLDEN (MAP 23) →  ROCHDALE CANAL →

HEBDEN BRIDGE

23A

Colden Water

HEBDEN BRIDGE

CALDER VALLEY

HERE IN THE CALDER VALLEY THE PENNINE CHAIN IS BROKEN AS THE SPRAWLING CONURBATIONS OF LANCS AND YORKS SPILL THROUGH THE GAP TO MEET.

Badger Fields Farm

Badger Lane

SCAMMERTON FARM

SIGNPOST TO BADGER FIELDS FARM

WINTERS COTTAGES

STONE SHED & WATERFALL

□23

STEPS

MYTHOLM

TO STOODLEY PIKE VIA EDGE END MOOR

DESCENDING TRACK

21

BROAD TRACK

TAKE THE TOW PATH FOR HEBDEN BRIDGE

A646

Rochdale Canal

23

TO BLACKSHAW HEAD

PASS THROUGH FARM'S GARDEN

FARM

ABANDONED GRAVEYARD IN WOODS – SPOOKY! 'WAINWRIGHT SIGN'

STEEP COBBLED PATH THROUGH GARDENS

UNDERBANK AVENUE

MAP 22

¼ mile
500m
APPROX SCALE
0
0

HEBDEN BRIDGE

30 MINS ALONG CANAL TOW PATH INTO HEBDEN BRIDGE

BRIDGE

ROUTE GUIDE AND MAPS

## HEBDEN BRIDGE    [see Map 22a]

It was along the Calder Valley that the Industrial Revolution was born and Hebden Bridge, a half-hour stroll east of the Pennine Way along the Rochdale Canal towpath, is well worth the short detour.

Since the mills closed it's attracted a large 'alternative' population (in 2005 it was named Europe's funkiest place to live) and as a result there are plenty of lively pubs, restaurants, interesting shops and a vibrant arts scene. The Picture House **cinema** (☎ 01422-842807) shows matinées at 3pm at the weekend and the main programme is at 7.45pm daily. There are regular performances at the **Little Theatre** (🖳 www.hebdenbridgelittletheatre.co.uk)

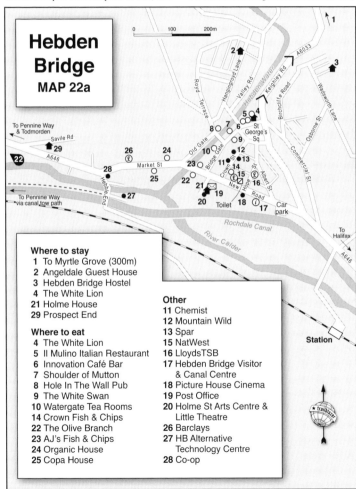

**Hebden Bridge MAP 22a**

0    100    200m

To Pennine Way & Todmorden

Savile Rd

To Pennine Way via canal tow path

Royd Terrace

Hangingroyd Lane

Valley Rd

Hebden Water

A6033

Keighley Rd

Birchcliffe Road

Wadsworth Lane

Osborne St

St George's Sq

Old Gate

Bridge Gate

Crown St

New Hope Road

Albert St

Commercial St

Market St

Hebble End

Toilet

Car park

Rochdale Canal

River Calder

To Halifax

A646

Station

trailblazer

### Where to stay
1 To Myrtle Grove (300m)
2 Angeldale Guest House
3 Hebden Bridge Hostel
4 The White Lion
21 Holme House
29 Prospect End

### Where to eat
4 The White Lion
5 Il Mulino Italian Restaurant
6 Innovation Café Bar
7 Shoulder of Mutton
8 Hole In The Wall Pub
9 The White Swan
10 Watergate Tea Rooms
14 Crown Fish & Chips
22 The Olive Branch
23 AJ's Fish & Chips
24 Organic House
25 Copa House

### Other
11 Chemist
12 Mountain Wild
13 Spar
15 NatWest
16 LloydsTSB
17 Hebden Bridge Visitor & Canal Centre
18 Picture House Cinema
19 Post Office
20 Holme St Arts Centre & Little Theatre
26 Barclays
27 HB Alternative Technology Centre
28 Co-op

beside the Holme St Arts Centre; see the website for details. See p25 for details about the Arts Festival in July.

If you need to save energy, visit the **HB Alternative Technology Centre** (☎ 01422 842121, 🖳 http://alternativetechnology.org. uk; Mon-Fri 10am-5pm, Sat noon-5pm, Sun noon-4pm; free but donations welcome) by the canal. The exhibitions change but feature aspects of energy use both in the home and outside.

### Transport
[See also pp45-50] There are frequent **trains** from Leeds, Bradford, Manchester and Preston. There are no direct **buses** from any major cities, but First operates regular services to Burnley, Rochdale, Todmorden and Halifax. Their E service does a circular route to Mytholm & Blackshaw Head. Keighley and District's No 500 goes to Oxenhope, Haworth and Keighley from here.

### Services
The **Hebden Bridge Visitor and Canal Centre** (☎ 01422-843831, 🖳 www.hebden bridge.co.uk; Apr-Oct Mon-Fri 9.30am-5.30pm, Sat 10.15am-5pm, Sun 10.30am-5pm; Nov-Mar Mon-Fri 10am-5pm, Sat & Sun 10.30am-4.15pm) is in the middle of the town. They are able to book accommodation (see box p13).

There are three major **banks**, all with **cash machines** and a **post office**. Mountain Wild on Crown St sells **walking gear** and there's a small Spar **supermarket** (8.30am-11pm weekdays) opposite and a **chemist** nearby. Alternatively try the Co-op (till 8.30am-9pm weekdays) on the main road.

### Where to stay
There are no campsites in town, but several B&Bs and hotels as well as a hostel, **Hebden Bridge Hostel** (☎ 01422-843183, 🖳 www.hebdenbridgehostel.co.uk; Easter to early Nov; 36 beds) on the eastern side of town. One dorm room sleeps six (two bunk beds and two single beds) for £12pp, seven rooms sleep four (£17pp) and there's a twin room for £50. Note that the hostel is vegetarian so fresh meat/fish cannot be brought onto the premises.

On the western edge of town is **Prospect End** (☎ 01422-843586, 🖳 www .prospectend.co.uk, 8 Prospect Tce, Savile Rd; 1D/1T, both en suite) charging from £27.50pp (single occupancy from £35). In order to reach it from the Way you'll have to walk in on the A646, not the towpath.

The very central **Holme House** (☎ 01422-847588, 🖳 www.holmehousehebden bridge.co.uk; 1T/2D en suite, bath available), on New Rd, is a classy Georgian house charging £75-90 (single occupancy £60-67.50) for B&B. They also have an apartment sleeping up to five people available only on a two-night self-catering basis £77.50-90 per night.

**Angeldale Guest House** (☎ 01422-847321, 🖳 www.angeldale.co.uk; 2D or T share bathroom/2D, T or F en suite; closed Jan to early Feb), at the top of Hangingroyd Lane, is also fairly central with rooms from £56 (en suite £66). During the week single occupancy costs from £40 but at the weekend the rate is the room rate.

**Myrtle Grove** (☎ 01422-846078 or ☎ 07905-147902, 🖳 www.myrtlegrove .btinternet.co.uk, Old Lees Rd; 1D en suite) is just north of the town centre up the hill, an organic and veggie-friendly place; two sharing costs £65-70, single occupancy by arrangement. Dogs (£5) also welcome if booked in advance.

**The White Lion Hotel** (☎ 01422-842197, 🖳 www.whitelionhotel.net, Bridge Gate; 1T/5D/4D, T or F, all en suite, bath available) charges from £79 for two sharing (single occupancy £59); a family room sleeping four costs from £115.

### Where to eat and drink
If sandwiches and full English breakfasts (FEBs) are getting a bit galling, make the most of the variety and choice in Hebden. There are some particularly good cafés along Market St. **Organic House** (☎ 01422-843429, 🖳 www.organic-house.co.uk; Mon-Fri 8.45am-5pm, Sat 9am-5.30pm, snacks only after 3pm, Sun 10am-5pm) does a range of wholesome dishes (all organic and Freetrade where possible); the menu includes both veggie and meat dishes and mains cost £6-10.

Nearby, *Copa House* (☎ 01422-845524; Tue-Fri & Sun 10am-4pm, Sat to 5pm) serves home-made soup, cakes and sandwiches; toasties cost £3.95 and Mediterranean platters are £5.95. Oh, and they do ice-cream cones for £1.20.

The *Innovation Café Bar* (☎ 01422-844094; Mon-Sat 9.45am-5pm, Sun 10.30am-5pm), in Hebden Bridge Mill, does home-made soups and pancakes (a mushroom pancake costs £5.50). Next door is *Il Mulino* (☎ 01422-845986, 🖥 www.ilmulino.co.uk; Mon-Sat 6-10pm) which does pizzas from £6.95. From Italy to Turkey, at *The Olive Branch* (☎ 01422-842299; daily noon-10pm) you can get a Turkish starter and a main course for £10 (Sun-Thur only).

On Bridge Gate, off the square, the *Shoulder of Mutton* serves pub grub from £5; the *White Swan* has similarly priced food. Nearby is the licensed *Watergate Tea Rooms* (☎ 01422-842978, 🖥 www .tandcakes.com; daily 10am-4.30pm) which does great home-made food such as a giant Yorkshire pudding with chips and gravy (£4.95). Both 'The Works' breakfast and a veggie version cost £6.95; a smaller version (£4) is also available.

Just across the pedestrian bridge over Hebden Water is the *Hole in the Wall*, a pub offering oxtail stew for £7.50 and fishfinger sandwiches for £3. *The White Lion* (see Where to stay) does pub food (Mon-Thur noon-3pm & 6-9pm, Fri & Sat noon-9pm, Sun noon-7pm) from around £8.

For fish and chips, there's *Crown* and *AJ's*; the latter does mussels and chips for £5.95. You can eat in or take away at both.

## CALDER VALLEY TO ICKORNSHAW                MAPS 22-31

### Route overview

Though it starts with a hefty climb out of the Calder Valley, this **17-mile (25km, 5½-7½hrs** plus time for walking to and from Haworth) section offers an array of landscapes from shady dells, dry-stone-walled pastures, the ever-present reservoirs and of course, heather-clad moorland. Route-finding has its moments, but others have managed; so can you!

Set off by zig-zagging up through **Mytholm**, an as-yet ungentrified outlier of Hebden Bridge. Behind you Stoodley Pike follows your every move, and soon you're clear of the valleyside and return among the pastures where the incongruous council terraces of **Colden** (Map 23) rise into view, grittily embedded below **Heptonstall Moor**. Once traversed, the peaty wastes drop down past a reservoir to the sheltered confluence of babbling brooks at **Graining Water** (Map 25), overlooked from one side by crags and from the other by the Pack Horse Inn (see p112).

An amble above this stream and a quiet road section leads to the **Walshaw Dean** series of reservoirs, forsaken before they get too tedious as you again climb the tawny moors to **Withins Height** (Map 27). Once crested you get a view of the dramatically situated ruin said to be the inspiration for the house in Emily Brontë's *Wuthering Heights* (see box p118).

Hereabouts paths leave the Way to Haworth (3½ miles, 6km, 1½hrs) and the full 'Brontë Experience' (see maps 27 and 28). Otherwise, all that remains is to drop down to **Ponden Reservoir** and decide whether to stay here or plod on to the mildly greater opportunities to be found around Ickornshaw and Cowling.

To get there the route climbs round the spur of the reservoir and up out of the Worth Valley onto **Ickornshaw Moor** (Map 30). As you come down the north side of the moor you'll spot several shooting huts; nearby Cowling has ancient shooting rights for the moorlands surrounding you.

Correctly negotiating the stiles and gates of pastures below brings you to the **waterfall** at Lumb Head Beck (Map 31) and a walled track that leads eventually to the A6068 on which lie Ickornshaw and Cowling.

## Route-finding trouble spots

Clear weather poses no problems but drifting aimlessly with the mist across Heptonstall Moor might be something you come to regret. However, once past the turn off to Clough Hole Bridge you should make it to the far side.

Withins Height Moor has a clear slabbed path, though you want to be sure you stick to the Pennine Way and not veer off into Haworth unnecessarily. And with your wits about you Ickornshaw Moor should pose no problems either; just remember to keep track after the shooters' huts while field-hopping your way to the waterfall from where you're nearly home and, who knows, maybe even dry.

### BLACKSHAW HEAD   [Map 22, p104]

Where the trail crosses Badger Lane there is *Badger Fields Farm* (☎ 01422-845161, 🖳 www.badgerfields.com; 2T/1D shared facilities, bath available; Apr-Oct) where Mrs Whitaker offers B&B for £64 for two sharing (£40 single occupancy), with drying facilities, evening meals for £14 and a packed lunch for £5.50. **Camping** is £4; use of a shower is £1.50 if have own towel and breakfast (£4-7) is available for campers if booked by the night before.

Blackshaw Head has no services but a **bus** (First's E) runs frequently to Hebden Bridge (see public transport map and table, pp45-50) and it's only a mile to the New Delight pub (see below) in Colden.

### COLDEN                              [Map 23]

Within a mile of leaving the valley, we come upon signs pointing the way to **Aladdin's Cave**, promising untold excesses such as sweets, cakes, groceries and drinks. This is *Highgate Farm* (☎ 01422-842897) run by the redoubtable May Stocks who has a natural instinct for what wayfarers want and has provided for them accordingly. Besides the shop (daily 7am-9pm), May allows basic **camping** for free; there are toilet facilities and a cold water tap.

*The New Delight* (☎01422-846178; pub Mon-Fri noon-2.30pm & 5pm-midnight; Sat & Sun noon-midnight; food served Mon-Fri noon-2pm & 5-8pm, Sat & Sun noon-5pm), at **Jack Bridge**, provides a haven for thirsty or just plain miserable Pennine Way walkers with ales including Mansfield Cask and the locally brewed Moorhouses.

Next door *Hebden Bridge Camping* (☎ 01422-844334 or ☎ 01422-844417, 🖳 www.hebdenbridgecamping.co.uk; open all year) charges £5 per tent and walker plus £2 per additional walker. Shower facilities are free; towels can be hired. Well-behaved dogs are welcome. A shop selling basic food supplies and camping gas is open during the summer season.

Further north, just over a mile off the Way, there's camping for £5pp at *Pennine Camp and Caravan Site* (off Map 24; ☎ 01422-842287; approx Apr-Oct), High Greenwood House. There's a shower (50p) and toilet facilities. To get there take the path down to Clough Hole Bridge (see Map 24) and turn left up the road for ¾ mile to the campsite.

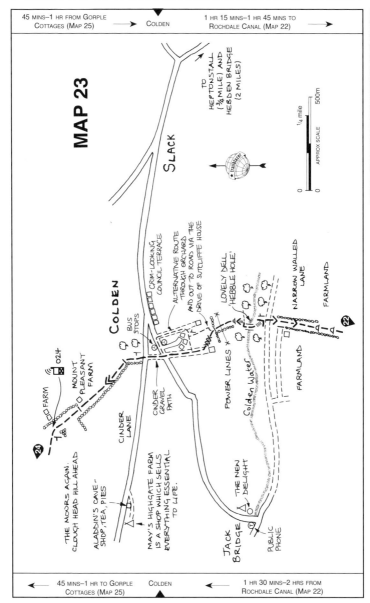

## MAP 23

45 MINS–1 HR FROM GORPLE COTTAGES (MAP 25) →

COLDEN

1 HR 15 MINS–1 HR 45 MINS TO ROCHDALE CANAL (MAP 22) →

TO HEPTONSTALL (¾ MILE) AND HEBDEN BRIDGE (2 MILES)

SLACK

¼ mile

500m

APPROX SCALE

★ Trailblazer

COLDEN

GRIM-LOOKING COUNCIL TERRACE

ALTERNATIVE ROUTE THROUGH ORCHARD AND OUT TO ROAD VIA THE DRIVE OF SUTCLIFFE HOUSE

LOVELY DELL 'HEBBLE HOLE'

NARROW WALLED LANE

FARMLAND

BUS STOPS

024

FARM

MOUNT PLEASANT FARM

CINDER/ GRAVEL PATH

POWER LINES

Colden Water

FARMLAND

FARMLAND

CINDER LANE

THE MOORS AGAIN. CLOUGH HEAD HILL AHEAD

ALADDIN'S CAVE – SHOP, TEA, PIES

MAY'S HIGHGATE FARM IS A SHOP WHICH SELLS EVERYTHING ESSENTIAL TO LIFE.

THE NEW DELIGHT

JACK BRIDGE

PUBLIC PHONE

← 45 MINS–1 HR TO GORPLE COTTAGES (MAP 25)

COLDEN

← 1 HR 30 MINS–2 HRS FROM ROCHDALE CANAL (MAP 22)

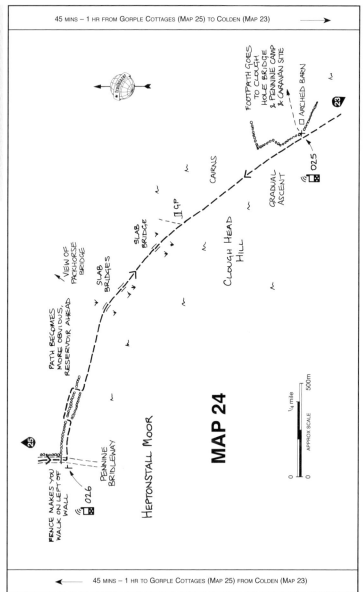

FOOTPATH GOES TO CLOUGH HOLE BRIDGE & PENNINE CAMP & CARAVAN SITE

☐ ARCHED BARN

28

025

GRADUAL ASCENT

CAIRNS

CLOUGH HEAD HILL

SLAB BRIDGE

IGP

VIEW OF PACKHORSE BRIDGE

SLAB BRIDGES

PATH BECOMES MORE OBVIOUS, RESERVOIR AHEAD

MAP 24

HEPTONSTALL MOOR

25

026

PENNINE BRIDLEWAY

FENCE MAKES YOU WALK ON LEFT OF WALL

¼ mile

500m

APPROX SCALE

0

0

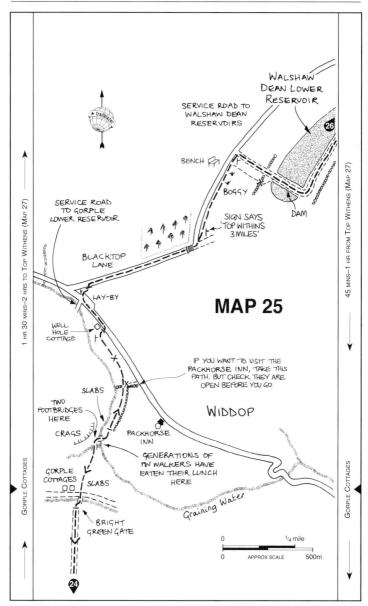

WALSHAW DEAN LOWER RESERVOIR

SERVICE RDAD TO WALSHAW DEAN RESERVOIRS

BENCH

**26**

BOGGY

SERVICE ROAD TO GORPLE LOWER RESERVOIR

SIGN SAYS 'TOP WITHINS 3 MILES'

DAM

BLACKTOP LANE

LAY-BY

**MAP 25**

WELL HOLE COTTAGE

IF YOU WANT TO VISIT THE PACKHORSE INN, TAKE THIS PATH. BUT CHECK THEY ARE OPEN BEFORE YOU GO.

SLABS

WIDDOP

TWO FOOTBRIDGES HERE

CRAGS

PACKHORSE INN

GENERATIONS OF PW WALKERS HAVE EATEN THEIR LUNCH HERE

GORPLE COTTAGES

SLABS

Graining Water

BRIGHT GREEN GATE

**24**

0        1/4 mile

0    APPROX SCALE    500m

1 HR 30 MINS–2 HRS TO TOP WITHENS (MAP 27)

45 MINS–1 HR FROM TOP WITHENS (MAP 27)

GORPLE COTTAGES

GORPLE COTTAGES

★ trailblazer

### WIDDOP [Map 25, p111]

The next pub north from Colden is the *Packhorse Inn* (Map 25; ☎ 01422-842803; 2D/1T, en suite, bath available; food served summer Tue-Sun noon-2pm & 7-9.30pm, Oct to Easter weekends only same hours), a few hundred metres off route. If you spent the night in Hebden, lunchtime could be about now but note that they're closed Mondays year-round and they also close in the afternoon; in the winter months they only open in the evening during the week. B&B costs from £48 per room (£43 single occupancy). They also have a self-catering apartment suitable for families or groups; contact them for details.

### PONDEN [Map 28, p114]

Ponden is now much smaller than it was when weaving was dominant in the area. **Ponden Mill** has been turned into a 'retail experience' and the houses along the Haworth road have been gentrified.

On the west side of the reservoir *Ponden Guest House* (☎ 01535-644154, 🖥 www.pondenhouse.co.uk; 2T shared bathroom/2D en suite) is a tastefully converted old barn right on the trail. Dogs by arrangement. Rooms cost £65-70 (single occupancy from £45) or you can **camp** round the back for £5pp (toilet/shower available). Evening meals (£18), breakfast for campers (£7) and packed lunches (£6) are available if booked in advance; alternatively you can walk the mile to The Old Silent Inn (see below), the nearest pub.

### STANBURY [Map 28, p114]

If Ponden is full and you have no intention of staying in Haworth, a walk down the road brings you to Stanbury and *The Old Silent Inn* (☎ 01535-647437, 🖥 www.old-silent-inn.co.uk; 1T/4D/1F, all en suite; food served Mon-Fri noon-2.15pm & 5.30-9pm, Sat noon-9pm, Sun noon-8pm), an upmarket hostelry which gained its name

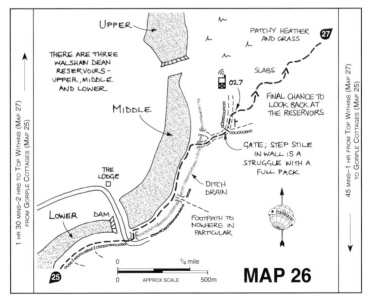

UPPER

PATCHY HEATHER AND GRASS **27**

THERE ARE THREE WALSHAN DEAN RESERVOIRS – UPPER, MIDDLE AND LOWER

SLABS

O27

FINAL CHANCE TO LOOK BACK AT THE RESERVOIRS

MIDDLE

GATE; STEP STILE IN WALL IS A STRUGGLE WITH A FULL PACK

THE LODGE

DITCH DRAIN

LOWER DAM

FOOTPATH TO NOWHERE IN PARTICULAR

★ trailblazer

0      ¼ mile

0                         500m
APPROX SCALE

**MAP 26**

**25**

1 HR 30 MINS–2 HRS TO TOP WITHINS (MAP 25) FROM GORPLE COTTAGES (MAP 27)

45 MINS–1 HR FROM TOP WITHINS (MAP 27) TO GORPLE COTTAGES (MAP 25)

ROUTE GUIDE AND MAPS

after Bonnie Prince Charlie hid out here in 1688 with a nod and a wink from the locals. To do likewise will cost £50-60 (single occupancy £45) for B&B. Dogs (£5) are welcome if booked in advance. The menu includes steak and Old Peculier pie (£9.35) and rack of lamb (£12.95).

## HAWORTH    [see Map 28a, p116]

The Pennine Way does not go through Haworth, but there are good reasons for taking the detour off the Way via the Brontë Bridge and Falls to seek whatever solace may be required: refreshment, accommodation (which is in short supply on the Way itself), literary inspiration; all are there in abundance but the extra 3½ miles (6km) down also involves 3½ miles (6km) back up!

This gritstone town's appeal is firmly based on its association with the Brontë

They won the Best Food Pub of the Year in the 2010 Great British pub awards.

If this doesn't suit, Keighley & District's No 664 **bus** stops here en route between Keighley and Haworth (see public transport map and table, pp45-50 for details).

sisters. Year-round the streets throng with visitors, most of whom have probably never read the works of Emily, Charlotte or Anne. However, such is the romantic appeal of the family, whose home can still be visited, that crowds continue to be drawn here from all over the world. Haworth is a major destination on the UK tour circuit for Japanese visitors; you'll have spotted PW signs in Japanese near Top Withins and others directing tourists up the, cobbled Main St.

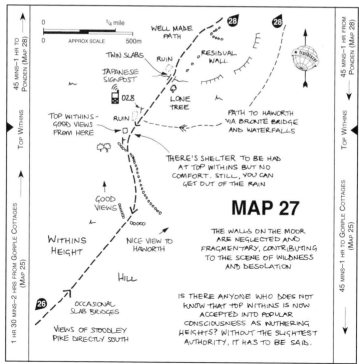

MAP 27

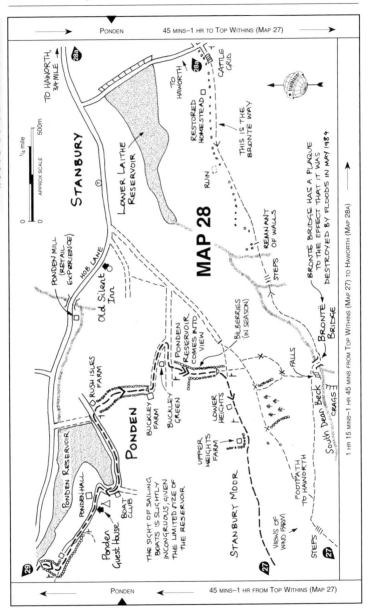

PONDEN     45 MINS–1 HR to TOP WITHINS (MAP 27)

TO HAWORTH, ¾ MILE

TO HAWORTH

CATTLE GRID

RESTORED HOMESTEAD

THIS IS THE BRONTË WAY

RUIN

STANBURY

LOWER LAITHE RESERVOIR

MAP 28

REMNANT OF WALLS

¼ mile    500m    APPROX SCALE

PONDEN MILL (RETAIL EXPERIENCE)

HOB LANE

OLD SILENT INN

ANCIENT STEPS

BRONTË BRIDGE HAS A PLAQUE TO THE EFFECT THAT IT WAS DESTROYED BY FLOODS IN MAY 1989

BRONTË BRIDGE

PONDEN RESERVOIR COMES INTO VIEW

BILBERRIES (IN SEASON)

RUSH ISLES FARM

PONDEN

BUCKLEY FARM

BUCKLEY GREEN

LOWER HEIGHTS

FALLS

South Dean Beck

CRAGS

UPPER HEIGHTS FARM

PONDEN RESERVOIR

BOAT CLUB

PONDEN HALL

Ponden Guest House

THE SIGHT OF SAILING BOATS IS SLIGHTLY INCONGRUOUS, GIVEN THE LIMITED SIZE OF THE RESERVOIR

STANBURY MOOR

VIEWS OF WIND FARM

FOOTPATH TO HAWORTH

STEPS

1 HR 15 MINS–1 HR 45 MINS FROM TOP WITHINS (MAP 27) TO HAWORTH (MAP 28A)

## Transport
[See also pp45-50] The **train station** is a stop on the Keighley and Worth Valley Railway Line (☎ 01535-645214, 🖥 www .kwvr.co.uk; return ticket £10, day rover £14), a preserved line which runs steam trips at weekends throughout the year and also daily during holiday periods between Keighley (where it links up with the main Leeds–Settle–Carlisle line) and Oxenhope. Oakworth, one of the other stops on the line, is where part of *The Railway Children* was filmed.

Keighley & District **bus** services (No 500, 664, 665 and 720) call here and connect with Keighley, Oxenhope, Stanbury, Bradford and Hebden Bridge.

For a **taxi** call Brontë Taxis (☎ 01535-644442).

## Services
Haworth has services aplenty including two **post offices**, a Spar **supermarket** (daily 7am-10.30pm), **pharmacy**, souvenir shops, a bookshop, newsagents' and numerous fudge outlets. The **tourist information centre** (☎ 01535-642329, 🖥 www.visit haworth.com; May-Aug Thu-Tue 9.30am-5.30pm, Wed 10am-5.30pm, Sep-Apr Thu-Tue 9.30am-5pm, Wed 10am-5pm) is at the top of the cobbled Main St in a commanding position that's hard to miss. They also do accommodation booking (see box p13).

There are **no banks** in Haworth but there is an **ATM** (cash machine) in the Spar supermarket near the station and in the Kings Arms pub.

Halfway up the cobbled Main St, on the corner of 'Purvs Lane', is **Spooks**, an interesting 'alternative' bookshop. If your walk isn't going quite as well as you'd planned you could have a tarot reading (£20) but perhaps the money would be better spent on an aromatherapy massage, also available here for £20.

The **Brontë Parsonage Museum**; ☎ 01535-642323, 🖥 www.bronte.info; daily Apr-Sep 10am-5.30pm, Oct-Mar 11am-5pm, closed Jan; £6.80) is at the top of the town. It tells the fascinating story of the family (see box p118) and their tragic life including the only son, Branwell, who gave his life up to riotous living. With such talented sisters, who could blame him?

## Where to stay
*Haworth YHA Hostel* (☎ 0845-371 9520, 🖥 haworth@yha.org.uk, Longlands Drive; open all year) is on the eastern side of town, 1½ miles up a long hill, passing most of the other services on the way. This grand Victorian mansion has 94 beds (17 rooms with 1-10 beds) but the popularity of the town means that it gets very busy at peak times. Adults are charged from £15, under 18s from £11.50. The hostel is open all day and meals are available.

At the top of the town on the western side is *The Thyme House* (☎ 01535-211860, 🖥 www.thethymehouse.co.uk; 1S/1D or T/ 2D, all with private facilities) a townhouse which does B&B for £80-115 and £65 for the single. One of the best B&Bs, *The Apothecary Guest House* (☎ 01535-643642, 🖥 www.theapothecaryguesthouse.co.uk; 86 Main St; 2S/3D/1T/1F, all with private facilities), is ideally located right in the heart of town, surrounded by places to eat. Their rates are £35 for a single, £55 for two sharing, £60-65 for the family room. *Heathfield B&B* (☎ 01535-640606, 🖥 www .heathfield-haworth.co.uk; 1D/1T or F/1D, T or F) is also right in the heart of town and has doubles and twins for £75-80 and family rooms from £90. Across the road is *Aitches Guest House* (☎ 01535-642501, 🖥 aitches@ talk21.com; 1T/2D/1F, all en suite, bath available) offering B&B from £60 for two sharing (£42 for single occupancy). Nearby is *Weavers* (☎ 01535-643822, 🖥 www .weaversmallhotel.co.uk; 1T/2D, all en suite with bath) a restaurant with rooms charging £90-110 or from £65 for single occupancy.

Halfway down the hill on Main St is *Haworth Tearooms & Guest House* (☎ 01535-644278, 🖥 www.haworthtearooms .co.uk; 1T/1D/1F, all en suite, bath available) where B&B is a reasonable £25pp (£35 for single occupancy); dogs are welcome if prebooked. *The Fleece Inn* (☎ 01535-642172, 🖥 www.fleece-inn.co.uk; 2S/1T/4D, all en suite, bath available) is one of the best pubs in town and has rooms for £75-85 for two sharing; a single is £50-55.

ROUTE GUIDE AND MAPS

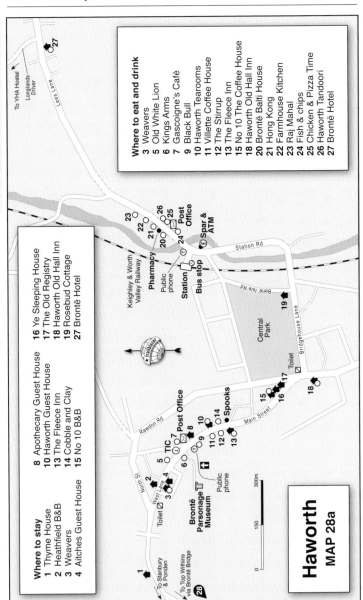

**Where to eat and drink**
3 Weavers
5 Old White Lion
6 Kings Arms
7 Gascoigne's Café
9 Black Bull
10 Haworth Tearooms
11 Villette Coffee House
12 The Stirrup
13 The Fleece Inn
15 No 10 The Coffee House
18 Haworth Old Hall Inn
20 Brontë Balti House
21 Hong Kong
22 Farmhouse Kitchen
23 Raj Mahal
24 Fish & chips
25 Chicken & Pizza Time
26 Haworth Tandoori
27 Brontë Hotel

**Where to stay**
1 Thyme House
2 Heathfield B&B
3 Weavers
4 Aitches Guest House
8 Apothecary Guest House
10 Haworth Guest House
13 The Fleece Inn
14 Cobble and Clay
15 No 10 B&B
16 Ye Sleeping House
17 The Old Registry
18 Haworth Old Hall Inn
19 Rosebud Cottage
27 Brontë Hotel

**Haworth**
MAP 28a

At the bottom of Main St *The Old Registry* (☎ 01535-646503, 🖳 www.the oldregistryhaworth.co.uk, 2-4 Main St; 7D/2D, T or F, all en suite, bath available; £75-100 Sun-Thur; £80-120 Fri & Sat) is furnished with an eye for detail and an emphasis on luxury and pampering. Dogs are welcome if booked in advance. They have a **bar** (Mon-Sat 6-8pm).

Almost next door at No 10 is the more modest-sized *No 10 B&B* (☎ 01535-644694, 🖳 www.10thecoffeehouse.co.uk; 2D en suite, bath available). One room overlooks the cobbled street, the other the valley; the latter has a four-poster bed and a spa bath. B&B costs from £80 (from £60 single occupancy). *Ye Sleeping House* (☎ 01535-645992, 🖳 www.yesleepinghouse. co.uk; 1S/2D, T or F, bath available) is the perfect place to do just that. B&B here is £29pp with shared bathroom or £39pp in the en suite room. Dogs are welcome if prebooked. Not far away is *Haworth Old Hall Inn* (☎ 01535-642709, 🖳 www .hawortholdhall.co.uk, Sun St; 1T/1D, both en suite) which charges from £65 for B&B (£50-65 for single occupancy).

*Rosebud Cottage* (☎ 01535-640321, 🖳 www.rosebudcottage.co.uk, 1 Belle Isle Rd; 1S/3D/1T, all en suite, bath available) is a well-run establishment charging £40 for the single and £80-85 for two sharing.

*Brontë Hotel* (☎ 01535-644112, 🖳 www.bronte-hotel.co.uk, Lees Lane; 3S/2T/3D/3F, most en suite, bath available) is a larger establishment not far from the YHA hostel and might be just the ticket for a group of walkers wanting accommodation under the same roof. It's geared for over-nighters with good clean rooms, and with ample scope for eating and drinking downstairs (see Where to eat and drink). You can expect to pay £28.50-38.50 for a single, £55-70 for two sharing and £75 for an en suite family room.

### Where to eat and drink

Three of Haworth's pubs, the *Old White Lion*, *Kings Arms*, and *Black Bull*, are clustered together at the top of the cobbled street. However, one of the best, *Haworth Old Hall Inn* (see Where to stay; bar open all day, food served Mon-Fri noon-3pm & 5-9pm, Sat & Sun noon-9pm) stands apart and is particularly recommended for its real ales. A range of bar meals in generous portions is available. Another place to consider is the *Brontë Hotel* (see Where to stay; food served Mon-Fri noon-2pm & 7-9pm, Sat noon-2pm & 7-9.30pm, Sun noon-8.30pm); it is open to non residents though it's quite far away if not staying there.

The cobbled Main St has a plethora of eating places. *The Fleece Inn* (see Where to stay; bar Mon-Thur noon-11pm, Fri & Sat 10am-11.30pm, Sun 10am-10.30pm; food served Mon-Fri noon-3pm & 5-9pm, Sat 10am-8pm & 10am-6pm) has a real fire (in winter) and real ales (Timothy Taylor) too. It's a good place to try some local food; the giant Yorkshire pudding is £7.95.

For lunches and afternoon teas you can't do better than *Villette Coffee House* (☎ 01535-644967; daily in season 8.30am-5/6pm – until the last customer leaves – and in winter till 4 or 4.30pm) where such delights as Yorkshire curd tarts, large flat Yorkshire Parkins, delicious sticky ginger buns and a rich spicy scone known as a Fat Rascal can all be savoured. Cream teas are £2.60 and their all-day breakfast is a feast for £4.99.

*No 10 The Coffee House* (see No 10 B&B; Thur-Sun & Bank Holiday Mondays 12.30-6pm) serves a variety of teas and freshly ground coffees, as well as home-made cakes baked daily on the premises, in a relaxing environment. A substantial afternoon tea (£15.50pp) is available on Saturday and Sunday.

*Haworth Tearooms* (see Where to stay; daily Apr-Dec 11am-4pm, Jan-Mar Fri-Tue 11am to about 4pm) is a good place for a cup of Yorkshire tea while *Gascoigne's* is a deli, smokehouse and café where you can get sandwiches for £3.95. At the art café *Cobbles and Clay* (☎ 01535-644218, 🖳 www.cobblesandclay.co.uk; daily 9am-5pm) you can paint a plate whilst enjoying their homemade soups (from £4.50).

At *The Stirrup Restaurant* (☎ 01535-642007, 🖳 www.thestirrup.co.uk; summer and holiday periods Wed 10am-6pm, Thur-Sun 10am-9.15pm; also Bank Hol Mons and Tue in July & Aug; winter Wed & Thur 10am-5.30pm, Fri & Sat 10am-9pm, Sun 10am-6.30pm) you can sit at a crisp, cotton tablecloth and tuck into a plate of Yorkshire ham, roast chicken and cheeses for £7.95. They do tasty home-made cakes (about £3.20) too. In the evening there is a set menu with two courses for £16.95 or three for £19.95.

At the other end of the street, on top of the hill, is *Weavers* (see Where to stay; Tue-Fri noon-2pm & 6.30-9.30pm; Sat 6-9.30pm) a curious mix of contemporary and rustic; where else have you seen leopard skin seats and old spinning spindles in the same room? If you feel you deserve a treat

why not try the Malham beef ribsteak for £18.50; alternatively they offer a set menu (two courses £15.50, three for £17.50) available at lunch (Wed-Fri noon-2pm) and all evening (Tue-Fri) for residents, Tue-Fri 6.30-7pm only for non residents.

In the eastern, non-touristy, part of town is a collection of takeaways and restaurants. *Raj Mahal* (☎ 01535-643890; 51 Mill Hey; Wed-Mon 5.30-11pm, closed Tue) is a notable Indian restaurant, or try the nearby *Brontë Balti* or *Haworth Tandoori*. There are also *takeaways* (a Chinese, *Hong Kong*, and *Chicken & Pizza Time*), a *fish and chip* shop, and the *Farmhouse Kitchen* over the road.

---

## ❏ The Brontës of Haworth

Haworth cannot be separated from the Brontës. Their home, the Parsonage, still stands and is open to the public, attracting tens of thousands of visitors every year from across the world. A shop sells the complete works in book form, on disc and on tape plus lavender-scented pot-pourris.

The churchyard above which the Parsonage stands can be a haunting place on a wet evening, calling to mind Mrs Gaskell's account of life in Haworth. Standing at the top of the village, the graveyard's eternal incumbents poisoned the springs which fed the pumps from which the villagers drew their water. Small wonder that typhoid and fever often afflicted the community. Mrs Gaskell's description sums up the oppressive nature of Haworth in Victorian times, an echo of which can be heard even today:

*The rain ceased, and the day was just suited to the scenery – wild and chill – with great masses of cloud, glooming over the moors, and here and there a ray of sunshine ...darting down into some deep glen, lighting up the tall chimney, or glistening on the windows and wet roof of the mill which lies couching at the bottom. The country got wilder and wilder as we approached Haworth; for the last four miles we were ascending a huge moor at the very top of which lies the dreary, black-looking village. The clergyman's house was at the top of the churchyard. So through that we went – a dreary, dreary place, literally paved with rain-blackened tombstones, and all on the slope.*
**Mrs Gaskell** *The Life of Charlotte Brontë*, 1857

The three Brontë sisters, Emily (*Wuthering Heights*, 1847), Charlotte (*Jane Eyre*, 1847) and Anne (*The Tenant of Wildfell Hall*, 1848), were brought up by their father and an aunt – after the death, in 1821 from cancer, of their mother – in the Parsonage where Reverend Brontë had taken a living in 1820. The only boy in the family, Branwell, had every hope and expectation lavished on him, taking precedence over his more talented sisters as the son, but squandered his life in drink and drugs, dying in 1848.

The lonely, unassuming sisters wrote under male pseudonyms but still their talents went largely unrecognised during their lifetimes and they all died comparatively young from the unhealthy conditions that plagued their village. Today their reputation as novelists endures, and *Wuthering Heights* in particular – set so obviously in the Haworth locality – continues to entrance readers with its vivid portrait of thwarted passion and unfulfilled lives shaped by the bleak, unforgiving landscape of the Yorkshire moors.

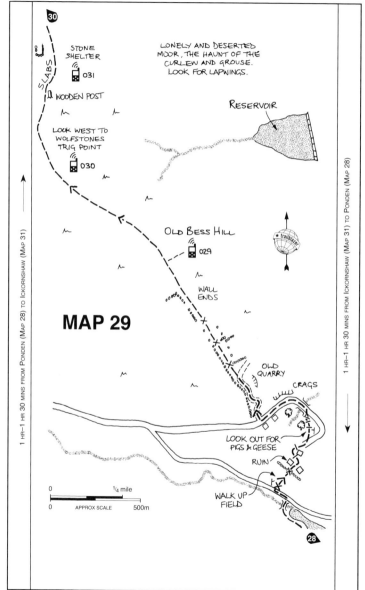

**30**

SLABS

STONE SHELTER

031

WOODEN POST

LOOK WEST TO WOLFSTONES TRIG POINT

030

LONELY AND DESERTED MOOR, THE HAUNT OF THE CURLEW AND GROUSE. LOOK FOR LAPWINGS.

RESERVOIR

trailbazer

OLD BESS HILL

029

WALL ENDS

**MAP 29**

OLD QUARRY

CRAGS

LOOK OUT FOR PIGS & GEESE

RUIN

WALK UP FIELD

**28**

1 HR–1 HR 30 MINS FROM PONDEN (MAP 28) TO ICKORNSHAW (MAP 31)

1 HR–1 HR 30 MINS FROM ICKORNSHAW (MAP 31) TO PONDEN (MAP 28)

0    1/4 mile

0    APPROX SCALE    500m

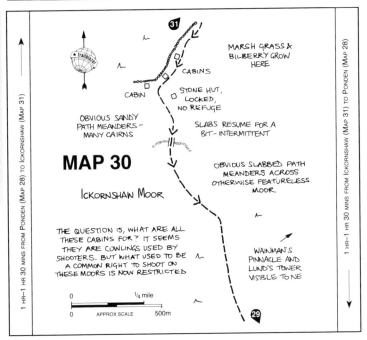

On the map:

**31**

MARSH GRASS & BILBERRY GROW HERE

★ trailblaze

CABINS

CABIN

STONE HUT, LOCKED, NO REFUGE

OBVIOUS SANDY PATH MEANDERS — MANY CAIRNS

SLABS RESUME FOR A BIT - INTERMITTENT

## MAP 30

Ickornshaw Moor

OBVIOUS SLABBED PATH MEANDERS ACROSS OTHERWISE FEATURELESS MOOR

THE QUESTION IS, WHAT ARE ALL THESE CABINS FOR? IT SEEMS THEY ARE COWLINGS USED BY SHOOTERS. BUT WHAT USED TO BE A COMMON RIGHT TO SHOOT ON THESE MOORS IS NOW RESTRICTED

WAINMAN'S PINNACLE AND LUND'S TOWER VISIBLE TO NE

0 ............ ¼ mile
0 ............ 500m
APPROX SCALE

**29**

ROUTE GUIDE AND MAPS

1 HR–1 HR 30 MINS FROM PONDEN (MAP 28) TO ICKORNSHAW (MAP 31)

1 HR–1 HR 30 MINS FROM ICKORNSHAW (MAP 31) TO PONDEN (MAP 28)

### ICKORNSHAW                    [Map 31]
The Pennine Way crosses the busy A6068 between Colne and Keighley at Ickornshaw. To blend in say 'Ick-<u>corn</u>-sher', with the emphasis on the 'corn' and no one need ever know your dark secret. Ickornshaw is an off-shoot of Cowling which is a quarter of a mile off route to the east (see below). The nearest B&B is *Winterhouse Barn* (☎ 01535-632234, 🖳 www.thepennineway.co .uk/winterhousebarn; 2T shared bathroom/ 2D en suite), where you'll pay £27.50-30pp (£35 single occupancy) or £4pp for **camping** in a field round the back with a toilet and shower block. Dogs are welcome if booked in advance. They don't do evening meals but are happy to take people to the Dog & Gun.

### COWLING                      [Map 31]
Cowling (🖳 www.cowlingweb.co.uk) has a useful **grocery shop** (Bains; ☎ 01535-634731; Mon-Fri 7.45am-1pm & 2-8.30pm, Sat 7.45-8.30pm, Sun 9am-3pm) which sells hot pies as well as sandwiches and is also licensed. At the time of writing the only restaurant here was closed though it is possible it may have reopened.

The nearest place for a meal is the *Dog & Gun* (☎ 01535-633855, 🖳 www.dog-and-gun-inn.co.uk; bar Mon-Sat 11.30am- 11pm, Sun to 10.30pm, food served daily noon-9pm) another mile down the road. The menu is extensive and includes the pie of the day (£5.75), a range of burgers (from £5.60) as well as fish dishes, baguettes and baked potatoes.

*Woodland House* (☎ 01535-637886, 🖳 www.woodland-house.co.uk; 2 Woodland St, 1T/1D en suite, 1T with private bathroom) is an especially walker-friendly B&B charging £35 for single occupancy and

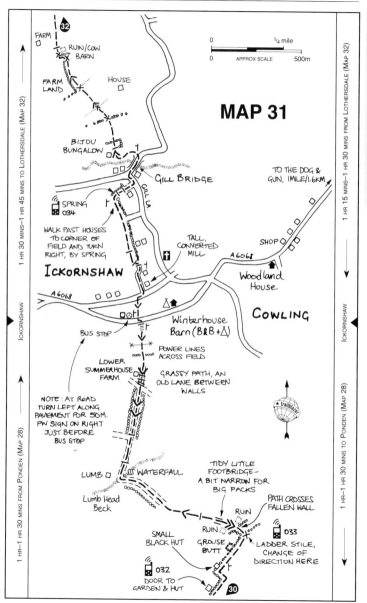

**MAP 31**

0 ............ ¼ mile
0 ............ APPROX SCALE ............ 500m

FARM

🏠32

RUIN/COW BARN

FARM LAND

HOUSE

BIJOU BUNGALOW

GILL BRIDGE

GILL LA

TO THE DOG & GUN, 1MILE/1.6KM

SPRING 034

WALK PAST HOUSES TO CORNER OF FIELD AND TURN RIGHT, BY SPRING

TALL, CONVERTED MILL

SHOP

A6068

Woodland House

ICKORNSHAW

A6068

COWLING

BUS STOP

Winterhouse Barn (B&B + △)

POWER LINES ACROSS FIELD

LOWER SUMMERHOUSE FARM

GRASSY PATH, AN OLD LANE BETWEEN WALLS

NOTE: AT ROAD TURN LEFT ALONG PAVEMENT FOR 50M. PW SIGN ON RIGHT JUST BEFORE BUS STOP

trailblazer

LUMB

WATERFALL

Lumb Head Beck

TIDY LITTLE FOOTBRIDGE- A BIT NARROW FOR BIG PACKS

RUIN

PATH CROSSES FALLEN WALL

RUIN

033

SMALL BLACK HUT

GROUSE BUTT

LADDER STILE, CHANGE OF DIRECTION HERE

032

DOOR TO GARDEN & HUT

🏠30

1 HR 30 MINS–1 HR 45 MINS TO LOTHERSDALE (MAP 32)

1 HR 15 MINS–1 HR 30 MINS FROM LOTHERSDALE (MAP 32)

ICKORNSHAW

ICKORNSHAW

1 HR–1 HR 30 MINS FROM PONDEN (MAP 28)

1 HR–1 HR 30 MINS TO PONDEN (MAP 28)

£55 for two sharing. Packed lunches (around £4.50) are available; they will take people down to the pub for an evening meal; you can get a taxi or walk back. They also offer luggage transfer between Hebden Bridge and Malham; contact them for details.

Transdev Lancashire Mainline (No 25), Keighley & District (No 79) and Little Red Bus (South Craven Village Bus; SCVB) operate **bus** services here (see public transport map and table, pp45-50) for details.

## ICKORNSHAW TO MALHAM                                    MAPS 31-41

### Route overview

This **17-mile (25km, 6¾-9¾hrs)** walk delivers you first class into the famed Yorkshire Dales and, better still, on the way drops you after 8 or 11 miles walking on the doorstep of two great cafés.

Leaving Ickornshaw via **Gill Bridge**, another 'up-and-over' pastoral interlude brings you to a wooded valley and **Lothersdale** (Map 32) from whose centre sprouts a huge out-of-place mill **chimney**. Lothersdale is the last of the South Pennine milltowns and the country begins to change as you prepare to traverse the riverine lowlands of the Aire Gap. It's something you'll hopefully get a fine view of from **Pinhaw Beacon** (Map 33) whose panorama can reveal Pen-y-ghent, 16 miles distant, the lowest of the Three Peaks and a challenge soon to come. Though off route, Earby (see p125) has more eating options and services than **Thornton-in-Craven** (Map 34).

The Way leaves Thornton, passing pristine retirement bungalows to cross a series of fields and reach the towpath of the **Leeds–Liverpool Canal** (Map 35) just before the unusual bridge-on-a-bridge at **East Marton**. Beyond the narrow boats is the charming Abbots Harbour (see p126), a perfect place to synchronise an arrival with a rumbling tummy.

At East Marton our route leaves the canal and takes to the green, wildflower-speckled fields again, climbing to diminutive **Scaleber Hill** (Map 36) from where the church tower of Gargrave jauntily signals '*Come hither, wayfarer!*'. **Gargrave** (Map 37), the Gateway to the Dales, is an interlude worth prolonging and it would be a glum walker indeed who did not avail themselves of the services of Dalesman Café (see p128). That done, the uphill road-walk out of the town soon branches off to cross **Eshton Moor** (Map 38; actually walls, plantations and pasture), an airy ramble to meet the meandering arcs of the River Aire for the second time; it was the Aire you crossed via the bridge in Gargrave. Riverside walking is on the agenda for the remaining two hours or so as you pass through **Airton** (Map 39) and **Kirkby Malham** to reach the tourist magnet that is **Malham**, venue for a thousand school field trips and the end of this section for Pennine wanderers.

### Route-finding trouble spots

Possible difficulties are limited to correctly **negotiating the rolling fields** and stiles before the Aire River; the sole moorland stretch over Pinhaw Beacon is straightforward. In the pastures signs get knocked down or overgrown and in the meadows, approaching Scaleber Hill or over Eshton Moor, a single clear path rarely develops. GPS lights the way of course, but even without a receiver a moment's contemplation will set you on the right track.

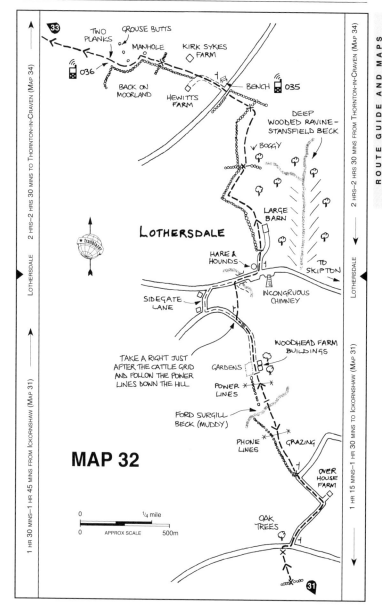

**33**
TWO PLANKS
GROUSE BUTTS
MANHOLE
KIRK SYKES FARM
036
BACK ON MOORLAND
HEWITTS FARM
BENCH
035
DEEP WOODED RAVINE – STANSFIELD BECK
BOGGY
LARGE BARN
LOTHERSDALE
HARE & HOUNDS
TO SKIPTON
SIDEGATE LANE
INCONGRUOUS CHIMNEY
TAKE A RIGHT JUST AFTER THE CATTLE GRID AND FOLLOW THE POWER LINES DOWN THE HILL
WOODHEAD FARM BUILDINGS
GARDENS
POWER LINES
FORD SURGILL BECK (MUDDY)
PHONE LINES
GRAZING
OVER HOUSE FARM
**MAP 32**
OAK TREES
**31**

0     ¼ mile
0     500m
APPROX SCALE

trailblazer

2 HRS–2 HRS 30 MINS TO THORNTON-IN-CRAVEN (MAP 34)

LOTHERSDALE

1 HR 30 MINS–1 HR 45 MINS FROM ICKORNSHAW (MAP 31)

2 HRS–2 HRS 30 MINS FROM THORNTON-IN-CRAVEN (MAP 34)

LOTHERSDALE

1 HR 15 MINS–1 HR 30 MINS TO ICKORNSHAW (MAP 31)

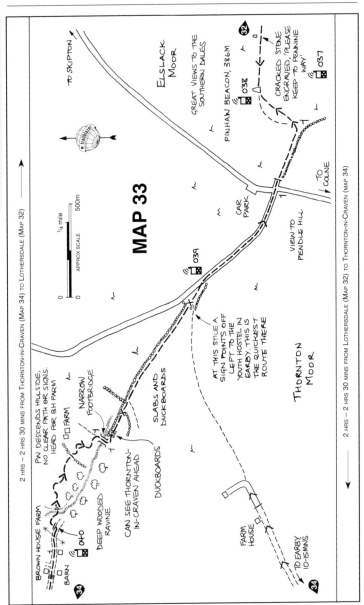

2 HRS – 2 HRS 30 MINS FROM THORNTON-IN-CRAVEN (MAP 32) TO LOTHERSDALE (MAP 32)

2 HRS – 2 HRS 30 MINS FROM LOTHERSDALE (MAP 32) TO THORNTON-IN-CRAVEN (MAP 34)

MAP 33

TO SKIPTON

ELSLACK MOOR

GREAT VIEWS TO THE SOUTHERN DALES

PINHAW BEACON, 386M

038

CRACKED STONE ENGRAVED, 'PLEASE KEEP TO PENNINE WAY'

037

32

1/4 mile

500m

APPROX SCALE

0

0

CAR PARK

TO COLNE

VIEW TO PENDLE HILL

039

AT THIS STILE A SIGN POINTS OFF LEFT TO THE YOUTH HOSTEL IN EARBY. THIS IS THE QUICKEST ROUTE THERE

THORNTON MOOR

PW DESCENDS HILLSIDE, NO CLEAR PATH OR SIGNS. HEAD FOR BH FARM

FARM

NARROW FOOTBRIDGE

SLABS AND DUCKBOARDS

DUCKBOARDS

DEEP WOODED RAVINE

CAN SEE THORNTON-IN-CRAVEN AHEAD

BROWN HOUSE FARM

BARN

040

FARM HOUSE

TO EARBY, 10-15MINS

34

34

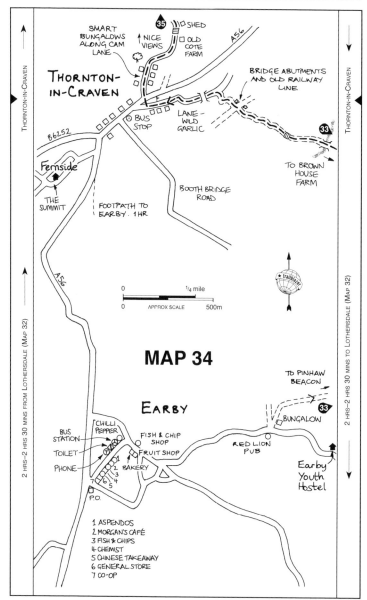

**35**
SHED
SMART BUNGALOWS ALONG CAM LANE
NICE VIEWS
OLD COTE FARM
A56

**THORNTON-IN-CRAVEN**

BRIDGE ABUTMENTS AND OLD RAILWAY LINE

**33**

B6252
BUS STOP
LANE - WILD GARLIC

TO BROWN HOUSE FARM

Fernside
THE SUMMIT
FOOTPATH TO EARBY. 1HR
BOOTH BRIDGE ROAD

A56

0    ¼ mile
APPROX SCALE    500m

★ trailblazer

**MAP 34**

**EARBY**

TO PINHAW BEACON

**33**

BUNGALOW

CHILLI PEPPER
BUS STATION
FISH & CHIP SHOP
TOILET
FRUIT SHOP
PHONE
1
2   BAKERY
3
7  6 4
5
P.O.

RED LION PUB

Earby Youth Hostel

1 ASPENDOS
2 MORGAN'S CAFÉ
3 FISH & CHIPS
4 CHEMIST
5 CHINESE TAKEAWAY
6 GENERAL STORE
7 CO-OP

THORNTON-IN-CRAVEN

THORNTON-IN-CRAVEN

2 HRS-2 HRS 30 MINS FROM LOTHERSDALE (MAP 32)

2 HRS-2 HRS 30 MINS TO LOTHERSDALE (MAP 32)

ROUTE GUIDE AND MAPS

## LOTHERSDALE [Map 32, p123]

The friendly *Hare and Hounds* (☎ 01535-630977; food served Easter-Oct Mon-Fri noon-2pm & 6-9pm, Sat & Sun noon-9pm, Nov to Easter Mon-Fri noon-2pm, Tue-Sun 6-9pm; the pub closes 3.30-6pm except on summer weekends) has good pub food for £8-13.

Little Red Bus's bookable South Craven Village Bus (SCVB) calls here (see public transport map and table, pp45-50).

## THORNTON-IN-CRAVEN [Map 34, p125]

*Fernside Cottage* (☎ 01282-842575, 💻 www.fernside-cottage.com; 1D/1T, en suite, bath available), The Summit, offers B&B for £70 (£55 single occupancy). They don't serve evening meals but will run guests to their local pub; you can get a taxi back. Fernside is about a five-minute walk from the centre of the village. Turn left off the A56 and follow the road till you see a turning off to the right called Thornton Heights; there is a sign here saying Fernside. Walk along Thornton Heights until it becomes The Summit. Fernside is on the right near the end of the houses.

Pennine Motor Services operate regular **buses** (No 215) along the A56 to Burnley and Skipton and Transdev Lancashire United's No 280 runs between Preston and Skipton (see public transport map and table, pp45-50).

See p25 for details of the village fête in July.

## EARBY [Map 34, p125]

Earby is quite a large community. However, the only accommodation here, 1½ miles (2km) off the trail on the way to Earby, is at the 22-bed *Earby YHA Hostel* (☎ 0845-371 9016, 💻 earby@yha .org.uk; Easter to Oct). Adults are charged from £17, under 18s from £13. It opens at 5pm and is self-catering only. One room is a twin, the other three rooms have six to eight beds. There's an excellent pub, *The Red Lion*, near the hostel, with plenty of real ales and friendly locals.

In Earby itself *Chilli Pepper* (☎ 01282-843943; Mon-Sat 5-11pm, Sun 3-11pm) is a good Indian restaurant and takeaway with a buffet (£9.50) on Wednesday and Sunday. There's also *Aspendos* with pizzas and kebabs to take away, *Morgan's Café* (Mon-Fri 8am-3pm, Sat 8.30am-3pm, Sun 9am-2.30pm), a *Chinese takeaway* and two *fish and chip* shops (both closed Sunday), a **fruit shop**, a **bakery**, a **post office**, a **general store**, a **chemist** and a Co-op **supermarket** (daily 8am-10pm).

If you've stayed at the hostel consider getting Pennine Motor Services' **bus** No 215 (see public transport map and table, pp45-50) up to Thornton-in-Craven in the morning if you don't want to walk.

## EAST MARTON [Map 35]

East Marton is a hidden treasure known only to canal users and walkers looking for a mooring or way station alongside the Pennine Way.

*Abbots Harbour* (☎ 01282-843207; Mon-Wed & Fri-Sat 10am-5pm, Sun 9am-5pm, closed Thurs) deserves an accolade for its atmosphere and food. This is a cracking good place to eat. A bacon sandwich is £2.70, all-day breakfast £6.95 and the lunch menu includes home-cooked favourites such as shepherd's pie (£9.25). You can also **camp** here; £5pp will see you securely ensconced, with a bathroom at your disposal. The *Cross Keys* (☎ 01282-844326; food served Mon-Fri noon-2.30pm & 5-8pm, Sat noon-9pm, Sun noon-7pm) is the nearest pub, up the lane facing the main road. The menu includes standard pub food, mains are around £9 and soup & sandwich costs £6.50.

Should you need to get out of town fast ring SD Cars (☎ 01282-814310) for a **taxi**. Transdev Lancashire United's **bus** No X80 stops in **West Marton**, a mile away, en route between Preston and Skipton (see public transport map and table, pp45-50).

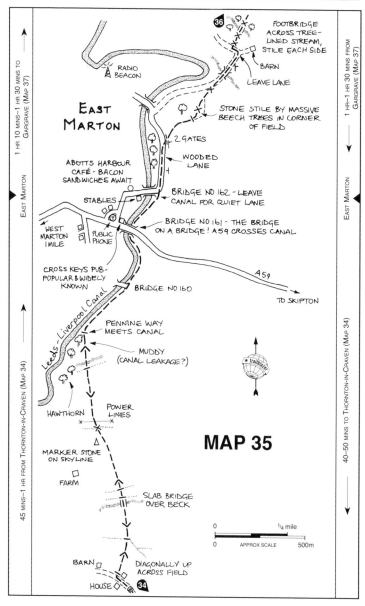

1 HR 10 MINS–1 HR 30 MINS TO GARGRAVE (MAP 37)

EAST MARTON

45 MINS–1 HR FROM THORNTON-IN-CRAVEN (MAP 34)

1 HR–1 HR 30 MINS FROM GARGRAVE (MAP 37)

EAST MARTON

40–50 MINS TO THORNTON-IN-CRAVEN (MAP 34)

FOOTBRIDGE ACROSS TREE-LINED STREAM, STILE EACH SIDE

36

BARN

LEAVE LANE

RADIO BEACON

EAST MARTON

STONE STILE BY MASSIVE BEECH TREES IN CORNER OF FIELD

2 GATES

WOODED LANE

ABOTTS HARBOUR CAFÉ - BACON SANDWICHES AWAIT

STABLES

BRIDGE NO 162 - LEAVE CANAL FOR QUIET LANE

WEST MARTON 1 MILE

PUBLIC PHONE

BRIDGE NO 161 - THE BRIDGE ON A BRIDGE! A59 CROSSES CANAL

CROSS KEYS PUB - POPULAR & WIDELY KNOWN

BRIDGE NO 160

A59

TO SKIPTON

Leeds–Liverpool Canal

PENNINE WAY MEETS CANAL

MUDDY (CANAL LEAKAGE?)

HAWTHORN

POWER LINES

MARKER STONE ON SKYLINE

FARM

MAP 35

SLAB BRIDGE OVER BECK

0      ¼ mile
0    APPROX SCALE    500m

BARN

HOUSE

DIAGONALLY UP ACROSS FIELD

34

trailblazer

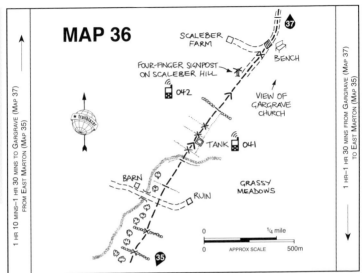

**MAP 36**

SCALEBER FARM

BENCH

FOUR-FINGER SIGNPOST ON SCALEBER HILL

042

VIEW OF GARGRAVE CHURCH

★ trailblazer

TANK  041

BARN

RUIN

GRASSY MEADOWS

0          1/4 mile

0          APPROX SCALE          500m

37

35

## GARGRAVE     [see Map 37a, p130]

This small attractive town has most things you will want. Say hello to the Aire river which you'll be following later in the day. See p26 for details of the agricultural show here in August.

### Services

All shops are on the main road and close together. There is a **pharmacy**, a well-stocked Co-op **supermarket** (Mon-Sat 8am-8pm, Sun 10am-6pm) with an **ATM** (cash machine), a **post office** (early closing Tue), a **butcher** and a **newsagent**.

### Transport

[See also pp45-50] Gargrave is a stop on the Leeds to Carlisle **railway** line. Pennine Motor Services **bus** No 210 and 580 call here. Little Red Bus's No 211 bus service operates on a similar route to the Pennine Motor Services No 210. Jacksons of Silsden's No 890 also calls here.

### Where to stay

Since the accommodation options are limited to two pubs and a campsite plan ahead or take a bus (see pp45-50) to Skipton (see

🖳 www.skiptonweb.co.uk/tourist for details of the many accommodation possibilities in Skipton as well as other information).

Coming off the Pennine Way, just before the bridge you'll pass **The Masons Arms** (☎ 01756-749304; 4D/2T, all en suite, bath available), on the corner close to the church, which has rooms costing from £65; single occupancy costs £45 but the full rate must be paid on a Saturday night. Dogs (£5) are welcome.

**The Old Swan Inn** (☎ 01756-749232; 1S/1D/1T/1D, T or F, all en suite, bath available) charges £70 (£40 for the single) B&B. Rates should be a bit lower if booked through 🖳 www.laterooms.com.

Carry on up that road and you'll get to, **Eshton Road Caravan Site** (☎ 01756-749229; open all year) with **camping** for £5pp. It is advisable to book ahead if wanting to stay here at a weekend in the summer months.

### Where to eat and drink

As you cross the bridge over the River Aire you will be facing **Dalesman Café** (☎ 01756-749250; Tue & Thu-Sun 9am-5pm,

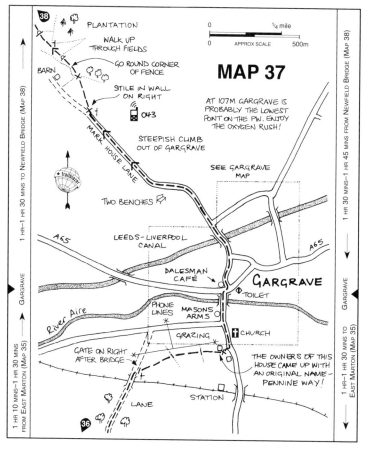

**MAP 37**

PLANTATION

WALK UP THROUGH FIELDS

GO ROUND CORNER OF FENCE

BARN

STILE IN WALL ON RIGHT

043

AT 107M GARGRAVE IS PROBABLY THE LOWEST POINT ON THE PW. ENJOY THE OXYGEN RUSH!

STEEPISH CLIMB OUT OF GARGRAVE

SEE GARGRAVE MAP

MARK HOUSE LANE

TWO BENCHES

LEEDS-LIVERPOOL CANAL

DALESMAN CAFÉ

GARGRAVE

TOILET

A65

River Aire

PHONE LINES

MASONS ARMS

GRAZING

CHURCH

GATE ON RIGHT AFTER BRIDGE

THE OWNERS OF THIS HOUSE CAME UP WITH AN ORIGINAL NAME – PENNINE WAY!

STATION

LANE

36

0        ¼ mile
0    APPROX SCALE    500m

ROUTE GUIDE AND MAPS

38  1 HR–1 HR 30 MINS TO NEWFIELD BRIDGE (MAP 38)

1 HR 30 MINS–1 HR 45 MINS FROM NEWFIELD BRIDGE (MAP 38)

GARGRAVE

GARGRAVE

1 HR 10 MINS–1 HR 30 MINS FROM EAST MARTON (MAP 35)

1 HR–1 HR 30 MINS TO EAST MARTON (MAP 35)

Wed 10am-5pm, also most Bank Holiday Mondays; Nov-Mar to 4.30pm), a well-primed place for some tucker. It offers a great range of good-value food: a 'Dalesman Lunch' with ham, Wensleydale cheese and chutney is £6; home-made cakes are £1.75; soup (always vegetarian) is £3.25 as well as indulgences such as quality ice-cream, mint cake, and around 200 different varieties of old-fashioned sweets sold out of jars in the old-fashioned way. Dogs are welcome.

Nearby is a very good Indian restaurant, **Bollywood Cottage** (☎ 01756-749252; Tue-

Sat 5.30-11pm, Sun 5.30-10.30pm). To eat in there are balti dishes from £5, tandooris from £7.

Just up West St is the **White Cottage Tea Room** (☎ 01756-748229; Mon/Thu/Fri 11am-5pm, Sat & Sun 10am-5pm; closed most of Nov). Everything is home made and the menu includes delicious triple-decker sandwiches (£6.95)– try and get through their ham with Wensleydale and chutney – and other dishes such as soups.

**The Masons Arms** (see Where to stay; food served daily noon-2pm & 6-9pm) is friendly; their interesting pub food costs around £8.

*The Old Swan Inn* (see Where to stay; bar noon to 11pm; food served summer Mon-Fri noon-3pm & 6-9pm, Sat noon-9pm, Sun noon-8pm) has a variety of traditionally themed rooms such as a flagstone floor 'Snug' has a TV and an open fire and a 'Parlour' with a pool table and a darts board. The menu is extensive and includes dishes such as fish pie, sausage and mash, and gammon steak; mains are around £9.95.

Not far from the Old Swan is a *fish and chip shop* (Wed 5-8pm, Thu-Sat noon-2pm 5-8pm, Sun 4-8pm).

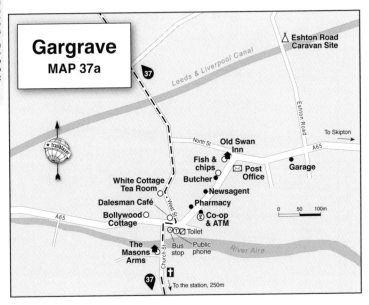

**Gargrave**

**MAP 37a**

Leeds & Liverpool Canal

Eshton Road Caravan Site

Eshton Road

To Skipton

A65

North St  **Old Swan Inn**

**Fish & chips**

☒ **Post Office**

**Garage**

**White Cottage Tea Room**

**Butcher**

**Dalesman Café**

● **Newsagent**

West St

● **Pharmacy**

**Bollywood Cottage**

A65

£ **Co-op & ATM**

Toilet

0   50   100m

**The Masons Arms**

Church St

Bus stop

Public phone

River Aire

To the station, 250m

### AIRTON                    [Map 39, p132]

Right by the left bank of the river, Airton is home to little more than two places to stay: *Quaker Hostel* (☎ 01729-830263; open all year; six bunk beds and space for six on the floor), attached to the Quaker Meeting House. The hostel has been refurbished and is due to reopen in April 2011. There are shower facilities (no bath) and access to two kitchens. However, bedding is not provided, dogs aren't accepted and there aren't any drying facilities. Advance booking is recommended; contact them for details of the rates.

The other place, towards the other end of the scale, is *Lindon Guesthouse* (☎

01729-830418, 🖳 www.lindonguesthouse. co.uk; 1T/2D en suite), which is a little way out of the village along the Malham road. The house is better appointed than the average Pennine Way walker may expect. B&B is £65 (£45 for single occupancy); packed lunches are available, as are evening meals subject to prior arrangement. Dogs are welcome if booked in advance but bedding for them is not provided.

Both Pennine Motor Services' **bus** No 210 and Little Red Bus's No 211 (see public transport map and table, pp45-50) call here en route between Skipton and Malham.

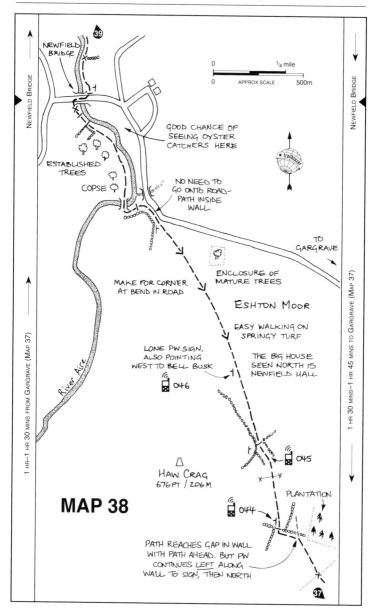

**MAP 38**

39

NEWFIELD BRIDGE

NEWFIELD BRIDGE

GOOD CHANCE OF SEEING OYSTER CATCHERS HERE

ESTABLISHED TREES

COPSE

NO NEED TO GO ONTO ROAD - PATH INSIDE WALL

TO GARGRAVE

ENCLOSURE OF MATURE TREES

MAKE FOR CORNER AT BEND IN ROAD

ESHTON MOOR

EASY WALKING ON SPRINGY TURF

THE BIG HOUSE SEEN NORTH IS NEWFIELD HALL

LONE PW SIGN, ALSO POINTING WEST TO BELL BUSK

046

River Aire

045

△
HAW CRAG
676FT / 206M

PLANTATION

044

PATH REACHES GAP IN WALL WITH PATH AHEAD. BUT PW CONTINUES **LEFT** ALONG WALL TO SIGN, THEN NORTH

37

NEWFIELD BRIDGE

1 HR-1 HR 30 MINS FROM GARGRAVE (MAP 37)

1 HR 30 MINS-1 HR 45 MINS TO GARGRAVE (MAP 37)

0        ¼ mile
0    APPROX SCALE    500m

★ trailblazer

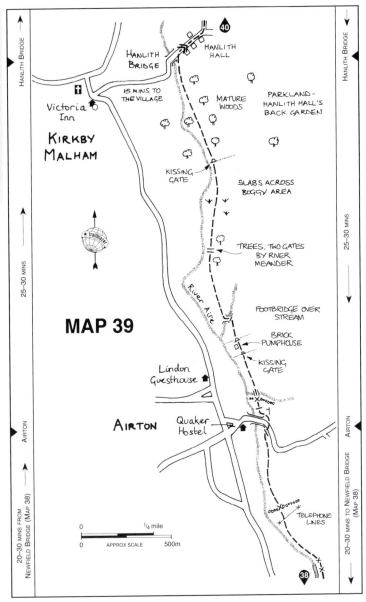

**MAP 39**

HANLITH BRIDGE

HANLITH HALL

40

15 MINS TO THE VILLAGE

Victoria Inn

KIRKBY MALHAM

PARKLAND – HANLITH HALL'S BACK GARDEN

MATURE WOODS

KISSING GATE

SLABS ACROSS BOGGY AREA

TREES, TWO GATES BY RIVER MEANDER

River Aire

FOOTBRIDGE OVER STREAM

BRICK PUMPHOUSE

KISSING GATE

Lindon Guesthouse

AIRTON

Quaker Hostel

TELEPHONE LINES

0   1/4 mile
0   APPROX SCALE   500m

38

HANLITH BRIDGE

25–30 MINS

AIRTON

20–30 MINS TO NEWFIELD BRIDGE (MAP 38)

HANLITH BRIDGE

25–30 MINS

AIRTON

20–30 MINS FROM NEWFIELD BRIDGE (MAP 38)

## KIRKBY MALHAM [Map 39]

Standing back from the river the village is another gem, carefully preserved by its inhabitants and unspoilt by anything as common as a shop. The church has a set of stocks into which anyone putting up a satellite dish would probably be clapped and pelted with rotting fruit.

But there is a pub, *The Victoria Inn* (☎ 01729-830499; food served Fri-Sun noon-3pm & Tue-Sun 6-9pm) which serves standard pub fare; main dishes are around £9. The pub closes in the afternoon but is open all day in the summer months.

Both Pennine Motor Services' No 210 and Little Red Bus's No 211 (see public transport map and table, pp45-50) call here en route between Skipton and Malham.

## MALHAM [see Map 41a, p135]

You would be wise to plan your overnight stay here on a weekday or certainly a non-holiday period. For no greater reason than its dramatic limestone amphitheatre this little stone village with its pretty river is among the most touristy places between Haworth and the Roman wall.

This was once a mining village known for calamine, the ore which produces zinc.

### Services

The **Yorkshire Dales National Park Information Centre** (☎ 01969-652380, 🖳 www.yorkshiredales.org.uk; Apr-Oct daily 10am-5pm, Nov-Mar Sat-Sun and daily in school holiday periods 10am-4pm) is just to the south of the village and is worth a visit for its interactive displays about the geology and history of the area. The staff are also able to help with accommodation booking (see box p13) and general information about the area and the Yorkshire Dales National Park.

The town's website (🖳 www.malhamdale.com) is also useful for information about the area in general, including yet

ROUTE GUIDE AND MAPS

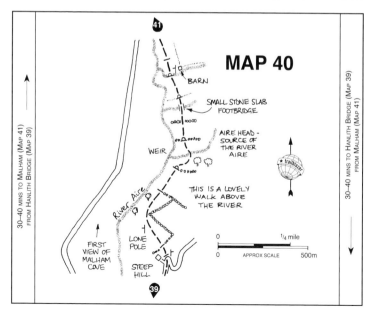

**MAP 40**

BARN

SMALL STONE SLAB FOOTBRIDGE

AIRE HEAD – SOURCE OF THE RIVER AIRE

WEIR

★ trailblazer

THIS IS A LOVELY WALK ABOVE THE RIVER

River Aire

FIRST VIEW OF MALHAM COVE

LONE POLE

STEEP HILL

0 ................ 1/4 mile
0 ........ APPROX SCALE ........ 500m

30-40 MINS TO MALHAM (MAP 41) FROM HANLITH BRIDGE (MAP 39)

30-40 MINS TO HANLITH BRIDGE (MAP 41) FROM MALHAM (MAP 41)

ROUTE GUIDE AND MAPS

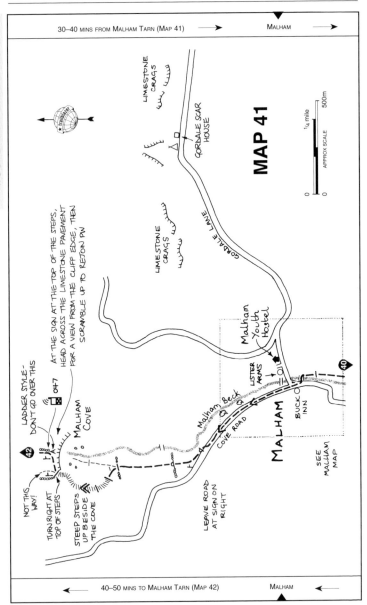

30–40 MINS FROM MALHAM TARN (MAP 41) →    MALHAM →

MAP 41

LIMESTONE CRAGS

GORDALE SCAR HOUSE

GORDALE LANE

0    0    1/4 mile    500m
APPROX SCALE

LIMESTONE CRAGS

Malham Youth Hostel

AT THE SIGN AT THE TOP OF THE STEPS,
HEAD ACROSS THE LIMESTONE PAVEMENT
FOR A VIEW FROM THE CLIFF EDGE, THEN
SCRAMBLE UP TO REJOIN PW

LADDER STYLE –
DON'T GO OVER THIS

047

MALHAM COVE

LISTER ARMS

Malham Beck

COVE ROAD

MALHAM

BUCK INN

40

42

NOT THIS WAY!

TURN RIGHT AT TOP OF STEPS

STEEP STEPS UP BESIDE THE COVE

LEAVE ROAD AT SIGN ON RIGHT

SEE MALHAM MAP

more accommodation (what follows below is a selection). **Gordale Gifts** is the place to stock up on new socks and bootlaces.

See p25 for details of various events held here in the summer.

### Transport
[See also pp45-50] Pennine Motor Services' No 210, Little Red Bus's No 211 and 212, and Jacksons of Silsden's No 890 **bus** services call here. For a 24-hour service call **Skipton Taxis** (☎ 01756-794994/701122).

### Where to stay
Even though there is a good supply of accommodation here visitor numbers are high so it's worth making advance reservations. If it's B&B you're after, note that during peak times some places will accept bookings only for a **two-day stay at weekends** and, as in some other places, solo travellers need expect no favours on pricing. As far as room quantities and ambience goes, most of the 'B&Bs' in Malham can be classified in the 'small hotel' category. It's a busy place.

To **camp** in an awesome setting walk one mile east to *Gordale Scar House* (Map 41; ☎ 01729-830333; Apr-Oct), where they charge £2.50 per person, £2 per tent. There's a toilet and shower block; a shower costs 10p.

North of the village there's spacious year-round camping at *Riverside Campsite* at Town Head Farm (☎ 01729-830287; Nov-Mar/Apr) where a tent with one person costs £6pp. There's also camping for £5pp at *Miresfield Farm* (see column opposite); toilets and showers are available.

There's **bunkhouse** accommodation at *Hill Top Farm* (☎ 01729-830320, 🖳 www. malhamdale.com/bunkbarn.htm); there are 32 spaces in six rooms for 2-15 people, showers, a drying room and a fully equipped kitchen and it costs £15pp. However, it is important to note that the bunkhouse is only available for sole occupancy (ie group bookings) in school holidays and at weekends.

Near the centre of the village is the very popular *Malham YHA Hostel* (bookings ☎ 0845-371 9529, 🖳 malham@yha.org. uk; open all year). The 82-bed (15 rooms

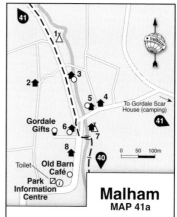

### Malham
### MAP 41a

**Where to stay and eat**
1 Riverside Campsite at Town Head Farm
2 Hill Top Farm Bunkhouse
3 Beck Hall B&B
4 Malham Youth Hostel
5 Lister Arms
6 The Buck Inn
7 Miresfield Farm (B&B & camping)
8 River House Hotel

with 2-8 beds) purpose-built hostel opens at 5pm; meals are available though as always there is a self-catering kitchen. There's also a **shop** selling basic foods such as tinned goods, milk, eggs and bread. Adults pay from £19, under 18s £14.50.

*Miresfield Farm* (☎ 01729-830414, 🖳 www.miresfield-farm.com; 5D/5T, all en suite) charges £32pp (£40-45 for single occupancy); dogs are welcome if booked in advance. *Beck Hall* (☎ 01729-830332, 🖳 www.beckhallmalham.com; 1T/6T or D/7D/4F, all en suite, bath available) is in a nice setting across a footbridge by the river and charges £28-44pp; dogs are welcome if prebooked.

If you're looking for more comfort try *The Buck Inn* (☎ 01729-830317, 🖳 www .buckinnmalham.co.uk; 2T/9D/1F, all en suite, bath available) on your left as you come into the village. The rooms cost £60-70 (single occupancy £45). Over the road the *Lister Arms* (☎ 01729-830330, 🖥 www .listerarms.co.uk; 5D/1T/3F, all en suite) charges £76-96 for two sharing (£60-65 for single occupancy) all with breakfast. Dogs (£10) are welcome if booked in advance.

Doubles or twins at *River House Hotel* (☎ 01729-830315, 🖥 www.riverhousehotel. co.uk; 2T/6D all en suite, bath available) cost from £75 (single occupancy from £55). Dogs (£5) by arrangement.

**Places to eat**

*Lister Arms* (see Where to stay; restaurant daily 6-9pm; bar food daily noon-3pm & 6-9pm) feels like the better of the two pubs and has a great restaurant menu. Main courses are £10-12. The bar menu has dishes for about £6-8. Pub grub is also served at *The Buck Inn* (see Where to stay; Mon-Sat noon-3pm & 6-9pm; Sun noon-9pm) – try

the Malham and Masham pie (beef, onions and mushrooms) for £11.25 – and at *Beck Hall* (see Where to stay; Tue-Sun 11.30am-5.30pm) where they sell salads, sandwiches, baked potatoes and they also do a cream tea (£3.25).

*River House Hotel* (see Where to stay) has a restaurant (Tue-Sat 6.30-8pm), which is also open to non-residents; booking is recommended.

There's also *Old Barn Café* (☎ 01729-830486; Feb-Nov Mon-Fri 9.30am-5pm, Sat and Sun to 5.30pm, Dec-Jan Sat & Sun 9.30am to dusk) near the Park Information Centre. An all-day breakfast costs £5.50-6, jacket potatoes are £4-4.95; they also serve home-made cakes as well as afternoon teas. You can also get tea and cake at *Gordale Gifts & Outdoor Wear* (see Services).

❑ **Peregrine falcon viewing**
Every year the RSPB run a peregrine-viewing site at Malham Cove (Map 41) where a resident pair of these raptors nest on the limestone cliffs. The site is right in the bowl of the cove and wardens are on hand with telescopes between 10.30am and 4.30pm daily from April to August. The national park centre in Malham (see p133) has more information. See also 🖥 www.yorkshiredales.org.uk/index/peregrines.htm.

## MALHAM TO HORTON-IN-RIBBLESDALE                    MAPS 41-48

**Route overview**

Catching your breath from the airy rim of **Malham Cove** you know you're in for a sensational day's walk, a full **15 miles (24kms, 6-8hrs)** of striding that, on a fine day, lifts the Pennine Way up into the best of your expectations. Limestone country envelopes the walker, its springy turf and expansive views returning the investment made so far in weary legs and peat-stained socks.

Gone are the smog-blackened gritstone farmsteads of Calderdale and the Worth Valley. At last you're in proper walking country. Look around from any of the summits today and for the first time in days no pinnacle, radio mast or obelisk mars the horizon.

The hills, too, are distinctively majestic. The massive bulk of **Fountains Fell** (Map 44; see box p144) and Pen-y-ghent are real mountains, challenges worthy of your effort and determination. Limestone, we salute you!

You don't get off quite scot-free. Towards the end of this stage, the ascent of **Pen-y-ghent** (Map 46), the 'hill of the winds', is the job in hand. A daunting climb with a series of steep rocky steps, it's easier than it looks. As is so often the case, it's the long downhill stretch to **Horton-in-Ribblesdale** (Map 48) that may well do you in.

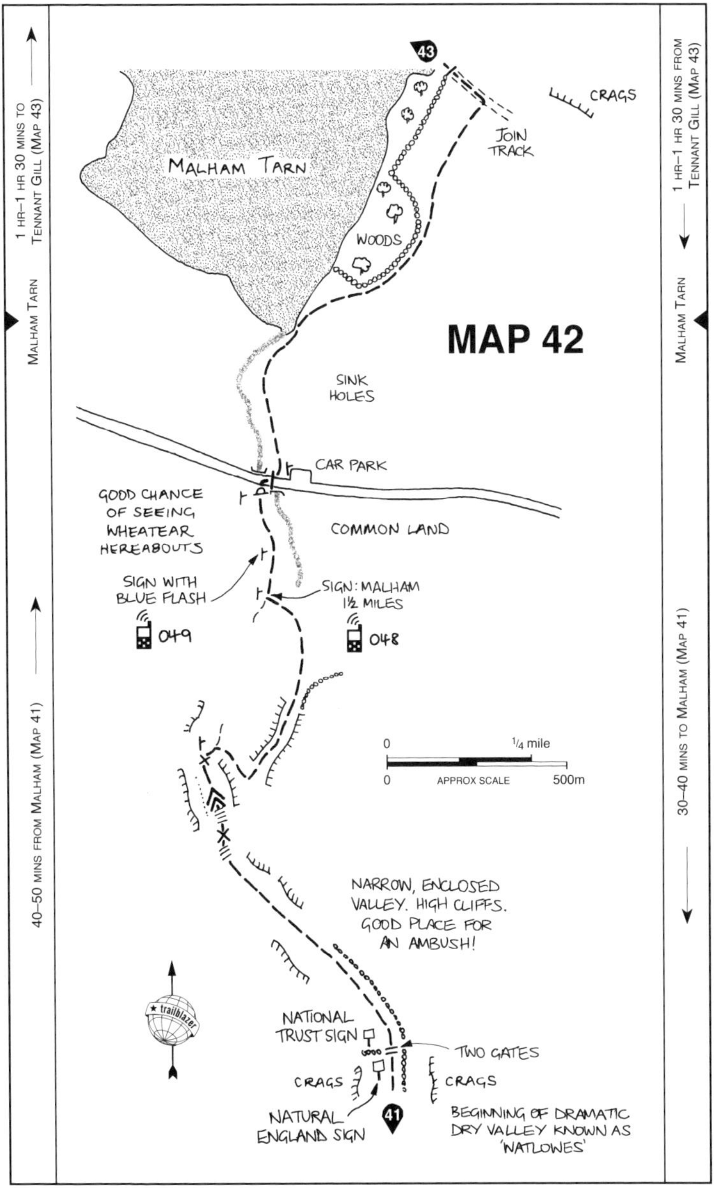

1 HR–1 HR 30 MINS TO
TENNANT GILL (MAP 43)

MALHAM TARN

1 HR–1 HR 30 MINS FROM
TENNANT GILL (MAP 43)

MALHAM TARN

43

CRAGS

JOIN
TRACK

MALHAM TARN

WOODS

**MAP 42**

SINK
HOLES

CAR PARK

GOOD CHANCE
OF SEEING
WHEATEAR
HEREABOUTS

COMMON LAND

SIGN WITH
BLUE FLASH

049

SIGN: MALHAM
1½ MILES

048

0     ¼ mile

0     APPROX SCALE     500m

30–40 MINS TO MALHAM (MAP 41)

40–50 MINS FROM MALHAM (MAP 41)

NARROW, ENCLOSED
VALLEY. HIGH CLIFFS.
GOOD PLACE FOR
AN AMBUSH!

★ trailblazer

NATIONAL
TRUST SIGN

TWO GATES

CRAGS

CRAGS

NATURAL
ENGLAND SIGN

41

BEGINNING OF DRAMATIC
DRY VALLEY KNOWN AS
'WATLOWES'

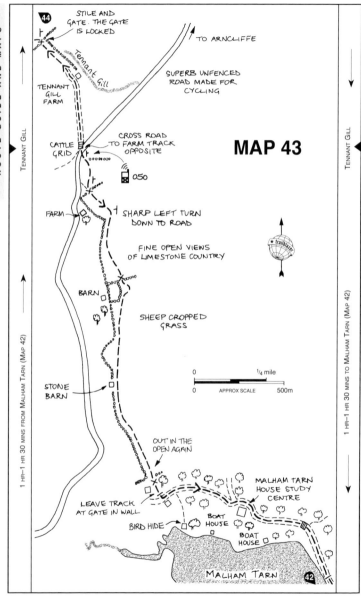

**44** STILE AND GATE. THE GATE IS LOCKED

TO ARNCLIFFE

Tennant Gill

SUPERB UNFENCED ROAD MADE FOR CYCLING

TENNANT GILL FARM

CATTLE GRID

CROSS ROAD TO FARM TRACK OPPOSITE

**MAP 43**

050

FARM

SHARP LEFT TURN DOWN TO ROAD

FINE OPEN VIEWS OF LIMESTONE COUNTRY

★ trailblazer

BARN

SHEEP CROPPED GRASS

0          ¼ mile
0    APPROX SCALE    500m

STONE BARN

OUT IN THE OPEN AGAIN

MALHAM TARN HOUSE STUDY CENTRE

LEAVE TRACK AT GATE IN WALL

BIRD HIDE

BOAT HOUSE

BOAT HOUSE

MALHAM TARN

**42**

TENNANT GILL

TENNANT GILL

1 HR–1 HR 30 MINS FROM MALHAM TARN (MAP 42)

1 HR–1 HR 30 MINS TO MALHAM TARN (MAP 42)

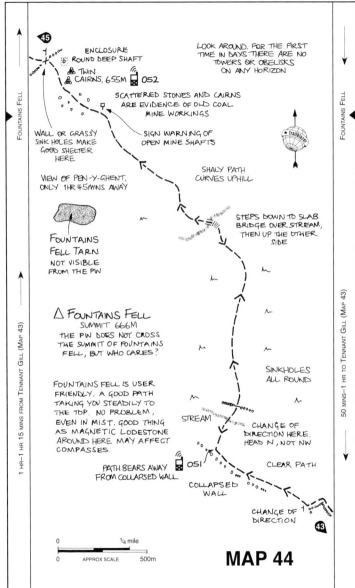

**45**

ENCLOSURE
ROUND DEEP SHAFT

TWIN
CAIRNS, 655M 📟 052

LOOK AROUND. FOR THE FIRST
TIME IN DAYS THERE ARE NO
TOWERS OR OBELISKS
ON ANY HORIZON

SCATTERED STONES AND CAIRNS
ARE EVIDENCE OF OLD COAL
MINE WORKINGS

WALL OR GRASSY
SINK HOLES MAKE
GOOD SHELTER
HERE

SIGN WARNING OF
OPEN MINE SHAFTS

VIEW OF PEN-Y-GHENT,
ONLY 1HR 45MINS AWAY

SHALY PATH
CURVES UPHILL

★ trailblazer

STEPS DOWN TO SLAB
BRIDGE OVER STREAM,
THEN UP THE OTHER
SIDE

FOUNTAINS
FELL TARN
NOT VISIBLE
FROM THE PW

△ FOUNTAINS FELL
SUMMIT 666M
THE PW DOES NOT CROSS
THE SUMMIT OF FOUNTAINS
FELL, BUT WHO CARES?

SINKHOLES
ALL ROUND

FOUNTAINS FELL IS USER
FRIENDLY. A GOOD PATH
TAKING YOU STEADILY TO
THE TOP. NO PROBLEM,
EVEN IN MIST. GOOD THING
AS MAGNETIC LODESTONE
AROUND HERE MAY AFFECT
COMPASSES.

STREAM

CHANGE OF
DIRECTION HERE.
HEAD N, NOT NW

PATH BEARS AWAY
FROM COLLAPSED WALL

📟 051

CLEAR PATH

COLLAPSED
WALL

CHANGE OF
DIRECTION

**43**

FOUNTAINS FELL

FOUNTAINS FELL

1 HR–1 HR 15 MINS FROM TENNANT GILL (MAP 43)

50 MINS–1 HR TO TENNANT GILL (MAP 43)

0          ¼ mile
0    APPROX SCALE    500m

**MAP 44**

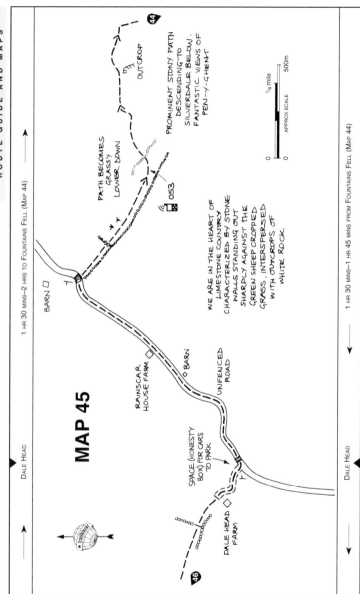

MAP 45

DALE HEAD

1 HR 30 MINS–2 HRS TO FOUNTAINS FELL (MAP 44)

BARN

RAINSCAR HOUSE FARM

BARN

UNFENCED ROAD

SPACE (HONESTY BOX FOR CARS TO PARK)

DALE HEAD FARM

46

PATH BECOMES GRASSY LOWER DOWN

053

OUTCROP

44

PROMINENT STONY PATH DESCENDING TO SILVERDALE BELOW. FANTASTIC VIEWS OF PEN-Y-GHENT

WE ARE IN THE HEART OF LIMESTONE COUNTRY CHARACTERIZED BY STONE WALLS STANDING OUT SHARPLY AGAINST THE GREEN SHEEP CROPPED GRASS, INTERSPERSED WITH OUTCROPS OF WHITE ROCK

¼ mile
APPROX SCALE
500m

DALE HEAD

1 HR 30 MINS–1 HR 45 MINS FROM FOUNTAINS FELL (MAP 44)

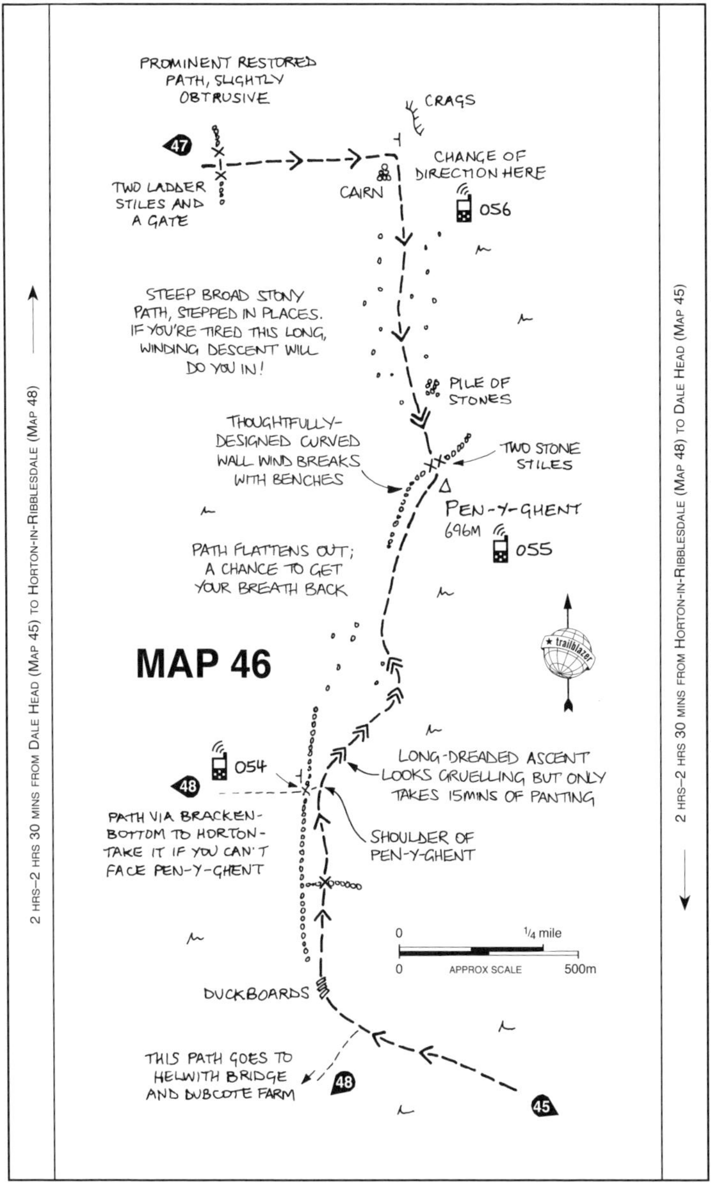

PROMINENT RESTORED PATH, SLIGHTLY OBTRUSIVE

CRAGS

**47**

CHANGE OF DIRECTION HERE

056

TWO LADDER STILES AND A GATE

CAIRN

STEEP BROAD STONY PATH, STEPPED IN PLACES. IF YOU'RE TIRED THIS LONG, WINDING DESCENT WILL DO YOU IN!

PILE OF STONES

THOUGHTFULLY-DESIGNED CURVED WALL WIND BREAKS WITH BENCHES

TWO STONE STILES

△ PEN-Y-GHENT 696m

055

PATH FLATTENS OUT; A CHANCE TO GET YOUR BREATH BACK

★ trailblazer

**MAP 46**

054

**48**

LONG-DREADED ASCENT LOOKS GRUELLING BUT ONLY TAKES 15MINS OF PANTING

PATH VIA BRACKEN-BOTTOM TO HORTON-TAKE IT IF YOU CAN'T FACE PEN-Y-GHENT

SHOULDER OF PEN-Y-GHENT

| 0 | | ¼ mile |
|---|---|---|
| 0 | APPROX SCALE | 500m |

DUCKBOARDS

THIS PATH GOES TO HELWITH BRIDGE AND DUBCOTE FARM

**48**

**45**

2 HRS–2 HRS 30 MINS FROM DALE HEAD (MAP 45) TO HORTON-IN-RIBBLESDALE (MAP 48)

2 HRS–2 HRS 30 MINS FROM HORTON-IN-RIBBLESDALE (MAP 48) TO DALE HEAD (MAP 45)

2 HRS–2 HRS 30 MINS FROM DALE HEAD (MAP 45) TO HORTON-IN-RIBBLESDALE (MAP 48) ⟶

1 HR 45 MINS–2 HRS 15 MINS FROM LING GILL BRIDGE (MAP 50) TO HORTON-IN-RIBBLESDALE (MAP 48) ⟶

ROUTE GUIDE AND MAPS

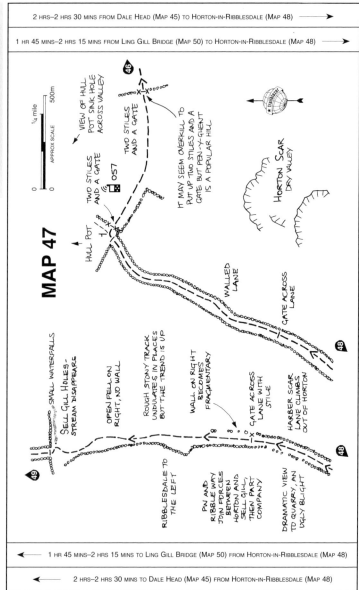

## MAP 47

¼ mile

APPROX SCALE

500m

VIEW OF HULL POT SINK HOLE ACROSS VALLEY

TWO STILES AND A GATE

O57

TWO STILES AND A GATE

HULL POT

IT MAY SEEM OVERKILL TO PUT UP TWO STILES AND A GATE BUT PEN-Y-GHENT IS A POPULAR HILL

46

HORTON SCAR DRY VALLEY

WALLED LANE

GATE ACROSS LANE

48

SMALL WATERFALLS

SELL GILL HOLES- STREAM DISAPPEARS

OPEN FELL ON RIGHT, NO WALL

ROUGH STONY TRACK UNDULATES IN PLACES BUT THE TREND IS UP

WALL ON RIGHT BECOMES FRAGMENTARY

GATE ACROSS LANE WITH STILE

HARBER SCAR LANE CLIMBS OUT OF HORTON

48

49

RIBBLESDALE TO THE LEFT

PW AND RIBBLE WAY JOIN FORCES BETWEEN HORTON AND SELL GILL, THEN PART COMPANY

DRAMATIC VIEW TO QUARRY, AN UGLY BLIGHT

⟵ 1 HR 45 MINS–2 HRS 15 MINS TO LING GILL BRIDGE (MAP 50) FROM HORTON-IN-RIBBLESDALE (MAP 48)

⟵ 2 HRS–2 HRS 30 MINS TO DALE HEAD (MAP 45) FROM HORTON-IN-RIBBLESDALE (MAP 48)

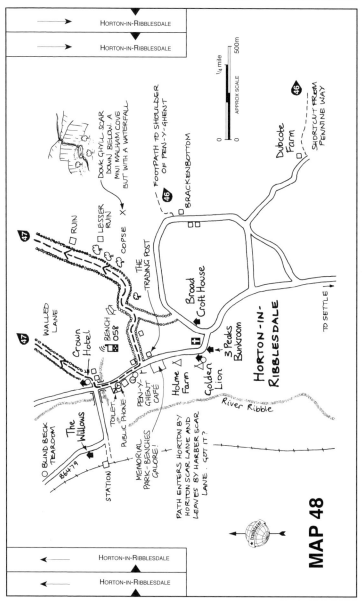

HORTON-IN-RIBBLESDALE

HORTON-IN-RIBBLESDALE

DOUK GHYLL SCAR DOWN BELOW. A MINI MALHAM COVE BUT WITH A WATERFALL

FOOTPATH TO SHOULDER OF PEN-Y-GHENT

500m

¼ mile

APPROX SCALE

0        0

46

BRACKENBOTTOM

DUBCOTE FARM

SHORTCUT FROM PENNINE WAY

46

RUIN

LESSER RUIN

COPSE X

THE TRADING POST

47

BROAD CROFT HOUSE

HORTON-IN-RIBBLESDALE

TO SETTLE

WALLED LANE

CROWN HOTEL

BENCH 058

3 PEAKS BUNKROOM

47

PEN-Y-GHENT CAFÉ

HOLME FARM

GOLDEN LION

TOILET

PUBLIC PHONE

RIVER RIBBLE

BLIND BECK TEAROOM

THE WILLOWS

B6479

STATION

MEMORIAL PARK - BENCHES GALORE!

PATH ENTERS HORTON BY HORTON SCAR LANE AND LEAVES BY HARBER SCAR LANE. GOT IT?

MAP 48

## Route-finding trouble spots

Even in poor weather and exacerbated by the elevations involved, it's hard to see anywhere the route might be lost. Pen-y-ghent up and down is as clear as a bell; the ascent of Fountains Fell is made easier by a good path, the only tricky spot being the unclear change of direction by the collapsed wall.

---

❑ **Fountains Fell** [see Map 44, p139]

Named after its original owners, the Cistercian monks of Fountains Abbey near Ripon, Fountains Fell possessed substantial coal deposits beneath its cap of millstone grit. It probably still does, but not in sufficient quantity to make extraction economically viable.

The most active period of coal extraction was the early 1800s when a road was constructed to the summit plateau where shafts were sunk. The remnants of this road now constitutes the generally agreeable gradient of the Pennine Way.

The output of coal was estimated at around 1000 tons a year which required some 10,000 packhorse loads to carry it away.

Very little now remains of the coal industry on Fountains Fell and the shafts have mostly been filled in. The ruins of the colliery building are in evidence but give no real idea of what was once a flourishing industry. We can spare a thought for the miners who had to work in this inhospitable place, spending the week in makeshift accommodation (known as 'shops') within yards of their labours and getting up in the small hours to trudge to work in all weathers.

---

## HORTON-IN-RIBBLESDALE
### [Map 48, p143]

There are no services along the route until you get to Horton, a famous landmark on the Pennine Way, as much for the presence of the Pen-y-ghent Café as for the charm of the village itself.

### Services

**Pen-y-ghent Café** (see also Where to eat and drink; ☎ 01729-860333; summer Mon & Wed-Fri 9am-5.30pm, Sat 8am-5.30pm, Sun 8.30am-5.30pm, closed Tue; opens later in the winter months), over the road, doubles as the **tourist information centre** (and can provide weather forecasts and also advice on accommodation) and also sells **camping gear**, snacks, maps and books. The Bayes family who run it are very helpful and friendly and provide a superb service for the walker. They are immensely knowledgeable about the area.

As well as operating a check-in/check-out service for day-walkers in the area, since the Pennine Way was opened they've been keeping a **Pennine Way book** for Wayfarers to sign as they pass. There are so many volumes there's now quite a library but it's a wonderful record of everyone who's passed along the Way. Be sure to sign it.

The Trading Post is a well-stocked **shop** (☎ 01729-860232; 🖳 www.horton tradingpost.co.uk; Mon-Tue 8.30am-5.30pm, Wed 8.30am-noon, Thu-Fri 8.30am-7pm, Sat 7am-8pm, Sun 7am-4pm; winter hours variable, check their website) which also serves sandwiches, pies and pasties.

**Post office** services (Mon 2-4pm, Thur 9.30am-noon) are provided in the Crown Hotel (see Where to stay).

### Transport

[See also pp45-50] Horton is a stop on Dales Rail and is also on the Leeds–Carlisle line (Northern Rail) so **trains** are frequent, making it an ideal place to begin or end a walk along the Way.

The only **bus** service (to Settle) is operated by Little Red Bus (B1).

For a **taxi** call Settle Taxis (☎ 01729-824824/822219).

## Where to stay
In the centre of the village *Holme Farm Camping* (☎ 01729-860281) costs £2 per tent plus £2 per person; there are shower (£1) and toilet facilities. At the southern end of the village is *3 Peaks Bunkroom* (☎ 01729-860380, 🖳 www.3peaksbunkroom .co.uk), a recently converted barn with 40 beds in two rooms (£15pp); if you stay here you will need a sleeping bag, pillow and towels. However, they tend to take group bookings and therefore are likely to send you to the Golden Lion (see below).

*Crown Hotel* (☎ 01729-860209, 🖳 www.crown-hotel.co.uk; 1S/3D/7D, T or F, all with private facilities, bath available) is particularly convenient as it's right on the Way. They charge £38pp £35 for the single.

The *Golden Lion Hotel* (☎ 01729-860206, 🖳 www.goldenlionhotel.co.uk; 2D/3T, all en suite) charges £40 for single occupancy (£60 Fri & Sat), otherwise it's £30pp. They also have 15 beds in a **bunk room** (£12pp) as well as space outside to pitch **tents** if Holme Farm campsite is full (you can use the pub's toilet when the pub is open).

*The Willows* (☎ 01729-860200, 🖳 www.the-willows-horton-in-ribblesdale. co.uk; 2D or F/1T or F, all with private facilities, bath available) charges £75-80 (£60-80 single occupancy; an extra bed in a room is £20); minimum booking of two nights at weekends between April and October. They offer luggage transfer to your next B&B (£6 per bag; minimum two bags)

and packed lunches (£6). Early breakfast (a bacon butty) is available from 6.30am.

*Broad Croft House* (☎ 01729-860302, 🖳 www.broadcroft.co.uk; 1D/1D or T/1T, both en suite) charges £70 (£55 for single occupancy). Packed lunches (£7) are also available. Generally they don't accept bookings for one night only at weekends in the main season.

## Where to eat and drink
As old as the Pennine Way itself, the legendary *Pen-y-ghent Café* (see Services for contact details and opening hours) is the obvious port of call being a 'One Stop Shop' for the walker as well as serving home-made cakes (about £2), sandwiches (£2.70), filling staples such as beans on toast, vegetable soup with a roll, and chilli con carne (£4.50). They also offer takeaway sandwiches – ham, or strong cheese (£1.95).

*The Crown Hotel* (see Where to stay; pub grub served daily noon-2pm & 6-9pm) has a nice garden round the back, and *The Golden Lion* (see Where to stay; bar food served summer daily noon-2pm & 6-9pm, Fri & Sat to 9.30pm; winter evenings only) offers the same type of fare at similar prices.

Just outside the village at its northern end is the *Blindbeck Tea Room* (☎ 01729-860396, 🖳 www.blindbeck.co.uk; Mon-Fri 10am-6pm, Sat & Sun usually 9am-6pm; they close earlier in the winter months) which serves home-made cakes and scones as well as hot and cold snacks.

---

### ❏ Fell running
Whilst puffing steadily up the Cam High Road (see Maps 51 and 52), you may be ignominiously overtaken by a wiry person in brief shorts, the scantiest of vests and strange-looking lightly studded shoes. He or she is a fell runner, a participant in a sport that is taken very seriously hereabouts.

The routes involve the muddiest tracks and the steepest hills, the sort of terrain that most people would dismiss as un-runnable. It goes to extremes too, and the **Three Peaks Challenge** is one of them. On this event people have to run 26 miles (42km) from Pen-y-ghent Café up three peaks – Pen-y-ghent, Whernside and Ingleborough – which you can see around you, and back in less than 12 hours; the fastest time is less than three hours. See also p25.

## HORTON-IN-RIBBLESDALE TO HAWES                    MAPS 48-55

### Route overview

A **14-mile (23km, 6¼-6¾hrs)** section, this stage involves a single long ascent up onto Dodd Fell to end with a relatively sudden drop down into Upper Wensleydale and the town of Hawes. For much of the way we follow wall-bound stony tracks, old packhorse trails (see box p153) used for centuries as thoroughfares over the wild limestone moors. It has to be said that these ever-present walls mute the exhilaration of being out on the moors and the rough track will get to your feet (though it's not as tough as the descent from Cross Fell in a few days' time).

Climbing out of Horton by way of **Harber Scar Lane** from the doorstep of the Crown Hotel, the lane passes gurgling potholes and tops out on **Jackdaw Hill** (Map 49; 400m/1312ft). It then follows a prominent 'green road' past more pot holes and limestone outcrops to reach the delightful **Ling Gill** (Map 50) ravine where the beck has carved a deep gash, creating a unique national nature reserve for trees, wildflowers and wildlife beyond the range of usual predators. So steep is it that even the signboard's invitation to considerably explore the interior of the reserve may not be enough to motivate you. However, it was closed at the time of writing but the Pennine Way goes right alongside it and you can look down into the deep wooded gorge.

The trail crosses **Ling Gill Bridge** and more uphill 'packhorsing' follows, the path easily followed to the high crossroads known as **Cam End**, halfway between Horton and Hawes. The view of Three Peaks country with Ribblehead Viaduct clearly visible in the wide valley between Ingleborough and Whernside is an impressive sight. Make the most of it for you must turn your back and follow the broad track of Cam High Road as it contours the hillside above dense forestry to reach **Kidhow Gate** (Map 53). Here farmers have been gathering their sheep for driving to market for as long as flocks have been grazed on the springy turf of these wide open moors.

Another 'green road', **West Cam Road**, leads along the shoulder of **Dodd Fell** high above the mysterious valley of Snaizeholme, a long level trudge enclosed by walls and fences that seem reluctant to end. But briefly end they do and you flit freely across the fells around and down **Rottenstone Hill** (Map 54) where **Hawes** (Map 55) beckons from far below. A smaller version of Haworth but without the 'Wutherobilia', Hawes is a welcoming village with all the services a walker could possibly need for rest and recuperation.

### Route-finding trouble spots

For most of this stage even a lame packhorse with a coal sack over its head would have no problems. For you, apart from the all-hay diet, the experience should be similar. Apart from the perimeter of Hawes itself, the sole drama might be coming off Rottenstone Hill in thick mist where the grassy path thins out until cairns lead to a stream crossing by a wall (GPS Waypoint 067, see p260).

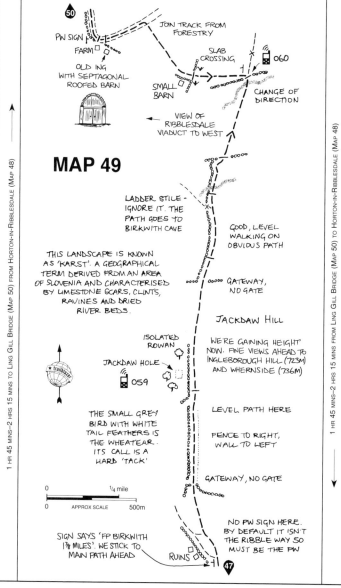

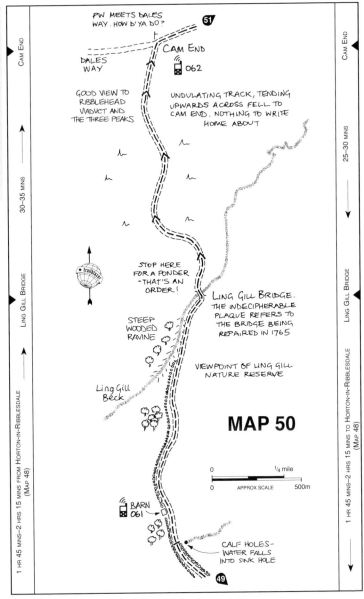

PW MEETS DALES WAY. HOW D'YA DO?

**51**

CAM END

📶 062

DALES WAY

GOOD VIEW TO RIBBLEHEAD VIADUCT AND THE THREE PEAKS

UNDULATING TRACK, TENDING UPWARDS ACROSS FELL TO CAM END. NOTHING TO WRITE HOME ABOUT

STOP HERE FOR A PONDER - THAT'S AN ORDER!

LING GILL BRIDGE. THE INDECIPHERABLE PLAQUE REFERS TO THE BRIDGE BEING REPAIRED IN 1765

STEEP WOODED RAVINE

VIEWPOINT OF LING GILL NATURE RESERVE

Ling Gill Beck

**MAP 50**

0 — 1/4 mile

0 — 500m
APPROX SCALE

📶 061 → BARN

CALF HOLES- WATER FALLS INTO SINK HOLE

**49**

ROUTE GUIDE AND MAPS

CAM END

25–30 MINS

LING GILL BRIDGE

1 HR 45 MINS–2 HRS 15 MINS TO HORTON-IN-RIBBLESDALE (MAP 48)

CAM END

30–35 MINS

LING GILL BRIDGE

1 HR 45 MINS–2 HRS 15 MINS FROM HORTON-IN-RIBBLESDALE (MAP 48)

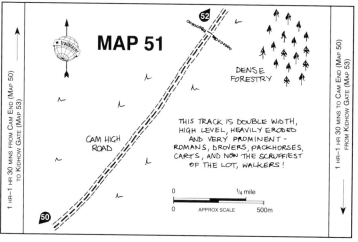

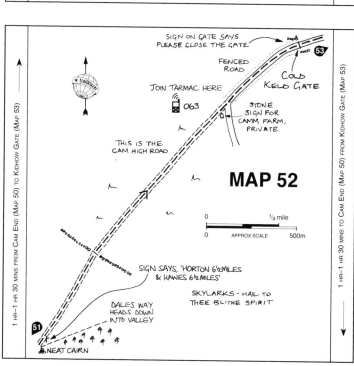

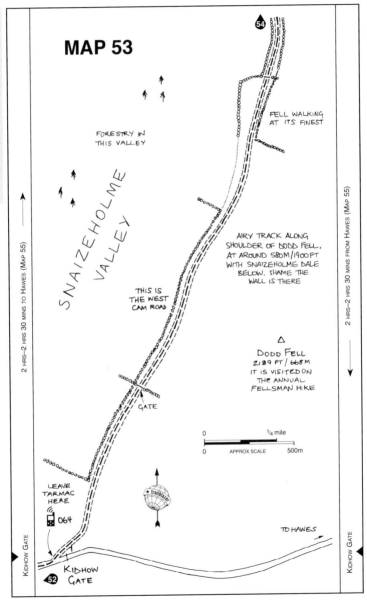

ROUTE GUIDE AND MAPS

**MAP 53**

54

FELL WALKING
AT ITS FINEST

FORESTRY IN
THIS VALLEY

SNAIZEHOLME
VALLEY

AIRY TRACK ALONG
SHOULDER OF DODD FELL,
AT AROUND 580M/1900FT
WITH SNAIZEHOLME DALE
BELOW. SHAME THE
WALL IS THERE

THIS IS
THE WEST
CAM ROAD

△
DODD FELL
2189 FT / 668M
IT IS VISITED ON
THE ANNUAL
FELLSMAN HIKE

GATE

0                    ¼ mile
0        APPROX SCALE        500m

★ trailblazer

LEAVE
TARMAC
HERE
064

TO HAWES

KIDHOW GATE

KIDHOW
GATE
52

2 HRS–2 HRS 30 MINS TO HAWES (MAP 55)

2 HRS–2 HRS 30 MINS FROM HAWES (MAP 55)

KIDHOW GATE

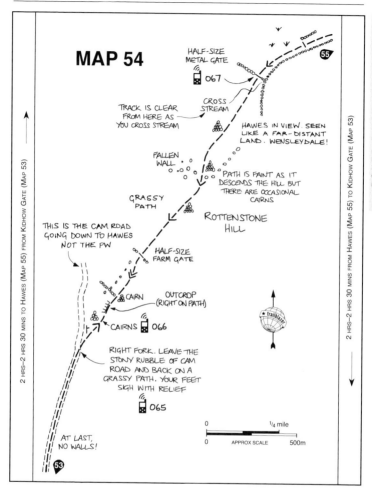

**MAP 54**

HALF-SIZE METAL GATE

🔊 067

CROSS STREAM

TRACK IS CLEAR FROM HERE AS YOU CROSS STREAM

HAWES IN VIEW. SEEN LIKE A FAR-DISTANT LAND. WENSLEYDALE!

FALLEN WALL

PATH IS FAINT AS IT DESCENDS THE HILL BUT THERE ARE OCCASIONAL CAIRNS

GRASSY PATH

ROTTENSTONE HILL

THIS IS THE CAM ROAD GOING DOWN TO HAWES NOT THE PW

HALF-SIZE FARM GATE

CAIRN

OUTCROP (RIGHT ON PATH)

CAIRNS 🔊 066

🌐 trailblazer

RIGHT FORK. LEAVE THE STONY RUBBLE OF CAM ROAD AND BACK ON A GRASSY PATH. YOUR FEET SIGH WITH RELIEF

🔊 065

0 — ¼ mile
0 — APPROX SCALE — 500m

AT LAST, NO WALLS!

▼ 53

*(left margin)* 2 HRS–2 HRS 30 MINS TO HAWES (MAP 55) FROM KIDHOW GATE (MAP 53)

*(right margin)* 2 HRS–2 HRS 30 MINS FROM HAWES (MAP 55) TO KIDHOW GATE (MAP 53)

*(top right)* **55**

## HAWES [Map 55a, p154]

There's nothing pretentious about Hawes. It's a down-to-earth Yorkshire town with a vibrant centre full of pubs and cafés. If you're in need of a break this could be the place to relax for a day or so. There's plenty to see: a good local museum, a traditional ropemaker – and this is the home of the world-famous Wensleydale cheese.

At the award-winning **Wensleydale Creamery** (☎ 01969-667664, 🖥 www .wensleydale.co.uk; Mon-Sat 9.30am-5pm, Sun 10am-4.30pm) the 900-year-old art of local cheese-making was nearly lost, only to be saved by the international popularity of Wensleydale-cheese-munching characters Wallace & Gromit. Blending Wensleydale

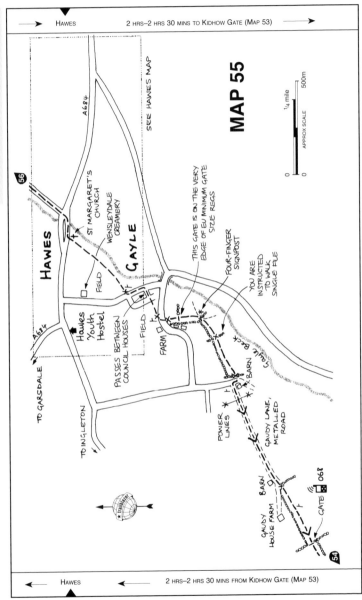

HAWES · 2 HRS–2 HRS 30 MINS TO KIDHOW GATE (MAP 53)

SEE HAWES MAP

A684

**MAP 55**

¼ mile · 500m
APPROX SCALE
0 · 0

St Margaret's Church
Wensleydale Creamery

**GAYLE**

**HAWES**

56

FIELD

THIS GATE IS ON THE VERY EDGE OF EU MINIMUM GATE SIZE REGS

FOUR-FINGER SIGNPOST

YOU ARE INSTRUCTED TO WALK SINGLE FILE

Hawes Youth Hostel

A684

PASSES BETWEEN COUNCIL HOUSES

FIELD

FARM

GAYLE BECK

TO GARSDALE

TO INGLETON

POWER LINES

BARN

GAUDY LANE, METALLED ROAD

trailblazer

BARN

GAUDY HOUSE FARM

GATE

890 068

54

HAWES · 2 HRS–2 HRS 30 MINS FROM KIDHOW GATE (MAP 53)

with cranberries soon became a best-seller, and now there's also Wensleydale & apricot and Wensleydale & ginger (stem ginger) for gourmet *fromageurs*. Phone in advance if you want to go on the Cheese Experience Tour (£2.50) as cheese is not made every day.

The **Dales Countryside Museum** (see Services; daily 10am-5pm, last entry to the museum 4pm; £3) is informative. Nearby the **Hawes Ropemaker** is not something you'll find in every town.

See p25 for details of events held here.

**Transport**

[See also pp45-50] The best way to **Garsdale station** for Northern Rail's Carlisle–Leeds services and Dales Rail's Blackpool to Carlisle train is by taxi, unless you are here at the right time to get one of Little Red Bus's No 113 services. Hawes is on a number of other **bus** routes (Arriva's X59, Dales and District's 156/157 and Royal Mail Postbus's No 364 route), though none is particularly frequent.

For a **taxi** try Cliff Ellis (☎ 01969-667598).

**Services**

The **Yorkshire Dales National Park Centre** and **Tourist Information Centre** (☎ 01969-666210, 🖳 www.yorkshiredales .org.uk; Feb-Dec daily 10am-5pm; closed some days in January so check in advance) are in the Dales Countryside Museum. Staff are able to do accommodation booking (see box p13) A useful **website** for information on the town is 🖳 www .wensleydale.org/ hawes.

The library has free **internet** access (Mon-Fri 9.30am-4.30pm; Thu 5.30-7pm).

There's a **Spar supermarket** (Mon-Fri 8am-6pm, Sat 8am-7.30pm, Sun 9am-5pm) while **Elijah Allen & Sons** is a wonderful old grocery store that shows how it used to be done and has been run by the same family since 1870. On Tuesdays there's a **street market**.

For **outdoor gear** there's Three Peaks, which has a selection of boots if yours have had it, or try Stewart R Cunningham (daily 9.30am-5pm).

There's a **launderette** (Mon-Sat 9.30am-4pm, closed Wed & Sun), a **post office** (early closing Wed) and both **banks** have cash machines. There's also a **chemist**, which doubles as a **wine merchant** so you can buy both the cause and the cure in one shop!

**Where to stay**

You can **camp** either side of the village. If you're feeling energetic head for *Bainbridge Ings Caravan and Camping Site* (☎ 01969-667354, 🖳 www.bainbridge-ings.co.uk; late Mar/Apr-end Oct), three-quarters of a

---

❑ **Packhorse roads**

The trackways that criss-cross the mid-Pennines are the remains of a once-thriving traffic in goods transported on the backs of packhorses.

These hardy animals were tough, stocky breeds known variously as jaggers after the German Jaeger ponies from which their stock came, or galloways after the Scottish breed particularly suited to carrying loads over rough country.

Wool, coal, hides, iron, lead, stone, charcoal and peat were carried down to the towns, the tracks used taking the shortest way across unenclosed country, often to avoid local taxes. Over the years the way would become heavily worn and sunken and we find names such as Hollow Way (Holloway) on maps where the traffic has cut a deep groove. Stones would be used to fill up holes and reinforce the road.

Most of the upland roads were abandoned when turnpike tollways were adopted for wheeled traffic and it was only farmers who continued to use the old tracks to get up onto the high fells. Now walkers use them more than farmers. With the advent of all-terrain quad bikes there was no need to follow the tracks; farmers simply ride straight across a field to the nearest gate.

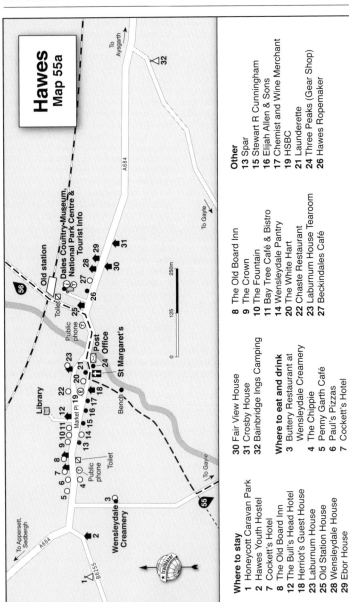

**Hawes**
**Map 55a**

Where to stay
1 Honeycott Caravan Park
2 Hawes Youth Hostel
7 Cockett's Hotel
8 The Old Board Inn
12 The Bull's Head Hotel
18 Herriot's Guest House
23 Laburnum House
25 Old Station House
28 Wensleydale House
29 Ebor House
30 Fair View House
31 Crosby House
32 Bainbridge Ings Camping

Where to eat and drink
3 Buttery Restaurant at
   Wensleydale Creamery
4 The Chippie
5 Penny Garth Café
6 Paul's Pizzas
7 Cockett's Hotel
8 The Old Board Inn
9 The Crown
10 The Fountain
11 Bay Tree Café & Bistro
14 Wensleydale Pantry
20 The White Hart
22 Chaste Restaurant
23 Laburnum House Tearoom
27 Beckindales Café

Other
13 Spar
15 Stewart R Cunningham
16 Elijah Allen & Sons
17 Chemist and Wine Merchant
19 HSBC
21 Launderette
24 Three Peaks (Gear Shop)
26 Hawes Ropemaker

mile east of Market Place, where you can pitch your tent in beautiful countryside for £5pp. There are toilet, shower (20p) and laundry (coin-operated machines) facilities and they sell milk and eggs. A bit nearer (on the B6255 to the west) but maybe too caravan-oriented is **Honeycott Caravan Park** (☎ 01969-667310, 🖵 www.honeycott. co.uk; Mar-Oct) which charges £5pp; there is a toilet and shower block. Booking is recommended, especially if you expect to arrive after 5pm.

It may have a comparatively bland exterior but inside **Hawes YHA Hostel** (bookings ☎ 0845-371 9120, 🖵 hawes@ yha.org.uk; Mar-Oct) has all the trimmings including 52 beds (14 rooms with 2-8 beds) for £15 (under 18s £11.50). It opens at 5pm and meals are available. There is also a self-catering kitchen and the hostel has a licence.

There's a clutch of **B&Bs** to the east of town which include **Ebor House** (☎ 01969-667337, 🖵 www.eborhouse. co.uk; Feb-Nov; 1T/5D, all with private facilities) which charges £65-80; single occupancy costs £55-60. They also offer packed lunches (£5). On the same street, **Wensleydale House** (☎ 01969-666020, 🖵 www.wensleydalehouse.co.uk; 2D or T/1D, all en suite, bath available) does B&B for £60-70 (single occupancy £45) and across the road **Crosby House** (☎ 01969-667322, 🖵 www.crosbyhousehawes.co.uk; 2D/1D or T, all en suite, bath available) is equally comfortable and charges from £64 (single occupancy £36).

**Laburnum House** (☎ 01969-667717, 🖵 www.stayatlaburnumhouse.co.uk, The Holme; 1T/2D/1F, all en suite, bath available; closed Jan) has rooms costing £60 (£35 single occupancy) and is just off Market Place, as is **Herriot's Guest House** (☎ 01969-667536, 🖵 www.herriotsinhawes. co.uk; 1S/1T/4D/1D, T or F, all en suite, bath available) which charges £37.50pp (£49.50 for single occupancy of a double/ twin room); they have an art gallery. Not far from the national park centre is **Old Station House B&B** (☎ 01969-666912, 🖵 www .oldstationhousehawes.co.uk; 2D or T/1F, all en suite) built in 1876 by the Midland Railway and refurbished in 2009. Dogs

are welcome; book in advance. B&B costs £30pp (£40 for single occupancy).

**Fair View House** (☎ 01969-667348, 🖵 www.fairview-hawes.co.uk; 2S share bathroom/2D/1F, all en suite) is another imposing Victorian property where B&B costs from £35pp.

Probably the best **hotel** is **Cockett's** (☎ 01969-667312, 🖵 www.cocketts.co.uk; 1S/1T/8D/1F, all en suite, bath available), which charges £72-92 for two sharing (two rooms have four-poster beds); the single is £45 but single occupancy of a room is £50. They can do a packed lunch (from £6.50).

Two people sharing a room at **The Old Board Inn** (☎ 01969-667223, 🖵 www.theoldboardinn.com; 1S/2D/2D or T, most en suite, bath available) pay £30-35pp (single occupancy in summer costs £40) while at **The Bull's Head Hotel** (☎ 01969-667437, 🖵 www.bullsheadhotel. com; 6D, T or F, en suite) the rate is from £60 (single occupancy £50-60). Dogs (£5) are welcome; booking is preferred.

### Where to eat and drink

**The Buttery Restaurant** at Wensleydale Creamery (see p151) is a fully licensed restaurant where few could resist a free cheese sample for a starter.

Back in town, **Bay Tree Café & Bistro** offers quiches and hot or cold filled baguettes with tasty fillings while the best dinner in town is waiting for you at **Cockett's** (see Where to stay; Wed-Mon 7-8.30pm) where a rack of lamb cutlets will cost £14.95. Well worth the slog from Horton, if not Edale itself!

Less fancy is **The White Hart** (bar open all day; food served daily noon-2pm & 7-8.30pm), a welcoming locals' pub, which will cook up a square meal for around £7-8. You can also get bar meals at **The Crown Inn**, **The Fountain** and **The Old Board Inn** (daily noon-2pm & 6.30-8pm). The latter does a mean plate of Cumberland sausage and Yorkshire pud for £7.25.

At the west end of the high street is **Penny Garth Café** (☎ 01969-667066, 🖵 www.pennygarthcafe.co.uk; Thu-Tue 9am-5pm, Wed 10am-4pm, they may close earlier in the winter), a legendary lunch stop for bikers but equally welcoming to Pennine Way walkers. They have picnic tables on the street out front where you can tuck into sausage, egg and chips (£4.50) and all-day breakfasts (£5.95) amongst other delights.

*Wensleydale Pantry* (☎ 01969-667202; daily 8.30am to 4.30pm; in the summer to 8pm Sun-Fri and 8.30pm Sat) has meals for around £8. The *Chaste Restaurant* (daily 10am-5pm) has a small outside terrace and does sandwiches for £4.95. Close by, *Laburnum House Tearoom* (see Where to stay; daily 10am-5pm, closed Jan and also may close earlier in the winter months) serves home-made food and also has a 'soup 'n' sandwich' menu in a nice setting.

Away from the hubbub of the main street is *Beckindales Café* which has an imaginative array of meals including chicken, ham and leek pie for £7.75.

For a takeaway there's *Paul's Pizzas* and *The Chippie* (cod, chips and mushy peas for £4.80).

## HAWES TO TAN HILL                    MAPS 55-64

### Route overview
This stage is back on par with the Malham section, a highly satisfying **16½-mile (27km, 8-10 hrs)** trek to the northern edge of the Yorkshire Dales. You start off ambling playfully through the meadows to the village of **Hardraw** (Map 56) where you must steel yourself for the 5-mile (8km) slog to the 716-metre (2349ft) summit of **Great Shunner Fell** (Map 59). However, the ascent is largely free of walls and climbing the shoulder of Great Shunner offers views east to the Buttertubs Pass road and west to the distinctive stepped peaks of the northern dales of which Great Shunner is one. On the far side cairns, slabs and our old friend peat bring us round to the enclosed perfection of **Swaledale** in whose verdant arms rests the village of **Thwaite** (Map 61). For once a fine café, part of Kearton Country Hotel (see p163) crops up right around lunchtime; a better place to recharge the batteries for the afternoon's exertions could not be found.

With digestion underway, the route leads first through the hay meadows surrounding the village to soar high above the valley of the infant River Swale along the exposed shoulder of **Kisdon Hill** (Map 62). Negotiating scree and rubble the path drops back into woodland and down to cross this river by a waterfall. Continuing straight soon brings you to curious little **Keld**, an isolated limestone settlement at the intersection with the Coast to Coast Path (another Trailblazer title which no walker's library should be without!). It's worth popping in to Keld for a look-see and an ice cream even if you're set on Tan Hill.

Refreshed again, you rise above Keld to traverse the upland valley of Stonesdale, a muddy prospect at times, and then, with a final flourish, soar like a bleating curlew onto **Stonesdale Moor** (Map 63). The lonely silhouette of the **Tan Hill Inn** (Map 64 and p164) soon crops up against the setting sun and a glass of Theakston's finest calls to you lovingly from the bar.

### Route-finding trouble spots
Even in mist, once set right on the path to Great Shunner Fell it would be hard to part from it and it's the same story coming off the far side into Thwaite.

Helpful signage is a bit sparse as you level off from the climb out of Thwaite around Kisdon House, but again the gradual descent into Keld is straightforward. Only the next stage, preoccupied with the latter reaches of the mushy Stonesdale

Valley, up to where it turns up onto Stonesdale Moor at Lad Gill could cause route-finding discord. Once on the moor it's plain sailing to Tan Hill but if you've failed to even get that far, the metalled road on the far side of Stonesdale Beck parallels the Way and also leads straight to the Inn.

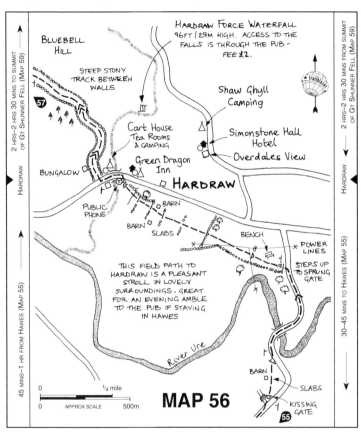

Map 56 illustration. Labels include: HARDRAW FORCE WATERFALL 96FT / 29M HIGH. ACCESS TO THE FALLS IS THROUGH THE PUB – FEE £2. BLUEBELL HILL. STEEP STONY TRACK BETWEEN WALLS. 57. 2 HRS–2 HRS 30 MINS TO SUMMIT OF GT SHUNNER FELL (MAP 59). HARDRAW. 45 MINS–1 HR FROM HAWES (MAP 55). Shaw Ghyll Camping. Cart House Tea Rooms & CAMPING. BUNGALOW. Green Dragon Inn. HARDRAW. Simonstone Hall Hotel. Overdales View. PUBLIC PHONE. BARN. BARN. SLABS. BENCH. POWER LINES. STEPS UP TO SPRUNG GATE. THIS FIELD PATH TO HARDRAW IS A PLEASANT STROLL IN LOVELY SURROUNDINGS. GREAT FOR AN EVENING AMBLE TO THE PUB IF STAYING IN HAWES. River Ure. BARN. SLABS. KISSING GATE. 55. 2 HRS–2 HRS 30 MINS FROM SUMMIT OF GT SHUNNER FELL (MAP 59). HARDRAW. 30–45 MINS TO HAWES (MAP 55). 0 ¼ mile. 0 APPROX SCALE 500m. MAP 56.

## HARDRAW [Map 56]

Hardraw's *Green Dragon Inn* (☎ 01969-667392, 🖳 www.greendragonhardraw .com; 5D/1T/1D, T or F, all en suite, bath available; food served daily 10am-9.30pm) is known for its fine ales. B&B is £35-40pp (£30-35 for room only); **camping** next door costs £8pp. Meals cost from £7. Two of the doubles are in the pub; the other rooms are in a separate building and dogs are welcome in these. From spring 2011 they plan to have two **bunkrooms**, each sleeping about 12 people (£15pp). Bathroom facilities will be shared but single sex; there are no cooking facilities. There is live music most Saturday nights in the summer; see p26 for details of the brass-band contest held here in September. For £2 (free for guests) you can visit the impressive Hardraw Force waterfall behind the pub.

**Camping** (Apr to end Oct) is also possible over the river at *Cart House Tea Rooms* (☎ 01969-667691, 🖳 www. hardrawforce.co.uk; Apr-Oct daily 10am-5pm; Nov & Feb-Apr weekends only 10am-4pm) for £3pp plus £2 per tent; shower (50p) and toilet facilities are available. The tea rooms serve snacks, light lunches and afternoon teas.

To the east of the village the very quiet *Shaw Ghyll Campsite* (☎ 01969-667359,

🖳 rogerstott@aol.com; March to end Oct) charges £16 per tent; booking is advised at any time. There is a toilet block and a shower costs 50p (in a meter).

If you're not too muddy or sweaty and feel like some luxury treat yourself at *Simonstone Hall Hotel* (☎ 01969-667255, 🖳 www.simonstonehall.com; 5D or T/13D, all en suite with bath). B&B costs from £155 per room and there is a fine restaurant (daily 7-9pm; open to non-residents). Dogs (£10) are welcome if booked in advance. You won't want to leave.

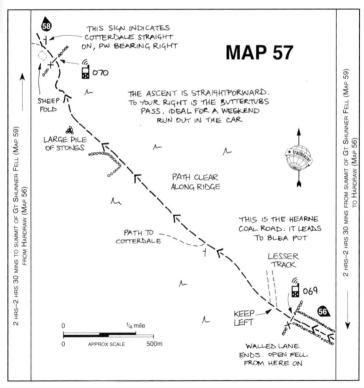

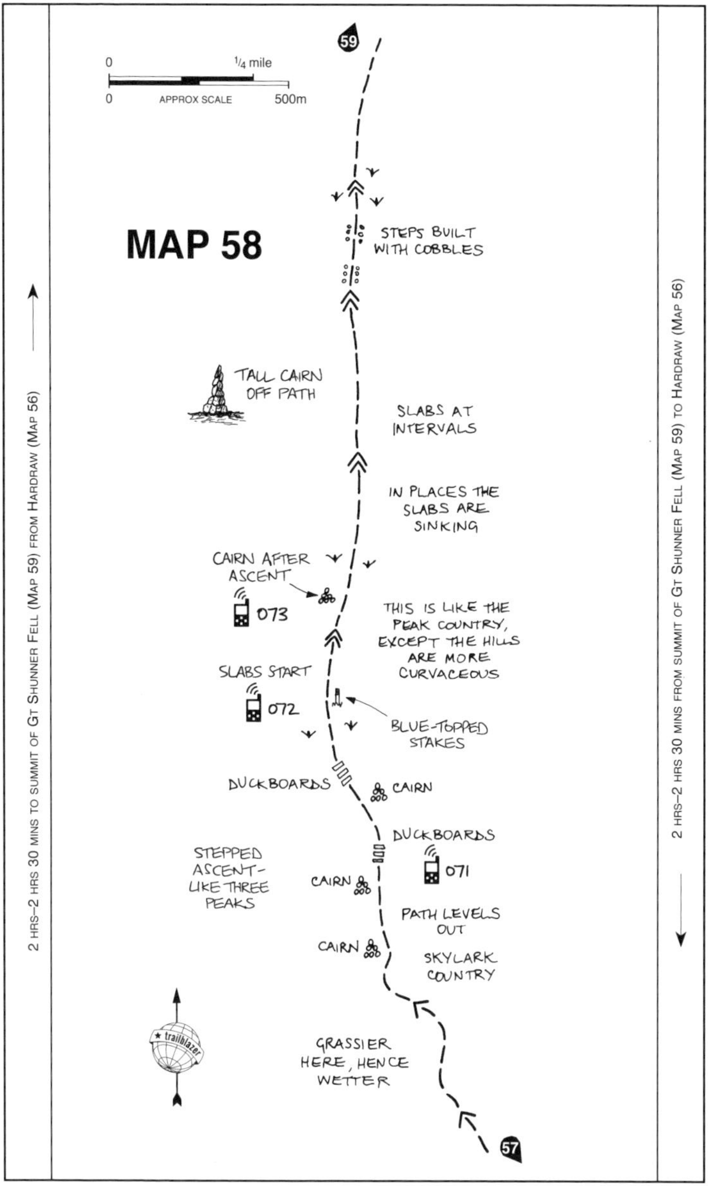

**MAP 58**

0 — ¼ mile
APPROX SCALE
0 — 500m

**59**

STEPS BUILT
WITH COBBLES

TALL CAIRN
OFF PATH

SLABS AT
INTERVALS

IN PLACES THE
SLABS ARE
SINKING

CAIRN AFTER
ASCENT

073

THIS IS LIKE THE
PEAK COUNTRY,
EXCEPT THE HILLS
ARE MORE
CURVACEOUS

SLABS START

072

BLUE-TOPPED
STAKES

DUCKBOARDS

CAIRN

DUCKBOARDS

071

STEPPED
ASCENT-
LIKE THREE
PEAKS

CAIRN

PATH LEVELS
OUT

CAIRN

SKYLARK
COUNTRY

trailblazer

GRASSIER
HERE, HENCE
WETTER

**57**

2 HRS–2 HRS 30 MINS TO SUMMIT OF GT SHUNNER FELL (MAP 59) FROM HARDRAW (MAP 56)

2 HRS–2 HRS 30 MINS FROM SUMMIT OF GT SHUNNER FELL (MAP 59) TO HARDRAW (MAP 56)

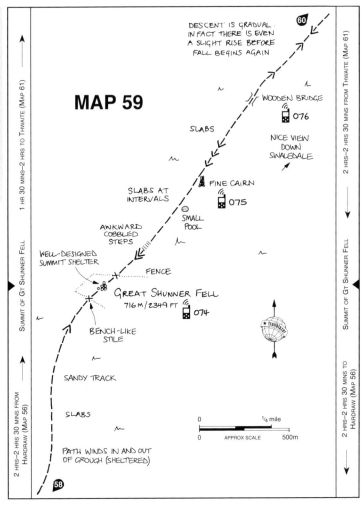

**MAP 59**

DESCENT IS GRADUAL.
IN FACT THERE IS EVEN
A SLIGHT RISE BEFORE
FALL BEGINS AGAIN

WOODEN BRIDGE
076

NICE VIEW
DOWN
SWALEDALE

SLABS

FINE CAIRN
075

SLABS AT
INTERVALS

SMALL
POOL

AWKWARD
COBBLED
STEPS

WELL-DESIGNED
SUMMIT SHELTER

FENCE

GREAT SHUNNER FELL
716 M / 2349 FT    074

★ trailblazer

BENCH-LIKE
STILE

SANDY TRACK

SLABS

0                    ¼ mile
0        APPROX SCALE        500m

PATH WINDS IN AND OUT
OF GROUGH (SHELTERED)

*Left margin:* ROUTE GUIDE AND MAPS  |  1 HR 30 MINS–2 HRS TO THWAITE (MAP 61)  |  SUMMIT OF GT SHUNNER FELL  |  2 HRS–2 HRS 30 MINS FROM HARDRAW (MAP 56)

*Right margin:* 2 HRS–2 HRS 30 MINS FROM THWAITE (MAP 61)  |  SUMMIT OF GT SHUNNER FELL  |  2 HRS–2 HRS 30 MINS TO HARDRAW (MAP 56)

**(Opposite – C1)** The glaciated valley known as High Cup (see p194) is one of the most impressive sights on the walk. © Chris Scott.

(See p161 for captions for **following colour pages**)

C1

C5

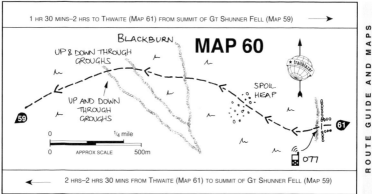

1 HR 30 MINS–2 HRS TO THWAITE (MAP 61) FROM SUMMIT OF GT SHUNNER FELL (MAP 59) ⟶

BLACKBURN

**MAP 60**

UP & DOWN THROUGH GROUGHS

UP AND DOWN THROUGH GROUGHS

★ trailblazer

SPOIL HEAP

**59**

**61**

0        ¼ mile
0    APPROX SCALE    500m

077

2 HRS–2 HRS 30 MINS FROM THWAITE (MAP 61) TO SUMMIT OF GT SHUNNER FELL (MAP 59) ⟵

ROUTE GUIDE AND MAPS

## ❑ Black (and red) grouse

Pennine Way walkers are unlikely to get as far as Bowes without seeing or at least hearing red grouse. Their distinctive nagging croak which has been likened to the warning 'go-back, go-back, go-back' is a familiar sound on wild heather moors, as familiar as the lonely bubbling call of the curlew or the insistent pipe of the golden plover.

While the red grouse is the primary target of many a landowner's gun, the black grouse is a different matter altogether. Shot almost to extinction across most of Northern England, it is now only plentiful in the Scottish hills where the vast space and better cover have enabled it to survive in some numbers. In the Pennines only a few remain and these are carefully protected by gamekeepers and conservationists alike. Most keepers now appreciate the bird for its own sake and, like their changing attitudes to birds of prey, are simply glad it has survived.

In Baldersdale black grouse have been seen near the former YHA hostel where their curious courtship ritual was described to me by the warden. The hen birds line up on the branch of a tree like spectators grabbing the best seats in the stands to watch the cock birds perform their 'lek', a display acted out on a piece of prepared ground on which they parade, each trying to outdo the others in their strutting and posturing. Their lyre-shaped tail feathers are fanned out in a magnificent demonstration to win the hens' affections.

(**Opposite – C5**) **Top**: Britain's highest pub, the Tan Hill Inn (see p164), stands at an altitude of 1732ft (528m). **Bottom**: Black faced sheep – familiar companions on the Way.

**Previous colour pages**
● **C2 (Top)** The Way at Colden near Hebden Bridge; and high on the horizon Stoodley Pike (**bottom left**, p103). (**Middle**): The Parsonage (see p115) where the Brontës lived and wrote is now a museum that's well worth the detour to Haworth. On the Way you'll pass the ruins of Top Withins (see p113), said to be the inspiration for Emily Brontë's *Wuthering Heights*. (**Bottom right**): The cobbled streets of Haworth are normally thronged with tourists.
● **C3 (Top left)**: Malham and Malham Cove (see p134-5), from the south. (**Middle left**): Entering the valley of Watlowes (see p137), heading north. (**Bottom left**): Watlowes, looking south. (**Right**): View towards Malham from the limestone pavement above Malham Cove.
● **C4 (Left)**: High Force (see p185). (**Right top**): Knock Old Man (p200) on Knock Fell above Dufton. (**Middle and bottom**): Greg's Hut (p201), the bothy near the summit of Cross Fell.

❏ **Kentucky Fried Turkeys versus Tan Hill Inn**
England's highest pub hit the news in 2007 when web-trawling lawyers behind the Kentucky Fried Chicken fast-food chain set out to sue the Tan Hill Inn for daring to use KFC's phrase 'Family Feast' on the online menu for their annual Christmas dinner. Googling the forbidden words results in over two million hits but the pub's owners were sternly informed that 'Family Feast' is a registered trademark of Kentucky Fried Chicken (Great Britain) Limited.

Arriving in April and signed by a 'Mr Giles Pratt' the owner assumed it was an overdue April Fool joke and initially ignored it. When the threats continued the owner rang her solicitors and was advised that the claim was indeed no joke. Of course the owner stood by her guns and local solicitors offered to take on the case for free.

A storm of media interest ensued and the pub's website crashed while jokes about the nutritional value of KFC's fare did the rounds. The KFC lawyers merely succeeded in making turkeys of themselves and the claim was withdrawn as they conceded a once-a-year traditional roast turkey Christmas dinner at a moorland pub could not be confused with a cardboard bucket full of fried chicken and chips with coleslaw and a fizzy drink.

## TAN HILL TO MIDDLETON-IN-TEESDALE          MAPS 64-72

### Route overview
Having spent a memorable night at Tan Hill Inn, today's **17-mile (25km, 7¼-9¾hrs)** day has the distinct novelty of starting off downhill. It's something you may appreciate if the Tan Hill Experience has hit you hard.

Downhill it may be but you're descending into the sheep-swallowing wastes of **Sleightholme Moor** (Map 65) and as you near Frumming Beck you may find your still-waking limbs forced into grough-hopping lunges over the peaty trenches until the path thankfully gains the better-drained northern bank. White-topped posts mark the way intermittently and all passes agreeably with the brook trickling by your side until you bridge it and take to a road which leads down to Sleightholme Farm. It's a stage of the walk during which the continuing peels of lapwing and curlew may quite possibly begin to get on your wick.

Having re-crossed Sleightholme Beck, you clamber up and over **Wytham Moor** (Map 67) and (if you don't take the Bowes Variant, see below) drop down to the River Greta at **God's Bridge**.

**Accommodation options** on *both* routes are rather lean until Middleton, so if you're not camping in the wilds, make sure you book ahead.

> **Bowes Variant** At Trough Heads Farm (Map 67; GPS waypoint 087, see p261) a branch of the Pennine Way heads off east for **8½ miles via Bowes** (see maps 67a-c) to reconverge at Baldersdale (totalling three extra miles). The Bowes Loop came about as an alternative route for those seeking a bed or a meal. However, there's not a lot at Bowes (see opposite) so you should phone ahead to make sure the pub/campsite are open. It's 1¼-1¾hrs from Bowes to the point where the paths converge at Baldersdale (Map 69, p177).
>
> This longer route has noticeably **fewer ups and downs** and is a little more scenically appealing, although route finding can have a few irritating moments.

Here at the Stainmore Gap you scurry under the A66 (Map 68) via a litter-strewn underpass. The roar of the traffic reminds you of the M62 back in the far distant past, before you'd earned your Pennine Way spurs. Depending on the wind, it takes till well after **Ravock Castle** (merely a scattering of stones) on top of Bowes Moor before you're finally free of the din.

You now drop into, and climb stiffly out of, Sled Dale over **Race Yate** (Map 69) to drop back among the reservoirs which now fill **Baldersdale**. Pat yourself on the back; this is the **halfway mark** on the Pennine Way. Yes, you're *only* halfway.

You may choose to overnight here; if so Clove Lodge (see below) is your only option. For those as yet unsatiated, it's six or seven miles to Middleton, including a hill climb over to **Lunedale** (Map 71) and another over **Harter Fell**; this may well dampen any excess energy you had stored up for the town, though it invites you in with a good range of accommodation, eating and re-provisioning options.

### Route-finding trouble spots
Irregular white-topped posts light the way across Sleightholme Moor; in thick mist a GPS may help. From there over the A66 to Baldersdale is clear, with the only other hitch – fair weather or foul – being the successful navigation over the walls and pastures leading up and around the shoulder of Harter Fell. The Bowes loop too has its confusions, mostly across the discreetly signed field.

### BOWES [Map 67a, p173]
There is little to do here but a stroll to the pub could include a look at the **churchyard** where Dickens found inspiration for the character of Smike in *Nicholas Nickleby*. See p26 for details of the farming show held here in September. **Bowes Castle** is a Norman keep dating from around 1087. It's managed by English Heritage and you are free to wander around the ruins at any time.

The **Ancient Unicorn** (☎ 01833-628321, 🖳 www.ancient-unicorn.com; 4T or D en suite/1F shared facilities, bath available) has great bar and restaurant meals (food served summer Tue-Sun noon-2pm, Tue-Sat 6-9pm, Sun & Mon 7-9pm; winter weekends only noon-2pm, Sun-Thur 7-9pm, Fri & Sat 6-9pm) and offers B&B for £35pp. Dogs are welcome as long as they don't climb on the beds.

**Campers** can pitch at *West End Farm* (☎ 01833-628239; Easter to Oct) for £3.50pp but the noise from the A66 may be a distraction. Toilet and shower facilities are available.

Central Coaches **bus** No 72 goes to Barnard Castle where other services connect with Darlington which is on the London to Edinburgh line (see transport map and table, pp45-50).

### BALDERSDALE [Map 69, p177]
These days all that's left in Baldersdale for the weary Pennine wayfarer is *Clove Lodge* (☎ 01833-650030, 🖳 www.clovelodge.co.uk; 1D/1T, en suite, bath available). In addition to the accommodation in the house they have a very cosy four-bed holiday cottage (1D/1D or T, en suite, bath available) though this is sometimes booked as a weekly let. B&B costs £35pp (£40 single occupancy). Dogs are allowed if you have phoned in advance. They also offer camping for £5pp and have a **camping barn** (£15pp) which sleeps up to six people and has a kitchen and shower room. An evening meal costs around £18, breakfast for £7 (for campers) and it's £5 for a packed lunch; book meals in advance. It's not a bad place to lay up for a rest day at the halfway point.

Alston Road Garage's **bus** service to/from Middleton calls here if prebooked (see public transport map and table, pp45-50).

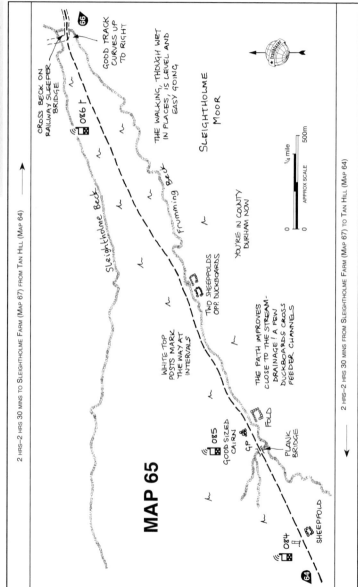

2 HRS–2 HRS 30 MINS TO SLEIGHTHOLME FARM (MAP 67) FROM TAN HILL (MAP 64)

**MAP 65**

CROSS BECK ON RAILWAY SLEEPER BRIDGE

GOOD TRACK CURVES UP TO RIGHT

THE WALKING, THOUGH WET IN PLACES, IS LEVEL AND EASY GOING

SLEIGHTHOLME MOOR

Sleightholme Beck

Frumming Beck

YOU'RE IN COUNTY DURHAM NOW

TWO SHEEPFOLDS OPP. DUCKBOARDS

WHITE TOP POSTS MARK THE WAY AT INTERVALS

THE PATH IMPROVES CLOSE TO THE STREAM-DRAINAGE! A FEW DUCKBOARDS CROSS FEEDER CHANNELS

FOLD

GP

PLANK BRIDGE

GOOD SIZED CAIRN

085

084

SHEEPFOLD

086

066

064

¼ mile

500m

0

0

APPROX SCALE

2 HRS–2 HRS 30 MINS FROM SLEIGHTHOLME FARM (MAP 67) TO TAN HILL (MAP 64)

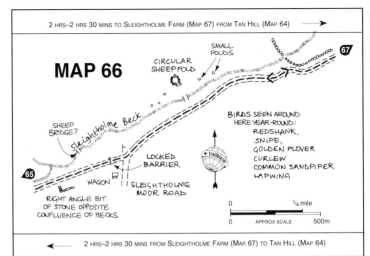

2 HRS–2 HRS 30 MINS TO SLEIGHTHOLME FARM (MAP 67) FROM TAN HILL (MAP 64) →

**MAP 66**

SMALL FOLDS

CIRCULAR SHEEP FOLD

67

Sleightholme Beck

SHEEP BRIDGE?

BIRDS SEEN AROUND HERE YEAR-ROUND:
REDSHANK,
SNIPE,
GOLDEN PLOVER
CURLEW
COMMON SANDPIPER
LAPWING

★ trailblazer

LOCKED BARRIER

65

WAGON

SLEIGHTHOLME MOOR ROAD

RIGHT ANGLE BIT OF STONE OPPOSITE CONFLUENCE OF BECKS

0          ¼ mile
0    APPROX SCALE    500m

← 2 HRS–2 HRS 30 MINS FROM SLEIGHTHOLME FARM (MAP 67) TO TAN HILL (MAP 64)

## ❏ Hannah Hauxwell

Right on the edge of Blackton Reservoir beside the Pennine Way stands the farm of Low Birk Hat (see Map 69, p177), home for many years to a remarkable woman. Hannah Hauxwell came to public attention through a number of television programmes and books (both formats are still available) telling the story of the life of someone living at subsistence level in Baldersdale as recently as the 1970s. With a cow which had one calf a year, she allowed herself £250 a year for living expenses, without electricity or gas, surviving the harsh winters by the simple expedient of putting on another coat.

Later Hannah Hauxwell became famous for her courage and her natural understanding of the world and its follies when she travelled for the cameras recording her impressions of cities around the world. Her curiosity and common-sense enabled her to put her finger on the unusual and get pleasure from the commonplace.

Now retired and living more comfortably nearby, Hannah will be long remembered by those who followed her adventures. Her farm where at one time her father alone supported a family of seven, both sets of parents, himself, his wife and their daughter, has since been much modernised and a glimpse over the wall reveals merely an echo of the hard livelihood it once accommodated. See also box p189.

**Hannah's Meadow** (see Map 70) Part of the legacy of Hannah Hauxwell has been the preservation of her farmland which has been given the status of a study area for meadow grasses and wild flowers.

Purchased by Durham Wildlife Trust in 1988, the site was later designated a Site of Special Scientific Interest (see p62) qualifying by having 23 of the 47 species of rare and characteristic plants listed by Natural England. The meadows were never ploughed, being cut for hay in August and thereafter grazed by cows resulting in herb-rich meadows. Numerous kinds of birds are visitors to the meadows and no fewer than 16 kinds of dung-beetle have been identified.

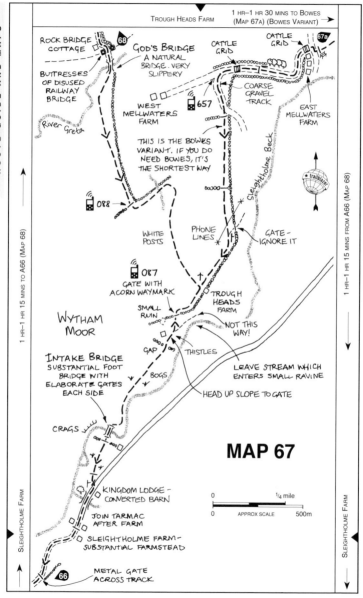

TROUGH HEADS FARM

1 HR–1 HR 30 MINS TO BOWES
(MAP 67A) (BOWES VARIANT)

ROCK BRIDGE COTTAGE

GOD'S BRIDGE
A NATURAL BRIDGE. VERY SLIPPERY

CATTLE GRID

CATTLE GRID

67A

BUTTRESSES OF DISUSED RAILWAY BRIDGE

COARSE GRAVEL TRACK

River Greta

WEST MELLWATERS FARM

657

EAST MELLWATERS FARM

THIS IS THE BOWES VARIANT. IF YOU DO NEED BOWES, IT'S THE SHORTEST WAY

Sleightholme Beck

088

WHITE POSTS

PHONE LINES

GATE – IGNORE IT

087

GATE WITH ACORN WAYMARK

WYTHAM MOOR

SMALL RUIN

TROUGH HEADS FARM

NOT THIS WAY!

GAP

THISTLES

LEAVE STREAM WHICH ENTERS SMALL RAVINE

INTAKE BRIDGE
SUBSTANTIAL FOOT BRIDGE WITH ELABORATE GATES EACH SIDE

BOGS

HEAD UP SLOPE TO GATE

CRAGS

**MAP 67**

KINGDOM LODGE – CONVERTED BARN

JOIN TARMAC AFTER FARM

SLEIGHTHOLME FARM – SUBSTANTIAL FARMSTEAD

METAL GATE ACROSS TRACK

66

0        ¼ mile
0                    500m
APPROX SCALE

★ trailblazer

ROUTE GUIDE AND MAPS

1 HR–1 HR 15 MINS TO A66 (MAP 68)

1 HR–1 HR 15 MINS FROM A66 (MAP 68)

SLEIGHTHOLME FARM

SLEIGHTHOLME FARM

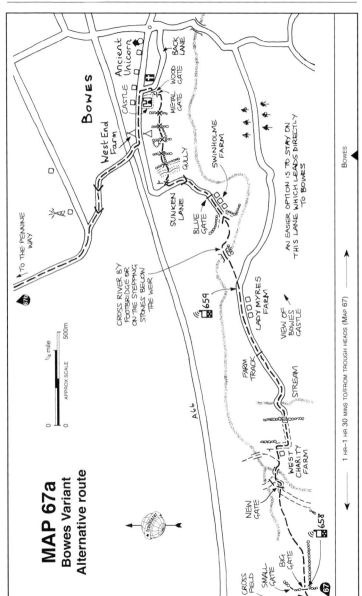

# MAP 67a
## Bowes Variant route

¼ mile

500m

APPROX SCALE

Bowes

West End Farm

TO THE PENNINE WAY

A66

CASTLE

Ancient Unicorn

BACK LANE

WOOD GATE

METAL GATE

GULLY

SUNKEN LANE

BLUE GATE

SWINHOLME FARM

AN EASIER OPTION IS TO STAY ON THIS LANE WHICH LEADS DIRECTLY TO BOWES

CROSS RIVER BY FOOTBRIDGE OR ON THE STEPPING STONES BELOW THE WEIR

659

LADY MYRES FARM

VIEW OF BOWES CASTLE

FARM TRACK

STREAM

WEST CHARITY FARM

NEW GATE

BIG GATE

SMALL GATE

CROSS FIELD

658

67

670

1 HR–1 HR 30 MINS TO/FROM TROUGH HEADS (MAP 67)

BOWES

1 HR 15 MINS–1 HR 45 MINS FROM BOWES (MAP 67A) TO BALDERSDALE (MAP 69)

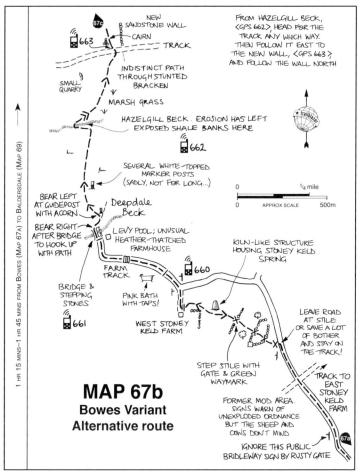

NEW SANDSTONE WALL

CAIRN

TRACK

663

SMALL QUARRY

INDISTINCT PATH THROUGH STUNTED BRACKEN

MARSH GRASS

FROM HAZELGILL BECK, <GPS 662>, HEAD FOR THE TRACK ANY WHICH WAY. THEN FOLLOW IT EAST TO THE NEW WALL, <GPS 663> AND FOLLOW THE WALL NORTH

HAZELGILL BECK. EROSION HAS LEFT EXPOSED SHALE BANKS HERE

662

trailblazer

SEVERAL WHITE-TOPPED MARKER POSTS (SADLY, NOT FOR LONG...)

0                    ¼ mile

0          APPROX SCALE          500m

BEAR LEFT AT GUIDEPOST WITH ACORN

Deepdale Beck

BEAR RIGHT AFTER BRIDGE TO HOOK UP WITH PATH

LEVY POOL; UNUSUAL HEATHER-THATCHED FARMHOUSE

FARM TRACK

BRIDGE & STEPPING STONES

661

PINK BATH WITH TAPS!

WEST STONEY KELD FARM

660

KILN-LIKE STRUCTURE HOUSING STONEY KELD SPRING

LEAVE ROAD AT STILE OR SAVE A LOT OF BOTHER AND STAY ON THE TRACK!

STEP STILE WITH GATE & GREEN WAYMARK

TRACK TO EAST STONEY KELD FARM

## MAP 67b
## Bowes Variant
## Alternative route

FORMER MOD AREA. SIGNS WARN OF UNEXPLODED ORDNANCE BUT THE SHEEP AND COWS DON'T MIND

IGNORE THIS PUBLIC BRIDLEWAY SIGN BY RUSTY GATE

67a

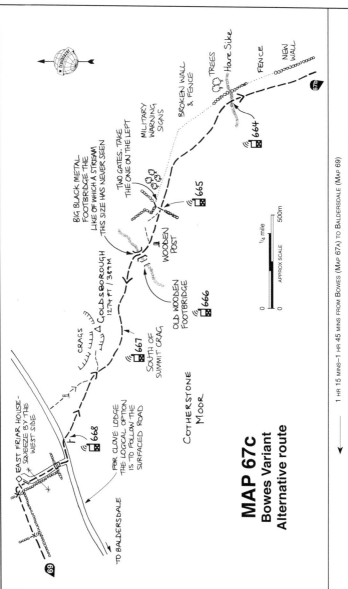

**MAP 67c**
**Bowes Variant**
**Alternative route**

1 HR 15 MINS–1 HR 45 MINS FROM BOWES (MAP 67A) TO BALDERSDALE (MAP 69)

ROUTE GUIDE AND MAPS

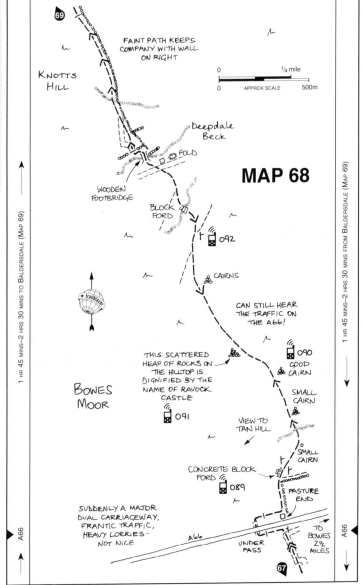

69

FAINT PATH KEEPS
COMPANY WITH WALL
ON RIGHT

KNOTTS
HILL

Deepdale
Beck

FOLD

**MAP 68**

0        ¼ mile

0     APPROX SCALE      500m

WOODEN
FOOTBRIDGE

BLOCK
FORD

092

CAIRNS

1 HR 45 MINS–2 HRS 30 MINS TO BALDERSDALE (MAP 69)

CAN STILL HEAR
THE TRAFFIC ON
THE A66!

THIS SCATTERED
HEAP OF ROCKS ON
THE HILLTOP IS
DIGNIFIED BY THE
NAME OF RAVOCK
CASTLE

090
GOOD
CAIRN

SMALL
CAIRN

BOWES
MOOR

091

VIEW TO
TAN HILL

SMALL
CAIRN

CONCRETE BLOCK
FORD

089

PASTURE
END

SUDDENLY A MAJOR
DUAL CARRIAGEWAY,
FRANTIC TRAFFIC,
HEAVY LORRIES –
NOT NICE

A66

UNDER
PASS

TO
BOWES
2½
MILES

67

1 HR 45 MINS–2 HRS 30 MINS FROM BALDERSDALE (MAP 69)

A66

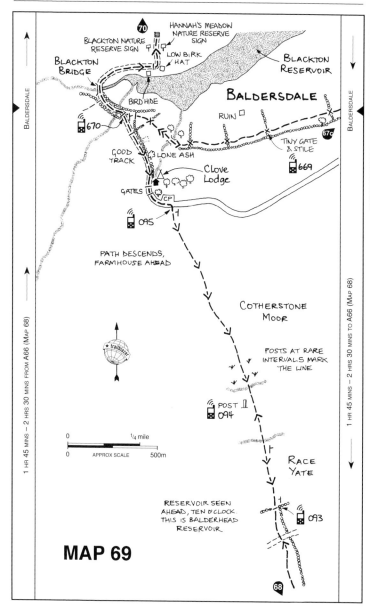

**MAP 69**

BALDERSDALE

HANNAH'S MEADOW NATURE RESERVE SIGN

BLACKTON NATURE RESERVE SIGN

BLACKTON BRIDGE

LOW BIRK HAT

BLACKTON RESERVOIR

BALDERSDALE

670

BIRD HIDE

RUIN

67c

GOOD TRACK

LONE ASH

TINY GATE & STILE

669

Clove Lodge

GATES

CP

095

PATH DESCENDS, FARMHOUSE AHEAD

COTHERSTONE MOOR

POSTS AT RARE INTERVALS MARK THE LINE

POST
094

RACE YATE

0       1/4 mile
0       APPROX SCALE      500m

★ trailblazer

RESERVOIR SEEN AHEAD, TEN O'CLOCK. THIS IS BALDERHEAD RESERVOIR

093

68

1 HR 45 MINS – 2 HRS 30 MINS FROM A66 (MAP 68)

1 HR 45 MINS – 2 HRS 30 MINS TO A66 (MAP 68)

70

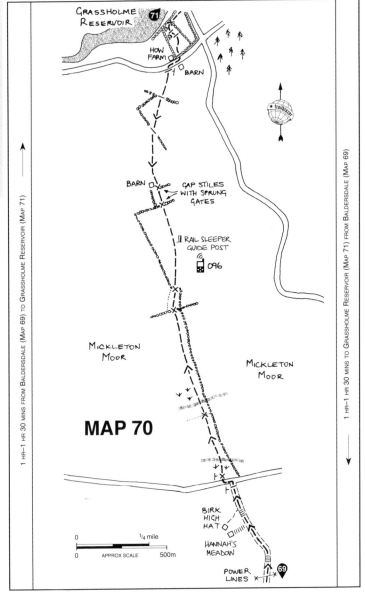

GRASSHOLME RESERVOIR **71**

HOW FARM

BARN

BARN

GAP STILES WITH SPRUNG GATES

RAIL SLEEPER GUIDE POST

096

MICKLETON MOOR

MICKLETON MOOR

**MAP 70**

BIRK HIGH HAT

HANNAH'S MEADOW

POWER LINES **69**

0    ¼ mile

0    APPROX SCALE    500m

1 HR–1 HR 30 MINS FROM BALDERSDALE (MAP 69) TO GRASSHOLME RESERVOIR (MAP 71)

1 HR–1 HR 30 MINS TO GRASSHOLME RESERVOIR (MAP 71) FROM BALDERSDALE (MAP 69)

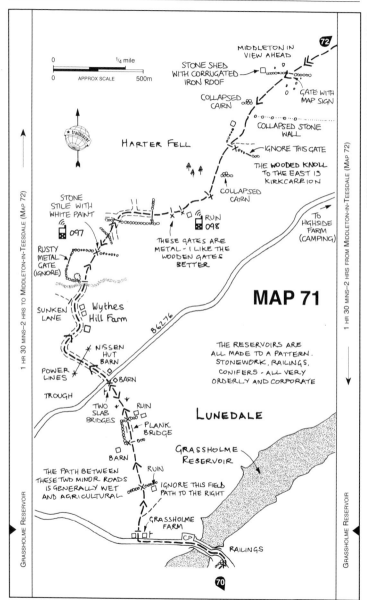

72

MIDDLETON IN VIEW AHEAD

STONE SHED WITH CORRUGATED IRON ROOF

GATE WITH MAP SIGN

COLLAPSED CAIRN

COLLAPSED STONE WALL

IGNORE THIS GATE

HARTER FELL

THE WOODED KNOLL TO THE EAST IS KIRKCARRION

COLLAPSED CAIRN

0 ¼ mile
0   APPROX SCALE   500m

trailblazer

STONE STILE WITH WHITE PAINT

097

098 RUIN

THESE GATES ARE METAL - I LIKE THE WOODEN GATES BETTER

TO HIGHSIDE FARM (CAMPING)

RUSTY METAL GATE (IGNORE)

SUNKEN LANE

Wythes Hill Farm

B6276

MAP 71

NISSEN HUT BARN

POWER LINES

TROUGH

BARN

THE RESERVOIRS ARE ALL MADE TO A PATTERN. STONEWORK, RAILINGS, CONIFERS - ALL VERY ORDERLY AND CORPORATE

LUNEDALE

TWO SLAB BRIDGES

RUIN

PLANK BRIDGE

GRASSHOLME RESERVOIR

BARN

THE PATH BETWEEN THESE TWO MINOR ROADS IS GENERALLY WET AND AGRICULTURAL

RUIN

IGNORE THIS FIELD PATH TO THE RIGHT

GRASSHOLME FARM

CP

RAILINGS

70

1 HR 30 MINS–2 HRS TO MIDDLETON-IN-TEESDALE (MAP 72)

1 HR 30 MINS–2 HRS FROM MIDDLETON-IN-TEESDALE (MAP 72)

GRASSHOLME RESERVOIR

GRASSHOLME RESERVOIR

## LUNEDALE    [Map 71, p179]

There's not much for walkers in Lunedale aside from scattered homesteads and farms but two miles (3km) along the B6276 (ie a stone's throw from Middleton itself by road) is the **campsite** at *Highside Farm* (off Map 71; ☎ 01833-640135, 💻 www .highsidefarm.co.uk; May-Sep), Bow Bank.

Pitching at the small site costs £8pp with showers, toilet and washing facilities and they can do you a breakfast in the morning if booked in advance.

Alston Road Garage's No 73 **bus** service calls here if prebooked; see public transport map and table, pp45-50 for details.

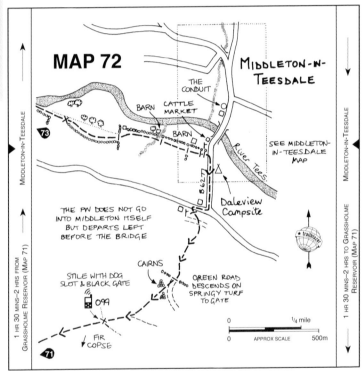

MAP 72

MIDDLETON-IN-TEESDALE

THE CONDUIT

BARN  CATTLE MARKET

BARN

River Tees.

SEE MIDDLETON-IN-TEESDALE MAP

Daleview Campsite

★ trailblazer

THE PW DOES NOT GO INTO MIDDLETON ITSELF BUT DEPARTS LEFT BEFORE THE BRIDGE

CAIRNS

GREEN ROAD DESCENDS ON SPRINGY TURF TO GATE

STILE WITH DOG SLOT & BLACK GATE

FIR COPSE

1 HR 30 MINS–2 HRS FROM GRASSHOLME RESERVOIR (MAP 71)

MIDDLETON-IN-TEESDALE

MIDDLETON-IN-TEESDALE

1 HR 30 MINS–2 HRS TO GRASSHOLME RESERVOIR (MAP 71)

0        ¼ mile
0    APPROX SCALE    500m

## MIDDLETON-IN-TEESDALE
### [Map 72a]

On the banks of the River Tees, this small town thrived during the 19th century when the now defunct lead-mining industry was in its heyday. It's mostly laid out along one street, with handsome architecture interspersed with a few quirky buildings.

See p25 for details of the carnival held here in July.

### Services

The **tourist information centre** (☎ 01833-641001, 💻 tic@middletonplus.myzen. co.uk; daily 10am-1pm), 10 Market Place, sells some interesting publications on the North Pennines but also has free information on the area and does accommodation booking (see box p13). For groceries try either the Co-op **supermarket** (daily 8am-

10pm), or R&L Armitage **off-licence and general store**.

There is also a **pharmacy**, a **post office** and Winter's **gear shop**, which stocks most camping fuels as well as boots and general walking kit. The Barclays Bank here has a **cash machine**. Early closing day for the town is Wednesday.

## Transport

[See also pp45-50] The nearest **train** station is Darlington, 25 miles (40km) away. To get there take Arriva's No 95/96 **bus** to Barnard Castle and change there for the No 75/76 service to Darlington. Alston Road Garage offers a bus service (No 73) to Langdon Beck and other villages in the area.

## Where to stay

Unless they stage the next G8 summit here there is plenty of choice. The most convenient campsite is *Daleview Caravan Park and Camp Site* (☎ 01833-640233, 🖳 www.daleviewcaravanpark.co.uk; Mar-Oct) which you pass on your way into town. They accept hikers (not family tents) and charge £4pp including a shower; there's a bar which also does food (Sat and Sun noon-2pm, daily 7-9pm).

Don't be put off by the grand appearance of *Grove Lodge* (☎ 01833-640798, 🖳 www .grovelodgeteesdale.co.uk; 2T/1D/1D, T or F, all en suite, bath available) just outside the town and with great views back to Kirkcarrion and Harter Fell; they welcome walkers as long as you don't shake yourself off in the hallway like a wet dog. The rooms upstairs cost £52 single occupancy or £82 for two sharing. The garden rooms (1T or D with kitchen/1T, both en suite with bath) can be separate or connected; dogs are welcome here if booked in advance. They can provide an evening meal (from an à la carte menu with dishes costing from £6.50) and a packed lunch (£5).

*Brunswick House* (☎ 01833-640393, 🖳 www.brunswickhouse.net; 2T/3D, en suite, bath available) is more central and their rooms cost £75 (£45 for single occupancy). They also do as good an evening meal (£22.50; at 7.30pm) as anywhere else in town and have a bar and

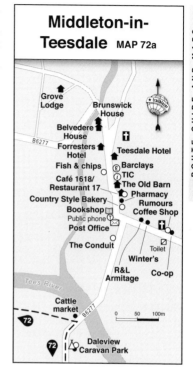

**Middleton-in-Teesdale** MAP 72a

Grove Lodge
Brunswick House
Belvedere House
B6277
Forresters Hotel
Teesdale Hotel
Fish & chips
Barclays
TIC
Café 1618/ Restaurant 17
The Old Barn
Pharmacy
Country Style Bakery
Rumours Coffee Shop
Bookshop
Public phone
Post Office
The Conduit
Toilet
Winter's
R&L Armitage
Co-op
Tees River
Cattle market
B6277
72
0  50  100m
72
Daleview Caravan Park

ROUTE GUIDE AND MAPS

can provide a packed lunch (£5). Next door is *Belvedere House* (☎ 01833-640884, 🖳 www.thecoachhouse.net; 1T/2D, all en suite, bath available) where a room for two sharing costs £55 (single occupancy £35). Dogs welcome, book in advance.

*The Forresters Hotel* (☎ 01833-641435, 🖳 www.forrestersmiddleton.co.uk; 2S/1D/5D or T; all en suite, bath available) is a flashy new place with a modern bar; all chrome fittings and shiny floors. They do B&B for £35pp based on two sharing or £45 for single occupancy. Dogs are welcome if they are clean.

For a change of style head over the road to *Teesdale Hotel* (☎ 01833-640264, 🖳 www.teesdalehotel.co.uk; 4S/4T/6D/1F, all en suite, bath available) an old stone-built coaching inn charging £70-80 and

£40-45 for a single. Dogs (£5) can stay if booked in advance.

*The Old Barn* (☎ 01833-640258, 🖳 www.theoldbarn-teesdale.co.uk; 2D/1T, all en suite) is a converted stone barn in the centre of town. This walker-friendly place charges £56 or £36 for single occupancy and can prepare a packed lunch (from £3.50). Just down the road is *Café 1618* (☎ 01833-640300; 3D, all en suite) which has two rooms in the house and one in a separate cottage; B&B costs £65-85 (single occupancy £55-70). Well-behaved dogs are welcome.

### Where to eat and drink

Closest to the Way is *The Conduit* (☎ 01833-640717; summer Mon-Sat 9am-5pm, Sun 10am-5pm, to 4pm in winter, closed Wed) where you can get an all-day breakfast for £5.70; they also serve lasagne, meat pies, home-made cakes and panini. Food is available to take away or eat in.

There are a couple more cafés with outside terraces: *Rumours Coffee Shop* with toasties from £3.95 and *Café 1618* (see Where to stay; Tue-Wed 10am-7pm, Thur-Sat till 11pm, Sun till 8pm; winter hours depend on demand; they may also open on Mondays in summer) which does all-day breakfasts for £7.25. They also own *Restaurant No 17* (daily 6-10pm) which opened in December 2010 and does not accept children aged under 12.

You can get sandwiches (from £3.30) at the *Country Style Bakery*. Opposite the TIC is a **fish and chips** shop (Tue-Sat).

The menu at *The Forresters* (see Where to stay; food served daily 11am-10pm) changes regularly but is likely to include sandwiches (from £4.25) as well as dishes such as beetroot risotto (£11.95). *Teesdale Hotel* (see Where to stay; daily noon-2.30pm, Mon-Fri 7-8.45pm, Sat & Sun 6.30-8.45pm) where a liver and bacon casserole costs £10.

## MIDDLETON-IN-TEESDALE TO DUFTON　　　MAPS 72-83

### Route overview

A thought-provoking **21 miles (32km, 9¾-10¾hrs)** it may well be, back over the Pennines to Dufton, but if fitness, weather and daylight are all combined in a serendipitous trinity, you're in for one of the best days between Edale and Kirk Yetholm. A gradual climb with barely a thigh-burning ascent nor a knee-popping ending, the wilderness evolves steadily as you trace the River Tees close to its source. Then, as you cross the watershed, the walk draws to an end with one of the Seven Wonders of the Pennine Way.

The riverside walk out of Middleton starts off in a fairly tame, dog-on-a-lead fashion with tedious stiles and vision-hampering woodland, but as you continue upstream, passing Holwick (Map 74) as you go, the spectacular effect of the river manifests itself as it cascades over unyielding dolerite sills to create the waterfalls of **Low Force** (Map 75) soon followed by the mesmerising powerhouse of High Force.

**High Force** (see box p185) may be on the souvenir spoon and tea towel circuit (at least from the PW side of the river you don't have to pay £1 to see it), but beyond the wild fell country of the North Pennines takes the path to a new dimension. Soon you cross the Tees at **Cronkley Bridge** (Map 77) where your day can end among the scattered, whitewashed communities of **Forest-in-Teesdale** or **Langdon Beck**. But who can resist recrossing the Tees and heading into the wilds of Upper Teesdale as it takes on the character of an upland Scottish burn. As the valley envelops you, at times you'll find yourself squeezed almost into the river itself as a trio of ankle-twisting rockfalls edge you awkwardly towards the running waters.

With those hurdles behind you, round a corner and you come face-to-face with the splendidly named **Cauldron Snout** (Map 78) churning down a series of jumbled rocks. Scrambling up alongside, the roar of the foaming torrent drowns out all other sounds. Now beneath the dam wall of **Cow Green Reservoir** which feeds the Snout, the wilderness is temporarily muted as you scoot along the access road to the isolated farmstead of **Birkdale** (Map 79; see box p189). But once through the farmyard you're out on the open moors again, crossing **Grain Beck** and facing the only mildly noteworthy climb of the day to a crest alongside Rasp Hill and its long abandoned mine workings.

Ahead of you **Maize Beck** (Maps 79 & 80) and its low-shelved cascades (waterfalls) glisten in the late afternoon sun and after a few soggy placements you join the stream and reach the **footbridge** raised tellingly high above the beck (GPS waypoint 105/671, see p262; not on all maps and *not* the one referred to on the wooden signs at Cow Green and below High Cup Nick). Before the bridge the Pennine Way crossed the stream hereabouts on stepping stones to follow the direct and well-marked path on the south side which leads straight to the rim of High Cup. For details on the now obsolete 'flood route' which stays north of the beck see p193. Whichever way you approach it (the southern route being far more dramatic), it's no exaggeration to proclaim that the colossal glacier-carved abyss of **High Cup** (Map 81) is a spectacular climax to a brilliant day. If the wind gusting up the valley is not too bad, sit back a while and take it all in; the remaining four miles along miners' tracks are straightforward, following the north rim of the valley with the silvery thread of High Cup Gill far below. It all

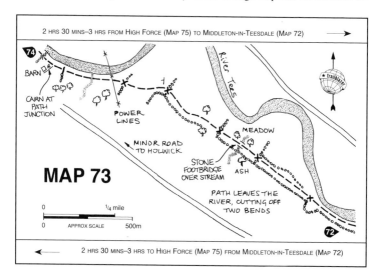

2 HRS 30 MINS–3 HRS FROM HIGH FORCE (MAP 75) TO MIDDLETON-IN-TEESDALE (MAP 72) ⟶

**74**

BARN

CAIRN AT PATH JUNCTION

POWER LINES

MINOR ROAD TO HOLWICK

**MAP 73**

River Tees

trailblazer

MEADOW

STONE FOOTBRIDGE OVER STREAM   ASH

PATH LEAVES THE RIVER, CUTTING OFF TWO BENDS

0           ¼ mile

0        APPROX SCALE        500m

**72**

⟵ 2 HRS 30 MINS–3 HRS TO HIGH FORCE (MAP 75) FROM MIDDLETON-IN-TEESDALE (MAP 72)

ends at the tidy village of **Dufton** (Map 83), a quintessential English hamlet with the inviting Stag Inn facing the hostel across the village green; one of the more delightful places to end a Pennine day.

## Route-finding trouble spots

With clear paths, farms tracks as well as water courses large and small running alongside you throughout this stage, it's hard to lose track of the path, even in poor visibility. The exception would be going against the grain and taking the old 'flood escape route' via Maize Beck Gorge (see p193) mentioned above. In misty or very wet conditions it's just not worth it.

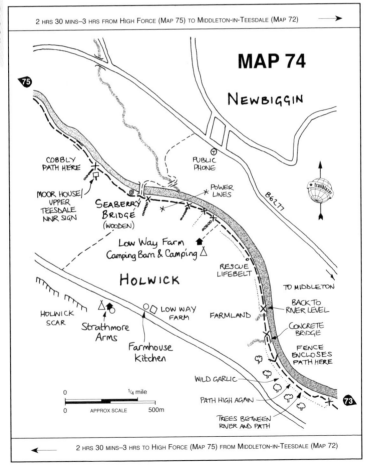

2 HRS 30 MINS–3 HRS FROM HIGH FORCE (MAP 75) TO MIDDLETON-IN-TEESDALE (MAP 72) →

MAP 74

NEWBIGGIN

COBBLY PATH HERE

MOOR HOUSE/ UPPER TEESDALE NNR SIGN

PUBLIC PHONE

SEABERRY BRIDGE (WOODEN)

POWER LINES

B6277

Low Way Farm Camping Barn & Camping △

HOLWICK

RESCUE LIFEBELT

TO MIDDLETON

BACK TO RIVER LEVEL

HOLWICK SCAR

Strathmore Arms

LOW WAY FARM

FARMLAND

CONCRETE BRIDGE

Farmhouse Kitchen

FENCE ENCLOSES PATH HERE

WILD GARLIC

PATH HIGH AGAIN

TREES BETWEEN RIVER AND PATH

0       ¼ mile
0    APPROX SCALE    500m

trailblazer

2 HRS 30 MINS–3 HRS TO HIGH FORCE (MAP 75) FROM MIDDLETON-IN-TEESDALE (MAP 72) ←

## HOLWICK [Map 74]

*Low Way Farm* (☎ 01629-592700) is run by the YHA and offers basic **camping** for £3pp and **camping barn** accommodation in two barns (one sleeping 20 and the other 8) for £7pp. Booking is recommended as the barns are sometimes taken by groups for sole use.

There are basic cooking facilities in the barns but if prebooked breakfast (£6) and evening meals (two courses from £12) are available at the *Farmhouse Kitchen* (☎ 01833-640506) by the main farm buildings.

There is a sign from the trail and the barns are only about 200 metres off the route. The Kitchen is open from Easter to October (Fri-Sun 10am-5pm) and serves country café fare such as soups, sandwiches, pies and baked potatoes.

Just over half a mile from the Way is the *Strathmore Arms* (☎ 01833-640362, ⌨ www.strathmorearms.co.uk; 1D/2T/1D, T or F, all en suite), a pub with rooms where B&B costs from £30pp. Dogs are welcome if booked in advance. **Campers** can use the nearby field for £5pp (washbasin/toilet facilities). If booked in advance B&B guests can have an evening meal; otherwise snacks are sold at the bar (Wed-Fri 6pm till when they close, Sat & Sun noon to when they close).

Alston Road Garage's No 73 **bus** service calls at Holwick if prebooked; see public transport map and table, pp45-50.

## HIGH FORCE [Map 75, p186]

*High Force Hotel* (☎ 01833-622222, ⌨ www.highforcehotel.com; 2S/1T/3D, all en suite, bath available) charges £40pp for B&B. Bar meals are served (summer daily noon-2.30pm & Mon-Sat 7-8.45pm, winter daily at lunch but Wed-Sat only in the evening); however, evening meals are available for residents every night. They also serve real ales.

---

❏ **High Force** [See Map 75, p186]

High Force is so big it has to claim some distinction over others. The highest? The biggest? These seem to belong elsewhere so what they say is it's the highest unbroken fall of water in England. The drop is 21 metres (70ft). It's certainly impressive, especially after rain when the water appears the colour of tea, tinged with the peat from the moors.

WA Poucher, the celebrated photographer and writer of a series of guides during the 1960s and '70s, said that it is a difficult subject to photograph well, facing northeast, hence having the wrong light conditions for effective photography. Its other problem, at least from the Pennine Way side of the river, is access for a good view. There are places where you can scramble through the undergrowth and cling on to the cliff edge but few where you can wield the camera effectively.

People have done some strange things here. Some have gone off the top, ending their lives in the torrent. Two boaters were stopped at the last minute from attempting to kayak off the top and a visitor from abroad slipped on the flat shelf at the lip and though saving himself, catapulted the infant on his back over the edge to its doom. There is an odd fascination about raging water which seems to compel some people to get just that little bit too close.

---

❏ **Important note – walking times**

Unless otherwise specified, all times in this book refer only to the time spent walking. You will need to add 20-30% to allow for rests, photography, checking the map, drinking water etc. When planning the day's hike count on 5-7 hours' actual walking.

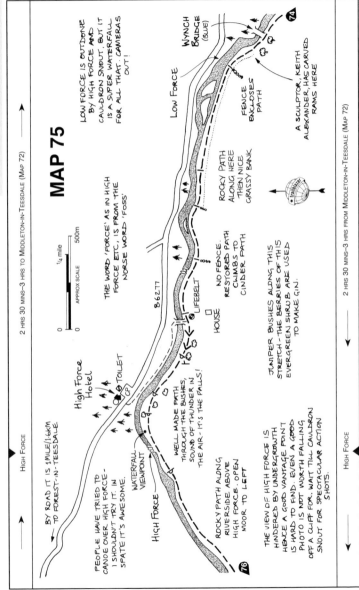

# MAP 75

2 HRS 30 MINS–3 HRS TO MIDDLETON-IN-TEESDALE (MAP 72)

2 HRS 30 MINS–3 HRS FROM MIDDLETON-IN-TEESDALE (MAP 72)

HIGH FORCE

LOW FORCE IS OUTDONE BY HIGH FORCE AND CAULDRON SNOUT, BUT IT IS A SUPER WATERFALL FOR ALL THAT. CAMERAS OUT!

WYNCH BRIDGE (BLUE)

LOW FORCE

FENCE ENCLOSES PATH

A SCULPTOR, KEITH ALEXANDER, HAS CARVED RAMS HERE

THE WORD 'FORCE' AS IN HIGH FORCE ETC, IS FROM THE NORSE WORD 'FOSS'

ROCKY PATH ALONG HERE THEN NICE GRASSY BANK

NO FENCE. RESTORED PATH CLIMBS TO CINDER PATH

B6277

LIFEBELT

HOUSE

JUNIPER BUSHES ALONG THIS STRETCH – THE BERRIES OF THIS EVERGREEN SHRUB ARE USED TO MAKE GIN.

¼ mile

500m

0

0

APPROX SCALE

BY ROAD IT IS 1MILE/1.6KM TO FOREST-IN-TEESDALE.

High Force Hotel

TOILET

CP

Waterfall VIEWPOINT

PEOPLE HAVE TRIED TO CANOE OVER HIGH FORCE - I SHOULDN'T TRY IT. IN SPATE IT'S AWESOME.

WELL MADE PATH THROUGH THE BUSHES, SOUND OF THUNDER IN THE AIR - IT'S THE FALLS!

HIGH FORCE

ROCKY PATH ALONG RIVERSIDE ABOVE HIGH FORCE. OPEN MOOR TO LEFT

THE VIEW OF HIGH FORCE IS HINDERED BY UNDERGROWTH HENCE A GOOD VANTAGE POINT IS HARD TO FIND. EVEN A GOOD PHOTO IS NOT WORTH FALLING OFF A CLIFF FOR. WAIT TILL CAULDRON SNOUT FOR SPECTACULAR ACTION SHOTS.

HIGH FORCE

76

74

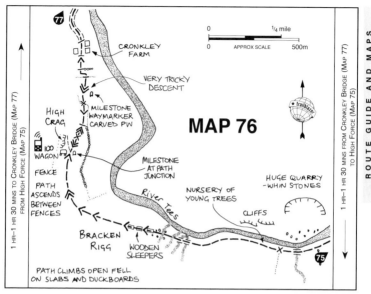

## FOREST-IN-TEESDALE  [off Map 77]

On reaching Cronkley Bridge the nearest place with accommodation is Forest-in-Teesdale, a scattered collection of houses along the B6277 with a **post office/shop** on the southern side of the village.

Alston Road Garage's No 73 **bus** service extends here if prebooked; see public transport map and table, pp45-50.

*The Dale* (☎ 01833-622303; 1D or T/1D, T or F, shared bathroom) is one of those stalwarts among Pennine Way B&Bs. Mrs Bonnett has catered for walkers for

many years and knows how to please them with massive helpings of good food, comfortable beds and a coal fire to sit by on cold days. Mr Bonnett works at the High Force waterfall and has some tales to tell. B&B costs £25pp and an evening meal £12 but they will take you to the pub if you prefer. They will also do a packed lunch for £4.50; all in all outstanding value for money. Dogs are also welcome, if booked in advance. You can find them by first locating the school then turning right at the top of the lane.

## LANGDON BECK     [Map 77, p188]

*Langdon Beck YHA Hostel* (☎ bookings 0845-371 9027, 🖳 langdonbeck@yha.org. uk; Mar-Nov) will be the chosen destination for many walkers, but note that the 31-bed (8 rooms with 2-7 beds) hostel gets booked up, particularly in the summer months, with groups doing their sustainable living courses for young people; walkers who booked weeks ahead will be rewarded by their forethought. Adults are charged from £17, under 18s from £13; meals are available.

If the hostel is full try the nearby *East Underhurth Farm* (☎ 01833-622062; 3D/ 1D, T or F, shared facilities, bath available), a working hill farm where B&B is £25pp. Evening meals (£10) and packed lunches (£5) are available; booking is preferred. Dogs are welcome subject to prior arrangement.

About a quarter of a mile north of the YHA hostel is *Langdon Beck Hotel* (☎ 01833-622267, 🖳 www.langdonbeckhotel. com; 2S/2D/3T, some en suite, some share

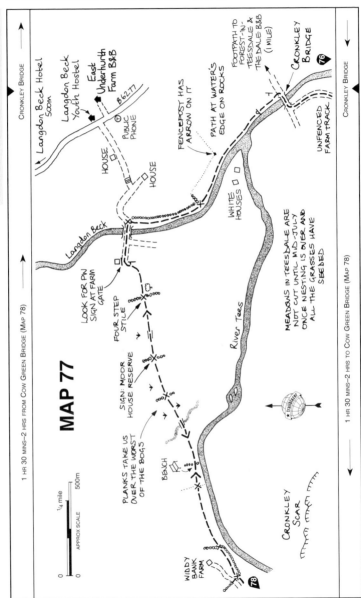

◄ CRONKLEY BRIDGE

1 HR 30 MINS–2 HRS FROM COW GREEN BRIDGE (MAP 78) →

**MAP 77**

0   ¼ mile
APPROX SCALE
0   500m

Langdon Beck Hotel 500m

Langdon Beck Youth Hostel

East Underhurth Farm B&B

B6277

HOUSE

Public Phone

HOUSE

HOUSE

Langdon Beck

LOOK FOR PN SIGN AT FARM GATE

FOUR STEP STILE

SIGN: MOOR HOUSE RESERVE

PLANKS TAKE US OVER THE WORST OF THE BOGS

BEACH

FENCEPOST HAS ARROW ON IT

PATH AT WATER'S EDGE ON ROCKS

WHITE HOUSES

FOOTPATH TO FOREST-IN-TEESDALE & THE DALE B&B (1 MILE)

CRONKLEY BRIDGE

76

UNFENCED FARM TRACK

River Tees

MEADOWS IN TEESDALE ARE NOT CUT UNTIL MID-JULY ONCE NESTING IS OVER AND ALL THE GRASSES HAVE SEEDED

CRONKLEY SCAR

WIDDY BANK FARM

78

trailblazer

◄ CRONKLEY BRIDGE

1 HR 30 MINS–2 HRS TO COW GREEN BRIDGE (MAP 78) →

facilities, bath available). B&B costs £80-90 for two sharing; the singles are £45. Dogs can stay (around £10). The pub (food served Mon-Sat noon-2pm, Sun noon-2.30pm and daily 7-9pm) has a great evening meal menu including a 9oz Teesdale sirloin steak with a plateload of trimmings for £13.05 as well as a few veggie options for around £8. They

also have specials such as shepherd's pie and steak pie; a roast is served on Sundays. Note that the hotel is closed completely on Mondays between October and Easter.

Alston Road Garage's No 73 **bus** runs from Langdon Beck to Middleton-in-Teesdale (see public transport map and table, pp45-50).

---

### ❏ Too Long a Winter

Even though these days a sealed road leads to it, walking past the front of Birkdale Farm (Map 79) you can't help but be struck by the homestead's strikingly remote location. Said to be the highest occupied farmhouse in England, it makes Emily Bronte's Withins Height (see p107) look like a shed at the back of the garden.

In the 1970s the farmer whose family had long rented the property from Lord Barnard's extensive Raby Estate were the subject of a TV documentary. The show depicted three groups of local characters: Brian and Mary Bainbridge farming at Birkdale, a brief glimpse of a chauffeur-driven Mrs Field from Middleton, a preposterous caricature cut out of an Agatha Christie novel, and the soon-to-become famous Hannah Hauxwell (see box p171).

Brian Bainbridge who helped dig out the Cow Green Reservoir behind Cauldron Snout was followed as he and his wife returned to the empty homestead after several years' absence to give the place another go. He was filmed from a circling helicopter rounding up sheep (or perhaps chasing them as they fled from the chopper) and staggering around the snowbound fells, staff in hand, hauling strays out of snow drifts. A decade earlier the disastrous winter of 1963 wiped out the then young farmer's entire flock and led him to eventually abandon Birkdale. He described that tragic year as just '*too long a winter*' for the sheep and so gave the programme its title.

Among other characters, a smiling, ruddy-faced fellow herder George Haw, was asked about the attraction of life on the moors. '*Well I don't know, it's just a living that's all... I can't say there's any attraction to it, like*'. Mary Bainbridge is mildly more upbeat to the same query '*I love the hills, the sheep, the loneliness*'.

*Too Long a Winter* also set the 46-year-old Daleswoman Hannah Hauxwell on her path to fame. Her story and presence are no less moving. Like a character out of a children's fairy tale, she is seen dragging her prize bull to market on a sleety winter's day; the outcome set to meet her financial needs for the coming year. Resigned but not necessarily devoted to a solitary life, she observes the wrong husband would not be worth having and is filmed at Mrs Field's annual harvest do tapping her feet in her giant-lapelled overcoat while all around her dance gaily. Like the Bainbridges (but not at all like the batty Mrs Field) Hauxwell's ingenuous innocence and ready acceptance of life's hardships set her apart and led to a staggering response from the viewing public; letters and food parcels came in from all over the country. Over the next twenty years other TV shows and books followed.

On her husband's death in 2006 Mary Bainbridge said 'He always thought the TV programme was a bit of a farce. Neither he nor I ever met Miss Hauxwell. I thought she was rather exploited.'

The video of *Too Long a Winter* is easily found on Amazon or eBay for a few pounds, along with what might be called the Hannah Hauxwell 'boxed set'. Tracing this prodigious output of 'Hannobilia' by director/producer Brian Cockcroft, ending in *Hannah USA*, you can't help feeling Mary Bainbridge may have had a point.

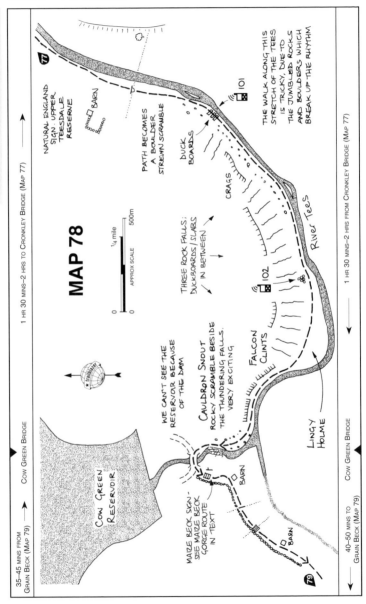

35–45 MINS FROM GRAIN BECK (MAP 79)

COW GREEN BRIDGE

1 HR 30 MINS–2 HRS TO CRONKLEY BRIDGE (MAP 77)

**MAP 78**

¼ mile

APPROX SCALE

0      500m

NATURAL ENGLAND SIGN - UPPER TEESDALE RESERVE

BARN

PATH BECOMES A BOULDER STREAM SCRAMBLE

DUCK BOARDS

101

CRAGS

THE WALK ALONG THIS STRETCH OF THE TEES IS TRICKY, DUE TO THE JUMBLED ROCKS AND BOULDERS WHICH BREAK UP THE RHYTHM

THREE ROCK FALLS; DUCKBOARDS / SLABS IN BETWEEN

102

FALCON CLINTS

River Tees

WE CAN'T SEE THE RESERVOIR BECAUSE OF THE DAM

CAULDRON SNOUT ROCKY SCRAMBLE BESIDE THE THUNDERING FALLS. VERY EXCITING

LINGY HOLME

COW GREEN RESERVOIR

MAIZE BECK SIGN - SEE MAIZE BECK GORGE ROUTE IN TEXT

BARN

BARN

79

40–50 MINS TO GRAIN BECK (MAP 79)

COW GREEN BRIDGE

1 HR 30 MINS–2 HRS FROM CRONKLEY BRIDGE (MAP 77)

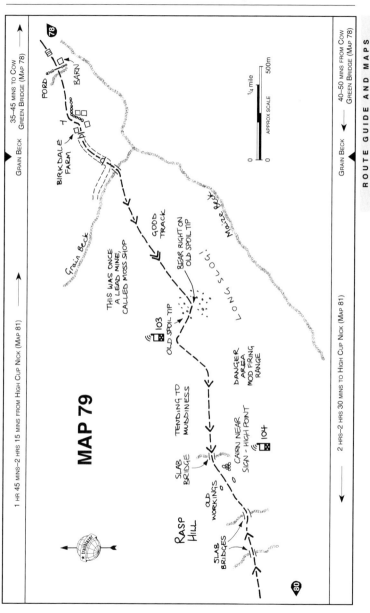

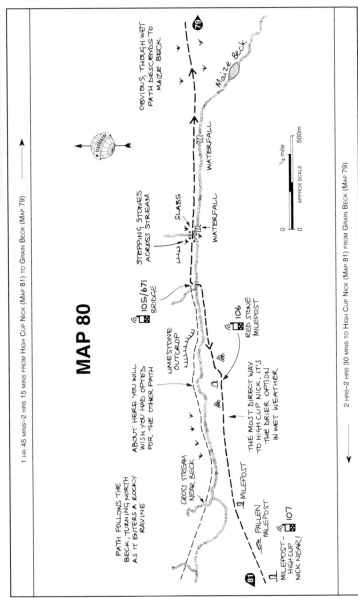

# MAP 80

1 HR 45 MINS–2 HRS 15 MINS FROM HIGH CUP NICK (MAP 81) TO GRAIN BECK (MAP 79)

2 HRS–2 HRS 30 MINS TO HIGH CUP NICK (MAP 81) FROM GRAIN BECK (MAP 79)

OBVIOUS, THOUGH WET PATH DESCENDS TO MAIZE BECK

Maize Beck

79

WATERFALL

WATERFALL

SLABS

STEPPING STONES ACROSS STREAM

APPROX SCALE

0 — ¼ mile
0 — 500m

105/67ↀ BRIDGE

ABOUT HERE YOU WILL WISH YOU HAD OPTED FOR THE OTHER PATH

LIMESTONE OUTCROP

106 RED STONE MILEPOST

THE MOST DIRECT WAY TO HIGH CUP NICK. IT'S THE DRIER OPTION IN WET WEATHER

II MILEPOST

PATH FOLLOWS THE BECK, TURNING NORTH AS IT ENTERS A ROCKY RAVINE

CROSS STREAM NEAR BECK

FALLEN MILEPOST

MILEPOST – HIGH CUP NICK NEAR! 107

81

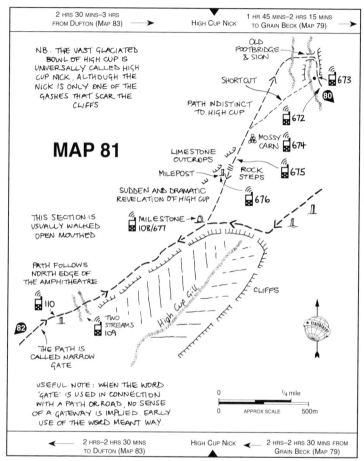

2 HRS 30 MINS–3 HRS FROM DUFTON (MAP 83) →

HIGH CUP NICK

1 HR 45 MINS–2 HRS 15 MINS TO GRAIN BECK (MAP 79) →

OLD FOOTBRIDGE & SIGN

SHORTCUT

**673**

PATH INDISTINCT TO HIGH CUP

**672**

**80**

NB. THE VAST GLACIATED BOWL OF HIGH CUP IS UNIVERSALLY CALLED HIGH CUP NICK, ALTHOUGH THE NICK IS ONLY ONE OF THE GASHES THAT SCAR THE CLIFFS

MOSSY CAIRN **674**

**MAP 81**

LIMESTONE OUTCROPS

ROCK STEPS **675**

MILEPOST

SUDDEN AND DRAMATIC REVELATION OF HIGH CUP

**676**

THIS SECTION IS USUALLY WALKED OPEN MOUTHED

MILESTONE 108/**677**

PATH FOLLOWS NORTH EDGE OF THE AMPHITHEATRE

**110**

CLIFFS

High Cup Gill

TWO STREAMS **109**

**82**

THE PATH IS CALLED NARROW GATE

trailblazer

USEFUL NOTE: WHEN THE WORD 'GATE' IS USED IN CONNECTION WITH A PATH OR ROAD, NO SENSE OF A GATEWAY IS IMPLIED. EARLY USE OF THE WORD MEANT WAY.

0 ¼ mile
0 APPROX SCALE 500m

← 2 HRS–2 HRS 30 MINS TO DUFTON (MAP 83)

HIGH CUP NICK

← 2 HRS–2 HRS 30 MINS FROM GRAIN BECK (MAP 79)

## The Maize Beck Gorge route　　　　　　[See Maps 80 and 81]

**Wooden warning signs** below Cow Green dam wall and at the walled enclosure above Dufton (see Maps 78 and 82) giving the grid ref '749270' refer to an **old footbridge** once used to cross upper Maize Beck in times of flood when the former stepping stone route (now also bridged; GPS waypoint 105/671, see p262) was unsafe. With the newer bridge these signs are now obsolete and confusing, an irony compounded by the fact that were Maize Beck really in spate, this 'escape route' via the old footbridge would be so soggy you might as well take your chances on the stepping stones submerged in the torrent!

The regular southern route is preferable in all ways but to some the Gorge route will be a curiosity. Just don't expect a well-trodden track. The first two waypoints (672 and 673) mark easy crossing points of Maize Beck. If there is too much water you can cross at the footbridge north of GPS waypoint 673. A very faint path leads from the footbridge to High Cup Gill or you can take a shortcut from waypoint 673 to the mossy cairn at 674 but there's no path between the two.

---

### ❑ High Cup

Northbound walkers come upon the massive glaciated valley of High Cup (also known as High Cup Nick) quite suddenly and are always surprised by this incredible sight. Suddenly the land drops away in front of you in a textbook U-shaped demonstration of the aftermath of glacial erosion. The sides are rimmed with strata of hard rock, basalt or dolerite, interspersed with jumbled scree and twinkling rivulets and from the head of the valley Maize Beck trickles down when it's not getting blown back in your face.

Strangely enough, none of the people who have seen fit to write about the Pennine Way has made much of it until recently. The curmudgeonly Wainwright hardly mentions it, others gloss over it and even JHB Peel in his invaluable book, *Along the Pennine Way*, loses the plot when it comes to describing High Cup Nick. Perhaps words are not needed as even the most unimaginative are impressed by the sight.

---

### DUFTON          [Map 83, p196]

This quiet and attractive little village is a lovely place to stop after a great day's walking, whichever direction you're taking. There is an agricultural show here in August; see p26 for details.

*Dufton YHA Hostel* (☎ bookings 0845-371 9734, 🖳 dufton@yha.org.uk; open all year; 32 beds – 8 rooms with 2-6 beds) opposite the pub is one of the best on the Way; meals are available and the hostel is licensed. Accommodation costs from £17pp, £13 for under 18s. Note that the hostel is sometimes booked by groups, particularly in the winter months, so reservations are recommended.

**Camping** at *Grandie Caravan Park* (☎ 01768-351573; Apr-Oct) costs £5 per person. They have space for up to 15 tents.

*Brow Farm* (☎ 01768-352865, 🖳 www.browfarm.com; 1T/2D, all en suite, bath available) offers B&B in comfortable rooms for £36pp.

*The Stag Inn* (☎ 01768-351608, 🖳 www.thestagdufton.co.uk) is known for its substantial bar meals (Tue-Sun noon-2pm, daily 6-8.45pm; bar closed on Mon

Jan-Mar) in the £8 range; dishes from the à la carte menu cost a bit more. It has a nicely appointed self-catering cottage (1T/1D, bath available) next door which can be booked through Cumbrian Cottages (☎ 01228-599960, 🖳 www.cumbrian-cottages. co.uk); the minimum booking is for three nights (from £180). Dogs are welcome in the cottage.

B&B for anything from one night or more is available a few doors along at *Hall Croft* (☎ 01768-352902, 🖳 hallcroft@ phonecoop.coop; 1T or D/2D, all with private facilities, bath available) where two people sharing pay £60 and single occupancy is £35. Dogs are welcome if booked in advance.

*Coney Garth* (☎ 01768-352582, 🖳 www.coneygarth.co.uk; 2T/1D or F, all en suite, bath available) offers a warm welcome and costs £30-35pp and has drying facilities on the Aga. They will do 'anything requested', including making up a tasty packed lunch. Evening meals provided if requested in advance. Posh camping is also available; contact them for details.

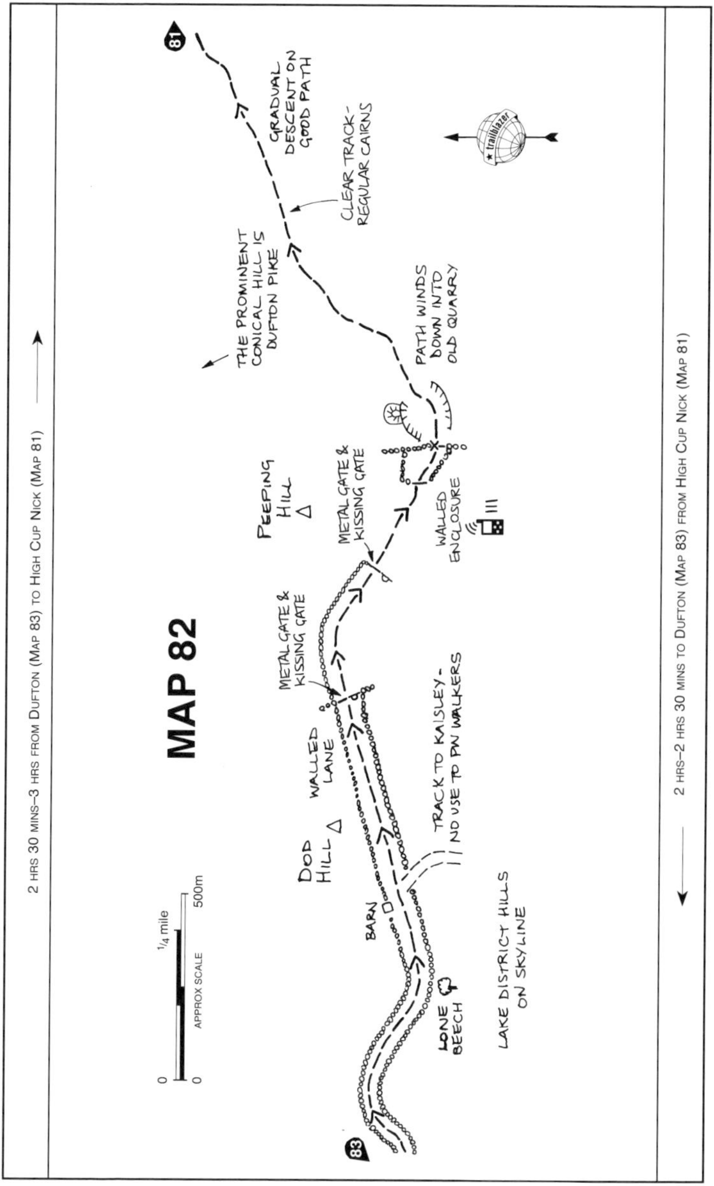
2 HRS 30 MINS–3 HRS FROM DUFTON (MAP 83) TO HIGH CUP NICK (MAP 81)
MAP 82
APPROX SCALE
0
1/4 mile
0
500m
83
81
LONE BEECH
BARN
DOD HILL
WALLED LANE
METAL GATE & KISSING GATE
TRACK TO KAISLEY - NO USE TO PW WALKERS
LAKE DISTRICT HILLS ON SKYLINE
PEEPING HILL
METAL GATE & KISSING GATE
WALLED ENCLOSURE
PATH WINDS DOWN INTO OLD QUARRY
THE PROMINENT CONICAL HILL IS DUFTON PIKE
CLEAR TRACK - REGULAR CAIRNS
GRADUAL DESCENT ON GOOD PATH
trailblazer
2 HRS–2 HRS 30 MINS TO DUFTON (MAP 83) FROM HIGH CUP NICK (MAP 81)

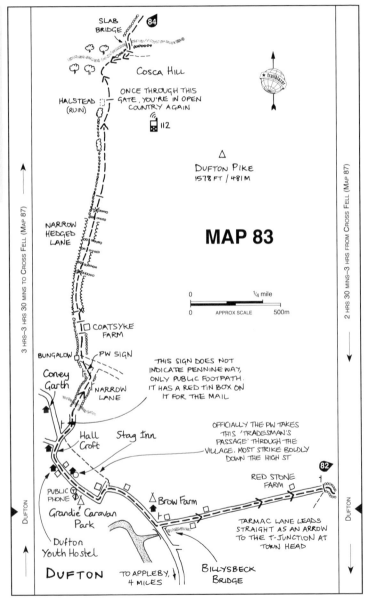

SLAB BRIDGE

84

Cosca Hill

ONCE THROUGH THIS GATE, YOU'RE IN OPEN COUNTRY AGAIN

📱 112

HALSTEAD (RUIN)

△ DUFTON PIKE
1578 FT / 481 M

**MAP 83**

0          ¼ mile
0    APPROX SCALE    500m

NARROW HEDGED LANE

COATSYKE FARM

BUNGALOW

PW SIGN

Coney Garth

NARROW LANE

THIS SIGN DOES NOT INDICATE PENNINE WAY, ONLY PUBLIC FOOTPATH. IT HAS A RED TIN BOX ON IT FOR THE MAIL

Hall Croft

Stag Inn

OFFICIALLY THE PW TAKES THIS 'TRADESMAN'S PASSAGE' THROUGH THE VILLAGE. MOST STRIKE BOLDLY DOWN THE HIGH ST

82

RED STONE FARM

PUBLIC PHONE

△ Brow Farm

Grandie Caravan Park

Dufton Youth Hostel

TARMAC LANE LEADS STRAIGHT AS AN ARROW TO THE T-JUNCTION AT TOWN HEAD

**DUFTON**

TO APPLEBY, 4 MILES

BILLYSBECK BRIDGE

*Sidebar left:* ROUTE GUIDE AND MAPS

*Vertical left:* 3 HRS–3 HRS 30 MINS TO CROSS FELL (MAP 87)

*Vertical right:* 2 HRS 30 MINS–3 HRS FROM CROSS FELL (MAP 87)

*Left margin:* DUFTON

*Right margin:* DUFTON

Robinson's operate a limited **bus** service (see public transport map and table, pp45-50) to Penrith and Appleby, the latter only four miles along the road (despite what the road sign near the campsite says). **Appleby** (🖳 www.visitcumbria.com/pen/ appleby.htm) is an attractive country town on the Carlisle–Leeds railway with banks, several pubs and a bakery or two, all settled around a bend in the River Eden. If you're due for a day off, you could a lot worse than scheduling it around Dufton and Appleby.

---

### ❑ Lead mining in the Pennines

The history of digging in the earth for lead in the Pennine hills goes back to the Romans and probably earlier, evidence having been uncovered that Romans further exploited existing workings soon after they arrived.

The growth in the building of abbeys and castles increased the demand for lead for the roofs and stained-glass windows but it was not until the 19th century that mining assumed industrial proportions as the demand for lead increased.

The industry started to suffer when cheaper foreign sources threatened local production and by the early years of the 20th century mining was in decline. Today there is no lead mining in Britain although some of the old pits have been re-opened to exploit other minerals found there such as barytes and fluorspar. The ore, galena, also has a use in producing X-ray equipment.

The ruins evident around Alston, and around Keld in Swaledale, are a reminder of the extensive industry involved in lead mining at one time. Old spoil tips, ruined mine buildings and the occasional remains of a chimney are all that is left of this activity, now long discarded as uneconomic. Traces of bell pits are often to be seen as hollows in the ground. They used to sink a shaft to a certain level then widen the bottom of the hole until it was unsafe to go further. Everything dug out went to the surface in a bucket, firstly by hand and then by a winch, sometimes drawn up on a wheel by a horse walking in a circle. It was a primitive industry in the early days, reliant on the muscle power of the miners themselves. With the advent of engineering, ways were found to mechanise production and so multiply the output, increasing profits for the owners.

Around Middleton-in-Teesdale mining rights were held by the London Lead Mining Company, a Quaker concern, active from the latter part of the 1700s until early in the 1900s when they pulled out in the face of cheap imported ore from Europe.

---

## DUFTON TO ALSTON                    MAPS 83-94

### Route overview

It won't have escaped your notice that the **21 miles (32km, 6½-8hrs)** between Dufton and Alston include the climb over Cross Fell. At 893m (2930ft) it is the Pennine Way's highest point and, excluding the peaks in the immediate vicinity and The Cheviot (which is not directly on the Way), Cross Fell stands up by quite a margin. Altogether this stage involves nearly 1100m of ascent. However, notwithstanding the possibility of losing the route in **bad visibility** (see p198), it will most likely be the prolonged trudge **down the infamous 'Corpse Road' miners' track** on the far side of Cross Fell to Garrigill that will do you in, starting with pulverising the soles of your feet.

You should also be acquainted with the fact that along the 16 miles to Garrigill the only places for refreshment are mountain streams and the only shelter are rabbit-filled sink holes and Greg's Hut (see box p201) so go well prepared. Though by now your Pennine route-finding instincts should be well honed, in anything less than perfect weather, this is a section to take seriously. Nobody should set off without adequate protective clothing, supplies and at the very least, a compass. The GPS waypoints (see pp262-3) on this section are particularly prolific for a reason. To be caught out in a rain- or even hailstorm in July or August is not at all unlikely and many a walker has struggled in to Greg's Hut in desperate straits, as the visitor's book testifies.

On the bright side, once you set your mind to it, the long haul up to the summit of Cross Fell is actually not so bad. It begins gently enough along farm lanes and byways skirting around **Dufton Pike** before a comparatively short and sharp haul up to **Knock Fell** (Map 85). Now, at less than 100m below Cross Fell, the lion's share of the climbing is behind you, but it's unlikely to be that simple...

If you're lucky the surreal geodesic forms atop Great Dun Fell (which you may have spotted from Dufton village green) will act as a beacon, but the chances are the weather may have begun to deteriorate. From Knock Fell once you gain the line of snow poles and slabs that lead to the **radar-tracking station access road**, navigation-wise you should be home free. From this point looking east you can see the back end of Cow Green Reservoir, the only obvious man-made feature in a grey-green vista of fells and dales.

The northbound descent to the windy col and climb onto **Little Dun Fell** (Map 86) can take the wind out of you, but now the views to both sides are potentially fantastic. Passing close by the source of the River Tees, the final haul onto the summit plateau and stone-cross shelter on **Cross Fell** (Map 87) is less severe; keeping track of the cairns will be the main priority in the mist.

The good news is, once off the summit plateau and securely installed on the miners' path leading past **Greg's Hut**, even the thickest pea souper with croutons and a side salad should not disorientate you from the track that unwinds and undulates and unwinds some more like a stuck record for every inch of the seven miles down to Garrigill. Corpse Road they call it, and you'll feel like one by the end of it. Over the years walkers have tried every trick in the book to save their soles from the purgatory of the rough, stony surface. But, as with so many Pennine days, it all ends happily at the diminutive haven of **Garrigill** (Map 91) where you can get a cup of tea in the village shop. Things could be worse.

Garrigill is a lovely place to end the tough hike over from Dufton and you may prefer to roll in the five miles to Alston with the 16½-mile hike to Greenhead on the Wall; it's flatter but less consistent. Those keen to power on to the dizzy heights of **Alston** (Map 94) beware, it's not the harmless riverside spindown that the map may suggest. Its latter half crumbles into a tedious negotiation of overgrown paths punctuated with numerous stiles, sprung gates and other walker's traps that will most likely finish you off as you stagger past the cemetery into the market town and a well-earned break. If staying at Alston Training and Adventure Centre here (see p208) you can take the path to it before reaching Alston (see Map 93, p206).

## Route-finding trouble spots

In good weather the route poses no great problems; Cross Fell may not exactly match the razor-edged profile of the Matterhorn but the globes of the tracking station atop Great Dun Fell are very distinctive landmarks. Even then, the actual trail gets a bit thin on the flat plateau from Knock Fell towards the tracking station access road. In poor visibility the frequent GPS waypoints are there if you want them; alternatively use a compass or the access road to get you up to Great Dun Fell's summit station. From there continue over the windy saddles to Cross Fell's flattened apex – oxygen is not needed.

Leaving the summit wind shelters again there is no distinct path but several small cairns march north. Otherwise a mist-blinded northward stagger will lead you eventually down to the unmissable Corpse Road track, Greg's Hut nearby and eventually a footsore arrival in Garrigill.

As noted earlier, the overgrown fields after you bridge the South Tyne on the way to Alston can also confound you, even if the river on your left is a guide.

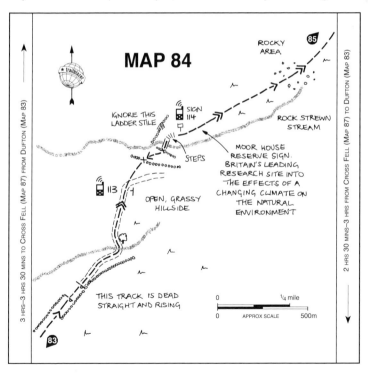

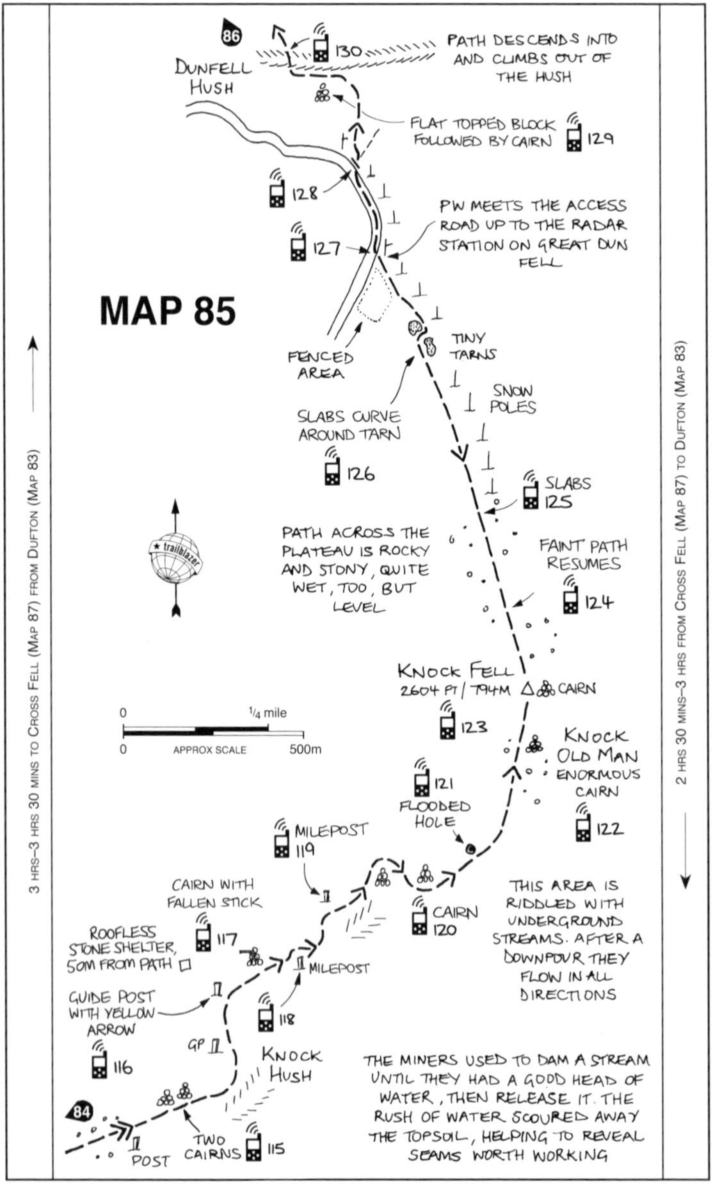

**MAP 85**

86

DUNFELL HUSH

130

PATH DESCENDS INTO AND CLIMBS OUT OF THE HUSH

FLAT TOPPED BLOCK FOLLOWED BY CAIRN 129

128

127

PW MEETS THE ACCESS ROAD UP TO THE RADAR STATION ON GREAT DUN FELL

FENCED AREA

TINY TARNS

SNOW POLES

SLABS CURVE AROUND TARN

126

SLABS 125

PATH ACROSS THE PLATEAU IS ROCKY AND STONY, QUITE WET, TOO, BUT LEVEL

FAINT PATH RESUMES 124

★ trailblazer

KNOCK FELL 2604 PT / 794M △ CAIRN

123

KNOCK OLD MAN ENORMOUS CAIRN

0        1/4 mile

0        APPROX SCALE        500m

121

FLOODED HOLE

122

MILEPOST 119

CAIRN WITH FALLEN STICK

117

ROOFLESS STONE SHELTER, 50M FROM PATH □

MILEPOST

CAIRN 120

THIS AREA IS RIDDLED WITH UNDERGROUND STREAMS. AFTER A DOWNPOUR THEY FLOW IN ALL DIRECTIONS

GUIDE POST WITH YELLOW ARROW

116

GP

118

KNOCK HUSH

84

POST

TWO CAIRNS 115

THE MINERS USED TO DAM A STREAM UNTIL THEY HAD A GOOD HEAD OF WATER, THEN RELEASE IT. THE RUSH OF WATER SCOURED AWAY THE TOPSOIL, HELPING TO REVEAL SEAMS WORTH WORKING

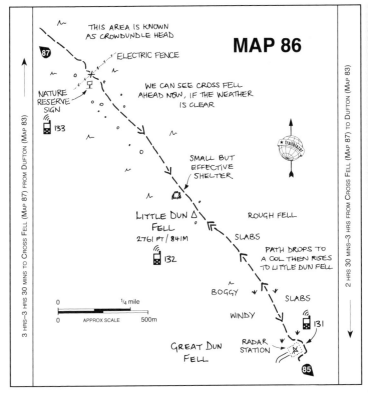

## ❑ Greg's Hut [See Map 87, p202]

Greg's Hut is a welcome and well-maintained bothy just over the summit of Cross Fell where walkers can take refuge or just pop in for a nose around. It holds a special place in the heart of many wayfarers. Originally it was used by lead miners whose tailing can be seen all around. They would stay here all week and walk home at the weekend. 'Greg' was actually John Gregory, a climber who died following an epic climbing accident in the Alps in 1968 in spite of the heroic efforts of his companion who held him on the rope and tended his injuries all night. Rescuers arrived too late.

Thanks to the efforts of the Mountain Bothies Association, the hut has been repaired and maintained. There are two rooms, the inner one has a raised sleeping platform with a stove, although fuel is scarce. Certainly you're unlikely to find any on the surrounding fell.

This is a classic mountain bothy, unique along the Pennine Way, and it's hard to drag yourself out of it in horrible conditions. The visitors' book could be published as it stands, telling a multitude of stories, most of them epics of embellishment or endurance.

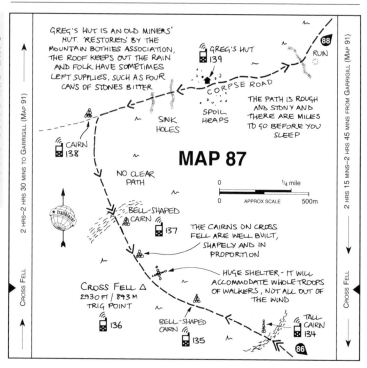

2 HRS–2 HRS 30 MINS TO GARRIGILL (MAP 91)

2 HRS 15 MINS–2 HRS 45 MINS FROM GARRIGILL (MAP 91)

CROSS FELL

GREG'S HUT IS AN OLD MINERS' HUT. 'RESTORED' BY THE MOUNTAIN BOTHIES ASSOCIATION, THE ROOF KEEPS OUT THE RAIN AND FOLK HAVE SOMETIMES LEFT SUPPLIES, SUCH AS FOUR CANS OF STONES BITTER

GREG'S HUT
139

RUIN

CORPSE ROAD

SPOIL HEAPS

SINK HOLES

THE PATH IS ROUGH AND STONY AND THERE ARE MILES TO GO BEFORE YOU SLEEP

CAIRN
138

NO CLEAR PATH

**MAP 87**

0        1/4 mile
0        APPROX SCALE        500m

BELL-SHAPED CAIRN
137

THE CAIRNS ON CROSS FELL ARE WELL BUILT, SHAPELY AND IN PROPORTION

HUGE SHELTER - IT WILL ACCOMMODATE WHOLE TROOPS OF WALKERS, NOT ALL OUT OF THE WIND

CROSS FELL △
2930 FT / 893 M
TRIG POINT
136

BELL-SHAPED CAIRN
135

TALL CAIRN
134

86

---

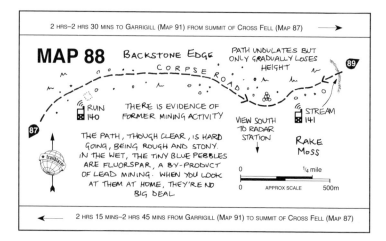

2 HRS–2 HRS 30 MINS TO GARRIGILL (MAP 91) FROM SUMMIT OF CROSS FELL (MAP 87)

**MAP 88**   BACKSTONE EDGE

PATH UNDULATES BUT ONLY GRADUALLY LOSES HEIGHT

CORPSE ROAD

89

87

RUIN
140

THERE IS EVIDENCE OF FORMER MINING ACTIVITY

STREAM
141

VIEW SOUTH TO RADAR STATION

RAKE MOSS

THE PATH, THOUGH CLEAR, IS HARD GOING, BEING ROUGH AND STONY. IN THE WET, THE TINY BLUE PEBBLES ARE FLUORSPAR, A BY-PRODUCT OF LEAD MINING. WHEN YOU LOOK AT THEM AT HOME, THEY'RE NO BIG DEAL

0        1/4 mile
0        APPROX SCALE        500m

2 HRS 15 MINS–2 HRS 45 MINS FROM GARRIGILL (MAP 91) TO SUMMIT OF CROSS FELL (MAP 87)

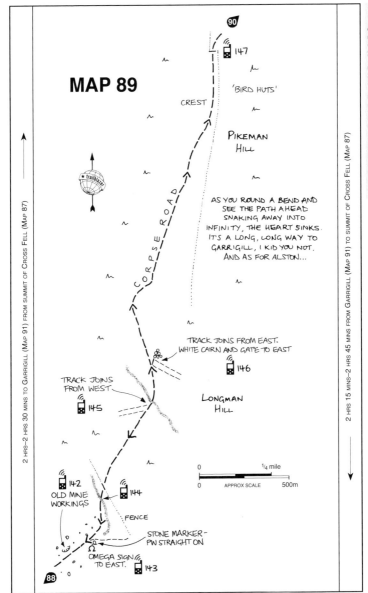

**MAP 89**

90

147

'BIRD HUTS'

CREST

PIKEMAN HILL

CORPSE ROAD

AS YOU ROUND A BEND AND
SEE THE PATH AHEAD
SNAKING AWAY INTO
INFINITY, THE HEART SINKS.
IT'S A LONG, LONG WAY TO
GARRIGILL, I KID YOU NOT,
AND AS FOR ALSTON...

TRACK JOINS FROM EAST.
WHITE CAIRN AND GATE TO EAST

146

TRACK JOINS
FROM WEST

145

LONGMAN HILL

0        ¼ mile
0    APPROX SCALE    500m

142
OLD MINE
WORKINGS

144

FENCE

STONE MARKER -
PW STRAIGHT ON

OMEGA SIGN
TO EAST.        143

88

2 HRS–2 HRS 30 MINS TO GARRIGILL (MAP 91) FROM SUMMIT OF CROSS FELL (MAP 87)

2 HRS 15 MINS–2 HRS 45 MINS FROM GARRIGILL (MAP 91) TO SUMMIT OF CROSS FELL (MAP 87)

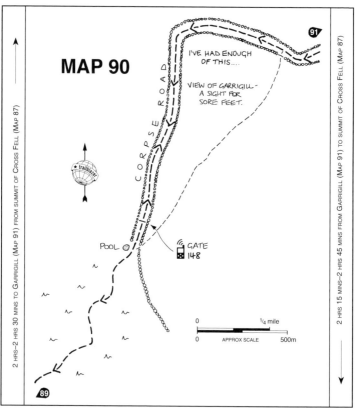

**MAP 90**

I'VE HAD ENOUGH OF THIS....

VIEW OF GARRIGILL – A SIGHT FOR SORE FEET.

CORPSE ROAD

★ trailblazer

POOL

GATE 148

0      ¼ mile

0    APPROX SCALE    500m

2 HRS – 2 HRS 30 MINS TO GARRIGILL (MAP 91) FROM SUMMIT OF CROSS FELL (MAP 87)

2 HRS 15 MINS – 2 HRS 45 MINS FROM GARRIGILL (MAP 91) TO SUMMIT OF CROSS FELL (MAP 87)

91

89

## GARRIGILL                    [Map 91]

Garrigill's **post office** (Mon & Wed-Fri 9am-5.30pm, Tue & Sat 9am-12.30pm) transacts the usual business and includes a **shop** (same hours) as well as selling **hot drinks**. It's also home to *Garrigill Post Office Guesthouse* (☎ 01434-381257, ☐ www.garrigill-guesthouse.co.uk; 2T shared bathroom; Easter to Oct). It's clean and comfortable but don't expect the rooms in this 300-year-old building to be palatial. B&B costs from £25pp; dogs are welcome.

Also on the village green is *Bridge View B&B* (☎ 01434-382448, ☐ www. bridgeview.org.uk; 1D, T or F, private bathroom) where B&B is £26pp for two/

three sharing (£31 for single occupancy); a packed lunch costs from £4. They have washing and drying facilities and the owner can offer a foot massage but this would only be possible for walkers without any blisters.

Nearby you'll also find *East View* (☎ 01434-381561, ☐ www.garrigillbed andbreakfast.co.uk; 1D or T/1D, shared bathroom) with rooms from £26pp. Dogs are welcome.

If you want to **camp** at Garrigill, you can pitch up behind the village hall. However, there are no facilities. Make a donation before you leave.

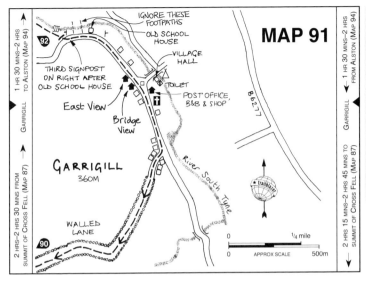

**MAP 91**

1 HR 30 MINS–2 HRS TO ALSTON (MAP 94)

1 HR 30 MINS–2 HRS FROM ALSTON (MAP 94)

GARRIGILL

2 HRS–2 HRS 30 MINS FROM SUMMIT OF CROSS FELL (MAP 87)

2 HRS 15 MINS–2 HRS 45 MINS TO SUMMIT OF CROSS FELL (MAP 87)

IGNORE THESE FOOTPATHS
OLD SCHOOL HOUSE
VILLAGE HALL
THIRD SIGNPOST ON RIGHT AFTER OLD SCHOOL HOUSE
East View
Bridge View
TOILET
POST OFFICE, B&B & SHOP
B6277
GARRIGILL 360M
River South Tyne
WALLED LANE
¼ mile
APPROX SCALE 500m

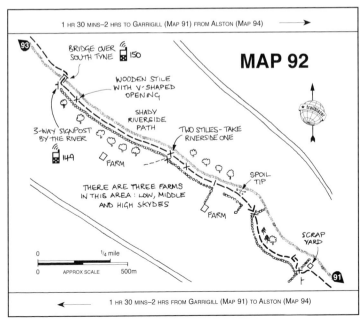

1 HR 30 MINS–2 HRS TO GARRIGILL (MAP 91) FROM ALSTON (MAP 94)

**MAP 92**

BRIDGE OVER SOUTH TYNE 150
WOODEN STILE WITH V-SHAPED OPENING
SHADY RIVERSIDE PATH
TWO STILES – TAKE RIVERSIDE ONE
3-WAY SIGNPOST BY THE RIVER 149
FARM
SPOIL TIP
THERE ARE THREE FARMS IN THIS AREA: LOW, MIDDLE AND HIGH SKYDES
FARM
SCRAP YARD
¼ mile
APPROX SCALE 500m

1 HR 30 MINS–2 HRS FROM GARRIGILL (MAP 91) TO ALSTON (MAP 94)

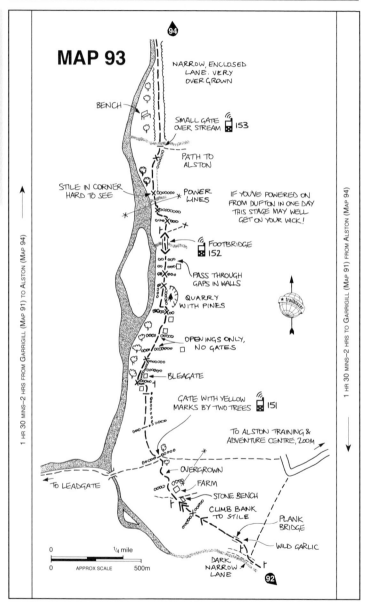

**MAP 93**

NARROW, ENCLOSED LANE. VERY OVERGROWN

BENCH

SMALL GATE OVER STREAM 📱 153

PATH TO ALSTON

STILE IN CORNER HARD TO SEE

POWER LINES

IF YOU'VE POWERED ON FROM DUFTON IN ONE DAY THIS STAGE MAY WELL GET ON YOUR WICK!

FOOTBRIDGE 📱 152

PASS THROUGH GAPS IN WALLS

★ trailblazer

QUARRY WITH PINES

OPENINGS ONLY, NO GATES

BLEAGATE

GATE WITH YELLOW MARKS BY TWO TREES 📱 151

TO ALSTON TRAINING & ADVENTURE CENTRE, 200M

OVERGROWN

FARM

STONE BENCH

TO LEADGATE

CLIMB BANK TO STILE

PLANK BRIDGE

WILD GARLIC

DARK, NARROW LANE

0    ¼ mile

0    APPROX SCALE    500m

92

1 HR 30 MINS–2 HRS FROM GARRIGILL (MAP 91) TO ALSTON (MAP 94)

1 HR 30 MINS–2 HRS TO GARRIGILL (MAP 91) FROM ALSTON (MAP 94)

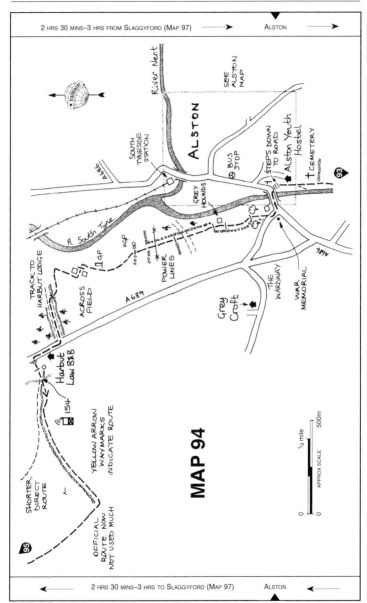

MAP 94

2 HRS 30 MINS–3 HRS FROM SLAGGYFORD (MAP 97) →    ALSTON →

River Nent

SEE ALSTON MAP

ALSTON

South Tyneside Station

A689

R South Tyne

GREY HOUNDS

BUS STOP

STEPS DOWN TO ROAD

Alston Youth Hostel

CEMETERY

93

TRACK TO HARBUT LODGE

GP

GP

POWER LINES

A686

THE WARDWAY

WAR MEMORIAL

ACROSS FIELD

A689

Grey Croft

Harbut Law B&B

154

YELLOW ARROW WAYMARKS INDICATE ROUTE

SHORTER, DIRECT ROUTE

95

OFFICIAL ROUTE NOW NOT USED MUCH

trailblazer

¼ mile        500m

APPROX SCALE

0        0

2 HRS 30 MINS–3 HRS TO SLAGGYFORD (MAP 97) ←    ALSTON ←

## ALSTON [Map 94a]

Alston is England's highest market town and its steep cobbled streets and 18th-century buildings give it a bit of character. It does, however, have a faint air of decline about it compared to other like-sized towns along the Way, although this could be an unfair impression following two days of remote hiking.

### Services

The **tourist information centre** (☎ 01434-382244, 🖳 www.eden.gov.uk/visit-eden-in-the-lake-district; mid Mar-Oct daily Mon, Tue, Fri & Sat 9.30am-5pm, Wed, Thur 10am-5pm, Sun 10am-4pm, Nov-Mar Mon & Fri 10am-5pm, Tue-Thur 10am-3pm, Sat 10am-4pm) is in the Town Hall on Front St They can book accommodation (see box p13). The **outdoor equipment shop** HI-Pennine Outdoor (Mon-Sat 10am-5pm, Sun 11am-5pm) is a good spot to replace worn-out socks, blister patches and the like.

**Alston Wholefoods** sells fairtrade chocolate, interesting cheeses (eg Northumberland Nettle, Swaledale Ewe) and environmentally friendly goods. There's also a **Co-op** (daily 7am-10pm), and a **chemist** (early closing Tue and Sat, closed Sun). The branches of HSBC and Barclays here have **cash machines**; there is also a **post office**.

### Transport

[See also pp45-50] Wright Bros seasonal No 888 **bus** operates to Hexham which is on the Newcastle to Carlisle railway line. Their No 680 (operated with Stagecoach/Telford's Coaches) goes to Carlisle, Brampton and Nenthead.

For a **taxi** try Hendersons (☎ 01434-381204) or Alston Taxis (☎ 0799-0593855).

**South Tyneside Railway** (☎ 01434-381696, 🖳 www.strps.org.uk) operates trains from Alston to Stonehaugh (2¼ miles) on 'Northern England's highest narrow-gauge railway'. Trains run daily in holiday periods from April to October and at weekends in December. Steam locomotives are used on some services; see the website or phone them for details. Volunteers are hoping to restore

the line from Stonehaugh to Slaggyford – the line originally went to Hexham.

### Where to stay

*Alston Training and Adventure Centre* (☎ 01434-381886, 🖳 www.alstontraining.co.uk; off Map 93), not far off the Pennine Way, offers **camping** (£4.50pp), **bunkhouse** accommodation (40+ beds; £13.50; bedding £4.80), breakfast (£6.25), evening meals (£9.50) and packed lunches (£4.50). Since they are sometimes fully booked by groups it is essential to book accommodation (and food) in advance.

Alternatively, if already in Alston, make your way past lots of derelict cars behind the Texaco garage to *Tyne Willows Caravan Park* (☎ 01434-382515; Mar to end Oct). It costs £5pp to **camp** on the bit of grass allocated for tents. There are toilet/shower facilities.

*Alston YHA Hostel* (☎ 0845-371 9301, 🖳 alston@yha.org.uk; Apr-Oct; 30 beds – 7 rooms with 2-6 beds) overlooks the South Tyne river; it offers meals and charges from £12.95 (from £9.95 for under 18s).

There are several pubs, some past their prime; you may find traditional B&Bs a better bet. Pubs with rooms include *The Victoria Inn* (☎ 01434-381194; 4S/2D/2F, some en suite) which charges £44-50 for two sharing and £30 for a single. *The Angel Inn* (☎ 01434-381363; 1S/1T/2D, shared facilities) down the hill does B&B for £59 (£35 for the single) and is used to walkers. *Cumberland Hotel* (☎ 01434-381875, 🖳 www.alstoncumberlandhotel.co.uk; 2D/3F, all en suite, bath available) charges £70 and £42 for single occupancy. Dogs are welcome.

*Alston House Hotel* (☎ 01434-382200, 🖳 www.alstonhousehotel.co.uk; 6D, T or F, all en suite, bath available) is the pick of the crop in town; B&B costs £100, from £40 for single occupancy. It has great food (see Where to eat and drink). Dogs (£5) are welcome.

Out of town (see Map 94) the award-winning *Grey Croft* (☎ 01434-381383, 🖳 www.greycroftalston.co.uk; 1D/1D, T or F, both en suite, bath available), Middle Park,

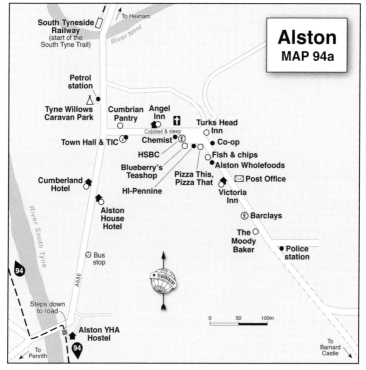

South Tyneside Railway (start of the South Tyne Trail)

To Hexham

River Nent

**Alston**
**MAP 94a**

Petrol station

Tyne Willows Caravan Park

Cumbrian Pantry

Angel Inn

Turks Head Inn

Cobbled & steep

Town Hall & TIC

Chemist

Co-op

HSBC

Fish & chips

Blueberry's Teashop

Alston Wholefoods

Pizza This, Pizza That

Post Office

Cumberland Hotel

HI-Pennine

Victoria Inn

Alston House Hotel

Barclays

River South Tyne

Bus stop

A686

The Moody Baker

Police station

★ trailblazer

Steps down to road

Alston YHA Hostel

0    50    100m

To Penrith

To Barnard Castle

The Raise, is a favourite among walkers; B&B is £64 (single occupancy costs £42). About a mile north of Alston, where the Pennine Way crosses the A689, is *Harbut Law* (☎ 01434-381950; 1D/1T, both en suite; Easter to Oct) a comfortable B&B charging £30pp.

### Where to eat and drink

Not all the pubs do great food; try *The Angel Inn* (see Where to stay; food served Mon-Thur noon-2pm & 6-9pm, Fri-Sun noon-3pm & 6-9pm). Alston House (see Where to stay) serves food in its *House Café* (Mon-Fri 10am-4pm, Sat & Sun 10am-9pm), with daytime snacks and salads for £4-6, as well as in its bar and **restaurant** (summer Mon-Sat 6-9pm, Sun 10am-9pm, winter Tue-Fri 6-9pm, Sat & Sun 10am-

9pm); the extensive menu includes dishes such as Cumbrian lamb shoulder (£12.50). *Cumberland Hotel* (see Where to stay) also serves food (daily noon-9pm).

*Blueberry's Tea Shop* (☎ 01434-381928; daily 9am-5pm; they may close earlier in the winter) serves lunches and an all-day breakfast from £3.50. In addition to the *fish and chip shop* the nearby *Moody Baker* (☎ 01434-382003; Mon & Wed-Sat 8.30am-4pm, Tue 8.30-2pm; they also may close earlier in the winter) co-operative has an excellent range of home-made food, to take away, focusing on local produce and organic ingredients where possible.

*Cumbrian Pantry* (☎ 01434-381406; Mon, Wed, Thu & Sun 9am-4pm, Fri & Sat 9am-5pm, closed Tue) prepares meals to be eaten in as well as food, such as sandwiches and cakes, to be eaten in or taken away. The fish and chips is £4 to takeaway.

The *Victoria Inn* (Tue-Sun 6-9pm) does curries and you can get a takeaway pizza at

*Pizza This Pizza That* (Mon, Wed, Thu, Sun 5-9pm, Fri & Sat 5-10pm, closed Tue).

The best place for a drink is the *Turks Head Inn* which does real ales.

## ALSTON TO GREENHEAD                     MAPS 94-102

### Route overview

Some days along the Pennine Way are classics, others are less memorable and today's **17-mile (27km, 7½-9½hrs)** walk from Alston to Greenhead falls into the latter category but fear not, there are only one or two like it and this is the last. It's also a sad day because around you the true Pennine chain comes to an end as you schlep along the South Tyne Valley. What hills continue on the far side of the Wall are really part of the Southern Uplands massif: England's sturdy backbone probes gently into Scotland's quivering belly.

No matter, the first objective is **Slaggyford** (Map 97), a name that suggests a glum colliery or worse, but which in reality is a residential village with no services except for a public telephone and a B&B. Here you join the course of a former railway now known as the **South Tyne Trail** which at one point is left for a mile or so in a pedantic struggle through fields and people's backyards before passing in and out of the viaduct at Burnstones. **Knarsdale** (see p217) is just a few minutes off the trail at this point. If you don't need a bed or food, continue north over the moor.

The **Maiden Way** (Map 98), a former Roman Road is now underfoot as you leave the valley and march more or less due north over marsh and marsh grass. You then descend to the more arable muck of the **Hartley Burn floodplain** (Map 99) before heading up again via a couple of farmyards onto the misery that dares call itself **Blenkinsopp Common** (Map 100), the crossing of which seems like an expedition over a country abandoned by man and beast. The '-sopp' suffix is a clue for once on the moor the path becomes indistinct or not worth following until you crest **Black Hill**, not unlike its sodden cousin in the northern Peak District all those miles ago, but without the blessings of a slab causeway.

You come upon a row of huge pylons and all that remains now is to cross the **A69** (Map 102) without getting run over – no thoughtful footbridge or underpass here. The village of Greenhead is in sight, arrived at by gingerly circumnavigating its golf course and dropping steeply into the dispersed hamlet. If the day is still young and your spirit untramelled, get a feed in Greenhead Hotel and consider powering on a few miles to Burnhead or Once Brewed. After tomorrow's thigh-stretching stage you may be glad you did.

Was it just us or is this stage a navigational headache at times? You're about to find out so read the **route-finding trouble spots** carefully.

### Alston to Greenhead: route-finding trouble spots

This stage is not helped by waymarking that at times verges on the extra sensory. The Way from Alston to Harbut Law (Map 94) on the A689 is easy enough but here ensues a sometimes discreetly signed arc back to the road at Castle Nook Farm (Map 95). Onwards to Slaggyford is merely the usual steeplechase of farm

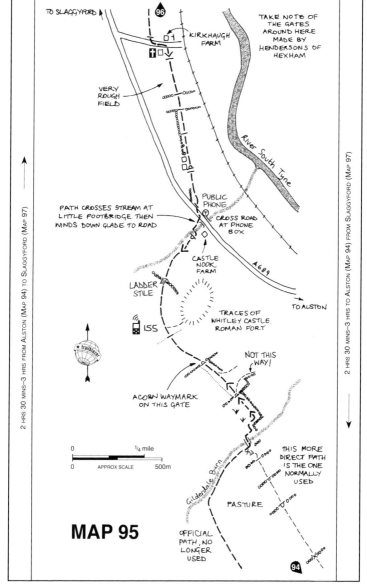

TO SLAGGYFORD

96

KIRKHAUGH FARM

TAKE NOTE OF THE GATES AROUND HERE MADE BY HENDERSONS OF HEXHAM

VERY ROUGH FIELD

River South Tyne

PATH CROSSES STREAM AT LITTLE FOOTBRIDGE THEN WINDS DOWN GLADE TO ROAD

PUBLIC PHONE

CROSS ROAD AT PHONE BOX

CASTLE NOOK FARM

A689

LADDER STILE

TO ALSTON

TRACES OF WHITLEY CASTLE ROMAN FORT

155

trailblazer

NOT THIS WAY!

ACORN WAYMARK ON THIS GATE

THIS MORE DIRECT PATH IS THE ONE NORMALLY USED

Gilderdale Burn

0    ¼ mile

0    APPROX SCALE    500m

PASTURE

**MAP 95**

OFFICIAL PATH, NO LONGER USED

94

2 HRS 30 MINS–3 HRS FROM ALSTON (MAP 94) TO SLAGGYFORD (MAP 97)

2 HRS 30 MINS–3 HRS TO ALSTON (MAP 94) FROM SLAGGYFORD (MAP 97)

walls and fences until you pass under the *correct* viaduct near Lintley Farm (Map 96) to rejoin the South Tyne river and the road to Slaggyford.

Joining the South Tyne Trail ('STT') along a former railway, watch out for a sign (if there is one) as the Pennine Way shoots off just after the bridge over Knar Burn (Map 97). It leads to the collection of houses known as Merry Knowe. Those in the 'merry know' may prefer to simply stick to the STT until it reaches Burnstones and slither down the left bank on the northern end of the viaduct (as most clearly do) to join up with the Maiden Way section. This too is not blindingly obvious until you make it to the A689 and over Hartley Burn (Map 99).

The next trick is projecting yourself accurately at Ulpham Farm (Map 100); a compass may be handy. And it will be again after you leave Greenriggs' yard. Once on the moor the Way supposedly turns west to join and follow a fence line north, but unless global warming has dried the land since this was written, looking west you wouldn't want to go there, even if they did sign it clearly. Instead tip-toe your way across the higher morass on a bearing of 300° or so to meet the point where the fence intercepts the more visible wall leading to Wain Rigg. Once crossed, the route down to the A69 and from there to Greenhead is less complicated, or at least near enough the end to be muddled (and muddied) through.

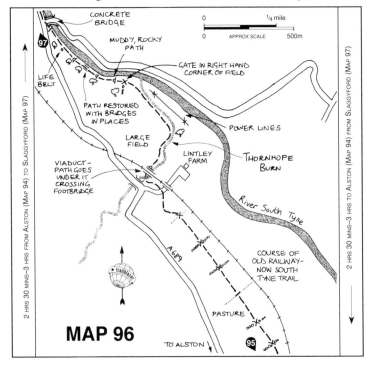

MAP 96

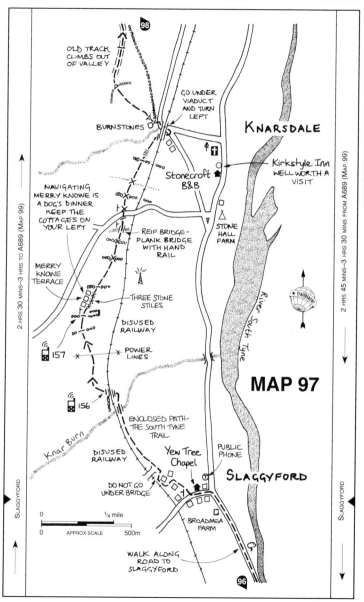

98

OLD TRACK CLIMBS OUT OF VALLEY

GO UNDER VIADUCT AND TURN LEFT

BURNSTONES

KNARSDALE

Kirkstyle Inn WELL WORTH A VISIT

Stonecroft B&B

NAVIGATING MERRY KNOWE IS A DOG'S DINNER. KEEP THE COTTAGES ON YOUR LEFT

REIF BRIDGE– PLANK BRIDGE WITH HAND RAIL

STONE HALL FARM

MERRY KNOWE TERRACE

THREE STONE STILES

DISUSED RAILWAY

157

POWER LINES

MAP 97

River South Tyne

156

ENCLOSED PATH– THE SOUTH TYNE TRAIL

Knar Burn

DISUSED RAILWAY

Yew Tree Chapel

PUBLIC PHONE

SLAGGYFORD

0        ¼ mile

0        500m
APPROX SCALE

DO NOT GO UNDER BRIDGE

BROADMEA FARM

WALK ALONG ROAD TO SLAGGYFORD

96

2 HRS 30 MINS–3 HRS TO A689 (MAP 99)

2 HRS 45 MINS–3 HRS 30 MINS FROM A689 (MAP 99)

SLAGGYFORD

SLAGGYFORD

ROUTE GUIDE AND MAPS

**MAP 98**

99

PW FOLLOWS THE
MAIDEN WAY, A
ROMAN ROAD

PASS STILE
ON LEFT

160

DON'T CROSS
THIS STILE

WET ALONG
THIS STRETCH

HEATHER
TO LEFT
OF FENCE

ROUGH FELL,
MARSH GRASS

0          1/4 mile

0          500m
APPROX SCALE

CROSS
WALL

GLENDUE
BURN

AS YOU DESCEND TO
THE ROAD, THE MARSH
GRASS IS WAIST HIGH

A689

TWO STILES AFTER
FORD, THEN DESCENT

159

TO ALSTON

FORD

DON'T TAKE THIS
TEMPTING TRACK,
STAY LEVEL

BARN

158

LEAVE TRACK TO
RIGHT (MAIDEN WAY)

PW FINGER
POST

97

2 HRS 30 MINS–3 HRS TO A689 (MAP 99) FROM SLAGGYFORD (MAP 97)

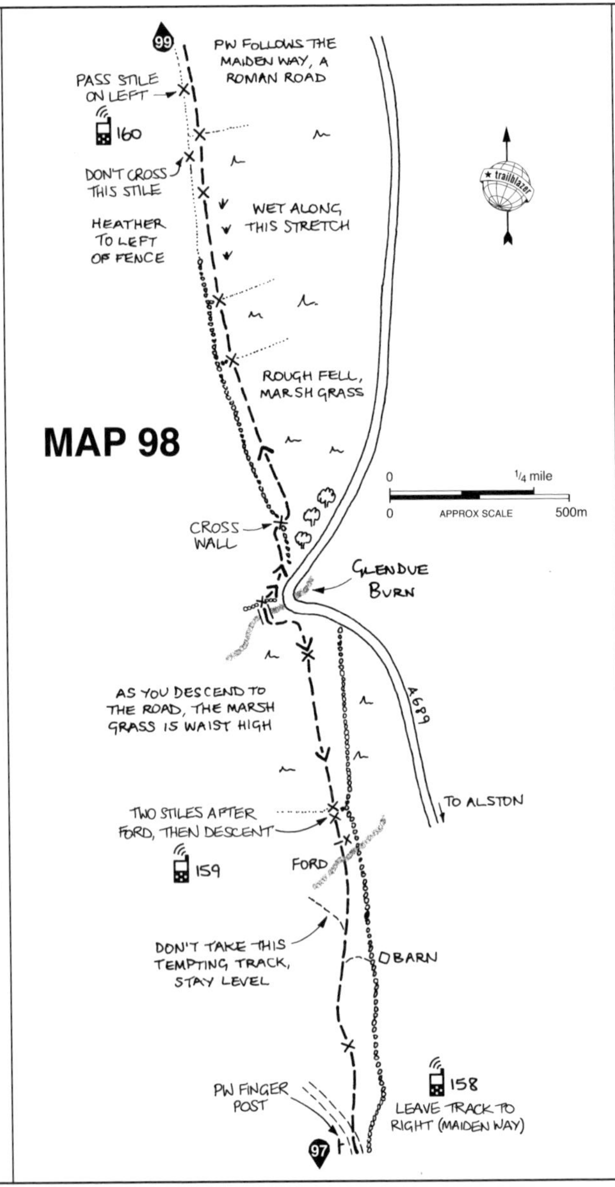

2 HRS 45 MINS–3 HRS 30 MINS FROM A689 (MAP 99) TO SLAGGYFORD (MAP 97)

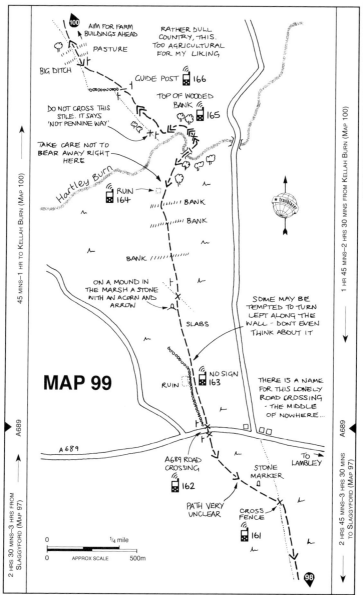

AIM FOR FARM BUILDINGS AHEAD

PASTURE

BIG DITCH

RATHER DULL COUNTRY, THIS. TOO AGRICULTURAL FOR MY LIKING

GUIDE POST 166

TOP OF WOODED BANK 165

DO NOT CROSS THIS STILE. IT SAYS 'NOT PENNINE WAY'

TAKE CARE NOT TO BEAR AWAY RIGHT HERE

Hartley Burn

RUIN 164

BANK

BANK

BANK

ON A MOUND IN THE MARSH A STONE WITH AN ACORN AND ARROW

SLABS

SOME MAY BE TEMPTED TO TURN LEFT ALONG THE WALL - DON'T EVEN THINK ABOUT IT

**MAP 99**

RUIN

NO SIGN 163

THERE IS A NAME FOR THIS LONELY ROAD CROSSING - THE MIDDLE OF NOWHERE...

A689

A689

TO LAMBLEY

A689 ROAD CROSSING

162

STONE MARKER

PATH VERY UNCLEAR

CROSS FENCE 161

0   ¼ mile

0   APPROX SCALE   500m

45 MINS–1 HR TO KELLAH BURN (MAP 100)

1 HR 45 MINS–2 HRS 30 MINS FROM KELLAH BURN (MAP 100)

2 HRS 30 MINS–3 HRS FROM SLAGGYFORD (MAP 97)

2 HRS 45 MINS–3 HRS 30 MINS TO SLAGGYFORD (MAP 97)

ROUTE GUIDE AND MAPS

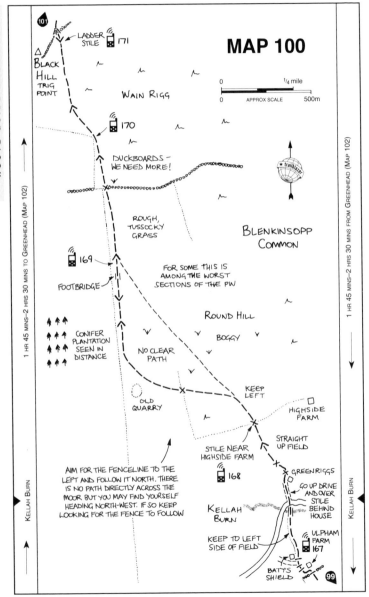

MAP 100

LADDER STILE

171

△ BLACK HILL TRIG POINT

WAIN RIGG

0        1/4 mile
0    APPROX SCALE    500m

★ trailblazer

170

DUCKBOARDS – WE NEED MORE!

ROUGH, TUSSOCKY GRASS

BLENKINSOPP COMMON

169

FOOTBRIDGE

FOR SOME THIS IS AMONG THE WORST SECTIONS OF THE PW

CONIFER PLANTATION SEEN IN DISTANCE

NO CLEAR PATH

ROUND HILL

BOGGY

OLD QUARRY

KEEP LEFT

HIGHSIDE FARM

STRAIGHT UP FIELD

AIM FOR THE FENCELINE TO THE LEFT AND FOLLOW IT NORTH. THERE IS NO PATH DIRECTLY ACROSS THE MOOR BUT YOU MAY FIND YOURSELF HEADING NORTH-WEST. IF SO KEEP LOOKING FOR THE FENCE TO FOLLOW

STILE NEAR HIGHSIDE FARM

168

GREENRIGGS

GO UP DRIVE AND OVER STILE BEHIND HOUSE

KELLAH BURN

KEEP TO LEFT SIDE OF FIELD

ULPHAM FARM 167

BATY'S SHIELD

99

1 HR 45 MINS–2 HRS 30 MINS TO GREENHEAD (MAP 102)

1 HR 45 MINS–2 HRS 30 MINS FROM GREENHEAD (MAP 102)

KELLAH BURN

KELLAH BURN

101

99

## SLAGGYFORD  [Map 97, p213]

If you're having a hard day or are on your own schedule, Slaggyford is only six miles from Alston.

Right in the village, *Yew Tree Chapel* (☎ 01434-382525, 🖳 www.yewtreechapel .co.uk; 2D or T/1T, all en suite with hip bath) has been spectacularly converted into an unusual B&B with two sharing paying from £70 (single occupancy from £40). Packed lunches (£6) and evening meals (£16) are also available for anyone without transport and if booked in advance. Dogs (£10) are also welcome. It's well worth a visit.

## KNARSDALE  [Map 97, p213]

A mile down the road you can **camp** at *Stonehall Farm* (☎ 01434-381349). At £4 it's basic, there's an outside toilet and a water tap. The pub, the Kirkstyle Inn, is just 50 metres down the road but note that it does not serve food every evening. Just before the pub is *Stonecroft* (☎ 01434-382995; 2T, en suite, bath available) where **B&B** costs £30pp (£35 single occupancy) and a packed lunch costs from £3.

Pennine Wayfarers are always looking for an excuse to stop at the *Kirkstyle Inn* (☎ 01434-381559; food served summer daily noon-2pm & Tue-Sat 6-9pm; winter Wed-Sun noon-2pm & Tue-Sat 6-9pm). From the choice of beers to the tasty bar menu and the atmosphere this place has everything walkers like and is the sort of hostelry you'll be hallucinating about when you're halfway between Byrness and Kirk Yetholm.

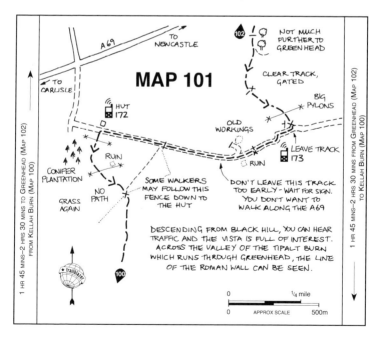

MAP 101

TO NEWCASTLE

A69

TO CARLISLE

NOT MUCH FURTHER TO GREEN HEAD

CLEAR TRACK, GATED

BIG PYLONS

HUT 172

OLD WORKINGS

LEAVE TRACK 173

RUIN

RUIN

CONIFER PLANTATION

GRASS AGAIN

NO PATH

SOME WALKERS MAY FOLLOW THIS FENCE DOWN TO THE HUT

DON'T LEAVE THIS TRACK TOO EARLY - WAIT FOR SIGN. YOU DON'T WANT TO WALK ALONG THE A69

DESCENDING FROM BLACK HILL, YOU CAN HEAR TRAFFIC AND THE VISTA IS FULL OF INTEREST. ACROSS THE VALLEY OF THE TIPALT BURN WHICH RUNS THROUGH GREENHEAD, THE LINE OF THE ROMAN WALL CAN BE SEEN.

1 HR 45 MINS–2 HRS 30 MINS TO GREENHEAD (MAP 102) FROM KELLAH BURN (MAP 100)

1 HR 45 MINS–2 HRS 30 MINS FROM GREENHEAD (MAP 102) TO KELLAH BURN (MAP 100)

0            1/4 mile

0      APPROX SCALE      500m

ROUTE GUIDE AND MAPS

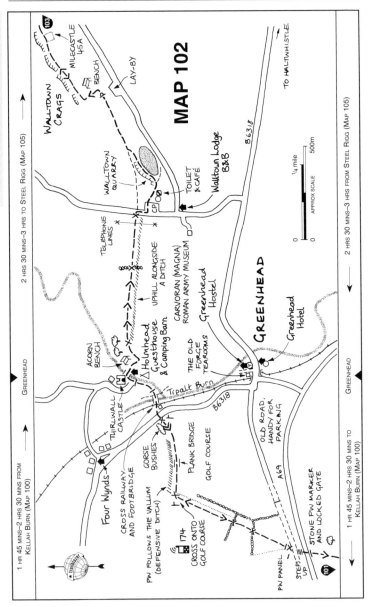

# MAP 102

1 HR 45 MINS–2 HRS 30 MINS FROM
KELLAH BURN (MAP 100)

2 HRS 30 MINS–3 HRS TO STEEL RIGG (MAP 105)

GREENHEAD

GREENHEAD

1 HR 45 MINS–2 HRS 30 MINS TO
KELLAH BURN (MAP 100)

2 HRS 30 MINS–3 HRS FROM STEEL RIGG (MAP 105)

103

MILECASTLE 45A

WALLTOWN CRAGS

BENCH

LAY-BY

TO HALTWHISTLE

WALLTOWN QUARRY

B6318

Walltown Lodge B&B

TOILET & CAFÉ

CP

TELEPHONE LINES

UPHILL ALONGSIDE A DITCH

CARVORAN (MAGNA) ROMAN ARMY MUSEUM

Greenhead Hostel

GREENHEAD

Greenhead Hotel

ACORN BENCH

Holmhead Guesthouse & Camping Barn

THE OLD FORGE TEAROOMS

Tipalt Burn

THIRLWALL CASTLE

B6318

Four Wynds

CROSS RAILWAY AND FOOTBRIDGE

GORSE BUSHES

PLANK BRIDGE

GOLF COURSE

OLD ROAD, HANDY FOR PARKING

A69

PW FOLLOWS THE VALLUM (DEFENSIVE DITCH)

174

CROSS ONTO GOLF COURSE

STEPS VP

PW PANEL

101

STONE PW MARKER AND LOCKED GATE

APPROX SCALE

¼ mile

500m

0

0

## GREENHEAD [Map 102]

Having arrived in the rather dispersed hamlet of Greenhead, you can take solace from the fact that you're very near **Britain's geographical centre**; a point equidistant from all shores. Not a lot of people know that.

The **Carvoran Roman Army Museum** (☎ 016977-47485, 🖥 www.vindolanda.com; Apr-Sep daily 10am-6pm, mid to end Mar & Oct 10am-5pm; £5/4.25/2.75) is well worth the short detour to see some fascinating Roman artefacts including coins, shoes and nails. The museum was refurbished over the winter of 2010-11; new features include a 3D film of a visualisation of the top of the wall from here to Vindolanda and additional exhibits about life in the Roman army.

### Transport

[See also pp45-50] The line for the Newcastle to Carlisle railway runs through Greenhead but services no longer stop here. However, Arriva's/Stagecoach's **bus** No 685 operates to Haltwhistle **railway** station, only 3 miles (5km) away. Greenhead is also a stop on the seasonal Hadrian's Wall bus route (AD122) and Telford's Coaches No 185.

### Where to stay, eat and drink

A converted Methodist chapel houses **Greenhead Hostel** (☎ 01697-747411, 🖥 www.greenheadhotelandhostel.co.uk; open all year; 40 beds), owned by the hotel over the road, where beds cost £15pp (YHA members £13.50; £10pp under 18s); breakfast (£1.95-8.50) and evening meals are available in the hotel. They also have a self-contained flat sleeping six (2S/2D) for £100 per night.

Nearby **Four Wynds Guest House** (☎ 01697-747972, 🖥 www.four-wynds guest-house.co.uk; 2T/1D or F, all en suite, Mar-Oct) has rooms for £68 based on two sharing (£38-40 single occupancy). Dogs are welcome as long as the proprietors have advance notice.

*Greenhead Hotel* (see Greenhead Hostel for contact details; 1D/1T/2T, D or F, all en suite, bath available; food served daily noon-8.30pm), in the middle of town, offers B&B in spacious rooms for £70 for two sharing and around £40 for single occupancy. Dogs are not permitted in the hotel though they have a dog pound outside. The hotel is your best bet for a **feed in the evening**.

Back on the Way, half a mile north of the village, *Holmhead Guest House* (☎ 01697-747402, 🖥 www.holmhead.com; 2T or D/2D, all en suite) is a multiple accommodation complex for Wall-bound wayfarers. The pleasant walk there crosses a river, follows a track along the bank, through sheep fields and thence to the homestead. B&B (£65-75 for two sharing, from £50 for single occupancy). The **camping barn** (£12.50pp plus £3.50 to hire a sleeping bag) sleeps five and has a kitchenette. There is also a **bunk barn** (£8pp) which sleeps up to seven people. Both barns have shower/toilet facilities. However, reservations are recommended as the barns are often booked by groups. They also have a small area where you can **camp** for £10 per pitch (basic toilet/shower facilities are available).

The *Old Forge Tea Rooms* (Tue-Fri 9.30am-4.30pm, Sat & Sun 9.30am-5pm) serves snacks on home-made bread and an all-day breakfast.

Alternatively try the **café** (Easter to end Oct, daily 10am-5pm) in the Walltown car park where you can get soup and a roll for £2. There's also a good B&B here: *Walltown Lodge* (☎ 01697-747514, 🖥 www.walltownlodge.com; 1T/2D, all en suite) charging £30-40pp (£10 single occupancy supplement). Dogs are not allowed in the house but they have dog kennels (£5). They also offer evening meals for £15 and packed lunches for £5; 24 hours' notice is required for meals.

❏ **Thirlwall Castle**
Thirlwall Castle was built in the 14th century by the powerful like-named family for protection and defence against border raiders. At that time the castle must have represented an impregnable stronghold to men armed only with spear and sword but by the 17th century these lawless times had passed and the Thirlwall family moved to more comfortable quarters in Hexham.

   As a reminder of a time when the Borders were the scene of raids and struggles, Thirlwall serves a purpose but we have more absorbing antiquities than this to investigate. Ahead lies The Wall!

## GREENHEAD TO BELLINGHAM                                 MAPS 102-112

### Route overview
Gird your loins for this is a tough one, a **22-mile (33km, 9-10½hrs)** stage that feels every bit of it thanks to over 900 galling metres of ascent; nearly as much as Day 1. You remember Day 1 don't you?

   Greenhead is left behind via the rather inflated if not bouncy ruin of Thirlwall Castle and at **Walltown Crags** you join **Hadrian's Wall** itself. As you follow the best-preserved part of the wall for eight miles it is the frequent **climbs and drops**, many stepped, which will account for the day's exertions. Indeed you may prefer to break this stage (or lengthen the previous day) by staying in or around **Once Brewed** (Map 105).

   The walk along the wall is now rather popular and for the first time since Malham you may feel a bit crowded by day-walking 'civilians'. If so, raise your eyes to the horizon and the views of the ramparts following the Whin Sill, swooping and soaring past the quacking wildfowl in **Crag Lough**.

   Soon enough you reach **Rapishaw Gap** (Map 106) and forsake the Wall-walking throng, north towards sunless forests and some fine walking. Revisionists and environmentalists condemn the post-war boom in plantation monoculture which anyway now seems to have had its day thanks to foreign imports. The trails which pass through them too are dismissed though today at least, your transit through **Wark Forest** (Map 107) generally avoids the main gravel drives for more agreeable and shady trails which never overstay their welcome. **Haughton Common** (Map 108) is a sunlit interlude and when you emerge from the forest ahead of Stonehaugh (off Map 109) the now not so distant Cheviots can be seen to the far north.

   Here ensues a pleasant mixture of pasture, farmland and quiet lanes until a radio mast indicates one more climb, **Shitlington Crag** (Map 111). Thereafter it's downhill all the way, the penultimate mile along the annoyingly busy B6320 until it bridges the North Tyne and leads you into town along the riverbank. This is actually a great day, overseen by the knowledge that journey's end is nigh. **Bellingham** awaits. Nobody gives up here.

### Route-finding trouble spots
In short: there are none. The initial section along the Wall follows as fine a landmark as you could wish for, and once you head into the badlands of the

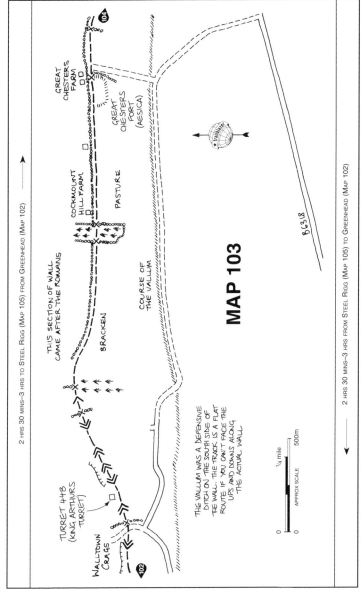

2 HRS 30 MINS–3 HRS TO STEEL RIGG (MAP 105) FROM GREENHEAD (MAP 102)

104

GREAT CHESTERS FARM

GREAT CHESTERS FORT (AESICA)

Trailblazer

COCKMOUNT HILL FARM

PASTURE

THIS SECTION OF WALL CAME AFTER THE ROMANS

BRACKEN

COURSE OF THE VALLUM

MAP 103

B6318

TURRET 44B (KING ARTHUR'S TURRET)

WALLTOWN CRAGS

102

THE VALLUM WAS A DEFENSIVE DITCH ON THE SOUTH SIDE OF THE WALL. THE TRACK IS A FLAT ROUTE IF YOU CAN'T FACE THE UPS AND DOWNS ALONG THE ACTUAL WALL

¼ mile

500m

APPROX SCALE

0

0

2 HRS 30 MINS–3 HRS FROM STEEL RIGG (MAP 105) TO GREENHEAD (MAP 102)

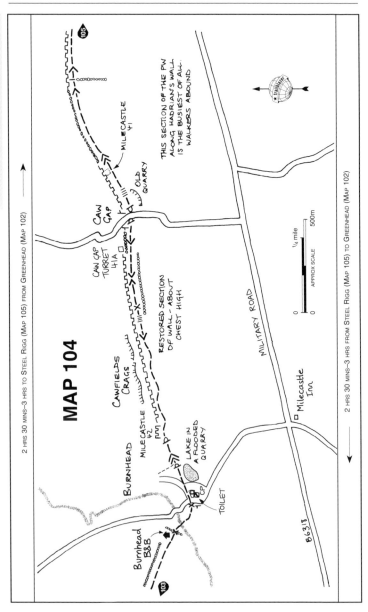

## MAP 104

2 HRS 30 MINS–3 HRS TO STEEL RIGG (MAP 105) FROM GREENHEAD (MAP 102)

2 HRS 30 MINS–3 HRS FROM STEEL RIGG (MAP 105) TO GREENHEAD (MAP 102)

105

THIS SECTION OF THE PW ALONG HADRIAN'S WALL IS THE BUSIEST OF ALL WALKERS ABOUND

MILECASTRE 41

OLD QUARRY

CAW GAP

CAW GAP TURRET 41A

CAWFIELDS CRAGS

RESTORED SECTION OF WALL – ABOUT CHEST HIGH

MILECASTLE 42

BURNHEAD

LAKE IN A FLOODED QUARRY

CP

TOILET

Burnhead B&B

103

MILITARY ROAD

Milecastle Inn

B6318

APPROX SCALE

¼ mile

500m

former cattle-thieving barbarians things do not deteriorate. Indeed this feels like one of the best-marked stages on the entire Pennine Way; an example for which Northumberland National Park should be praised.

## BURNHEAD [Map 104]

Right on the Pennine Way so you may well walk into it, you'll get a warm welcome at *Burnhead* (☎ 01434-320841, 🖳 www .burnheadbedandbreakfast.co.uk; 2T, en suite); they charge £35pp (no single occupancy supplement) and packed lunches (£5) are available on request.

*Milecastle Inn* (☎ 01434-321372, 🖳 www.milecastle-inn.co.uk; food served Easter to end Oct daily noon-8.45pm, daily noon-2.30pm & 6-8.30pm the rest of the year) on Military Road is just 10 minutes' walk away for an evening meal.

### ❏ Hadrian's Wall

The Roman Emperor Hadrian first conceived the project after visiting Britain in AD122 and finding out for himself the extent of the difficulty faced by the occupying army in northern Britain. It was impossible to hold any kind of control over the lawless tribes in the area that is now called Scotland so, as the Chinese had done nearly 400 years earlier, it was decided to build a defensive wall. The line of the wall, drawn from the Solway to the Tyne, followed the fault-line of the Whin Sill, an 'escarpment' of resistant dolerite which acted as a natural east–west barrier.

The Wall ran for approximately 80 Roman miles (73 modern miles or 117km) and had turrets or milecastles every (Roman) mile and larger forts at intervals along its length. The forts would have had a garrison of 500 cavalry or 1000 foot soldiers, and milecastles were manned by 50 men. The Wall was made of stone and turf and would have been five metres high and with a defensive ditch, the vallum, set between two mounds of earth, running the length of the southern side. Behind that ran a road to supply and provision the troops manning the wall.

The construction of the Wall was supervised by the Imperial Legate, Aulus Platorius Nepos, and construction took ten years. It remained in use for 200 years but as the Romans withdrew it fell into disuse and gradually the stones were plundered to build farmsteads and roads. Thirlwall Castle (see Map 102) is among the many local buildings with stones from the Roman Wall.

Today English Heritage, the National Trust and the National Park authorities preserve and protect what remains of the wall, keeping it tidy and providing the information that we need to help us imagine what it was all for. It's well worth visiting **Housesteads Fort** (off Map 106; ☎ 01434-344363; daily Apr-Sep 10am-6pm, Oct-Mar 10am-4pm; adult £4.80; free to NT and English Heritage members), just before the Way heads north. You'll be pleased to know the communal latrines are particularly well preserved.

The information we have about the history of the Wall is fragmentary and circumstantial, historians having disputed for centuries over the finer details. What is certain is that the Wall is an extraordinary example of military might whilst demonstrating perhaps the futility of human endeavour. How can you hold back the tide of human expansion by anything so transient as a wall? Impressive, inspiring, unique, yes, but ultimately a failure. When we turn our back on it and head north into Wark Forest, the sight of the Whin Sill is like a breaking wave. The Wall blends into the landscape. The northern tribes had only to wait.

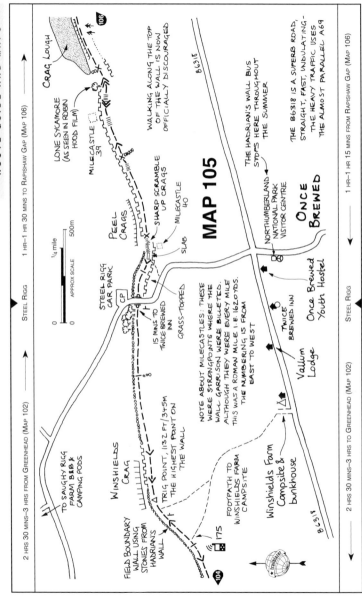

## MAP 105

2 HRS 30 MINS–3 HRS FROM GREENHEAD (MAP 102)  STEEL RIGG  1 HR–1 HR 30 MINS TO RAPISHAW GAP (MAP 106)

2 HRS 30 MINS–3 HRS TO GREENHEAD (MAP 102)  STEEL RIGG  1 HR–1 HR 15 MINS FROM RAPISHAW GAP (MAP 106)

CRAG LOUGH

LONE SYCAMORE (AS SEEN IN ROBIN HOOD FILM)

WALKING ALONG THE TOP OF THE WALL IS NOW OFFICIALLY DISCOURAGED

B6318

THE B6318 IS A SUPERB ROAD, STRAIGHT, FAST, UNDULATING — THE HEAVY TRAFFIC USES THE ALMOST PARALLEL A69

MILECASTLE 39

THE HADRIAN'S WALL BUS STOPS HERE THROUGHOUT THE SUMMER

PEEL CRAGS

SHARP SCRAMBLE UP CRAGS

MILECASTLE 40

SLAB

NORTHUMBERLAND NATIONAL PARK VISITOR CENTRE

Once Brewed

STEEL RIGG CAR PARK

CP

GRASS-TOPPED

15 MINS TO TWICE BREWED INN

NOTE ABOUT MILECASTLES: THESE WERE STRONGPOINTS WHERE THE WALL GARRISON WERE BILLETED. ALTHOUGH THEY WERE EVERY MILE THIS WAS A ROMAN MILE I.E. 1620 YDS. THE NUMBERING IS FROM EAST TO WEST

TWICE BREWED INN

Once Brewed Youth Hostel

Vallum Lodge

TO SAUGHY RIGG FARM B&B & CAMPING PODS

WINSHIELDS CRAG

TRIG POINT, 1132 FT/345M THE HIGHEST POINT ON THE WALL

FOOTPATH TO WINSHIELDS FARM CAMPSITE

Winshields Farm Campsite & bunkhouse

FIELD BOUNDARY WALL USING STONES FROM HADRIAN'S WALL

175

B6318

104

0  1/4 mile
0  500m
APPROX SCALE

* Trailblazer

## ONCE BREWED [Map 105]

Not really a village, Once Brewed is about half a mile south of the Way on the B6318, better known for nearly two millennia as the 'Military Road'. Doubtless the origins of the name torment your curiosity. The Twice Brewed Inn, a staging post between Carlisle and Newcastle, gained its name around 1710 when General Wade found the local ale so weak he advised that it be brewed again. When the hostel was opened in the 1930s, the YHA's patron, Lady Trevelyan, remarked that she hoped her cup of tea would be brewed once, not twice like the General's ale and so the name was born.

See p25 for details of the Roman Wall show held here in June.

## Services

The **Northumberland National Park Visitor Centre** acts as a **tourist information centre** (TIC; ☎ 01434-344396, 🖳 www. northumberlandnationalpark.org.uk; daily mid-March to Oct 9.30am-5pm, Nov to mid-Mar Sat & Sun 10am-3pm) and thus the staff can book accommodation (see box p13) and provide information on the area. There are also drinks machines (hot and cold) and an area where you can buy snacks. Visit 🖳 www.hadrians-wall.org for the whole story on the area, including more regional accommodation.

**Internet access** is available at The Twice Brewed Inn (see Where to stay).

## Transport

[See also pp45-50] The Hadrian's Wall **Bus** Service (Apr-Oct; designated route 'AD122' in honour of the Wall's inauguration by the Emperor Hadrian) stops outside the visitor centre. Many of these buses also stop at the **railway station** at Haltwhistle on the Carlisle–Newcastle line with frequent trains coming and going throughout the day. Wright's No 681 also stops here.

For a **taxi**, call Sprouls Taxis (☎ 01434-321064 or ☎ 07712-321064) or Turnbulls (☎ 01434-320105).

## Where to stay and eat

The obvious choice for **campers** is **Winshields Farm** (☎ 01434-344243, 🖳 www.winshields.co.uk) right by the main road, where the charge is £7pp. They also have a **bunkhouse** sleeping 12 for £10pp; book in advance as sometimes this is used by groups. Everyone can use the shower/toilet facilities and a cooked breakfast (Apr-Oct) can be provided as well as packed lunches. There is also a shop on site selling food essentials but there's no kitchen, just a microwave oven.

***Once Brewed YHA Hostel*** (☎ 0845-371 9753, 🖳 oncebrewed@yha.org.uk; open all year) is a purpose-built hostel with 77 beds, mostly in four-bedded rooms. Meals are available and beds cost from £17pp (from £13 for under 18s).

Other accommodation in the area includes the superior ***Vallum Lodge*** (☎ 01434-344248, 🖳 www.vallum-lodge.co .uk; 3T/2D/1F, all en suite, bath available; mid Mar-Oct) charging £80 for two sharing and £69 for single occupancy.

Between the YHA hostel and Vallum Lodge is ***The Twice Brewed Inn*** (☎ 01434-344534, 🖳 www.twicebrewedinn. co.uk; 2S/3D & 3T en suite/3D & 3T, share facilities) with a single for £34, basic doubles/twins from £56 and en suites for £72-84. The pub has broadband **internet** (£1 for 30 mins) and free wifi and the menu (food served daily summer noon-8.30pm, to 9pm Fri & Sat, winter daily noon-8pm, to 8.30pm Fri & Sat) has some good vegetarian options.

Another great spot is ***Saughy Rigg Farm*** (off Map 105; ☎ 01434-344120, 🖳 www.saughyrigg.co.uk; 2S/3D/4T/2F, all en suite, one room with bath); B&B costs £50 for a single and £75-85 for two sharing. They will provide evening meals (a main course costs from £12; check out the sample menu on their website) and a packed lunch is £5. They have a bar with draught beer. Dogs (£5) are welcome if booked in advance. For those on a budget try one of their three '**camping pods**', small wooden shelters costing £40 for a pod sleeping four and £50 for a pod sleeping six; each pod has a heater and is lockable. Pod guests can use a bathroom with shower in the house. Bedding (£2) can be rented and breakfast (£6) can be provided. Booking is recommended for the pods, especially in the main season. The pleasingly isolated farm is about half a mile north of Hadrian's Wall along the road from the Steel Rigg car park.

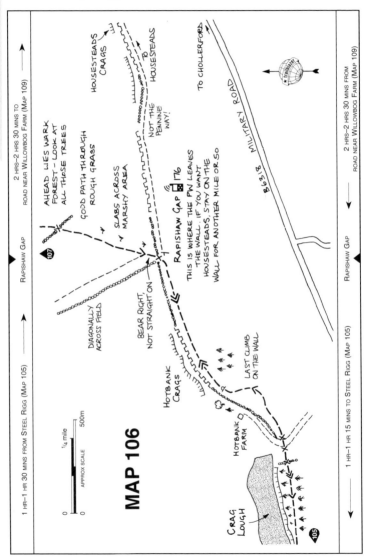

# MAP 106

1/4 mile
APPROX SCALE    500m

1 HR–1 HR 30 MINS FROM STEEL RIGG (MAP 105)
RAPISHAW GAP
2 HRS–2 HRS 30 MINS TO ROAD NEAR WILLOWBOG FARM (MAP 109)

1 HR–1 HR 15 MINS TO STEEL RIGG (MAP 105)
RAPISHAW GAP
2 HRS–2 HRS 30 MINS FROM ROAD NEAR WILLOWBOG FARM (MAP 109)

HOUSESTEADS CRAGS

TO HOUSESTEADS

AHEAD LIES WARK FOREST – LOOK AT ALL THOSE TREES

GOOD PATH THROUGH ROUGH GRASS

NOT THE PENNINE WAY!

SLABS ACROSS MARSHY AREA

Rapishaw Gap 176

THIS IS WHERE THE PW LEAVES THE WALL. IF YOU WANT HOUSESTEADS, STAY ON THE WALL FOR ANOTHER MILE OR SO

TO CHOLLERFORD

B6318 MILITARY ROAD

DIAGONALLY ACROSS FIELD

BEAR RIGHT, NOT STRAIGHT ON

HOTBANK CRAGS

LAST CLIMB ON THE WALL

HOTBANK FARM

CRAG LOUGH

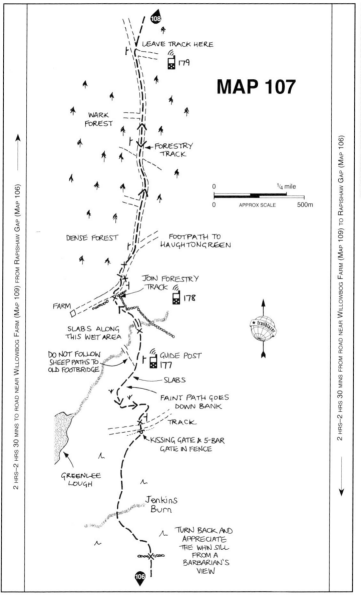

## STONEHAUGH [off Map 109]

Aside from licking dew off the grass, there are hardly any opportunities for refreshments on the route today except at the forestry outpost of Stonehaugh, eight miles from Bellingham, where, if you feel that you simply cannot walk any further, you could head for the Forestry Commission's **Stonehaugh Camp Site** (☎ 01434-230798; Easter to Sep), which charges £7.50 for a single tent plus £5pp. It's a mile off the route and there are no shops for five miles although they can provide provisions and a packed lunch if you call ahead; however, they may request a deposit. There are also toilet/shower facilities. The community hall provides breakfasts (Sat & Sun 8.30-10am).

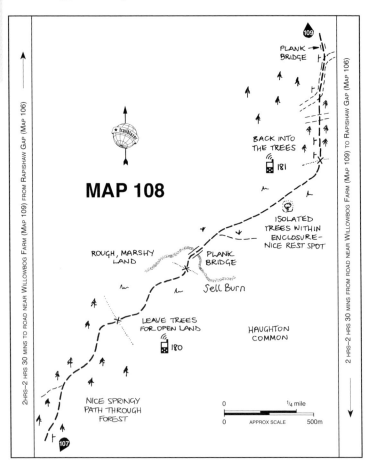

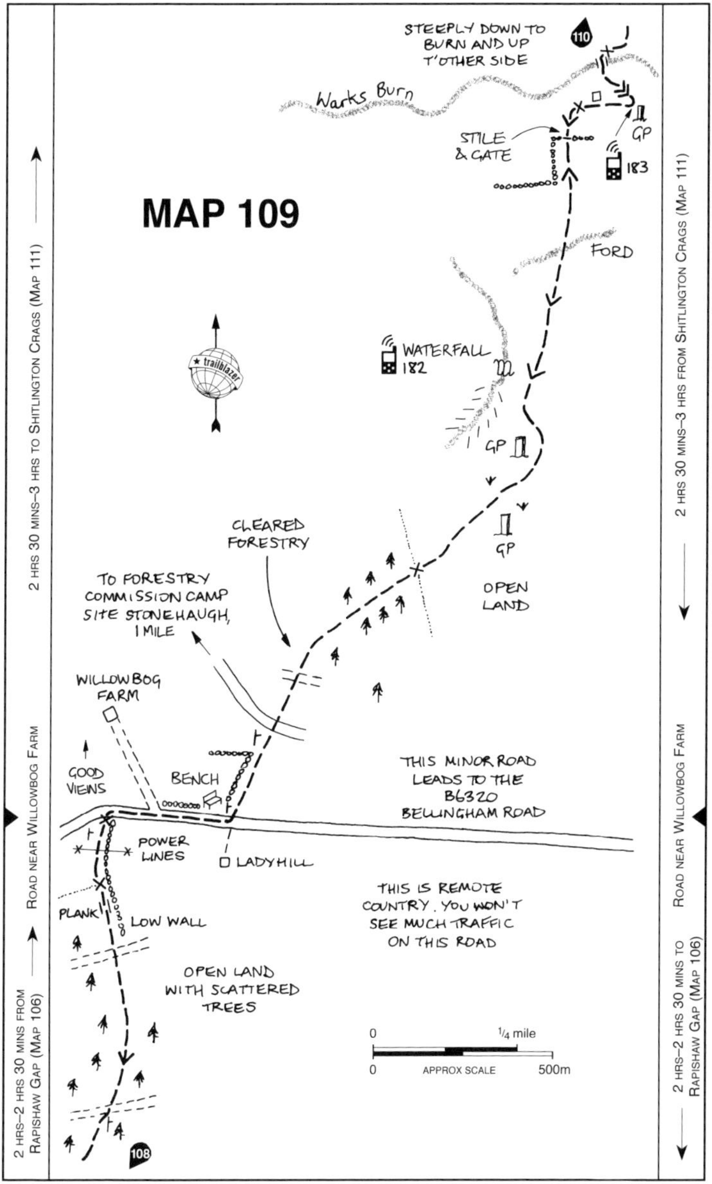

ROUTE GUIDE AND MAPS

STEEPLY DOWN TO BURN AND UP T'OTHER SIDE

110

Warks Burn

STILE & GATE

GP

183

FORD

MAP 109

WATERFALL 182

GP

2 HRS 30 MINS–3 HRS TO SHITLINGTON CRAGS (MAP 111)

2 HRS 30 MINS–3 HRS FROM SHITLINGTON CRAGS (MAP 111)

CLEARED FORESTRY

GP

OPEN LAND

TO FORESTRY COMMISSION CAMP SITE STONEHAUGH, 1 MILE

WILLOWBOG FARM

GOOD VIEWS

BENCH

LADYHILL

THIS MINOR ROAD LEADS TO THE B6320 BELLINGHAM ROAD

ROAD NEAR WILLOWBOG FARM

POWER LINES

PLANK

LOW WALL

OPEN LAND WITH SCATTERED TREES

THIS IS REMOTE COUNTRY, YOU WON'T SEE MUCH TRAFFIC ON THIS ROAD

ROAD NEAR WILLOWBOG FARM

108

0          1/4 mile

0    APPROX SCALE    500m

2 HRS–2 HRS 30 MINS FROM RAPISHAW GAP (MAP 106)

2 HRS–2 HRS 30 MINS TO RAPISHAW GAP (MAP 106)

## HETHERINGTON [Map 110]

Two miles further on, *Hetherington Farm* (☎ 01434-230260; 2D both en suite/1T shared bathroom), just a few hundred metres from the Way, welcomes walkers and offers very comfortable B&B. A double with a four-poster bed costs £80, the other double is £60 (£35 single occupancy); the twin is £52 (£28 single occupancy). The owner will take you to a pub in Wark in the evening for a meal.

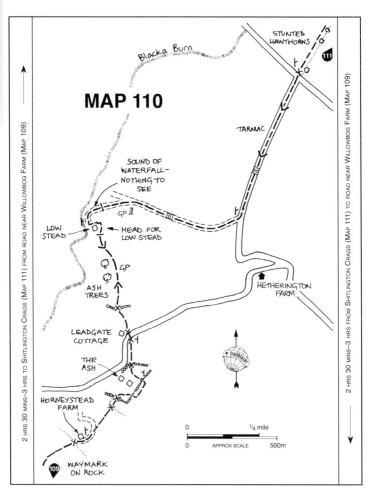

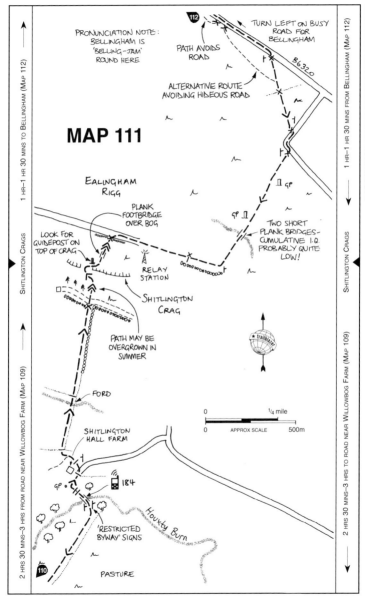

MAP 111

PRONUNCIATION NOTE: BELLINGHAM IS 'BELLING-JAM' ROUND HERE

TURN LEFT ON BUSY ROAD FOR BELLINGHAM

PATH AVOIDS ROAD

B6320

ALTERNATIVE ROUTE AVOIDING HIDEOUS ROAD

EALINGHAM RIGG

PLANK FOOTBRIDGE OVER BOG

LOOK FOR GUIDEPOST ON TOP OF CRAG

RELAY STATION

GP

GP

TWO SHORT PLANK BRIDGES- CUMULATIVE I.Q. PROBABLY QUITE LOW!

SHITLINGTON CRAG

PATH MAY BE OVERGROWN IN SUMMER

FORD

SHITLINGTON HALL FARM

0        ¼ mile
0        APPROX SCALE        500m

GP

184

Houxty Burn

'RESTRICTED BYWAY' SIGNS

PASTURE

110

112

1 HR—1 HR 30 MINS TO BELLINGHAM (MAP 112)

SHITLINGTON CRAGS

2 HRS 30 MINS—3 HRS FROM ROAD NEAR WILLOWBOG FARM (MAP 109)

1 HR—1 HR 30 MINS FROM BELLINGHAM (MAP 112)

SHITLINGTON CRAGS

2 HRS 30 MINS—3 HRS TO ROAD NEAR WILLOWBOG FARM (MAP 109)

trailblazer

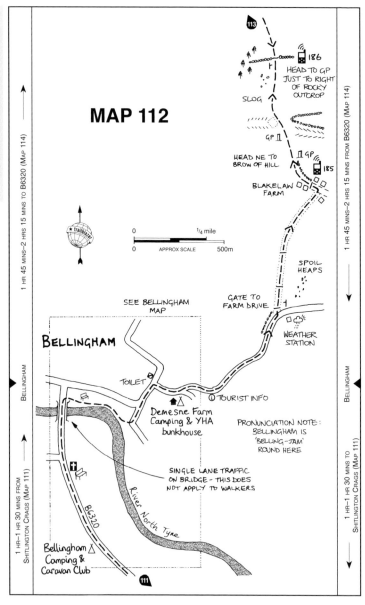

ROUTE GUIDE AND MAPS

**MAP 112**

113

186

HEAD TO GP
JUST TO RIGHT
OF ROCKY
OUTCROP

SLOG

GP

HEAD NE TO
BROW OF HILL

GP

185

BLAKELAW
FARM

1 HR 45 MINS–2 HRS 15 MINS TO B6320 (MAP 114)

1 HR 45 MINS–2 HRS 15 MINS FROM B6320 (MAP 114)

0     ¼ mile
0   APPROX SCALE   500m

★ trailblazer

SPOIL
HEAPS

GATE TO
FARM DRIVE

WEATHER
STATION

SEE BELLINGHAM
MAP

BELLINGHAM

BELLINGHAM

TOILET

① TOURIST INFO

Demesne Farm
Camping & YHA
bunkhouse

PRONUNCIATION NOTE:
BELLINGHAM IS
'BELLING-JAM'
ROUND HERE

River North Tyne

B6320

SINGLE LANE TRAFFIC
ON BRIDGE - THIS DOES
NOT APPLY TO WALKERS

Bellingham
Camping &
Caravan Club

111

1 HR–1 HR 30 MINS FROM
SHITLINGTON CRAGS (MAP 111)

1 HR–1 HR 30 MINS TO
SHITLINGTON CRAGS (MAP 111)

## BELLINGHAM [Map 112a]

This old market town on the North Tyne is the last place on the Pennine Way offering most things you may need. Note Bellingham is pronounced Belling-jam.

See p26 for details of the show held here in August.

### Services

The **heritage and tourist information centre** (☎ 01434-220050, 🖳 www.bellingham-heritage.org.uk; Easter to Oct Mon-Sat 9.30am-1pm & 1.30-4.30pm, to 5pm mid-May to Sep; Nov to Easter Mon, Wed, Fri 10am-3pm), on the road out of town to the east, has displays on local history; they can also book accommodation (see box p13). There's a **library** (Tue 10am-noon, Wed 1.30-4.30pm & 5-7pm, Fri 10am-noon & 1.30-4.30pm) which offers free **internet access**, a **post office**, **chemist**, **bakery** and a Co-op **supermarket** (Mon-Sat 8am-10pm, Sun 10am-10pm). Coleman fuel and gas canisters are sold at Bellingham Country Stores. Barclays has a **cash machine** but the Lloyds TSB branch doesn't.

### Transport

[See also pp45-50] Bellingham is a stop on Tyne Valley Coaches' No 880 **bus** (Apr-Oct) route. For a **taxi** call Bellingham Taxis ☎ 01434-220570 or ☎ 0781-550 3927 or Howard Snaith Coaches ☎ 01830-520609.

### Where to stay

Before the bridge on your way to town you'll pass *Bellingham Camping and Caravan Club* (☎ 01434-220175; mid Mar to Oct) which charges £5.50-8.50pp (for backpackers) and has wooden camping pods for £40 (sleeping up to four); there are toilet and shower facilities.

Closer to the town centre *Demesne Farm Campsite and Bunkhouse* (☎ 01434-220258 or ☎ 07967-396345, 🖳 www.demesnefarmcampsite.co.uk; open all year) has camping for £5; its 15-bed self-catering **bunkhouse** (from £16; £13 for under 18s) is

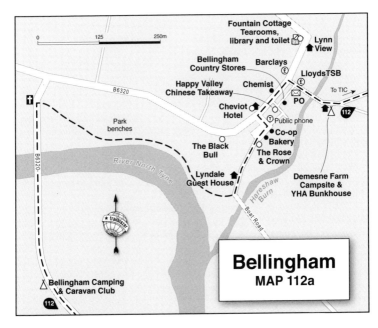

**Bellingham**
**MAP 112a**

effectively the Bellingham YH so it can be booked through the YHA (see p15). It has a well-equipped kitchen and a sitting area.

*Lynn View* (☎ 01434-220344; 1T/2D, shared bathroom; Mar-Nov) offers B&B for only £54 (£30 for single occupancy). Dogs are accepted as long as they don't sleep on the bed.

*Lyndale Guest House* (☎ 01434-220361, 🖳 www.lyndaleguesthouse.co.uk; 1S/1T/2D, most en suite, bath available) is a bright and friendly place charging £70 (£40 for the single, £55 for single occupancy). One of the doubles and the single are on a separate floor with a bathroom in between and thus are suitable for a family. They are happy to do a load of washing/drying (£5) and also have a drying room for boots. If they are full they can take you to their daughter who does B&B (*Carlton Guest House*, ☎ 01434-220132; 2T shared bathroom; £30pp) on Boat Rd nearby.

If you'd like to stay in a pub *The Cheviot Hotel* (☎ 01434-220696, 🖳 www .thecheviothotel.co.uk; 1S/3T/2D/1F, all en suite, bath available) is the best choice at £70 for two sharing or £38.50 for the single.

### Where to eat and drink
*Fountain Cottage Tea Rooms* (summer Tue-Sun 10am-5pm), in the library, does light lunches and teas. *The Cheviot Hotel* (see Where to stay; food served Mon-Sat noon-2pm, Sun noon-2.30pm & daily 6.30-10pm; takeaways available till 10pm) is the best of the pubs, with favourites such as steak and ale pie (£8.50) or fish & chips (£8.50; takeaway for £4.70) and a carvery on Sunday. *The Black Bull* (open evenings only) and *Rose and Crown* also do pub grub.

Besides the tearoom and the pubs your only options are the *Happy Valley Chinese takeaway* or a snack from the **bakery**.

## BELLINGHAM TO BYRNESS
**MAPS 112-120**

### Route overview
It's only **15 miles (24km, 7¼-9hrs)** from Bellingham to the lonesome frontier outpost of Byrness, a place of minimal services and interest other than as the penultimate overnight stop on the Pennine Way.

The good news is that this stage is, in local vernacular 'a dolly', an easy and occasionally thrilling section and just what a personal trainer would recommend prior to your upcoming trans-Cheviot marathon.

Once you've climbed out of the North Tyne valley onto the moors it's an enjoyable day too, far from noisy roads as you meander through knee-deep heather over **Deer Play** (Map 114), **Whitley Pike** (Map 115) and around **Padon Hill's** (Map 116) distinctive cairn.

At this point a short, steep and sodden ascent alongside **Redesdale Forest** leads to a interminable slalom of irksome bog- and puddle-dodging between the plantation's northern edge and a fence. You'll need to be nimble-footed if you want to keep your feet dry.

When this ends at a **Forestry Commission sign** (Map 117) welcoming Pennine Way walkers the fun, such as it's been, ends. From here on you're trudging up and down, a little left, a little right along a forestry road that you're warned is used by logging machinery.

Soon the A68 comes into both earshot and view and you converge with it near **Blakehopeburn** car park (Map 119). Here the last mile or so to **Byrness** (Map 120) is a pleasant walk through woodland and along the River Rede, a gentle end to a thankfully undemanding if soggy-bottomed day. Just as well for tomorrow requires heroic commitment.

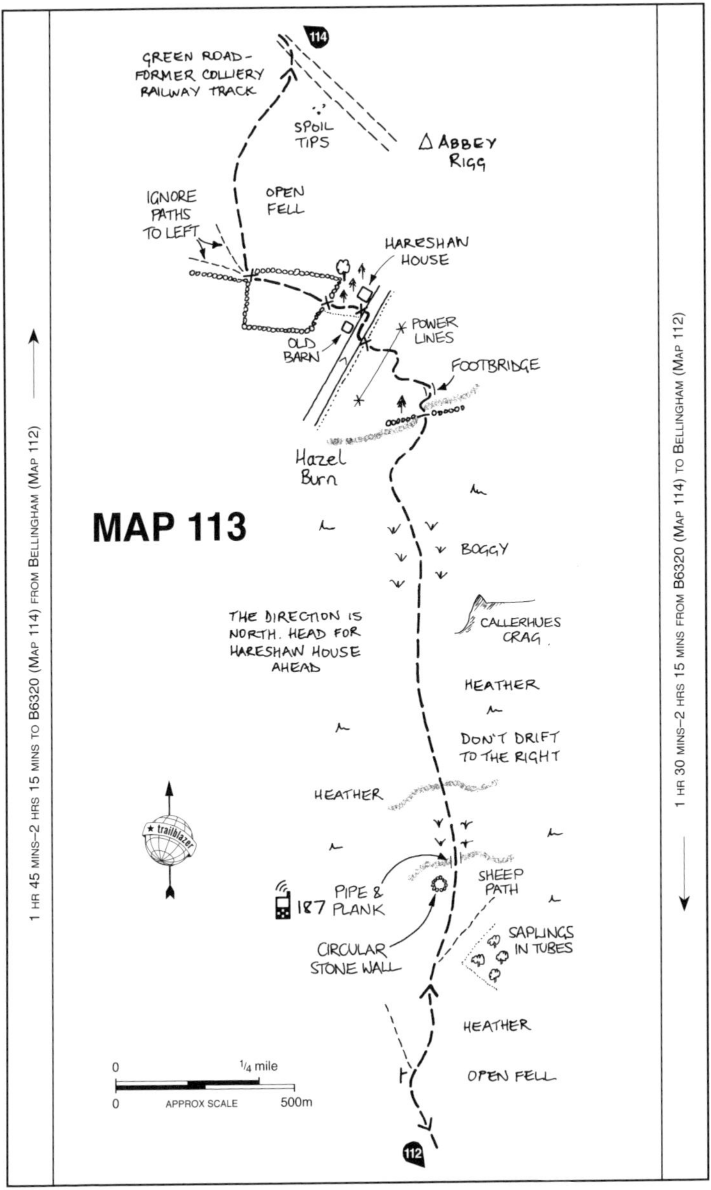

GREEN ROAD - FORMER COLLIERY RAILWAY TRACK

114

SPOIL TIPS

△ ABBEY RIGG

IGNORE PATHS TO LEFT

OPEN FELL

HARESHAN HOUSE

POWER LINES

OLD BARN

FOOTBRIDGE

Hazel Burn

**MAP 113**

BOGGY

CALLERHUES CRAG

THE DIRECTION IS NORTH. HEAD FOR HARESHAN HOUSE AHEAD

HEATHER

DON'T DRIFT TO THE RIGHT

HEATHER

★ trailblazer

187 PIPE & PLANK

CIRCULAR STONE WALL

SHEEP PATH

SAPLINGS IN TUBES

HEATHER

OPEN FELL

0      1/4 mile

0      APPROX SCALE      500m

112

1 HR 45 MINS–2 HRS 15 MINS TO B6320 (MAP 114) FROM BELLINGHAM (MAP 112)

1 HR 30 MINS–2 HRS 15 MINS FROM B6320 (MAP 114) TO BELLINGHAM (MAP 112)

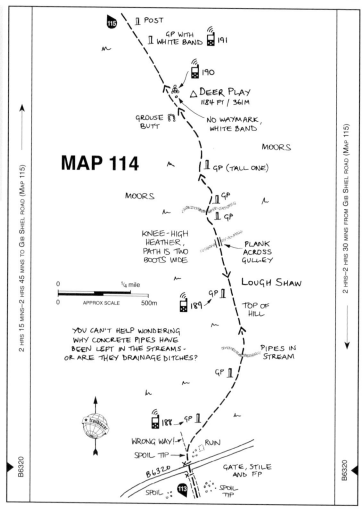

## MAP 114

2 HRS 15 MINS–2 HRS 45 MINS TO GIB SHIEL ROAD (MAP 115)

2 HRS–2 HRS 30 MINS FROM GIB SHIEL ROAD (MAP 115)

115

POST

GP WITH WHITE BAND

191

190

△ DEER PLAY
1184 FT / 361M

NO WAYMARK, WHITE BAND

GROUSE BUTT

MOORS

GP (TALL ONE)

MOORS

GP

GP

KNEE-HIGH HEATHER, PATH IS TWO BOOTS WIDE

PLANK ACROSS GULLEY

LOUGH SHAW

GP

189

TOP OF HILL

0          ¼ mile
0          500m
APPROX SCALE

YOU CAN'T HELP WONDERING WHY CONCRETE PIPES HAVE BEEN LEFT IN THE STREAMS - OR ARE THEY DRAINAGE DITCHES?

PIPES IN STREAM

GP

trailblazer

188     GP

WRONG WAY!

RUIN

SPOIL TIP

B6320

GATE, STILE AND FP

SPOIL

113

SPOIL TIP

B6320

B6320

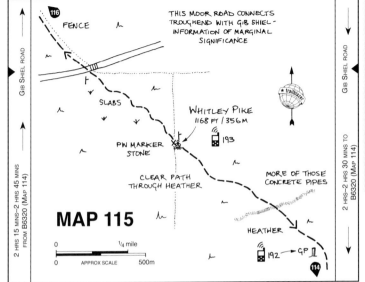

## Route-finding trouble spots

In very bad visibility the route may get a little thin as it branches around a bog below Callerhues Crag (Map 113) on the way to Hareshaw House. Soon after, at the B6320 you must make sure you set off at the right bearing, NNW, to lock on to the line of guideposts leading to Deer Play hill then down and up again to Whitley Pike.

The descent from here to the minor road crossing (Map 115), Padon Hill (Map 116), Brownrigg Head and all that follows is straightforward if irritating with extremes of unavoidable peat mush and mindless forestry roads.

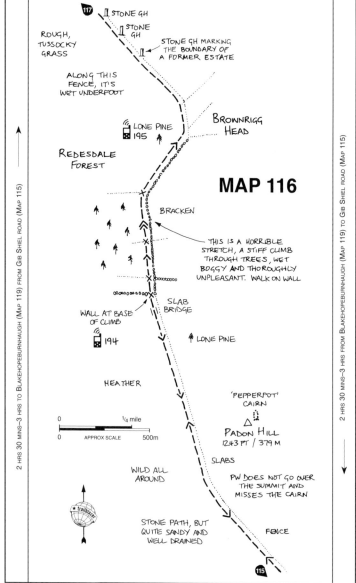

117 STONE GH

STONE GH

STONE GH MARKING
THE BOUNDARY OF
A FORMER ESTATE

ROUGH,
TUSSOCKY
GRASS

ALONG THIS
FENCE, IT'S
WET UNDERFOOT

BROWNRIGG
HEAD

LONE PINE
195

REDESDALE
FOREST

**MAP 116**

BRACKEN

THIS IS A HORRIBLE
STRETCH, A STIFF CLIMB
THROUGH TREES, WET
BOGGY AND THOROUGHLY
UNPLEASANT. WALK ON WALL

SLAB
BRIDGE

WALL AT BASE
OF CLIMB
194

LONE PINE

HEATHER

0        ¼ mile

0        APPROX SCALE        500m

'PEPPERPOT'
CAIRN

PADON HILL
1243 PT / 379 M

SLABS

PW DOES NOT GO OVER
THE SUMMIT AND
MISSES THE CAIRN

WILD ALL
AROUND

★ trailblaze

STONE PATH, BUT
QUITE SANDY AND
WELL DRAINED

FENCE

115

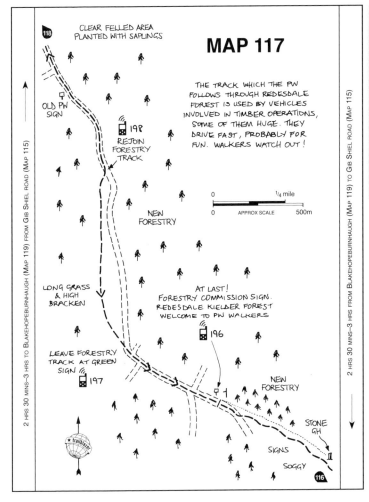

CLEAR FELLED AREA
PLANTED WITH SAPLINGS

# MAP 117

THE TRACK WHICH THE PW
FOLLOWS THROUGH REDESDALE
FOREST IS USED BY VEHICLES
INVOLVED IN TIMBER OPERATIONS,
SOME OF THEM HUGE. THEY
DRIVE FAST, PROBABLY FOR
FUN. WALKERS WATCH OUT!

OLD PW
SIGN

198
REJOIN
FORESTRY
TRACK

NEW
FORESTRY

0        ¼ mile

0        APPROX SCALE        500m

AT LAST!
FORESTRY COMMISSION SIGN.
REDESDALE KIELDER FOREST
WELCOME TO PW WALKERS

196

LONG GRASS
& HIGH
BRACKEN

LEAVE FORESTRY
TRACK AT GREEN
SIGN

197

NEW
FORESTRY

★ trailblazer

STONE
GH

SIGNS

SOGGY

2 HRS 30 MINS–3 HRS TO BLAKEHOPEBURNHAUGH (MAP 119) FROM GIB SHIEL ROAD (MAP 115)

2 HRS 30 MINS–3 HRS FROM BLAKEHOPEBURNHAUGH (MAP 119) TO GIB SHIEL ROAD (MAP 115)

118

116

ROUTE GUIDE AND MAPS

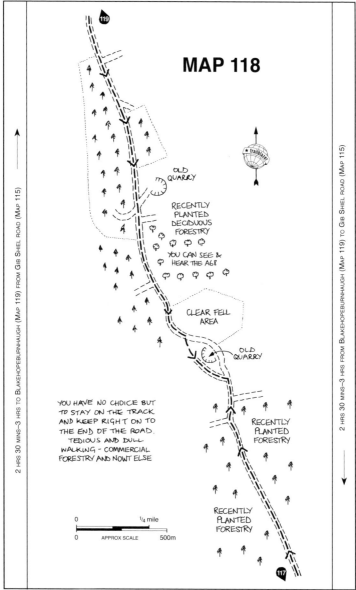

ROUTE GUIDE AND MAPS

**MAP 118**

★ trailblazer

2 HRS 30 MINS–3 HRS TO BLAKEHOPEBURNHAUGH (MAP 119) FROM GIB SHIEL ROAD (MAP 115)

2 HRS 30 MINS–3 HRS FROM BLAKEHOPEBURNHAUGH (MAP 119) TO GIB SHIEL ROAD (MAP 115)

OLD QUARRY

RECENTLY PLANTED DECIDUOUS FORESTRY

YOU CAN SEE & HEAR THE A68

CLEAR FELL AREA

OLD QUARRY

RECENTLY PLANTED FORESTRY

YOU HAVE NO CHOICE BUT TO STAY ON THE TRACK AND KEEP RIGHT ON TO THE END OF THE ROAD. TEDIOUS AND DULL WALKING – COMMERCIAL FORESTRY AND NOWT ELSE

RECENTLY PLANTED FORESTRY

0          ¼ mile

0     APPROX SCALE     500m

119

117

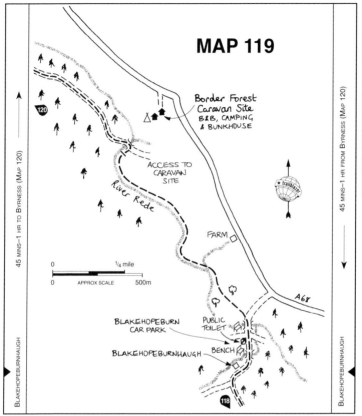

# MAP 119

Border Forest
Caravan Site
B&B, CAMPING
& BUNKHOUSE

ACCESS TO
CARAVAN
SITE

River Rede

FARM

A68

★ trailblaze

120

45 MINS–1 HR TO BYRNESS (MAP 120)

45 MINS–1 HR FROM BYRNESS (MAP 120)

0          ¼ mile

0                        500m
APPROX SCALE

BLAKEHOPEBURN
CAR PARK

PUBLIC
TOILET

BLAKEHOPEBURNHAUGH          BENCH

BLAKEHOPEBURNHAUGH

BLAKEHOPEBURNHAUGH

118

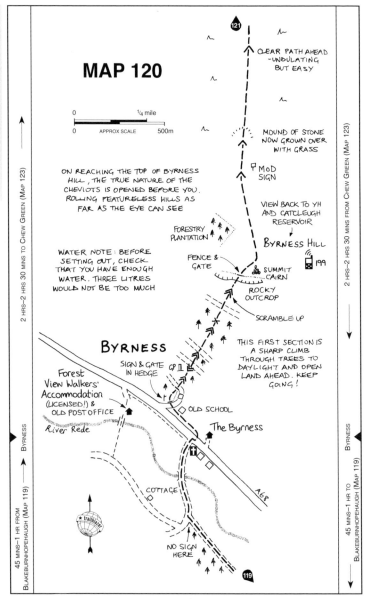

**MAP 120**

0      ¼ mile
0     APPROX SCALE     500m

CLEAR PATH AHEAD
-UNDULATING
BUT EASY

MOUND OF STONE
NOW GROWN OVER
WITH GRASS

MoD SIGN

VIEW BACK TO YH AND CATCLEUGH RESERVOIR

BYRNESS Hill
199

ON REACHING THE TOP OF BYRNESS HILL, THE TRUE NATURE OF THE CHEVIOTS IS OPENED BEFORE YOU. ROLLING FEATURELESS HILLS AS FAR AS THE EYE CAN SEE

WATER NOTE: BEFORE SETTING OUT, CHECK THAT YOU HAVE ENOUGH WATER. THREE LITRES WOULD NOT BE TOO MUCH

FORESTRY PLANTATION

FENCE & GATE

SUMMIT CAIRN

ROCKY OUTCROP

SCRAMBLE UP

THIS FIRST SECTION IS A SHARP CLIMB THROUGH TREES TO DAYLIGHT AND OPEN LAND AHEAD. KEEP GOING!

BYRNESS

SIGN & GATE IN HEDGE

GP

Forest View Walkers' Accommodation (LICENSED!) & OLD POST OFFICE

River Rede

OLD SCHOOL

The Byrness

COTTAGE

A68

★ trailblazer

NO SIGN HERE

119

121

2 HRS–2 HRS 30 MINS TO CHEW GREEN (MAP 123)

45 MINS–1 HR FROM BLAKEBURNHOPEHAUGH (MAP 119)   →   BYRNESS

2 HRS–2 HRS 30 MINS FROM CHEW GREEN (MAP 123)

BYRNESS   ◄   45 MINS–1 HR TO BLAKEBURNHOPEHAUGH (MAP 119)

## BYRNESS [Map 120]

These days this collection of buildings strung out along the A68 offers **barely enough** to fortify you for the final hurdle, so arrive prepared.

*The Byrness* (☎ 01830-520231, 🖳 www.thepennineway.co.uk/thebyrness; 1D en suite/2T private facilities) is a former hotel offering B&B for £30pp; evening meals are available from an à la carte menu (mains £7-12). They also do hot drinks and snacks (summer daily 10.30am-5pm, winter Thur-Sun 10.30am-5pm). Dogs are welcome.

*Forest View Walkers' Accommodation* (☎ 01830-520425, 🖳 www.forestview byrness.co.uk; open all year; 20 beds) has rooms (2, 3 or 4 beds) in two converted forestry cottages; a bed costs from £17 (£15 for under 18s). Evening meals (two courses

for £8) are available; it's licensed and is open to non residents. They also have a shop (4-10pm) selling a wide range of foods and provide DB&B nearby at the *Old Post Office* (2D/1T, shared bathroom) for £36pp.

You'll pass round the back of *Border Forest Caravan Park* (see Map 119; ☎ 01830-520259, 🖳 www.borderforest.com) with **camping** (Mar-Oct) for £7pp including toilet/shower facilities. There is no shop on site but they do have a microwave oven. They also have two plain, en suite (one with bath) **motel-type rooms** for £40; breakfast is not served. Dogs are welcome.

Munro's operate a **bus** service (No 131) here and Byrness is also a stop on National Express's NX383 service (see the public transport map and table, pp45-50).

## BYRNESS TO KIRK YETHOLM MAPS 120-135

### Route overview

Of all the challenges met so far these **27 miles (43km, 10½-14hrs)**, across the Cheviot massif, will be the most demanding. It's as if every stage has been a preparation for today and your mental preparation must be right. You can do it. Keep telling yourself that. The proud fraternity of Penninites has done it before you and there is no reason why you should not take your place among them.

Few walkers normally tackle 27 miles in a single day, but this is the Last Day so you can risk a burnout. Rude stone shelters on some summits and the two refuge huts (see below) are the only protection if things turn nasty.

For those who decide to make **two days** of it, you'll enjoy it even more. Wild camping offers the freedom of the hills but it might be necessary to drop down off the exposed plateau. Alternatively you could spend the night in one of the two identical **refuge huts** (Map 125 and Map 131) with room for up to six on the floor. There's no water at either although notes tell you where to look.

Just after the second refuge hut – about six or seven miles before Kirk Yetholm – a path leads down to *Mount Hooley YHA Bunkhouse* (off Map 131; ☎ 01668-216358, 🖳 paulineatthetop@hotmail.com; £13pp/£10 for students; 24 beds). There is one four-bed room, two with nine beds and a twin; cooking facilities, bedding and a drying room are provided and meals are available; book in advance particularly in the summer). It's about 1½ miles from the Pennine Way and involves a steep descent of over 200 metres into College Valley and a steep climb back up the next day.

Aside from wild camping, the refuge huts and the bunkhouse, the only accommodation between Byrness and Kirk Yetholm is at Trows Farm and Barrowburn Farm in Upper Coquetdale, 1½ miles from the summit of Windy Gyle (Map 127; see p250). There is an alternative; at around Mile 15 a crossroads

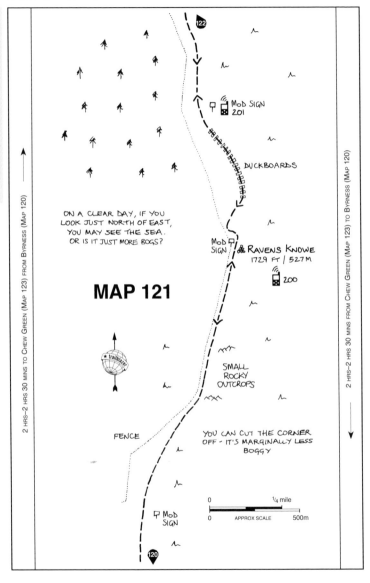

2 HRS–2 HRS 30 MINS TO CHEW GREEN (MAP 123) FROM BYRNESS (MAP 120)

2 HRS–2 HRS 30 MINS FROM CHEW GREEN (MAP 123) TO BYRNESS (MAP 120)

122

MoD SIGN
201

DUCKBOARDS

ON A CLEAR DAY, IF YOU
LOOK JUST NORTH OF EAST,
YOU MAY SEE THE SEA.
OR IS IT JUST MORE BOGS?

MoD
SIGN

RAVENS KNOWE
1729 FT / 527 M

200

**MAP 121**

★ trailblazer

SMALL
ROCKY
OUTCROPS

YOU CAN CUT THE CORNER
OFF – IT'S MARGINALLY LESS
BOGGY

FENCE

0        1/4 mile

0    APPROX SCALE    500m

MoD
SIGN

120

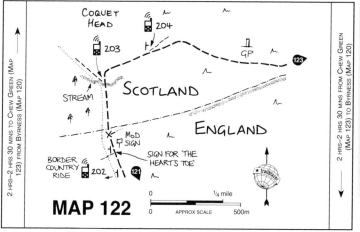

2 HRS–2 HRS 30 MINS TO CHEW GREEN (MAP 123) FROM BYRNESS (MAP 120)

2 HRS–2 HRS 30 MINS FROM CHEW GREEN (MAP 123) TO BYRNESS (MAP 120)

Inside map:

COQUET HEAD

204

203

GP

123

Scotland

STREAM

England

MoD SIGN

SIGN FOR 'THE HEART'S TOE'

BORDER COUNTRY RIDE

202

121

★ trailblazer

0        ¼ mile
**MAP 122**
0        500m
APPROX SCALE

just after Windy Gyle gives the opportunity to descend to Cocklawfoot road end, nine miles from Kirk Yetholm where Valleydene B&B (see p256) will pick you up. You can also ask Joyce at Forest View Walkers' Accommodation in Byrness (see p243) to pick you up and drop you off from the track at Trows Farm, about 1½ miles south of Windy Gyle (£5 per journey).

Extensive and maybe even excessive **slabbing** helps make the single day's effort all the more achievable, primarily as rhythm-maintaining tram rails. Although you gain height while still half asleep, the ascent to **Windy Gyle** (Map 127), followed by the intermittently slabbed climb to the **Auchope Cairn duckboard promenade** (Map 130) may take the wind out of you, even if at this point you have broken the back of the day. The final significant climb up **The Schil** (Map 131) will be enough though; altogether a day's total of **over 1600m** or a vertical mile.

As for the so-called low-level or high-level finale; both diverge for about 1½ miles (2.7km) though the former takes just ninety minutes, the latter a little longer. If weather, energy and daylight are all on your side it's well worth the effort to watch your last Pennine sunset from the heights of **White Law** (Map 133) or thereabouts before spilling down over moorland and pasture to a bridge a mile by road from town.

At last you pull back your shoulders and pick up your dragging feet. There's no point in looking beaten. The villagers in **Kirk Yetholm** (Map 135) don't care one way or the other, but you have your pride. Your walk is over. At the Border Hotel don't expect curiosity, sympathy or admiration, just their book to sign if you ask. You read there the comments of fellow lengthsmen and women, mostly nonchalant or triumphant, some philosophical. Add yours if you like as you

ROUTE GUIDE AND MAPS

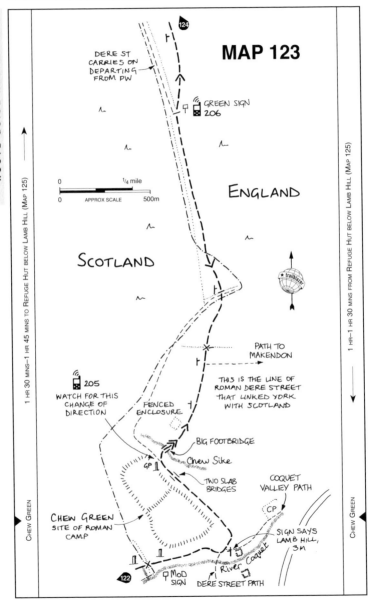

**MAP 123**

DERE ST CARRIES ON DEPARTING FROM PW

GREEN SIGN 206

ENGLAND

0 — ¼ mile
0 — APPROX SCALE — 500m

SCOTLAND

★ trailblazer

PATH TO MAKENDON

205 WATCH FOR THIS CHANGE OF DIRECTION

THIS IS THE LINE OF ROMAN DERE STREET THAT LINKED YORK WITH SCOTLAND

FENCED ENCLOSURE

BIG FOOTBRIDGE

Chew Sike

GP

TWO SLAB BRIDGES

COQUET VALLEY PATH

CP

CHEW GREEN SITE OF ROMAN CAMP

SIGN SAYS LAMB HILL, 3M

122

MoD SIGN

River Coquet

DERE STREET PATH

1 HR 30 MINS–1 HR 45 MINS TO REFUGE HUT BELOW LAMB HILL (MAP 125)

1 HR–1 HR 30 MINS FROM REFUGE HUT BELOW LAMB HILL (MAP 125)

CHEW GREEN

CHEW GREEN

celebrate with a beer, the traditional end to what you'll probably now agree is still Britain's most challenging long-distance trail.

## Route-finding trouble spots

Once the fenceline slabs set in after Lamb Hill there's very little to distract you from the path. Up to that point waymarking and paths are reasonably clear. From Auchope Cairn the knee-popping descent to the second hut is well trodden, as is the trail round and up to The Schil and down to the ladder style leading to the **high or low route** split both of which roll unambiguously down to Kirk Yetholm.

All in all, even in poor visibility this very long day is made much easier by good waymarking and orientation aids (aka 'slabs and fence lines'). All you have to do is last the distance.

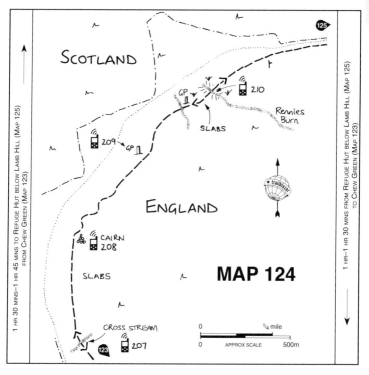

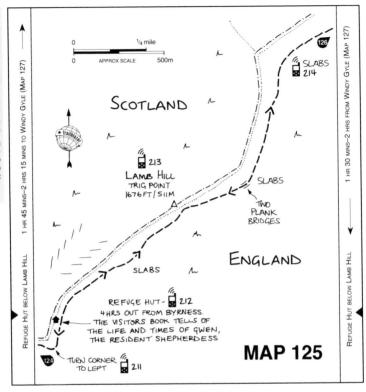

0 ¼ mile

0     APPROX SCALE    500m

SCOTLAND

★ trailblazer

213

LAMB HILL
TRIG POINT
1676FT / 511M

SLABS

TWO
PLANK
BRIDGES

SLABS

ENGLAND

REFUGE HUT - 212
4HRS OUT FROM BYRNESS.
THE VISITORS BOOK TELLS OF
THE LIFE AND TIMES OF GWEN,
THE RESIDENT SHEPHERDESS

**MAP 125**

124   TURN CORNER
TO LEFT   211

126

SLABS
214

1 HR 45 MINS–2 HRS 15 MINS TO WINDY GYLE (MAP 127)

1 HR 30 MINS–2 HRS FROM WINDY GYLE (MAP 127)

REFUGE HUT BELOW LAMB HILL

REFUGE HUT BELOW LAMB HILL

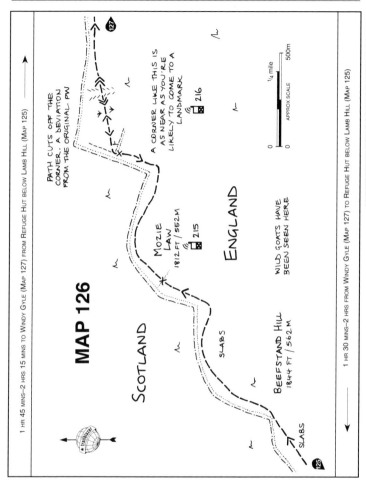

**MAP 126**

SCOTLAND

ENGLAND

PATH CUTS OFF THE
CORNER. A DEVIATION
FROM THE ORIGINAL PW

A CORNER LIKE THIS IS
AS NEAR AS YOU'RE
LIKELY TO COME TO A
LANDMARK

216

MOZIE
LAW
1812 FT / 562 M   215

WILD GOATS HAVE
BEEN SEEN HERE

SLABS

BEEFSTAND HILL
1844 FT / 562 M

SLABS

¼ mile

500m

APPROX SCALE

trailblazer

ROUTE GUIDE AND MAPS

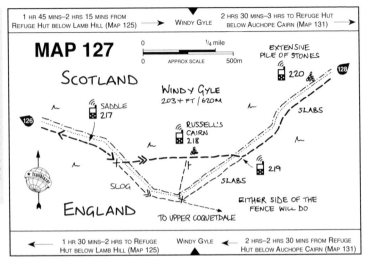

1 HR 45 MINS–2 HRS 15 MINS FROM REFUGE HUT BELOW LAMB HILL (MAP 125) →

WINDY GYLE

2 HRS 30 MINS–3 HRS TO REFUGE HUT BELOW AUCHOPE CAIRN (MAP 131) →

**MAP 127**

0 — ¼ mile
0 — APPROX SCALE — 500m

SCOTLAND

EXTENSIVE PILE OF STONES

220

128

WINDY GYLE 2034 FT / 620M

SADDLE 217

126

RUSSELL'S CAIRN 218

SLABS

219

SLOG

SLABS

ENGLAND

EITHER SIDE OF THE FENCE WILL DO

TO UPPER COQUETDALE

★ trailblazer

1 HR 30 MINS–2 HRS TO REFUGE HUT BELOW LAMB HILL (MAP 125) ←

WINDY GYLE ←

2 HRS–2 HRS 30 MINS FROM REFUGE HUT BELOW AUCHOPE CAIRN (MAP 131)

**UPPER COQUETDALE [off Map 127]**

Upper Coquetdale is about 1½ miles from Windy Gyle. **Barrowburn Farm** (☎ 01669-621176, 🖳 www.barrowburn.com; 1D/1T, shared bathroom). Here you can get **B&B** in the farmhouse for £25pp or self cater in 'The Deer Hut' which sleeps up to six (2T plus 2 fold out beds) for £60.

There is also a simple **camping barn** that sleeps up to 17 people. It costs £80 for sole use or £10pp for groups of fewer than eight people. You can **camp** outside for £5 per tent. Dogs are welcome. Evening meals (£15), packed lunches (£5) and a full English breakfast for campers (£6.50) are available if booked in advance. They also have a **tea room** (☎ 01669-650312; Wed-Sun 11am-5pm) which serves soups, sandwiches and cakes as well as a Sunday lunch in winter.

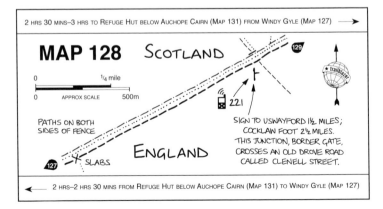

2 HRS 30 MINS–3 HRS TO REFUGE HUT BELOW AUCHOPE CAIRN (MAP 131) FROM WINDY GYLE (MAP 127) →

**MAP 128** SCOTLAND

0 — ¼ mile
0 — APPROX SCALE — 500m

129

★ trailblazer

PATHS ON BOTH SIDES OF FENCE

221

ENGLAND

SIGN TO USWAYFORD 1½ MILES; COCKLAWN FOOT 2½ MILES. THIS JUNCTION, BORDER GATE, CROSSES AN OLD DROVE ROAD CALLED CLENELL STREET.

127

SLABS

2 HRS–2 HRS 30 MINS FROM REFUGE HUT BELOW AUCHOPE CAIRN (MAP 131) TO WINDY GYLE (MAP 127) ←

ROUTE GUIDE AND MAPS

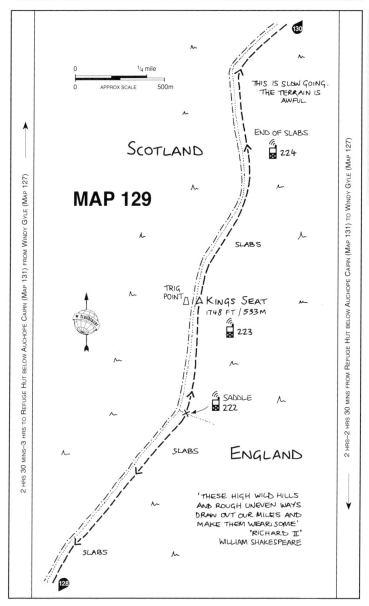

MAP 129

SCOTLAND

130

THIS IS SLOW GOING.
THE TERRAIN IS
AWFUL

END OF SLABS

📱 224

SLABS

TRIG
POINT △ Kings Seat
1748 FT / 533M

📱 223

★ trailblazer

📱 SADDLE
222

SLABS

ENGLAND

'THESE HIGH WILD HILLS
AND ROUGH UNEVEN WAYS
DRAW OUT OUR MILES AND
MAKE THEM WEARISOME'
"RICHARD II"
WILLIAM SHAKESPEARE

SLABS

128

0    ¼ mile
0    APPROX SCALE    500m

2 HRS 30 MINS–3 HRS TO REFUGE HUT BELOW AUCHOPE CAIRN (MAP 131) FROM WINDY GYLE (MAP 127)

2 HRS–2 HRS 30 MINS FROM REFUGE HUT BELOW AUCHOPE CAIRN (MAP 131) TO WINDY GYLE (MAP 127)

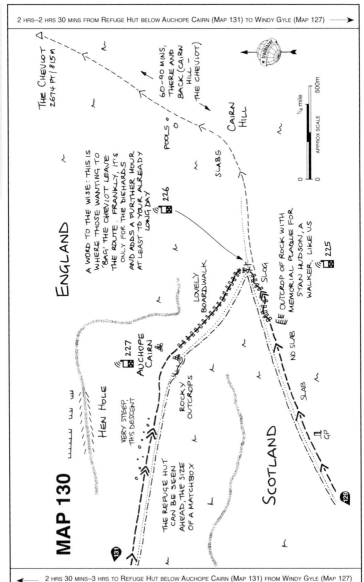

ROUTE GUIDE AND MAPS

**MAP 130**

HEN HOLE

ENGLAND

THE CHEVIOT
2674 PT / 815 M

A WORD TO THE WISE: THIS IS WHERE THOSE WANTING TO 'BAG' THE CHEVIOT LEAVE THE ROUTE. FRANKLY, IT'S ONLY FOR THE DIEHARDS AND ADDS A FURTHER HOUR AT LEAST TO YOUR ALREADY LONG DAY

60–90 MINS, THERE AND BACK (CAIRN HILL – THE CHEVIOT)

CAIRN HILL

POOLS

SLABS

126

LOVELY BOARDWALK

AUCHOPE CAIRN

127

VERY STEEP, THIS DESCENT

ROCKY OUTCROPS

SLOG

OUTCROP OF ROCK WITH MEMORIAL PLAQUE FOR STAN HUDSON, A WALKER, LIKE US

225

NO SLAB

SLAB

GP

SCOTLAND

THE REFUGE HUT CAN BE SEEN AHEAD, THE SIZE OF A MATCHBOX

131

129

¼ mile
APPROX SCALE
500m

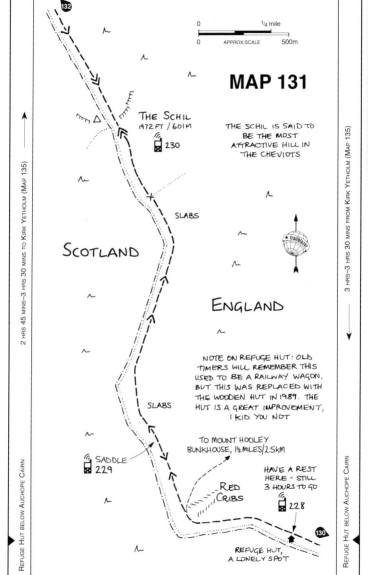

**MAP 131**

THE SCHIL IS SAID TO
BE THE MOST
ATTRACTIVE HILL IN
THE CHEVIOTS

THE SCHIL
1972 FT / 601M
📶 230

SCOTLAND

SLABS

ENGLAND

SLABS

NOTE ON REFUGE HUT: OLD
TIMERS WILL REMEMBER THIS
USED TO BE A RAILWAY WAGON,
BUT THIS WAS REPLACED WITH
THE WOODEN HUT IN 1989. THE
HUT IS A GREAT IMPROVEMENT,
I KID YOU NOT

📶 SADDLE
229

TO MOUNT HOOLEY
BUNKHOUSE, 1½ MILES/2.5KM

HAVE A REST
HERE - STILL
3 HOURS TO GO
📶 228

Red
Cribs

REFUGE HUT,
A LONELY SPOT

2 HRS 45 MINS–3 HRS 30 MINS TO KIRK YETHOLM (MAP 135)

3 HRS–3 HRS 30 MINS FROM KIRK YETHOLM (MAP 135)

REFUGE HUT BELOW AUCHOPE CAIRN

REFUGE HUT BELOW AUCHOPE CAIRN

¼ mile

500m
APPROX SCALE

132

130

ROUTE GUIDE AND MAPS

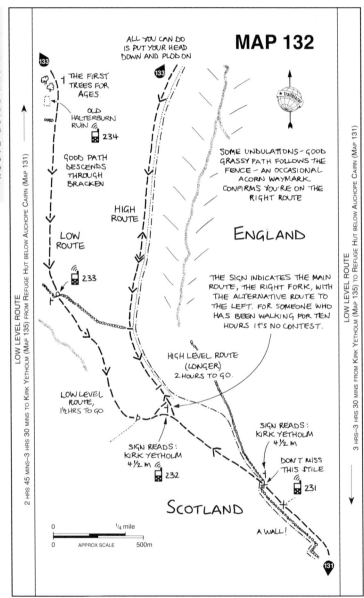

**MAP 132**

133

ALL YOU CAN DO
IS PUT YOUR HEAD
DOWN AND PLOD ON

133

THE FIRST
TREES FOR
AGES

OLD
HALTERBURN
RUIN 234

GOOD PATH
DESCENDS
THROUGH
BRACKEN

SOME UNDULATIONS - GOOD
GRASSY PATH FOLLOWS THE
FENCE - AN OCCASIONAL
ACORN WAYMARK
CONFIRMS YOU'RE ON THE
RIGHT ROUTE

HIGH
ROUTE

LOW
ROUTE

ENGLAND

233

THE SIGN INDICATES THE MAIN
ROUTE, THE RIGHT FORK, WITH
THE ALTERNATIVE ROUTE TO
THE LEFT. FOR SOMEONE WHO
HAS BEEN WALKING FOR TEN
HOURS IT'S NO CONTEST.

HIGH LEVEL ROUTE
(LONGER)
2 HOURS TO GO.

LOW LEVEL
ROUTE,
1½ HRS TO GO.

SIGN READS:
KIRK YETHOLM
4½ M 232

SIGN READS:
KIRK YETHOLM
4½ M

DON'T MISS
THIS STILE
231

SCOTLAND

A WALL!

131

0          ¼ mile
0    APPROX SCALE    500m

LOW LEVEL ROUTE
2 HRS 45 MINS–3 HRS 30 MINS TO KIRK YETHOLM (MAP 135) FROM REFUGE HUT BELOW AUCHOPE CAIRN (MAP 131)

LOW LEVEL ROUTE
3 HRS–3 HRS 30 MINS FROM KIRK YETHOLM (MAP 135) TO REFUGE HUT BELOW AUCHOPE CAIRN (MAP 131)

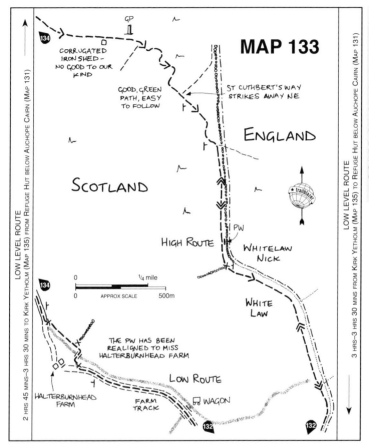

LOW LEVEL ROUTE
2 HRS 45 MINS–3 HRS 30 MINS TO KIRK YETHOLM (MAP 135) FROM REFUGE HUT BELOW AUCHOPE CAIRN (MAP 131)

LOW LEVEL ROUTE
3 HRS–3 HRS 30 MINS FROM KIRK YETHOLM (MAP 135) TO REFUGE HUT BELOW AUCHOPE CAIRN (MAP 131)

134

GP

**MAP 133**

CORRUGATED IRON SHED – NO GOOD TO OUR KIND

GOOD, GREEN PATH, EASY TO FOLLOW

ST CUTHBERT'S WAY STRIKES AWAY NE

ENGLAND

SCOTLAND

trailblazer

PW

HIGH ROUTE

WHITELAW NICK

0          ¼ mile
0          APPROX SCALE          500m

134

WHITE LAW

THE PW HAS BEEN REALIGNED TO MISS HALTERBURNHEAD FARM

LOW ROUTE

HALTERBURNHEAD FARM

FARM TRACK

WAGON

132

132

## KIRK YETHOLM [Map 135]

It's probably fair to say that only a fraction of the people who have heard of this pleasant little village would have done so if the Pennine Way did not end here. As it is, it offers a perfect and well-appointed spin down to your big walk. See p25 for details of Yetholm Festival week held in June.

### Transport

[See pp45-50] First Borders operates the No 81 **bus** to Kelso (20-35 mins) from where you can catch Perryman's No 67 to Berwick-upon-Tweed or Munro's No 52 to Edinburgh for mainline rail and coach connections.

For a **taxi** call Peter Hogg Taxis on ☎ 01835-863755 or ☎ 01835-863039.

### Places to stay, eat and drink

*Valleydene* (☎ 01573-420286, 🖥 www. valleydene.freeuk.com; 2T/2D/1F some en suite, bath available) is a friendly establishment which charges £25pp for two sharing an en suite room, £22 in a standard room (single occupancy from £25). Dogs are welcome. They offer a very useful service of picking you up at Cocklawfoot halfway along the leg from Byrness (see Map 128, p250) and dropping you back there the next morning for £15 for a one-night stay and £5 for a two-night stay.

*Mill House* (☎ 01573-420604, 🖥 www.millhouseyetholm.co.uk; 1T/1D/1T, D or F, all en suite, bath available) is a comfortable place with wi-fi throughout the

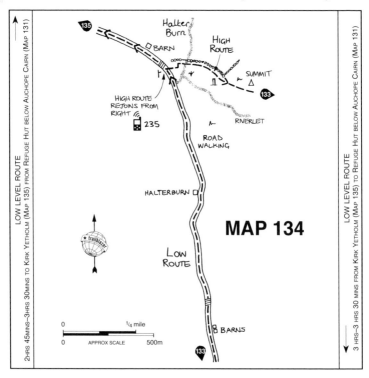

**MAP 134**

(**Opposite**) **Top**: On Windy Gyle in the Cheviots: the big 27-mile final section (see p243). **Bottom**: The Border Hotel in Kirk Yetholm marks the end of the Pennine Way.

house, a drying room for walking gear and a hot tub for guests' use. B&B costs £35-45pp for two sharing, single occupancy £50. Packed lunches are available (£6.50).

**The Border Hotel** (☎ 01573-420237, 💻 www.theborderhotel.com; 1D/3D or T/1D, T or F, all en suite, bath available; food served daily noon-2pm & 6-9pm) has a characterful bar where the big book of 'Pennine Lengthspersons' awaits your contribution. Anyone who has finished the Pennine Way is still stood a free half courtesy

of Broughton Ales. B&B costs from £45pp. Dogs are welcome (on a lead). The **menu** here offers a knee-weakening range of dishes to help pile back the calories burned up during the haul over from Byrness.

Round the corner **Kirk Yetholm SYHA Hostel** (☎ 01573-420639, bookings Mon-Fri 9am-5pm ☎ 0845-293 7373, 💻 reservations@syha.org.uk; Apr-Sep) costs £16-18 (£12-13.50 for under 18s) and has 20 beds as well as washing and drying facilities. Self-catering only.

## TOWN YETHOLM                    [Map 135]

It could be one more mile too many but in Town Yetholm you'll find a **shop** (Mon-Fri 7am-6pm, Sat 7am-5pm, Sun 9am-5pm) and a **post office** (closed afternoons, Wed and Sat). There's also the **Plough Hotel** (☎ 01573-420215, 💻 www

.ploughhotelyetholm.co.uk; 3D/2T, most en suite, bath available) where B&B costs £60 (£35 for single occupancy). Dogs are welcome. The food (served daily noon-2.30pm & 6-8.30pm to 9pm at the weekend) here is excellent and may include a tasty lamb hot pot (£8.75).

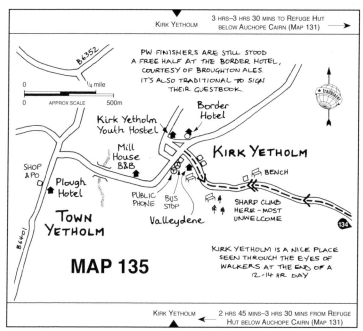

KIRK YETHOLM — 3 HRS–3 HRS 30 MINS TO REFUGE HUT BELOW AUCHOPE CAIRN (MAP 131) →

PW FINISHERS ARE STILL STOOD A FREE HALF AT THE BORDER HOTEL, COURTESY OF BROUGHTON ALES. IT'S ALSO TRADITIONAL TO SIGN THEIR GUESTBOOK.

Border Hotel

Kirk Yetholm Youth Hostel

Mill House B&B

**KIRK YETHOLM**

BENCH

SHOP & PO

Plough Hotel

PUBLIC PHONE    BUS STOP

SHARP CLIMB HERE – MOST UNWELCOME

**TOWN YETHOLM**

Valleydene

134

KIRK YETHOLM IS A NICE PLACE SEEN THROUGH THE EYES OF WALKERS AT THE END OF A 12-14 HR DAY

**MAP 135**

KIRK YETHOLM — 2 HRS 45 MINS–3 HRS 30 MINS FROM REFUGE HUT BELOW AUCHOPE CAIRN (MAP 131)

0    ¼ mile
0    APPROX SCALE    500m

* trailblazer

ROUTE GUIDE AND MAPS

**(Opposite) Top**: Whitley Pike (p237) on the long haul between Bellingham and Byrness. **Bottom**: The short, often busy, section along Hadrian's Wall (see p220, © Chris Scott).

# Map key

| | | | | | | |
|---|---|---|---|---|---|---|
| ♠ | Where to stay | ▥ | Library/bookstore | ● | Other | |
| ○ | Where to eat and drink | ◐ | Internet | CP | Car park | |
| Δ | Campsite | ⛪ | Museum/gallery | ◷ | Bus station | |
| ⊠ | Post Office | ✝ | Church/cathedral | ◔ | Bus stop | |
| £ | Bank/ATM | ☏ | Telephone | ▭○▭ | Rail line & station | |
| ⓘ | Tourist Information | ✓ | Public toilet | | Park | |
| | | □ | Building | 📱082 | GPS waypoint | |

| | | | | | |
|---|---|---|---|---|---|
| | Pennine Way | | Cattle grid | | Bog or marsh |
| | Other path | | Bridge | | Hedge |
| | 4 x 4 track | | Stone wall | | Trees/woodland |
| | Tarmac road | | Water | | Rough grassland |
| | Steps | | Cleft/small valley | | Trig point |
| | Slope/ Steep slope | | Crags | GP | Guide post |
| | Stile | | Stream | | Signpost |
| | Gate | | River | ㉔ | Map continuation |

# APPENDIX – GPS WAYPOINTS

Each GPS waypoint below was taken on the route at the reference number marked on the map as below. This list of GPS waypoints is also available in downloadable form from the Trailblazer website – ⌨ http://trailblazer-guides.com/gps-waypoints.

## Edale

| MAP NO | REF | GPS WAYPOINT | | DESCRIPTION |
|--------|-----|--------------|--|-------------|
| Map 3 | 001 | 53° 22.514' | 01° 52.925' | Sign: to Edale Head; keep left |
| Map 3 | 002 | 53° 22.821' | 01° 52.959' | Kinder Low summit |
| Map 4 | 003 | 53° 23.820' | 01° 52.587' | Kinder Downfall |
| Map 4 | 004 | 53° 24.464' | 01° 54.279' | Snake Inn Path junction |
| Map 7 | 005 | 53° 27.679' | 01° 51.588' | Bleaklow Head summit |
| Map 7 | 006 | 53° 27.955' | 01° 51.801' | Milestone by fence |
| Map 8 | 007 | 53° 28.515' | 01° 54.359' | Fence above Reaps Farm |

## Crowden

| MAP NO | REF | GPS WAYPOINT | | DESCRIPTION |
|--------|-----|--------------|--|-------------|
| Map 10 | 008 | 53° 31.409' | 01° 54.785' | Cross stream joining Crowden Great Brook |
| Map 11 | 009 | 53° 31.718' | 01° 54.280' | Slabs start on Meadowgrain Clough |
| Map 12 | 010 | 53° 32.332' | 01° 53.144' | Black Hill summit |
| Map 12 | 011 | 53° 33.038' | 01° 52.659' | Wooden shelter |
| Map 15 | 012 | 53° 34.747' | 01° 57.494' | Last gate before Standedge Cutting |
| Map 15 | 013 | 53° 34.890' | 01° 57.640' | Milestone and signpost before Standedge Cutting |

## Standedge

| MAP NO | REF | GPS WAYPOINT | | DESCRIPTION |
|--------|-----|--------------|--|-------------|
| Map 15 | 014 | 53° 35.371' | 01° 58.958' | Millstone Edge trig point |
| Map 16 | 015 | 53° 35.862' | 01° 59.683' | Oldham Way, path divides, turn right |
| Map 17 | 016 | 53° 36.908' | 02° 00.943' | White Hill summit trig point |
| Map 18 | 017 | 53° 38.475' | 02° 02.460' | Shelter of sorts |
| Map 18 | 018 | 53° 38.635' | 02° 02.615' | Blackstone Edge trig point |
| Map 18 | 019 | 53° 39.008' | 02° 02.506' | Aiggin Stone, turn left |
| Map 18 | 020 | 53° 38.968' | 02° 02.876' | Cross drainage ditch, then turn right |
| Map 20 | 021 | 53° 41.401' | 02° 03.195' | Slabs start after Warland reservoir |
| Map 20 | 022 | 53° 42.676' | 02° 02.530' | Withen's Gate; Calderdale Way path to left |

## Hebden

| MAP NO | REF | GPS WAYPOINT | | DESCRIPTION |
|--------|-----|--------------|--|-------------|
| Map 22 | 023 | 53° 44.337' | 02° 02.790' | Sign to Badger Fields Farm after Calder ascent |

## Colden

| MAP NO | REF | GPS WAYPOINT | | DESCRIPTION |
|--------|-----|--------------|--|-------------|
| Map 23 | 024 | 53° 45.516' | 02° 03.070' | Pennine Way path goes away from the wall after Mt Pleasant Fm |
| Map 24 | 025 | 53° 45.831' | 02° 03.398' | Junction with path to Clough Hole Bridge near arched barn |
| Map 24 | 026 | 53° 46.389' | 02° 04.894' | Pennine Way meets Pennine Bridleway. Turn right to Gorple reservoirs |
| Map 26 | 027 | 53° 48.002' | 02° 02.817' | Path leaves track after signpost |
| Map 27 | 028 | 53° 48.963' | 02° 01.592' | Junction with Japanese guidepost after Top Withins ruins |

## Ponden

| MAP NO | REF | GPS WAYPOINT | | DESCRIPTION |
|--------|-----|--------------|--|-------------|
| Map 29 | 029 | 53° 50.789' | 02° 01.885' | Old Bess Hill |
| Map 29 | 030 | 53° 51.212' | 02° 02.349' | High point with trig point to west |
| Map 29 | 031 | 53° 51.470' | 02° 02.544' | Stone shelter |
| Map 31 | 032 | 53° 52.241' | 02° 02.649' | Wooden door to garden with trees and hut |

**Ponden** *(continued from p259)*

| MAP NO | REF | GPS WAYPOINT | | DESCRIPTION |
|---|---|---|---|---|
| Map 31 | 033 | 53° 52.334' | 02° 02.548' | Ladder stile; change direction |

**Ickornshaw**

| | | | | |
|---|---|---|---|---|
| Map 31 | 034 | 53° 53.154' | 02° 03.182' | Spring after terraced houses |
| Map 32 | 035 | 53° 55.111' | 02° 03.871' | Pass bench by road |
| Map 32 | 036 | 53° 55.216' | 02° 04.355' | Wall ends, two plank bridges |
| Map 33 | 037 | 53° 55.275' | 02° 04.852' | Cracked 'Pennine Way' slab |
| Map 33 | 038 | 53° 55.278' | 02° 05.030' | Pinhaw Beacon summit trig point |
| Map 33 | 039 | 53° 55.430' | 02° 05.973' | Turn left off road |
| Map 33 | 040 | 53° 55.883' | 02° 07.244' | Gate under pylon near Brown House Farm |

**Thornton**

| | | | | |
|---|---|---|---|---|
| Map 36 | 041 | 53° 58.233' | 02° 07.316' | Concrete tank, slight ascent |
| Map 36 | 042 | 53° 58.436' | 02° 07.035' | Four-finger signpost on Scaleber Hill |

**Gargrave**

| | | | | |
|---|---|---|---|---|
| Map 37 | 043 | 53° 59.466' | 02° 06.920' | Cross stile in wall to enter field |
| Map 38 | 044 | 54° 00.166' | 02° 07.606' | Pennine Way sign by junction of walls in field corner |
| Map 38 | 045 | 54° 00.410' | 02° 07.703' | Path goes between two walls |
| Map 38 | 046 | 54° 00.562' | 02° 07.825' | Lone PW sign also pointing west to Bell Busk |

**Malham**

| | | | | |
|---|---|---|---|---|
| Map 41 | 047 | 54° 04.395' | 02° 09.408' | Top of Malham Cove, turn north |
| Map 42 | 048 | 54° 05.041' | 02° 10.073' | Signpost to Malham |
| Map 42 | 049 | 54° 05.124' | 02° 09.828' | Signpost with blue flash |
| Map 43 | 050 | 54° 07.066' | 02° 10.612' | Meet and cross road, sign at end of wall |
| Map 44 | 051 | 54° 07.530' | 02° 11.339' | Path bears away from collapsed wall |
| Map 44 | 052 | 54° 08.609' | 02° 12.095' | Fountains Fell cairn |
| Map 45 | 053 | 54° 08.604' | 02° 13.029' | Meet wall coming down Fountains Fell |
| Map 46 | 054 | 54° 09.037' | 02° 15.043' | Bracken Bottom turn off; shoulder of Pen-y-ghent climb |
| Map 46 | 055 | 54° 09.361' | 02° 14.835' | Pen-y-ghent summit |
| Map 46 | 056 | 54° 09.794' | 02° 14.952' | Turn left after cairn |
| Map 47 | 057 | 54° 09.840' | 02° 16.276' | Left turn near Hull Pot after gate between two stiles |
| Map 48 | 058 | 54° 08.906' | 02° 17.357' | Bench near Horton-in-Ribblesdale |

**Horton**

| | | | | |
|---|---|---|---|---|
| Map 49 | 059 | 54° 10.316' | 02° 17.446' | Jackdaw Hole (trees) |
| Map 49 | 060 | 54° 11.405' | 02° 17.189' | Turn left up hill to viaduct view |
| Map 50 | 061 | 54° 11.780' | 02° 18.204' | Barn |
| Map 50 | 062 | 54° 13.169' | 02° 18.242' | Meet Cam End Road, turn north-east |
| Map 52 | 063 | 54° 14.413' | 02° 16.420' | Join tarmac |
| Map 53 | 064 | 54° 14.757' | 02° 15.673' | Leave tarmac for West Cam Road above Snaizeholme |
| Map 54 | 065 | 54° 16.638' | 02° 14.461' | Leave West Cam Road to right |
| Map 54 | 066 | 54° 16.980' | 02° 13.957' | First cairn after path junction |
| Map 54 | 067 | 54° 17.386' | 02° 13.612' | Half gate, path bends right |
| Map 55 | 068 | 54° 17.500' | 02° 13.297' | Gate before Gaudy House Farm |

**Hawes**

| | | | | |
|---|---|---|---|---|
| Map 57 | 069 | 54°19.453' | 02°13.123' | Walled lane ends |

**Hawes** (*continued from opposite*)

| MAP NO | REF | GPS WAYPOINT | | DESCRIPTION |
|--------|-----|--------------|---|-------------|
| Map 57 | 070 | 54°20.050' | 02°14.068' | Sheepfold to left after gate |
| Map 58 | 071 | 54°20.514' | 02°14.390' | Duckboards between cairns |
| Map 58 | 072 | 54°20.687' | 02°14.507' | Slabs start |
| Map 58 | 073 | 54°21.351' | 02°14.465' | Cairn after ascent |
| Map 59 | 074 | 54°22.257' | 02°13.969' | Great Shunner Fell summit |
| Map 59 | 075 | 54°22.617' | 02°13.531' | Handsome cairn |
| Map 59 | 076 | 54°22.915' | 02°13.091' | Wooden bridge |
| Map 60 | 077 | 54°22.878' | 02°11.463' | Join walled lane down to Thwaite |

**Thwaite**

| Map 61 | 078 | 54°22.867' | 02°09.571' | Wall above meadow; rough ascent follows |
|--------|-----|------------|------------|------------------------------------------|
| Map 61 | 079 | 54°22.935' | 02°09.135' | Kisdon House |

**Keld**

| Map 62 | 080 | 54°24.665' | 02°09.945' | Gate in fence on open fell |
|--------|-----|------------|------------|----------------------------|
| Map 63 | 081 | 54°25.880' | 02°10.446' | Pole with no sign |
| Map 63 | 082 | 54°26.343' | 02°10.107' | Cairn |
| Map 64 | 083 | 54°26.585' | 02°09.949' | Guidepost near Tan Hill |

**Tan Hill Inn**

| Map 65 | 084 | 54°27.968' | 02°08.150' | Guidepost opposite sheepfold |
|--------|-----|------------|------------|-------------------------------|
| Map 65 | 085 | 54°28.091' | 02°07.827' | Big cairn |
| Map 65 | 086 | 54°28.534' | 02°06.285' | Gatepost before railway sleeper bridge |
| Map 67 | 087 | 54°29.739' | 02°03.673' | Gate before Trough Heads Farm |
| Map 67 | 088 | 54°30.182' | 02°03.924' | Gate in wall |

**Bowes alternative route – OS only**

| Map 67 | 087 | 54°29.739' | 02°03.673' | Gate before Trough Heads Farm |
|--------|-----|------------|------------|-------------------------------|
| Map 67 | 657 | 54°30.278' | 02°03.317' | Coarse gravel track joins farm track |
| Map 67a | 658 | 54°30.350' | 02°02.578' | Big gate after East Mellwaters Farm |
| Map 67a | 659 | 54°30.445' | 02°01.445' | Leave road after Lady Myres Farm |

**Bowes**

| Map 67b | 660 | 54°31.536' | 02°02.392' | West Stoney Keld Farm track |
|---------|-----|------------|------------|-----------------------------|
| Map 67b | 661 | 54°32.036' | 02°03.041' | Bridge behind Levy Pool Farmhouse |
| Map 67b | 662 | 54°32.215' | 02°03.102' | Hazelgill Beck |
| Map 67b | 663 | 54°32.334' | 02°02.595' | Pennine Way crosses track |
| Map 67c | 664 | 54°32.409' | 02°03.059' | Cross Hare Sike |
| Map 67c | 665 | 54°32.591' | 02°03.190' | Gate before Goldsborough crag |
| Map 67c | 666 | 54°33.066' | 02°03.471' | Big black metal footbridge across stream |
| Map 67c | 667 | 54°33.117' | 02°04.170' | South of Goldsborough Crags summit |
| Map 67c | 668 | 54°33.221' | 02°04.537' | Meet Baldersdale Road |
| Map 69 | 669 | 54°33.268' | 02°05.308' | Tiny gate/stile |
| Map 69 | 670 | 54°33.295' | 02°06.145' | Main route and Bowes variant route converge at Baldersdale |

**Cross A66**

| Map 68 | 089 | 54°30.779' | 02°04.150' | Guidepost by ford at wall corner |
|--------|-----|------------|------------|----------------------------------|
| Map 68 | 090 | 54°31.098' | 02°04.176' | Good cairn |
| Map 68 | 091 | 54°31.182' | 02°04.303' | Hill top cairn – Ravock Castle |
| Map 68 | 092 | 54°31.587' | 02°04.600' | Guidepost before you drop to ford stream |
| Map 69 | 093 | 54°32.412' | 02°05.363' | Gate in wall |
| Map 69 | 094 | 54°32.716' | 02°05.499' | Post |

## Cross A66 *(continued from p261)*

| MAP NO | REF | GPS WAYPOINT | | DESCRIPTION |
|---|---|---|---|---|
| Map 69 | 095 | 54°33.224' | 02°05.951' | Path joins road |
| Map 69 | 670 | 54°33.295' | 02°06.145' | Main route and Bowes variant route converge at Baldersdale |

### Baldersdale

| | | | | |
|---|---|---|---|---|
| Map 70 | 096 | 54°34.727' | 02°06.527' | Rail sleeper guidepost |
| Map 71 | 097 | 54°36.152' | 02°07.152' | Stone stile with white paint |
| Map 71 | 098 | 54°36.297' | 02°06.826' | Ruined barn |
| Map 72 | 099 | 54°36.832' | 02°05.451' | Stile with dog slot by black gate |

### Middleton-in-Teesdale

| | | | | |
|---|---|---|---|---|
| Map 76 | 100 | 54°38.921' | 02°12.722' | Rail wagon near hill top |

### Langdon Beck

| | | | | |
|---|---|---|---|---|
| Map 78 | 101 | 54°39.048' | 02°15.757' | First rockfall; duckboards |
| Map 78 | 102 | 54°38.868' | 02°16.361' | Cairn after second rockfall |
| Map 79 | 103 | 54°38.447' | 02°18.943' | Old spoil tip |
| Map 79 | 104 | 54°38.304' | 02°20.068' | Cairn near sign – high point |
| Map 80 | 105 | 54°38.092' | 02°21.489' | Bridge at Maize Beck crossing |

### Maize Beck alternative route – OS only

| | | | | |
|---|---|---|---|---|
| Map 80 | 671 | 54°38.092' | 02°21.489' | Bridge at Maize Beck crossing |
| Map 81 | 672 | 54°38.093' | 02°23.134' | Path reaches lower gorge |
| Map 81 | 673 | 54°38.083' | 02°23.222' | West side of gorge |
| Map 81 | 674 | 54°38.081' | 02°23.395' | Mossy cairn |
| Map 81 | 675 | 54°38.031' | 02°23.443' | Eroded limestone pavement |
| Map 81 | 676 | 54°37.549' | 02°23.512' | Milepost – close to High Cup Nick |
| Map 81 | 677 | 54°37.503' | 02°23.566' | Alternative route meets main route at milepost |
| Map 80 | 106 | 54°38.088' | 02°22.249' | Red stone milepost |
| Map 80 | 107 | 54°37.912' | 02°23.333' | Milepost; getting near to High Cup Nick |
| Map 81 | 108 | 54°37.503' | 02°23.566' | Alternative route meets main route at milepost |
| Map 81 | 109 | 54°37.629' | 02°24.497' | Cross two streams |
| Map 81 | 110 | 54°37.592' | 02°24.648' | Mileposton west side of High Cup |
| Map 82 | 111 | 54°37.168' | 02°25.822' | Walled enclosure – easy track down |

### Dufton

| | | | | |
|---|---|---|---|---|
| Map 83 | 112 | 54°38.260' | 02°28.702' | Halstead (ruin) out on open land |
| Map 84 | 113 | 54°38.911' | 02°28.072' | Path leaves track to left and contours hill at signpost |
| Map 84 | 114 | 54°39.088' | 02°27.833' | Sign |
| Map 85 | 115 | 54°39.244' | 02°27.433' | Two cairns close together |
| Map 85 | 116 | 54°39.314' | 02°27.204' | Guidepost with yellow mark |
| Map 85 | 117 | 54°39.431' | 02°26.831' | Cairn with fallen stick |
| Map 85 | 118 | 54°39.649' | 02°26.602' | Milepost |
| Map 85 | 119 | 54°39.736' | 02°26.402' | Milepost |
| Map 85 | 120 | 54°39.800' | 02°26.337' | Cairn before bend in path, above Knock Hush |
| Map 85 | 121 | 54°39.843' | 02°26.243' | Flooded hole |
| Map 85 | 122 | 54°39.901' | 02°26.029' | Knock Old Man – enormous cairn |
| Map 85 | 123 | 54°39.987' | 02°25.912' | Knock Fell summit |
| Map 85 | 124 | 54°40.110' | 02°25.927' | Faint path resumes |
| Map 85 | 125 | 54°40.171' | 02°26.005' | Pass west of slabs |

**Dufton** *(continued from opposite)*

| MAP NO | REF | GPS WAYPOINT | | DESCRIPTION |
|--------|-----|--------------|---|-------------|
| Map 85 | 126 | 54°40.368' | 02°26.128' | Slabs curve around tarn |
| Map 85 | 127 | 54°40.620' | 02°26.293' | Join tracking station access road |
| Map 85 | 128 | 54°40.718' | 02°26.395' | Leave access road |
| Map 85 | 129 | 54°40.825' | 02°26.639' | Flat topped block followed by cairn before Dun Fell Hush |
| Map 85 | 130 | 54°40.859' | 02°26.765' | North edge of Dunfell Hush |
| Map 86 | 131 | 54°41.057' | 02°26.900' | Just east of Great Dun Fell Radar station |
| Map 86 | 132 | 54°41.466' | 02°27.500' | Little Dun Fell summit |
| Map 86 | 133 | 54°41.845' | 02°28.071' | Nature Reserve sign |
| Map 87 | 134 | 54°42.061' | 02°28.506' | Tall cairn on edge of summit plateau |
| Map 87 | 135 | 54°42.156' | 02°28.818' | Bell-shaped cairn |
| Map 87 | 136 | 54°42.183' | 02°29.088' | Cross Fell summit |
| Map 87 | 137 | 54°42.282' | 02°29.142' | Another bell-shaped cairn, before steep drop |
| Map 87 | 138 | 54°42.654' | 02°29.427' | Path from Cross Fell meets Corpse Rd at cairn |
| Map 87 | 139 | 54°42.770' | 02°28.789' | Greg's Hut |
| Map 88 | 140 | 54°43.045' | 02°28.035' | Very ruined ruin |
| Map 88 | 141 | 54°43.037' | 02°26.852' | Stream |
| Map 89 | 142 | 54°43.061' | 02°26.725' | Old mine workings |
| Map 89 | 143 | 54°43.113' | 02°26.547' | Omega sign to east |
| Map 89 | 144 | 54°43.290' | 02°26.340' | Path crosses stream |
| Map 89 | 145 | 54°43.526' | 02°26.124' | A track joins from west |
| Map 89 | 146 | 54°43.633' | 02°26.064' | A track joins from east; white cairn/gate to east |
| Map 89 | 147 | 54°44.528' | 02°25.768' | Path leaves wall near 'bird huts' |
| Map 90 | 148 | 54°45.085' | 02°25.163' | Gate at walled lane down to Garrigill |

**Garrigill**

| MAP NO | REF | GPS WAYPOINT | | DESCRIPTION |
|--------|-----|--------------|---|-------------|
| Map 92 | 149 | 54°46.678' | 02°25.408' | Three-way signpost by river |
| Map 92 | 150 | 54°46.812' | 02°25.712' | Bridge over South Tyne |
| Map 93 | 151 | 54°47.097' | 02°26.234' | Gate with yellow marks by two trees |
| Map 93 | 152 | 54°47.854' | 02°26.369' | Footbridge |
| Map 93 | 153 | 54°48.196' | 02°26.400' | Small gate over stream meets path to Alston |

**Alston**

| MAP NO | REF | GPS WAYPOINT | | DESCRIPTION |
|--------|-----|--------------|---|-------------|
| Map 94 | 154 | 54°49.225' | 2°27.727' | Take direct route to Gilderdale Burn crossing |
| Map 95 | 155 | 54°49.795' | 2°28.634' | Approaching Whitley Castle |
| Map 97 | 156 | 54°52.271' | 2°30.722' | Leave South Tyne Trail at sliding gate, head up hill |
| Map 97 | 157 | 54°52.425' | 2°30.794' | Gate leading to Merry Knowe terrace |
| Map 98 | 158 | 54°53.244' | 2°30.636' | Leave track to right (Maiden Way) |
| Map 98 | 159 | 54°53.497' | 2°30.556' | Two stiles after ford, then descent |
| Map 98 | 160 | 54°54.952' | 2°31.098' | Pass stile on left |
| Map 99 | 161 | 54°55.101' | 2°31.195' | Cross stile in fence |
| Map 99 | 162 | 54°55.238' | 2°31.509' | A689 road crossing |
| Map 99 | 163 | 54°55.435' | 2°31.601' | Pass ruin behind wall |
| Map 99 | 164 | 54°55.935' | 2°31.814' | Ruin |
| Map 99 | 165 | 54°56.144' | 2°31.655' | Top of the wooded bank |
| Map 99 | 166 | 54°56.234' | 2°31.923' | Guidepost |
| Map 100 | 167 | 54°56.391' | 2°32.271' | Ulpham Farm barn with red doors |
| Map 100 | 168 | 54°56.897' | 2°32.513' | Stile near Highside Farm |

## Alston (*continued from p263*)

| MAP NO | REF | GPS WAYPOINT | | DESCRIPTION |
|--------|-----|------|------|-------------|
| Map 100 | 169 | 54°57.332' | 2°33.267' | Fenceline – no clear path, follow fence north |
| Map 100 | 170 | 54°57.629' | 2°33.332' | Corner of wall on left |
| Map 100 | 171 | 54°57.938' | 2°33.512' | Ladder stile east of Black Hill summit |
| Map 101 | 172 | 54°58.179' | 2°33.649' | After pylons, join track near hut |
| Map 101 | 173 | 54°58.395' | 2°33.613' | Leave track to left |
| Map 102 | 174 | 54°58.345' | 2°32.683' | Turn right, go along edge of golf course |

## Greenhead

| | | | | |
|--------|-----|------|------|-------------|
| Map 105 | 175 | 55°00.151' | 2°24.367' | Junction with path to Winshields Farm Campsite |
| Map 106 | 176 | 55°00.705' | 2°20.555' | Rapishaw Gap; leave Wall, north-north-east |
| Map 107 | 177 | 55°01.557' | 2°20.622' | Guidepost after slabs |
| Map 107 | 178 | 55°01.875' | 2°20.679' | Join forestry track, turn right |
| Map 107 | 179 | 55°02.468' | 2°20.563' | Leave forestry track to right |
| Map 108 | 180 | 55°02.893' | 2°20.149' | Leave trees for open land |
| Map 108 | 181 | 55°03.378' | 2°19.094' | Back into the forest |
| Map 109 | 182 | 55°04.880' | 2°17.807' | Waterfall |
| Map 109 | 183 | 55°05.239' | 2°17.592' | Turn left downhill to river |
| Map 111 | 184 | 55°06.741' | 2°16.060' | Near Houxty Burn |

## Bellingham

| | | | | |
|--------|-----|------|------|-------------|
| Map 112 | 185 | 55°09.349' | 2°14.456' | Guidepost |
| Map 112 | 186 | 55°09.591' | 2°14.529' | Gate in wall after stiff ascent |
| Map 113 | 187 | 55°10.068' | 2°14.492' | Pipe and plank |
| Map 114 | 188 | 55°11.476' | 2°14.879' | Guidepost after crossing B6320 |
| Map 114 | 189 | 55°11.892' | 2°14.716' | Guidepost after Lough Shaw summit |
| Map 114 | 190 | 55°12.381' | 2°14.950' | Cairn west of Deer Play summit |
| Map 114 | 191 | 55°12.506' | 2°15.176' | Guidepost with white band |
| Map 115 | 192 | 55°12.630' | 2°15.257' | Guidepost |
| Map 115 | 193 | 55°12.905' | 2°16.088' | Whitley Pike |
| Map 116 | 194 | 55°14.118' | 2°17.523' | Wall at base of climb |
| Map 116 | 195 | 55°14.573' | 2°17.319' | Lone pine after forest climb |
| Map 117 | 196 | 55°15.251' | 2°18.998' | Forestry Commission sign, track starts |
| Map 117 | 197 | 55°15.673' | 2°19.087' | Leave track to left for parallel path |
| Map 117 | 198 | 55°16.013' | 2°19.296' | Rejoin forestry track |

## Byrness

| | | | | |
|--------|-----|------|------|-------------|
| Map 120 | 199 | 55°19.389' | 2°21.429' | Byrness Hill summit |
| Map 121 | 200 | 55°20.966' | 2°20.797' | Ravens Knowe |
| Map 121 | 201 | 55°21.496' | 2°21.074' | Ministry of Defence (MoD) sign |
| Map 122 | 202 | 55°21.581' | 2°21.142' | 'Border Country Ride' on left |
| Map 122 | 203 | 55°21.943' | 2°21.164' | After stream, turn right |
| Map 122 | 204 | 55°22.031' | 2°20.936' | Guidepost. Fork left down to Chew Green |
| Map 123 | 205 | 55°22.346' | 2°20.127' | Turn right along Dere St, away from Chew Green |
| Map 123 | 206 | 55°23.326' | 2°20.017' | Green sign as you leave Dere Street |
| Map 124 | 207 | 55°23.677' | 2°20.070' | Cross stream |
| Map 124 | 208 | 55°23.944' | 2°19.976' | Cairn |
| Map 124 | 209 | 55°24.130' | 2°19.753' | Guidepost |
| Map 124 | 210 | 55°24.319' | 2°19.441' | Gully (Rennies Burn) |
| Map 125 | 211 | 55°24.401' | 2°18.700' | Turn corner to left |

**Byrness** *(continued from opposite)*

| MAP NO | REF | GPS WAYPOINT | | DESCRIPTION |
|---|---|---|---|---|
| Map 125 | 212 | 55°24.573' | 2°18.560' | First refuge hut |
| Map 125 | 213 | 55°24.807' | 2°17.952' | Lamb Hill summit |
| Map 125 | 214 | 55°25.219' | 2°17.536' | Turn right, slabs |
| Map 126 | 215 | 55°25.720' | 2°16.232' | Mozie Law summit |
| Map 126 | 216 | 55°25.712' | 2°15.644' | Turn left towards sign |
| Map 127 | 217 | 55°25.891' | 2°14.266' | Saddle. Steeply up to Windy Gyle |
| Map 127 | 218 | 55°25.821' | 2°13.700' | Windy Gyle summit (Russell's Cairn) |
| Map 127 | 219 | 55°25.923' | 2°13.269' | Rejoin wall |
| Map 127 | 220 | 55°26.004' | 2°13.156' | Extensive pile of stones |
| Map 128 | 221 | 55°26.281' | 2°12.203' | Sign for Uswayford |
| Map 129 | 222 | 55°26.726' | 2°11.580' | Saddle |
| Map 129 | 223 | 55°26.988' | 2°11.483' | Kings Seat |
| Map 129 | 224 | 55°27.631' | 2°11.194' | Slabs end |
| Map 130 | 225 | 55°28.002' | 2°10.154' | Outcrop with memorial plaque |
| Map 130 | 226 | 55°28.071' | 2°09.900' | Ahead for The Cheviot, left for Auchope Cairn |
| Map 130 | 227 | 55°28.340' | 2°10.349' | Auchope Cairn |
| Map 131 | 228 | 55°28.509' | 2°11.670' | Second refuge hut |
| Map 131 | 229 | 55°29.022' | 2°12.215' | Saddle |
| Map 131 | 230 | 55°29.675' | 2°12.374' | The Schil summit |
| Map 132 | 231 | 55°30.196' | 2°12.943' | Stile not to be missed |
| Map 132 | 232 | 55°30.308' | 2°13.357' | High and Low routes diverge |
| Map 132 | 233 | 55°30.748' | 2°14.115' | Saddle, wall, Guidepost |
| Map 132 | 234 | 55°31.232' | 2°14.065' | Old Halterburn ruin. Trees |
| Map 134 | 235 | 55°32.546' | 2°15.252' | High route rejoins from right |

### ❏ St Cuthbert's Way and other continuations

In the unlikely event right now that you want to extend your walk, **St Cuthbert's Way** is a 66-mile (106km) trail that runs from Kirk Yetholm to Lindisfarne Castle on Holy Island, reached via a causeway off the Northumberland coast. That would round off your adventure in tremendous style.

If you still just can't stop walking there's also a link to the **Southern Upland Way** and with a certain amount of ingenuity to the **West Highland Way** and from there on to the **Great Glen Way**. It's therefore possible to walk from Derbyshire to Inverness, a great challenge for anyone with the stamina and the time.

The pastime of walking the long-distance trails grows on you. Getting back to normal life is hard. You're likely to find that everyday cares are less important now that you've communed with curlews and breathed the wind on Windy Gyle. One of the attractions of walking is the tangible sense of being out of the everyday world yet bonded to a community with different values from the common herd:

*We are Pilgrims, Master; we shall go*
*Always a little further: it may be*
*Beyond that last blue mountain barred with snow,*
*Across that angry or that glimmering sea.*

So it is that the Trailblazer marketing department feels compelled to alert you to the full range of its **British Walking Guides** series listed on pp270-2. For you my friend, the walking is *not* over.

# INDEX

Page references in **bold** type refer to maps

## The Inca Trail, Cusco & Machu Picchu
*Alexander Stewart*, 4th edn, £12.99
ISBN 978-1-905864-15-7, 352pp, 74 maps, 40 colour photos
The Inca Trail, from Cusco to Machu Picchu, is South America's
most popular trek. Practical guide including detailed trail maps,
plans of Inca sites, plus guides to Cusco and Machu Picchu. Route
guides to other trails in the area: the Santa Teresa Trek and the
Choquequirao Trek as well as the Vilcabamba Trail plus the routes
linking them. This entirely rewalked and rewritten fourth edition
includes a new history of the Incas by Hugh Thomson.

## New Zealand – The Great Walks *Alex Stewart*, 2nd edn, £12.99
ISBN 978-1-905864-11-9, 272pp, 60 maps, 40 colour photos
New Zealand is a wilderness paradise of incredibly beautiful landscapes. There is no better way to experience it than on one of the
nine designated Great Walks, the country's premier walking tracks
which provide outstanding hiking opportunities for people at all
levels of fitness. Also includes detailed guides to Auckland, Wellington, Taumarunui, Nelson, Queenstown, Te Anau and Oban.

## Kilimanjaro – the trekking guide to Africa's highest
mountain *Henry Stedman*, 3rd edn, £12.99
ISBN 978-1-905864-24-9, 368pp, 40 maps, 30 photos
At 19,340ft the world's tallest freestanding mountain, Kilimanjaro
is one of the most popular destinations for hikers visiting Africa.
It's possible to walk up to the summit: no technical skills are necessary. Includes town guides to Nairobi and Dar-Es-Salaam, and a
colour guide to flora and fauna. Includes Mount Meru.

## Nepal Trekking and the Great Himalaya Trail
*Robin Boustead*, 1st edn, £14.99, ISBN 978-1-905864-31-7
256pp, 8pp colour maps, 40 colour photos
This guide includes the most popular routes in Nepal – the Everest,
Annapurna and Langtang regions – as well as the newest trekking
areas for true trailblazers. This is the first guide to chart The Great
Himalaya Trail, the route which crosses Nepal from east to west.
Extensive planning sections.

## Tour du Mont Blanc *Jim Manthorpe*, 1st edn, £11.99
ISBN 978-1-905864-12-6, 176pp, 50 maps, 30 colour photos
At 4807m (15,771ft), Mont Blanc is the highest mountain in western
Europe, and one of the most famous mountains in the world. The
trail (105 miles, 168km) that circumnavigates the massif, passing
through France, Italy and Switzerland, is the most popular long distance walk in Europe. Includes Chamonix and Courmayeur guides.

## Scottish Highlands – The Hillwalking Guide 2nd edn, £12.99
*Jim Manthorpe*, 320pp, 86 maps, ISBN 978-1-905864-21-8
Covers 60 day-hikes in the following areas: ● Loch Lomond, the
Trossachs and Southern Highlands ● Glen Coe and Ben Nevis
● Central Highlands ● Cairngorms and Eastern Highlands
● Western Highlands ● North-West Highlands ● The Far North
● The Islands. Plus: 3- to 4-day hikes linking some regions.

# TRAILBLAZER
## British Walking Guides

Coast to Coast PATH

Hadrian's Wall PATH

Pennine Way

Cotswold Way

South Downs WAY

The Ridgeway

Cornwall Coast PATH

Offa's Dyke PATH

Pembrokeshire Coast Path

Peddars Way NORFOLK COAST PATH

*'The same attention to detail that distinguishes its other guides
has been brought to bear here'.*
**THE SUNDAY TIMES**

# Title list – www.trailblazer-guides.com

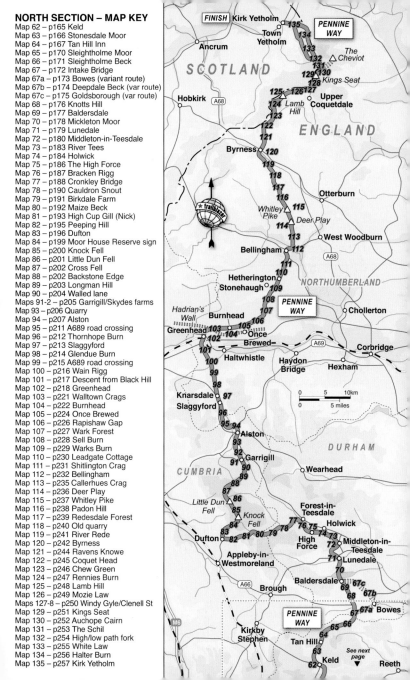

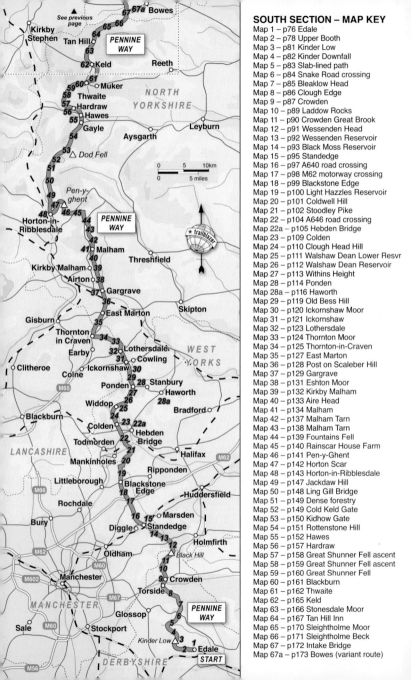